AFGHANISTAN
TO
ZIMBABWE

. . . .

AFGHANISTAN
TO
ZIMBABWE

· · · · · · · · · · · ·

COUNTRY FACTS
THAT HELPED ME WIN
THE NATIONAL
GEOGRAPHIC BEE

by
Andrew Wojtanik

NATIONAL GEOGRAPHIC
Washington, D.C

To my sister, Jessica,
who sees the world in a special way

Acknowledgments:
There are a number of people I would like to thank who have been supportive for so long and have given me the motivation to reach my goals:
- my parents, Daniel and Dianna Wojtanik, who have been behind me every step of the way ever since the day I was born and who have given valuable advice throughout my life
- my grandparents, Raymond and Ruth Rippley, who also backed me one hundred percent and encouraged me to pursue my goals and accomplish them
- my entire family living in the Kansas City area, who have been extremely supportive, especially Denise Brame, who has given me many important geography books
- my aunt and uncle, Virginia and Edward Pryze, who gave me my first subscription to *National Geographic Kids* magazine
- all of my relatives living in western New York, who cheered me on as I competed in the National Geographic Bee. To this day, I am a die-hard Buffalo Bills fan because of them (yes, this *is* a good thing!)
- Mr. and Mrs. Vince Stonestreet, who provided the best world atlases I have ever owned
- the Lakewood Middle School community, including Mr. Scott Currier, who went out of his way to support me while I was competing in the Geographic Bee
- Mrs. Julie Larsen, my sixth-grade social studies teacher, who shared with me her tremendous love for geography
- my friends who rooted for me in the Bee and challenged me to compete at the highest level.
Lastly, I need to acknowledge National Geographic for giving me the opportunity to share my knowledge of the world. Special thanks goes to David B. Miller, Geoffrey W. Hatchard (the runner-up in the 1992 National Geographic Bee who now works for NGMaps!), Verónica E. Betancourt, David M. Seager, Andrew Murphy, Suzanne Fonda, and the rest of the National Geographic staff for their hard work and dedication in making this project a reality.

The text type is set in New Caledonia; headlines are set in Clarendon

Library of Congress Cataloging-in-Publication Data
Wojtanik, Andrew.
  Afghanistan to Zimbabwe : country facts that helped me win the National Geographic Bee / by Andrew Wojtanik.
    p. cm.
  Includes bibliographical references (p.   ) and index.
  ISBN 0-7922-7981-6 (Paperback)
  ISBN 0-7922-7442-3 (Library)
  1. Geography—Encyclopedias. I. National Geographic Society (U.S.) II. Title.
  G63.W64 2005
  910'.3—dc22
                    2004026137

Front cover photograph: Mark Thiessen, NGP

Printed in the United States of America

Contents

Note from the Author

There is definitely something about geography that catches my eye. Maybe it is the fact that I like to look at atlases to gain a perspective of lands that are far away. It could be because of the satisfaction I get from planning family vacations. Or possibly, it is the cultures and histories of the interesting places around the world that compel my mind. But most likely, it is a combination of all of these that first sparked my interest in the study of the world's features.

It wasn't until the sixth grade that I heard about the National Geographic Bee, a geography competition that boasts more than five million fourth- through eighth-grade students across the country every year. After winning my first "Bee title" at the school level, I was ecstatic and officially "hooked" on geography. I put up a good fight at the state competition in Hays, Kansas, but fell just short of moving on.

But my growing knowledge of the world produced a better result the following year. I advanced to the national competition in Washington, D.C., where I met other people who enjoy geography as much as I do. Unfortunately, I lost in the preliminaries and ended up watching the finals from the audience rather than as a contestant on stage.

It wasn't until my third and final try (I was an eighth grader) that I reached out and snatched my goal to make the "top ten" at the national competition. Just proceeding that far was an extraordinary achievement for me, but the excitement didn't quite end there. If someone had told me before I embarked on this long trip that I would actually win the next Geographic Bee, I probably would have laughed in disbelief…but you never know when a surprise will be thrown your way.

After answering many geographical questions correctly and surviving an intense final round, I was declared the champion of the 2004 National Geographic Bee. It was an accomplishment that exceeded all expectations, but one that could not have been achieved without lots of hard work.

When Alex Trebek, host of the hit game show *JEOPARDY!* and moderator of the National Geographic Bee, asked me how I studied for the contest, I smiled and gave an answer that wasn't exactly expected. I explained how I had created a 400-page "study guide," which consisted of information about the physical, political, and environmental features for each of the world's 192 countries. I believe that this guide, along with a decent memory (and a little luck), were major contributors to my success.

A mere three months later—just when I thought all the hype from the Bee had died down—I received a telephone call from National Geographic regarding my geography fact book. I responded by asking in an excited tone, "Publish? What do you mean, you want to publish it?" The surprises never end.

It is a great privilege to have the ability to share my love for geography with others who have the same interest as I do. I encourage you to get involved in the Geographic Bee if you're the right age, and I hope this book can be useful on your fantastic journey. I also recommend getting your hands on a detailed atlas for visual reference so you can find the exact location of the features listed in this book.

When competing in the Geographic Bee, always keep this information in the back of your mind: Even if you don't advance to the national finals, you will walk away with the satisfaction of gaining a wider knowledge of the world. Geography is a truly amazing subject if you are willing to expand your horizons and go beyond your boundaries to a place you have never seen before. Because of this, there is nothing to lose by participating in the next year of competition.

So, whether you are preparing for the National Geographic Bee or would just like to own a new geography reference, *Afghanistan to Zimbabwe* is the book for you!

Andrew Wojtanik

Things You Need to Know

Geography is a huge subject, as you probably have already discovered for yourself. It would be impossible to list every fact about every country. So I had to make some choices when I put my book together. I selected key things that I thought would help me study for the National Geographic Bee. Then I organized them in a way that made sense to me.

First, I listed each of the world's 192 independent countries in alphabetical order. Then I decided what facts I needed to know about each and organized them into three categories: physical, political, and environmental/economic. Within each of these categories I listed topics that fit the category and put these in the same order for each country. Of course, if a topic didn't apply to a country, I didn't list it. For example, you won't find rain forests listed for Iceland.

I was selective in what I listed for each country. In the case of physical features and political regions, only major ones are included. For some countries a mountain range will be named but no peaks will be singled out. That's because I only listed peaks that were at least 8,000 feet (2,400 meters) high. In countries that have several peaks that exceed this elevation, I listed the ones that I thought were the most significant or well known. The same is true for rivers. In some cases you will see rivers on the country map but no rivers listed in the text. That's because these rivers are usually less than a hundred miles long. For depressions, only those that are at least 50 feet (15 meters) below sea level are listed.

For the most part, features and places are listed in alphabetical order. The major exception is cities. These are listed in order of population, from largest to smallest. I only listed capital cities, a country's largest city, or cities that had at least a million people. Ethnic/racial groups are listed largest to smallest; religions are listed by number of followers, largest to smallest; and languages are listed in order of the number of people who speak them, largest to smallest. The top natural resources and major exports are listed in order of importance, as are the leading agricultural products.

There are two "Region" categories, one in physical and one in political, so don't think this is an error. Also, the heading "Independence" does not necessarily refer to when a country became free from control by another country. It generally marks the commonly accepted date for when the country became an independent political entity. Finally, all accents and diacritical marks have been intentionally omitted from the text, although they do appear on the maps.

All of the maps in this book were created by the cartographers at National Geographic as part of the Xpeditions Atlas, an online collection of maps intended for use by students. (The maps can be printed or downloaded from the Society's Web site: www.nationalgeographic.com/xpeditions/atlas/. The same Web site also offers blank outline maps of each country.) In some cases, places that I mention in my text are not labeled on the country map. Likewise, some places on the country map are not included in my text, and sometimes the name on a map is different from what I have in my text. That's because I use the commonly accepted international place-names, while the map may use the local spelling. Remember, to get the maximum benefit from this study guide, you will need to supplement it with up-to-date atlases and other reference books.

THE WORLD

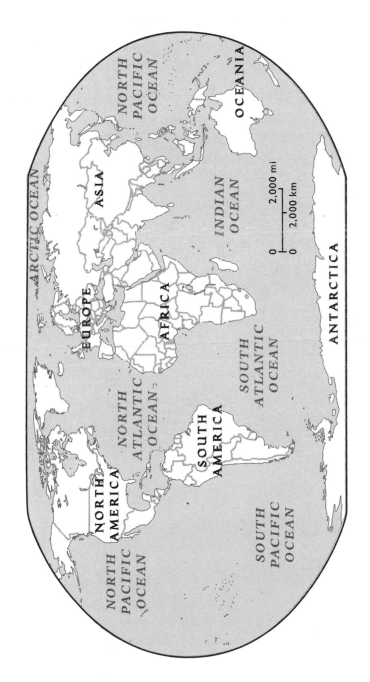

ARCTIC OCEAN

ASIA

EUROPE

NORTH PACIFIC OCEAN

OCEANIA

AFRICA

INDIAN OCEAN

2,000 mi
0
2,000 km
0

ANTARCTICA

NORTH AMERICA

NORTH ATLANTIC OCEAN

SOUTH AMERICA

SOUTH ATLANTIC OCEAN

NORTH PACIFIC OCEAN

SOUTH PACIFIC OCEAN

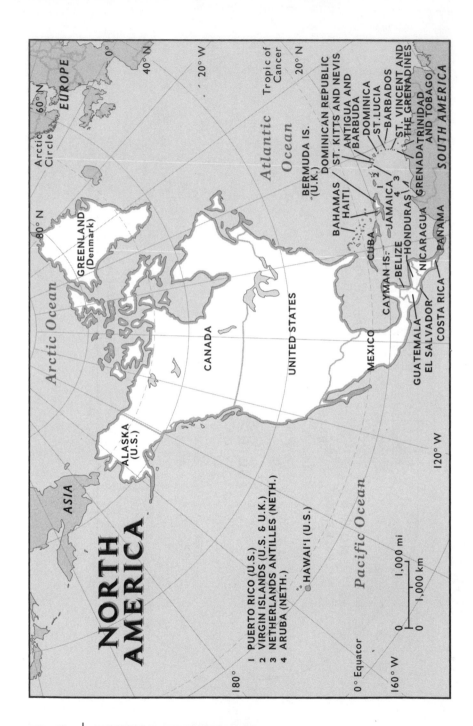

NORTH AMERICA

ASIA

Arctic Ocean

GREENLAND
(Denmark)

60° N
Arctic
Circle

EUROPE

0°

80° N

40° N

20° W

CANADA

ALASKA
(U.S.)

1 PUERTO RICO (U.S.)
2 VIRGIN ISLANDS (U.S. & U.K.)
3 NETHERLANDS ANTILLES (NETH.)
4 ARUBA (NETH.)

HAWAI'I (U.S.)

UNITED STATES

Atlantic
Ocean

Tropic of
Cancer

20° N

BERMUDA IS.
(U.K.)

DOMINICAN REPUBLIC
ST. KITTS AND NEVIS
ANTIGUA AND
BARBUDA
DOMINICA
ST. LUCIA
BARBADOS
ST. VINCENT AND
THE GRENADINES
GRENADA TRINIDAD
AND TOBAGO

BAHAMAS
HAITI
CUBA

JAMAICA

CAYMAN IS.

BELIZE
HONDURAS
NICARAGUA

MEXICO

GUATEMALA
EL SALVADOR
COSTA RICA

PANAMA

SOUTH AMERICA

Pacific Ocean

0 1,000 mi
0 1,000 km

0° Equator

160° W

120° W

180°

SOUTH AMERICA

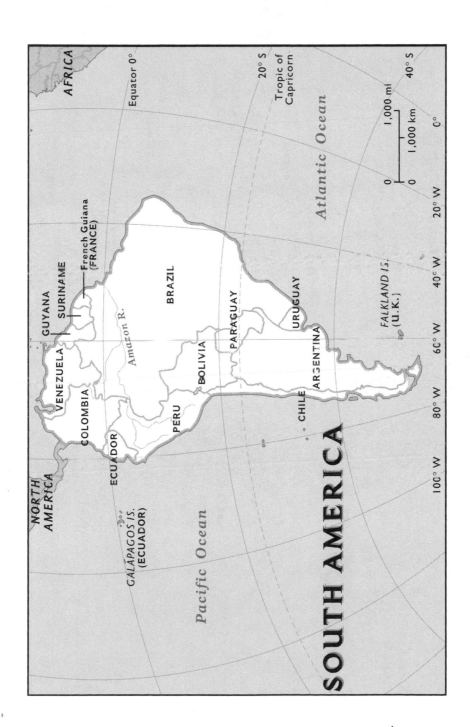

SOUTH AMERICA

NORTH
AMERICA

AFRICA

Equator 0°

20° S

Tropic of
Capricorn

40° S

Atlantic Ocean

French Guiana
(FRANCE)

SURINAME

GUYANA

VENEZUELA

BRAZIL

Amazon R.

COLOMBIA

ECUADOR

GALÁPAGOS IS.
(ECUADOR)

PERU

BOLIVIA

PARAGUAY

URUGUAY

CHILE

ARGENTINA

FALKLAND IS.
(U. K.)

Pacific Ocean

100° W

80° W

60° W

40° W

20° W

0°

1,000 mi

1,000 km

EUROPE

NORTH
AMERICA

Atlantic
Ocean

ICELAND

IRELAND

UNITED
KINGDOM

NORWAY

DENMARK

North
Sea

NETH.

BELGIUM

LUX.

GERMANY

FRANCE

MONACO

ANDORRA

SPAIN

PORTUGAL

GIBRALTAR (U.K.)

Norwegian Sea

SWEDEN

FINLAND

ESTONIA

LATVIA

LITH.

RUSS.

POLAND

CZECH
REP.

LIECH.

SWITZ. AUSTRIA

SLOVENIA

ITALY

VATICAN
CITY

SAN
MARINO

CROATIA

BOSN. &
HERZG.

SERB. &
MONT.

ALBANIA

MACEDONIA

Mediterranean Sea

AFRICA

MALTA

GREECE

BELARUS

UKRAINE

SLOVAKIA

HUNGARY

ROMANIA

BULGARIA

TURKEY

Black Sea

GEORGIA

AZER.

MOLDOVA

RUSSIA

KAZ.

Caspian
Sea

ASIA

ASIA

CYPRUS

Arctic
Circle

Meridian of Greenwich 0°
(London)

60° N

40° N

40° W

20° W

0°

20° E

40° E

60° E

500 mi

500 km

0

0

ASIA

Tropic of Cancer

180°
20° N
40° N
60° N
160° E
Equator 0°
20° S

OCEANIA

Pacific Ocean

120° E

Arctic Ocean

JAPAN

NORTH KOREA

SOUTH KOREA

TAIWAN

PHILIPPINES

RUSSIA

MONGOLIA

CHINA

VIETNAM
CAMBODIA

LAOS

THAI.

BRUNEI

MALAYSIA

SINGAPORE

INDONESIA

TIMOR-LESTE
(EAST TIMOR)

EUROPE

KAZAKHSTAN

KYRGYZSTAN

TAJIKISTAN

BHUTAN

MYANMAR
(BURMA)

100° E

GEORGIA

ARMENIA

AZERBAIJAN

UZB.

TURKM.

NEPAL

INDIA

BANGLADESH

SRI
LANKA

80° E

TURKEY

SYRIA

IRAQ

IRAN

AFGHAN.

PAKISTAN

U.A.E.

MALDIVES

Indian Ocean

LEBANON
ISRAEL
JORDAN

KUWAIT
BAHRAIN
QATAR

SAUDI
ARABIA

YEMEN

OMAN

Arabian
Sea

AFRICA

Atlantic Ocean

1,000 mi

1,000 km

0

0

AFRICA

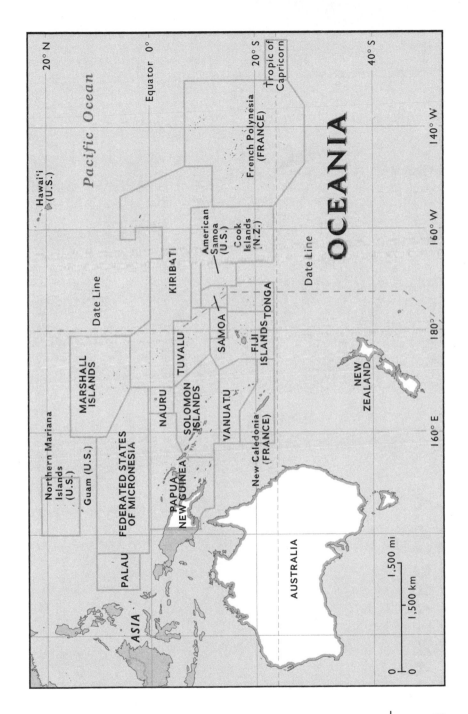

OCEANIA

Pacific Ocean

20° N
Equator 0°
20° S
Tropic of Capricorn
40° S

140° W
160° W
180°
160° E

Hawai'i (U.S.)

Date Line

KIRIBATI

American Samoa (U.S.)

French Polynesia (FRANCE)

Cook Islands (N.Z.)

Date Line

SAMOA

TONGA

FIJI ISLANDS

NEW ZEALAND

Northern Mariana Islands (U.S.)

MARSHALL ISLANDS

Guam (U.S.)

NAURU

TUVALU

VANUATU

FEDERATED STATES OF MICRONESIA

SOLOMON ISLANDS

New Caledonia (FRANCE)

PALAU

PAPUA NEW GUINEA

ASIA

AUSTRALIA

1,500 mi

1,500 km

0
0

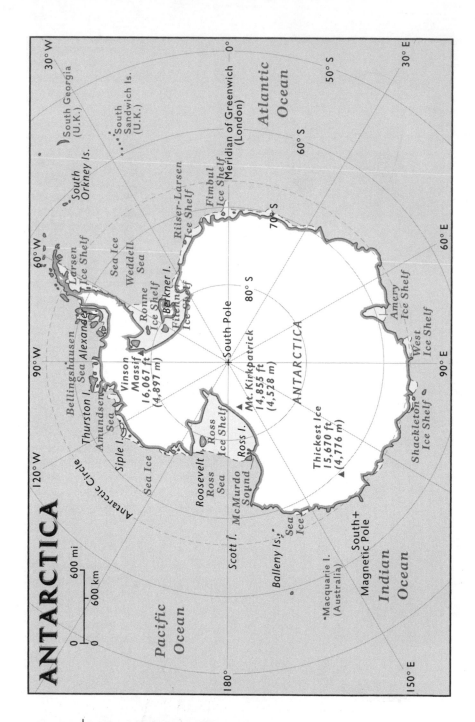

ANTARCTICA

30° W

South Georgia (U.K.)

South Sandwich Is. (U.K.)

South Orkney Is.

Meridian of Greenwich (London)

0°

Atlantic Ocean

30° E

50° S

60° S

70° S

Fimbul Ice Shelf

Riiser-Larsen Ice Shelf

Larsen Ice Shelf

Sea Ice

Weddell Sea

Berkner I.

Filchner Ice Shelf

Ronne Ice Shelf

60° W

Bellingshausen Sea

Thurston I.

Alexander I.

80° S

South Pole

60° E

Amery Ice Shelf

90° W

Vinson Massif 16,067 ft (4,897 m)

ANTARCTICA

West Ice Shelf

90° E

Mt. Kirkpatrick 14,855 ft (4,528 m)

Amundsen Sea

Siple I.

Sea Ice

120° W

Roosevelt I.

Ross Sea

Ross Ice Shelf

Ross I.

McMurdo Sound

Thickest Ice 15,670 ft (4,776 m)

Shackleton Ice Shelf

Arctic Circle

600 mi

600 km

0

0

Pacific Ocean

Scott I.

Balleny Is.

Sea Ice

Macquarie I. (Australia)

South Magnetic Pole

Indian Ocean

150° E

180°

AFGHANISTAN

Country Name: Transitional Islamic State of Afghanistan
Continent: Asia
Area: 251,773 sq mi / 652,090 sq km
Population: 28,717,000
Population Density: 114 people per sq mi / 44 people per sq km
Capital: Kabul

PHYSICAL:

Highest Point: Nowshak 24,557 ft / 7,485 m
Lowest Point: Amu Darya (river) 846 ft / 258 m
Mountain Ranges:

Hindu Kush: •cover most of Afghanistan •extend into Tajikistan, Pakistan, and China •includes the Safed Koh Range

Peaks (minimum elevation of 8,000 ft / 2,400 m):

Nowshak: •located in the Hindu Kush •highest point in Afghanistan

Passes:

Khyber: •located in the Safed Koh Range •crosses the border into Pakistan

Rivers:
    Amu Darya: ●forms all of the Afghanistan-Uzbekistan border ●forms part of Afghanistan's border with Turkmenistan and Tajikistan
    Helmand: ●has its source in the Hindu Kush mountains ●extends into Iran

POLITICAL:
Independence: August 19, 1919 (from the United Kingdom)
Former Name: Republic of Afghanistan
Bordering Countries: Pakistan, Tajikistan, Iran, Turkmenistan, Uzbekistan, China (6)
Regions:
    Rigestan: ●arid desert region in southern Afghanistan
Administrative Divisions: Badakhshan, Badghis, Baghlan, Balkh, Bamian, Farah, Faryab, Ghazni, Ghowr, Helmand, Herat, Jowzjan, Kabol, Kandahar, Kapisa, Khost, Konar, Kondoz, Laghman, Lowgar, Nangarhar, Nimruz, Nurestan, Oruzgan, Paktia, Paktika, Parvan, Samangan, Sar-e Pol, Takhar, Vardak, Zabol (32 provinces)
Ethnic/Racial Groups: Pashtun, Tajik, Hazara, Uzbek
Religion: Islam (primarily Sunni and Shiite)
Languages: Pashtu, Afghan Persian (Dari), Uzbek, Turkmen
Currency: afghani
Current President: Hamid Karzai
Cities (capital, largest, or with at least a million people):
    Kabul: ●located in eastern Afghanistan ●city in the Kabol province ●capital of Afghanistan ●most populated city in Afghanistan (2,956,000 people) ●located in the Hindu Kush

ENVIRONMENTAL/ECONOMIC:
Climate: arid to semi-arid with cold winters/hot summers
Natural Resources: natural gas, petroleum, coal, copper, chromite
Agricultural Products: opium, wheat, fruits and nuts, wool
Major Exports: opium, fruits and nuts, handwoven carpets, wool, cotton
Natural Hazards: earthquakes, floods, droughts

ALBANIA
Country Name: Republic of Albania
Continent: Europe
Area: 11,100 sq mi / 28,748 sq km
Population: 3,135,000
Population Density: 282 people per sq mi / 109 people per sq km
Capital: Tirana

PHYSICAL:
Highest Point: Golem Korab 9,068 ft / 2,764 m
Lowest Point: Adriatic Sea 0 ft / 0 m (sea level)

Mountain Ranges:
   Pindus: •located in southern Albania •extend into Greece
Peaks (minimum elevation of 8,000 ft / 2,400 m):
   Golem Korab: •on the Albania-Macedonia border •highest point in Albania
Seas:
   Adriatic: •forms part of the western coast of Albania •feeds into the Ionian Sea
   Ionian: •forms part of the southwestern coast of Albania •feeds into the
      Mediterranean Sea
Straits:
   Strait of Otranto: •forms part of the southwestern coast of Albania •separates
      Albania from Italy •connects the Adriatic and Ionian Seas
Lakes:
   Ohrid: •located in eastern Albania •on the Albania-Macedonia border
   Prespa: •located in eastern Albania •on the border with Macedonia and Greece
   Scutari: •located in northwestern Albania •on the Albania-Serbia and Montenegro
      border

POLITICAL:
Independence: November 28, 1912 (from the Ottoman Empire)
Former Name: People's Socialist Republic of Albania
Bordering Countries: Serbia and Montenegro, Greece, Macedonia (3)
Administrative Divisions: Beratit, Dibres, Durresit, Elbasanit, Fierit,
   Gjirokastres, Korces, Kukesit, Lezhes, Shkodres, Tirane, Vlores (12 counties)

Ethnic/Racial Groups: Albanian, Greek
Religions: Islam, Christianity (Albanian Orthodox, Roman Catholic)
Languages: Albanian (Tosk), Greek
Currency: lek
Current President: Alfred Moisiu
Cities (capital or with at least a million people):
  Tirana: •located in central Albania •city in Tirane county •capital of Albania •most
    populated city in Albania (367,000 people)

ENVIRONMENTAL/ECONOMIC:
Climate: mild temperature, cool and wet winters/hot and dry summers
Natural Resources: oil, natural gas, coal, chromium, copper
Agricultural Products: wheat, corn, potatoes, vegetables, meat
Major Exports: textiles and footwear, asphalt, metals and metallic ores, crude oil
Natural Hazards: earthquakes, tsunamis, floods, droughts

ALGERIA
Country Name: People's Democratic Republic of Algeria
Continent: Africa
Area: 919,595 sq mi / 2,381,741 sq km
Population: 31,746,000
Population Density: 35 people per sq mi / 13 people per sq km
Capital: Algiers

PHYSICAL:
Highest Point: Tahat 9,573 ft / 2,918 m
Lowest Point: Chott Melrhir 131 ft / 40 m below sea level
Mountain Ranges:
    Ahaggar: •located in southern Algeria
    Atlas: •located in northern Algeria •extend into Morocco and Tunisia
Peaks (minimum elevation of 8,000 ft / 2,400 m):
    Tahat: •located in the Ahaggar Mountains •highest point in Algeria
Plateau Regions:
    Hauts Plateaux: •located in northern Algeria •extend into Morocco •high basin in
    the Atlas Mountains
Depressions:
    Chott Melrhir: •located near the Grand Erg Oriental •lowest point in Algeria
Deserts:
    Grand Erg Occidental: •located in central Algeria
    Grand Erg Oriental: •located in eastern Algeria •extends into Tunisia
    Sahara: •covers most of Algeria •extends into Western Sahara (claimed by Morocco),
    Mauritania, Mali, Niger, Libya, and Tunisia •largest desert in the world
    Tenere: •located in southern Algeria •extends into Niger
Seas:
    Alboran •(sometimes labeled as part of the Mediterranean): •forms part of the
    northwestern coast of Algeria •feeds into the Atlantic Ocean
    Mediterranean: •forms the northern coast of Algeria •feeds into the Atlantic Ocean

POLITICAL:
Independence: July 5, 1962 (from France)
Bordering Countries: Morocco, Mali, Libya, Tunisia, Niger, Mauritania, Western
    Sahara (claimed by Morocco) (7)
Administrative Divisions: Adrar, Ain Defla, Ain Temouchent, Alger, Annaba,
    Batna, Bechar, Bejaia, Biskra, Blida, Bordj Bou Arreridj, Bouira, Boumerdes, Chlef,
    Constantine, Djelfa, El Bayadh, El Oued, El Tarf, Ghardaia, Guelma, Illizi, Jijel,
    Khenchela, Laghouat, Mascara, Medea, Mila, Mostaganem, M'Sila, Naama, Oran,
    Ouargla, Oum el Bouaghi, Relizane, Saida, Setif, Sidi Bel Abbes, Skikda, Souk Ahras,
    Tamanghasset, Tebessa, Tiaret, Tindouf, Tipaza, Tissemsilt, Tizi Ouzou, Tlemcen
    (48 provinces)
Ethnic/Racial Groups: Arab-Berber
Religion: Islam (predominantly Sunni)
Languages: Arabic, French, Berber dialects
Currency: Algerian dinar
Current President: Abdul Aziz Butaflika
Cities (capital, largest, or with at least a million people):
    Algiers: •located in northern Algeria •city in the Alger province •capital of Algeria
    •most populated city in Algeria (3,060,000 people) •chief port on the Mediterranean

ENVIRONMENTAL/ECONOMIC:
Climate: arid to semi-arid with mild and wet winters/hot and dry summers along the coast, hot and dry in the desert
Natural Resources: oil, natural gas, iron ore, phosphates, uranium
Agricultural Products: wheat, barley, oats, grapes, sheep
Major Exports: petroleum, natural gas, petroleum products
Natural Hazards: earthquakes, mudslides, floods, droughts, desertification

ANDORRA
Country Name: Principality of Andorra
Continent: Europe
Area: 181 sq mi / 468 sq km
Population: 67,000
Population Density: 370 people per sq mi / 143 people per sq km
Capital: Andorra La Vella

PHYSICAL:
Highest Point: Coma Pedrosa 9,666 ft / 2,946 m
Lowest Point: Riu Runer 2,756 ft / 840 m
Mountain Ranges:
  Pyrenees: •cover the entire country •extend into France and Spain
Peaks (minimum elevation of 8,000 ft / 2,400 m):
  Coma Pedrosa: •located in the Pyrenees •on the Andorra-Spain border

POLITICAL:
Independence: 1278 (formed under joint sovereignty of France and Spain)
Bordering Countries: Spain, France (2)
Administrative Divisions: Andorra la Vella, Canillo, Encamp, La Massana, Escaldes-Engordany, Ordino, Sant Julia de Loria (7 parishes)
Ethnic/Racial Groups: Spanish, Andorran, Portuguese, French
Religion: Christianity (predominantly Roman Catholic)
Languages: Catalan, French, Castilian, Portuguese
Currency: euro
Heads of State: President of France and Bishop of Urgel (Spain)
Current Head of Government: Marc Forne Molne
Cities (capital, largest, or with at least a million people):
  Andorra La Vella: ●located in western Andorra ●city in the Andorra la Vella parish ●capital of Andorra ●most populated city in Andorra (21,000 people) ●located in the Pyrenees

ENVIRONMENTAL/ECONOMIC:
Climate: temperate with snowy and cold winters/warm and dry summers
Natural Resources: hydropower, mineral water, timber, iron ore, lead
Agricultural Products: rye, wheat, barley, oats, sheep
Major Exports: tobacco products, furniture
Natural Hazards: avalanches

ANGOLA
Country Name: Republic of Angola
Continent: Africa
Area: 481,354 sq mi / 1,246,700 sq km
Population: 13,087,000
Population Density: 27 people per sq mi / 10 people per sq km
Capital: Luanda

PHYSICAL:
Highest Point: Morro de Moco 8,596 ft / 2,620 m
Lowest Point: Atlantic Ocean 0 ft / 0 m (sea level)
Peaks (minimum elevation of 8,000 ft / 2,400 m):
  Morro de Moco: ●located near the Bie Plateau ●highest point in Angola
Plateau Regions:
  Bie Plateau: ●located in central Angola
Deserts:
  Namib: ●located in southwestern Angola ●extends into Namibia
Oceans:
  Atlantic: ●forms the western coast of Angola

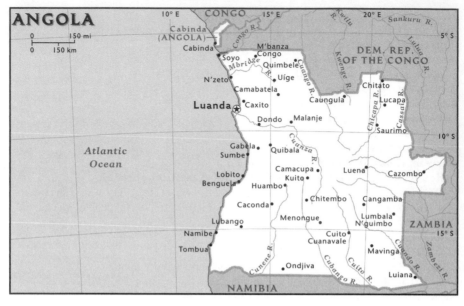

ANGOLA

Rivers:

> Congo: • has its mouth in the Atlantic Ocean • forms part of the Angola-Democratic
> Republic of the Congo border • extends into Democratic Republic of the Congo
> Cuango: • has its source in the Bie Plateau • forms part of the Angola-Democratic
> Republic of the Congo border • extends into Democratic Republic of the Congo
> Cubango: • has its source in the Bie Plateau • forms part of the Angola-Namibia
> border • extends into Namibia
> Zambezi: • extends into Zambia

Deltas:

> Congo River Delta: • mouth of the Congo River • feeds into the Atlantic Ocean
> • borders Angola and Democratic Republic of the Congo

POLITICAL:

Independence: November 11, 1975 (from Portugal)

Former Name: People's Republic of Angola

Bordering Countries: Democratic Republic of the Congo, Namibia, Zambia, Republic
of the Congo (4)

Administrative Divisions: Bengo, Benguela, Bie, Cabinda, Cuando Cubango,
Cuanza Norte, Cuanza Sul, Cunene, Huambo, Huila, Luanda, Lunda Norte, Lunda
Sul, Malanje, Moxico, Namibe, Uige, Zaire (18 provinces)

Ethnic/Racial Groups: Ovimbundu, Kimbundu, Bakongo

Religions: indigenous beliefs, Christianity (Roman Catholic, Protestant)

Languages: Portuguese, Bantu

Currency: kwanza

Current President: Jose Eduardo dos Santos
Cities (capital, largest, or with at least a million people):
    Luanda: •located in northwestern Angola •city in the Luanda province •capital of
    Angola •most populated city in Angola (2,623,000 people) •chief port on the
    Atlantic Ocean

ENVIRONMENTAL/ECONOMIC:
Climate: semi-arid in the south and along the coast with cool summers/hot winters
Natural Resources: oil, diamonds, iron ore, phosphates, copper
Agricultural Products: bananas, sugarcane, coffee, sisal, livestock
Major Exports: crude oil, diamonds, refined petroleum products, natural gas
Natural Hazards: flooding

ANTIGUA AND BARBUDA
Country Name: Antigua and Barbuda
Continent: North America
Area: 171 sq mi / 442 sq km
Population: 74,000
Population Density: 433 people per sq mi / 167 people per sq km
Capital: Saint John's

PHYSICAL:
Highest Point: Boggy Peak 1,319 ft / 402 m
Lowest Point: Caribbean Sea 0 ft / 0 m (sea level)
Oceans:
    Atlantic: •forms the entire coast of Antigua and Barbuda
Islands:
    Antigua: •largest island in Antigua and Barbuda •surrounded by the Atlantic Ocean
    Barbuda: •island in Antigua and Barbuda •surrounded by the Atlantic Ocean

POLITICAL:
Independence: November 1, 1981 (from the United Kingdom)
Administrative Divisions: Saint George, Saint John, Saint Mary, Saint Paul, Saint
    Peter, Saint Philip (6 parishes) •Barbuda, Redonda (2 dependencies)
Ethnic/Racial Groups: black, British, Portuguese, Lebanese, Syrian
Religion: Christianity (predominantly Protestant with some Roman Catholic)
Languages: English, local dialects
Currency: East Caribbean dollar
Current Prime Minister: Baldwin Spencer
Cities (capital, largest, or with at least a million people):
    Saint John's: •located on the island of Antigua •city in the Saint John parish
    •capital of Antigua and Barbuda •most populated city in Antigua and Barbuda
    (28,000 people) •chief port on the Atlantic Ocean

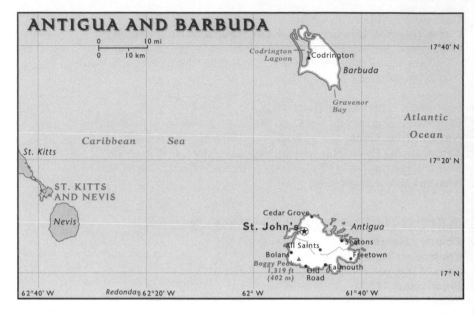

ANTIGUA AND BARBUDA

0   10 mi
0   10 km

17°40' N

Codrington Lagoon   Codrington

Barbuda

Gravenor Bay

Atlantic Ocean

Caribbean Sea

St. Kitts

17°20' N

ST. KITTS AND NEVIS

Nevis

Cedar Grove

St. John's ⭑   *Antigua*

All Saints   Seatons

Boland   Freetown

Boggy Peak 1,319 ft (402 m)   Old Road   Falmouth

17° N

62°40' W   Redonda   62°20' W   62° W   61°40' W

ENVIRONMENTAL/ECONOMIC:

Climate: tropical marine, little change in temperature

Agricultural Products: cotton, fruit, vegetables, bananas, livestock

Major Exports: petroleum products, manufactures, machinery and transport equipment, food, and live animals

Natural Hazards: hurricanes, tropical storms, droughts

ARGENTINA

Country Name: Argentine Republic
Continent: South America
Area: 1,073,518 sq mi / 2,780,400 sq km
Population: 36,925,000
Population Density: 34 people per sq mi /13 people per sq km
Capital: Buenos Aires

PHYSICAL:

Highest Point: Cerro Aconcagua 22,834 ft / 6,960 m
Lowest Point: Valdes Peninsula 131 ft / 40 m below sea level
Mountain Ranges:

    Andes: •located in western Argentina •extend into Chile and Bolivia
    Sierra de Cordoba: •located in central Argentina

Peaks (minimum elevation of 8,000 ft / 2,400 m):
Cerro Aconcagua: •located in the Andes •highest point in South America
Grasslands/Prairies:
Gran Chaco: •located in northern Argentina •extends into Paraguay
Pampas: •located in central Argentina
Depressions:
Valdes Peninsula: •located on the southeastern coast of Argentina •lowest point in South America
Oceans:
Atlantic: •forms the eastern coast of Argentina
Islands:
Islas Malvinas: •group of islands off the southeast coast •claimed by Argentina •administered by the United Kingdom as the Falkland Islands
Tierra del Fuego: •group of islands south of mainland Argentina •name of the largest island in the group •bordered by the Atlantic Ocean •western half belongs to Chile
Straits:
Strait of Magellan: •forms part of the southern coast of Argentina •separates Tierra del Fuego from mainland Argentina •connects the Pacific and Atlantic Oceans
Rivers:
Paraguay: •tributary of the Parana River •forms part of the Argentina-Paraguay border •extends into Brazil
Parana: •has its mouth in the Rio de la Plata Estuary •forms part of the Argentina-Paraguay border •extends into Brazil

Uruguay: •has its mouth in the Rio de la Plata Estuary •forms all of the Argentina-Uruguay border •extends into Brazil

Deltas:
Rio de la Plata Estuary: •mouth of the Parana and Uruguay Rivers •feeds into the Atlantic Ocean •borders Argentina and Uruguay

Waterfalls:
Iguazu Falls: •located in northeastern Argentina •part of the Iguazu River •on the Argentina-Brazil border

POLITICAL:
Independence: July 9, 1816 (from Spain)
Bordering Countries: Chile, Paraguay, Brazil, Bolivia, Uruguay (5)
Regions:
Patagonia: •high plateau in southern Argentina •located east of the Andes
Administrative Divisions: Buenos Aires, Catamarca, Chaco, Chubut, Cordoba, Corrientes, Entre Rios, Formosa, Jujuy, La Pampa, La Rioja, Mendoza, Misiones, Neuquen, Rio Negro, Salta, San Juan, San Luis, Santa Cruz, Santa Fe, Santiago del Estero, Tierra del Fuego, Tucuman (23 provinces) •Buenos Aires Federal District (1 federal district)
Ethnic/Racial Groups: European (mainly Spanish and Italian), Amerindian
Religion: Christianity (predominantly Roman Catholic)
Languages: Spanish, English, Italian, German, French
Currency: Argentine peso
Current President: Nestor Kirchner
Cities (capital, largest, or with at least a million people):
Buenos Aires: •located in eastern Argentina •city in the Buenos Aires province •Buenos Aires Federal District is located in center of city •capital of Argentina •most populated city in Argentina (13,349,000 people) •chief port on the Rio de la Plata Estuary
Cordoba: •located in central Argentina •city in the Cordoba province •on the edge of the Sierra de Cordoba
Rosario: •located in central Argentina •city in the Santa Fe province •chief port on the Parana River
Mendoza: •located in western Argentina •city in the Mendoza province •on the edge of the Andes

ENVIRONMENTAL/ECONOMIC:
Climate: mostly temperate, arid in the south
Natural Resources: lead, zinc, tin, copper, iron ore
Agricultural Products: sunflower seeds, lemons, soybeans, livestock
Major Exports: edible oils, fuels and energy, cereals, feed, motor vehicles
Natural Hazards: earthquakes, pamperos (windstorms), floods

ARMENIA

Country Name: Republic of Armenia
Continent: Asia
Area: 11,484 sq mi / 29,743 sq km
Population: 3,220,000
Population Density: 280 people per sq mi / 108 people per sq km
Capital: Yerevan

PHYSICAL:
Highest Point: Aragats 13,419 ft / 4,090 m
Lowest Point: Debed (river) 1,312 ft / 400 m
Mountain Ranges:
   Lesser Caucasus: ● cover most of the country ● extend into Georgia, Turkey, and
      Azerbaijan
Peaks (minimum elevation of 8,000 ft / 2,400 m):
   Aragats: ● located in the Lesser Caucasus ● highest point in Armenia
Lakes:
   Sevan: ● located in central Armenia ● surrounded by the Lesser Caucasus
Rivers:
   Aras: ● forms all of the Armenia-Iran border ● forms part of the Armenia-Turkey
      border ● extends into Turkey and Azerbaijan

POLITICAL:
Independence: September 21, 1991 (from the Soviet Union)
Former Names: Armenian Soviet Socialist Republic, Armenian Republic
Bordering Countries: Azerbaijan, Turkey, Georgia, Iran (4)
Administrative Divisions: Aragatsotn, Ararat, Armavir, Gegharkunik, Kotayk, Lorri, Shirak, Syunik, Tavush, Vayots Dzor, Yerevan (11 provinces)
Ethnic/Racial Groups: Armenian, Russian
Religion: Christianity (primarily Armenian Apostolic)
Languages: Armenian, Russian
Currency: dram
Current President: Robert Kocharian
Cities (capital, largest, or with at least a million people):
Yerevan: ●located in central Armenia ●city in the Yerevan province ●capital of Armenia ●most populated city in Armenia (1,079,000 people)

ENVIRONMENTAL/ECONOMIC:
Climate: Highland continental with hot summers/cold winters
Natural Resources: gold, copper, molybdenum, zinc, alumina
Agricultural Products: fruits (especially grapes), vegetables, livestock
Major Exports: diamonds, mineral products, foodstuffs
Natural Hazards: earthquakes, droughts

AUSTRALIA
Country Name: Commonwealth of Australia
Continent: Australia/Oceania
Area: 2,969,906 sq mi / 7,692,024 sq km (largest in Australia/Oceania)
Population: 19,917,000 (largest in Australia/Oceania)
Population Density: 6.7 people per sq mi / 2.6 people per sq km (least dense in Australia/Oceania)
Capital: Canberra

PHYSICAL:
Highest Point: Mount Kosciuszko 7,310 ft / 2,228 m
Lowest Point: Lake Eyre 52 ft / 16 m below sea level (lowest point in Australia/Oceania)
Mountain Ranges:
Australian Alps: ●located in southeastern Australia
Flinders Ranges: ●located in southern Australia
Great Dividing Range: ●located in eastern Australia
Macdonnell Ranges: ●located in central Australia
Depressions:
Lake Eyre: ●located in central Australia ●lowest point in Australia/Oceania

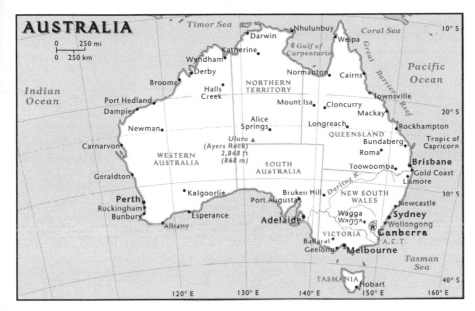

Grasslands/Prairies:
    Nullarbor Plain: •located in southern Australia •north of the Great Australian Bight

Plateau Regions:
    Kimberley Plateau: •located in northwestern Australia
    Lake Eyre Basin: •located in central Australia
    Murray River Basin: •located in southern Australian •between the Flinders
       Ranges and the Great Dividing Range

Deserts:
    Gibson: •located in western Australia
    Great Sandy: •located in western Australia
    Great Victoria: •located in southern Australia
    Simpson: •located in central Australia
    Tanami: •located in northern Australia

Oceans:
    Indian: •forms the western and southern coasts of Australia •forms part of the
       northern coast of Australia
    Pacific: •forms part of the eastern coast of Australia

Seas:
    Arafura Sea: •forms part of the northern coast of Australia
    Coral Sea: •forms part of the eastern coast of Australia
    Tasman Sea: •forms part of the southeastern coast of Australia
    Timor Sea: •forms part of the northern coast of Australia

Gulfs:
    Gulf of Carpentaria: •forms part of the northern coast of Australia •feeds into the Arafura Sea
    Joseph Bonaparte: •forms part of the northern coast of Australia •feeds into the Timor Sea
    Spencer: •forms part of the southern coast of Australia
Bays:
    Great Australian Bight: •forms part of the southern coast of Australia •feeds into the Indian Ocean
Straits:
    Bass: •forms part of the southwestern coast of Australia •separates the island of Tasmania from mainland Australia •connects the Indian Ocean and the Tasman Sea
    Torres: •forms part of the northern coast of Australia •separates Australia from Papua New Guinea •connects the Arafura and Coral Seas
Lakes:
    Eyre: •located in southern Australia •located on the Lake Eyre Basin •lowest point in Australia/Oceania •largest lake in Australia/Oceania
    Torrens: •located in southern Australia
Rivers:
    Darling: •tributary of the Murray River • has its source in the Great Dividing Range •along with the Murray River, it forms the longest river in Australia/Oceania
    Murray: •has its mouth in the Indian Ocean •has its source in the Australian Alps •including its tributary the Darling River, the Murray forms the longest river in Australia/Oceania
Peninsulas:
    Cape York: •bordered by the Coral Sea, Gulf of Carpentaria, and Torres Strait
    Eyre: •bordered by the Indian Ocean, Great Australian Bight, and Spencer Gulf
Islands:
    Tasmania: •an island southeast of mainland Australia •bordered by the Indian Ocean, Tasman Sea, and Bass Strait •a state of Australia

POLITICAL:
Independence: January 1, 1901(from the United Kingdom)
Regions:
    Arnhem Land: •located in Australia's Northern Territory •Aboriginal homeland
Administrative Divisions: New South Wales, Queensland, South Australia, Tasmania, Victoria, Western Australia (6 states) •Australian Capital Territory, Northern Territory (2 territories)
External Territories: Ashmore and Cartier Islands, Christmas Island, Cocos Islands, Coral Sea Islands, Heard and McDonald Islands, Norfolk Island (6)
Ethnic/Racial Groups: white, Asian, Aboriginal
Religion: Christianity (Anglican, Roman Catholic)
Languages: English, indigenous languages

Currency: Australian dollar
Current Prime Minister: John Howard
Cities (capital, largest, or with at least a million people):
Sydney: •located in southeastern Australia •city in the New South Wales state
•most populated city in Australia (4,277,000 people) •chief port on the Tasman Sea
Melbourne: •located in southeastern Australia •city in the Victoria state •chief port
on the Bass Strait
Brisbane: •located in eastern Australia •city in the Queensland state •chief port on
the Coral Sea
Perth: •located in southwestern Australia •city in the Western Australia state •a
major port on the Indian Ocean
Adelaide: •located in southern Australia •city in the South Australia state •a major
port on the Indian Ocean
Canberra: •city in the Australian Capital Territory •capital of Australia (373,000 people)

ENVIRONMENTAL/ECONOMIC:
Climate: mostly arid to semi-arid, temperate in the south and east, tropical in the north
Natural Resources: bauxite, coal, iron ore, copper, tin
Agricultural Products: wheat, barley, sugarcane, fruits, cattle
Major Exports: coal, gold, meat, wool, alumina
Natural Hazards: cyclones, severe droughts, forest fires

AUSTRIA
Country Name: Republic of Austria
Continent: Europe
Area: 32,378 sq mi / 83,858 sq km
Population: 8,157,000
Population Density: 252 people per sq mi / 97 people per sq km
Capital: Vienna

PHYSICAL:
Highest Point: Grossglockner 12,461 ft / 3,798 m
Lowest Point: Neusiedler See 377 ft / 115 m
Mountain Ranges:
Alps: •cover most of southern Austria •extend into Switzerland, Liechtenstein,
Italy, and Germany
Peaks (minimum elevation of 8,000 ft / 2,400 m):
Grossglockner: •located in the Alps •highest point in Austria
Passes:
Brenner: •located in the Alps •crosses the border into Italy
Lakes:
Constance: •located in northwestern Austria •on the border with Germany and
Switzerland •fed by the Rhine River
Neusiedler See: •located in eastern Austria •on the Austria-Hungary border

Rivers:

Danube: •forms part of the Austria-Germany border •extends into Germany, Slovakia, and Hungary

Drava: •has its source in the Alps •extends into Slovenia

Inn: •tributary of the Danube •forms part of the Austria-Germany border •has its source in the Swiss Alps

Rhine: •forms part of the Austria-Liechtenstein border •extends into Switzerland and Germany

POLITICAL:

Independence: 1156 (from Bavaria)

Bordering Countries: Germany, Italy, Hungary, Czech Republic, Slovenia, Switzerland, Slovakia, Liechtenstein (8)

Administrative Divisions: Burgenland, Carinthia, Lower Austria, Salzburg, Styria, Tirol, Upper Austria, Vienna, Vorarlberg (9 states)

Ethnic/Racial Groups: primarily German

Religion: Christianity (Roman Catholic, Protestant)

Languages: German, Slovene, Croatian, Hungarian

Currency: euro

Current President: Heinz Fischer

Cities (capital, largest, or with at least a million people):

Vienna: •located in northeastern Austria •city in the Vienna state •capital of Austria •most populated city in Austria (2,179,000 people) •chief port on the Danube River

Climate: temperate with cold and rainy or snowy winters/moderate summers
Natural Resources: iron ore, oil, timber, magnesite, lead
Agricultural Products: grains, potatoes, sugar beets, wine, dairy products
Major Exports: machinery and equipment, motor vehicles and parts, paper, metal goods, chemicals
Natural Hazards: landslides, avalanches, earthquakes

AZERBAIJAN

Country Name: Republic of Azerbaijan
Continent: Asia
Area: 33,436 sq mi / 86,600 sq km
Population: 8,233,000
Population Density: 246 people per sq mi / 95 people per sq mi
Capital: Baku

PHYSICAL:
Highest Point: Bazar Dyuzi 14,652 ft / 4,466 m
Lowest Point: Caspian Sea 92 ft / 28 m below sea level
Mountain Ranges:

Caucasus: •located in northern Azerbaijan •extend into Russia and Georgia
Lesser Caucasus: •located in western Azerbaijan •extend into Armenia and Georgia

Peaks (minimum elevation of 8,000 ft / 2,400 m):
Bazar Dyuzi: •located in the Caucasus •on the Azerbaijan-Russia border •highest point in Azerbaijan
Depressions:
Caspian Sea: •located in eastern Azerbaijan •lowest point in Azerbaijan
Lakes:
Caspian Sea: •forms the eastern coast of Azerbaijan •also borders Russia and Iran •largest lake in the world
Rivers:
Aras: •has its mouth in the Caspian Sea •forms part of the Azerbaijan-Iran border •extends into Turkey

POLITICAL:
Independence: August 30, 1991 (from the Soviet Union)
Former Name: Azerbaijan Soviet Socialist Republic
Bordering Countries: Armenia, Iran, Georgia, Russia, Turkey (5)
Regions:
Nagorno-Karabakh: •mountainous region in western Azerbaijan •located in the Lesser Caucasus
Administrative Divisions: Abseron, Agcabadi, Agdam, Agdas, Agstafa, Agsu, Astara, Balakan, Barda, Beylaqan, Bilasuvar, Cabrayil, Calilabad, Daskasan, Davaci, Fuzuli, Gadabay, Goranboy, Goycay, Haciqabul, Imisli, Ismayilli, Kalbacar, Kurdamir, Lacin, Lankaran, Lerik, Masalli, Neftcala, Oguz, Qabala, Qax, Qazax, Qobustan, Quba, Qubadli, Qusar, Saatli, Sabirabad, Saki, Salyan, Samaxi, Samkir, Samux, Siyazan, Susa, Tartar, Tovuz, Ucar, Xacmaz, Xanlar, Xizi, Xocali, Xocavand, Yardimli, Yevlax, Zangilan, Zaqatala, Zardab (59 rayons) •Ali Bayramli, Baki, Ganca, Lankaran, Mingacevir, Naftalan, Saki, Sumqayit, Susa, Xankandi, Yevlax (11 cities) •Naxcivan(1 autonomous republic)
Ethnic/Racial Groups: Azeri, Dagestani, Russian, Armenian
Religion: primarily Islam
Languages: Azeri, Russian, Armenian
Currency: Azerbaijani manat
Current President: Ilham Aliyev
Cities (capital, largest, or with at least a million people):
Baku: •located in eastern Azerbaijan •capital of Azerbaijan •most populated city in Azerbaijan (1,816,000 people) •chief port on the Caspian Sea

ENVIRONMENTAL/ECONOMIC:
Climate: dry, semi-arid steppe
Natural Resources: oil, natural gas, iron ore, nonferrous metals, alumina
Agricultural Products: cotton, grain, rice, grapes, cattle
Major Exports: oil and gas, machinery, cotton, foodstuffs
Natural Hazards: droughts

BAHAMAS

Country Name: Commonwealth of the Bahamas
Continent: North America
Area: 5,382 sq mi / 13,939 sq km
Population: 311,000
Population Density: 58 people per sq mi / 22 people per sq km
Capital: Nassau

B

PHYSICAL:

Highest Point: Mount Alvernia 207 ft / 63 m
Lowest Point: Atlantic Ocean 0 ft / 0 m (sea level)
Oceans:
   Atlantic: •surrounds the islands of the Bahamas
Islands:
   Andros: •largest island in the Bahamas •surrounded by the Atlantic Ocean
   Great Inagua: •second largest island in the Bahamas •surrounded by the Atlantic Ocean

POLITICAL:

Independence: July 10, 1973 (from the United Kingdom)
Administrative Divisions: Acklins and Crooked Islands, Bimini, Cat Island,
   Exuma, Freeport, Fresh Creek, Governor's Harbour, Green Turtle Cay, Harbour
   Island, High Rock, Inagua, Kemps Bay, Long Island, Marsh Harbour, Mayaguana,
   New Providence, Nicholls' Town and Berry Islands, Ragged Island, Rock Sound,
   Sandy Point, San Salvador and Rum Cay (21 districts)
Ethnic Groups: black, white
Religion: Christianity (Baptist, Anglican, Roman Catholic)
Languages: English, Creole
Currency: Bahamian dollar
Current Prime Minister: Perry Gladstone Christie
Cities (capital, largest, or with at least a million people):
   Nassau: •located on New Providence island •city in the New Providence district
      •capital of the Bahamas •most populated city in the Bahamas (222,000 people)
      •chief port on the Atlantic Ocean

ENVIRONMENTAL/ECONOMIC:

Climate: tropical marine, moderated by the Gulf Stream current
Natural Resources: salt, aragonite, timber, arable land
Agricultural Products: citrus, vegetables, poultry

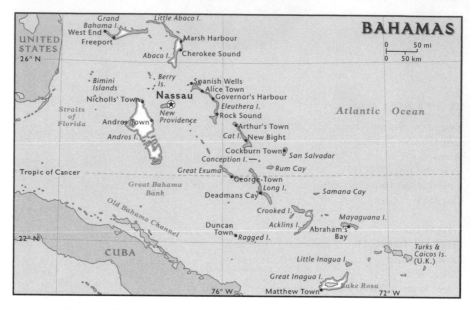

Major Exports: fish and crawfish, rum, salt, chemicals, fruits and vegetables
Natural Hazards: hurricanes, tropical storms

BAHRAIN

Country Name: Kingdom of Bahrain
Continent: Asia
Area: 277 sq mi / 717 sq km
Population: 678,000
Population Density: 2,448 people per sq mi / 946 people per sq km
Capital: Manama

PHYSICAL:
Highest Point: Jabal ad Dukhan 400 ft / 122 m
Lowest Point: Persian Gulf 0 ft / 0 m (sea level)
Gulfs:
Persian: •forms the northern coast of Bahrain
Gulf of Bahrain: •forms the western, southern, and eastern coasts of Bahrain
Islands:
Bahrain: •largest island in Bahrain •surrounded by Persian Gulf and Gulf of Bahrai

POLITICAL:

Independence: August 15, 1971 (from the United Kingdom)

Former Name: Dilmun

Administrative Divisions: Al Hadd, Al Manamah, Al Mintaqah al Gharbiyah, Al Mintaqah al Wusta, Al Mintaqah ash Shamaliyah, Al Muharraq, Ar Rifa wa al Mintaqah al Janubiyah, Jidd Hafs, Madinat Hamad, Madinat Isa, Juzur Hawar, Sitrah (12 municipalities)

Ethnic/Racial Groups: Arab, Asian, Iranian

Religion: Islam (Sunni, Shiite)

Languages: Arabic, English, Farsi, Urdu

Currency: Bahraini dinar

Current King: Hamad bin Isa Al Khalifa

Cities (capital, largest, or with at least a million people):
   Manama: •located on the island of Bahrain •city in the Al Manamah municipality •capital of Bahrain •most populated city in Bahrain (139,000 people) •chief port on the Persian Gulf

ENVIRONMENTAL/ECONOMIC:

Climate: arid with mild winters/hot summers

Natural Resources: petroleum, natural gas, fish, pearls

Agricultural Products: fruits, vegetables, poultry, shrimp

Major Exports: petroleum and petroleum products, aluminum, textiles

Natural Hazards: droughts, dust storms

BANGLADESH

Country Name: People's Republic of Bangladesh
Continent: Asia
Area: 56,997 sq mi / 147,570 sq km
Population: 146,733,000
Population Density: 2,620 people per sq mi / 994 people per sq km
Capital: Dhaka

PHYSICAL:
Highest Point: Keokradong 4,035 ft / 1,230 m
Lowest Point: Bay of Bengal 0 ft / 0 m (sea level)
Grasslands/Prairies:
　　Sundarbans: •located in southern Bangladesh •borders the Bay of Bengal •extends
　　　　into India
Bays:
　　Bay of Bengal: •forms the southern coast of Bangladesh •feeds into the Indian Ocean
Rivers:
　　Brahmaputra: •tributary of the Ganges •extends into India
　　Ganges: •has its mouth in the Bay of Bengal •extends into India
　　Jamuna: •tributary of the Ganges •joins with the Brahmaputra

Deltas:
> Mouths of the Ganges: •mouth of the Ganges •feed into the Bay of Bengal •extend into India

POLITICAL:
Independence: December 16, 1971 (from West Pakistan)
Former Name: East Pakistan
Bordering Countries: India, Myanmar (2)
Administrative Divisions: Barisal, Chittagong, Dhaka, Khulna, Rajshahi, Sylhet (6 divisions)
Ethnic/Racial Groups: Bengali
Religions: Islam, Hinduism
Languages: Bangla (Bengali), English
Currency: taka
Current Prime Minsiter: Khaleda Zia
Cities (capital, largest, or with at least a million people):
> Dhaka: •located in central Bangladesh •city in the Dhaka division •capital of Bangladesh •most populated city in Bangladesh (12,560,000 people)
> Chittagong: •located in southeastern Bangladesh •city in the Chittagong division • chief port on the Bay of Bengal
> Khulna: •located in southwestern Bangladesh •city in the Khulna division •located near the Sundarbans in the Mouths of the Ganges

ENVIRONMENTAL/ECONOMIC:
Climate: tropical, mild winters/hot summers/warm and rainy monsoon seasons
Natural Resources: natural gas, arable land, timber, coal
Agricultural Products: rice, jute, tea, wheat, beef
Major Exports: garments, jute and jute goods, leather, frozen fish and seafood
Natural Hazards: droughts, cyclones, heavy rains, floods

BARBADOS

Country Name: Barbados
Continent: North America
Area: 166 sq mi / 430 sq km
Population: 253,000
Population Density: 1,524 people per sq mi / 588 people per sq km (most dense in North America)
Capital: Bridgetown

PHYSICAL:
Highest Point: Mount Hillaby 1,115 ft / 340 m
Lowest Point: Atlantic Ocean 0 ft / 0 m (sea level)
Oceans:
> Atlantic: •forms the entire coast of Barbados

BARBADOS

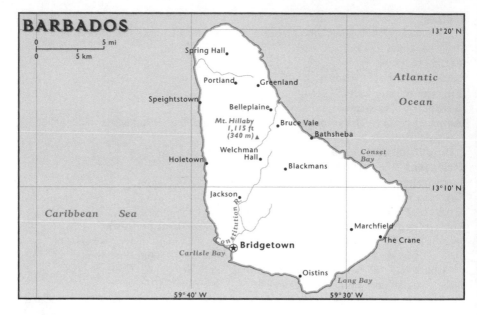

POLITICAL:

Independence: November 30, 1966 (from the United Kingdom)

Administrative Divisions: Christ Church, Saint Andrew, Saint George, Saint James, Saint John, Saint Joseph, Saint Lucy, Saint Michael, Saint Peter, Saint Philip, Saint Thomas (11 parishes)

Ethnic/Racial Groups: predominantly black

Religion: Christianity (Protestant, Roman Catholic)

Language: English

Currency: Barbadian dollar

Current Prime Minister: Owen Arthur

Cities (capital, largest, or with at least a million people):
> Bridgetown: •located on the island of Barbados •city in the Saint Michael parish •capital of Barbados •most populated city in Barbados (140,000 people) •chief port on the Atlantic Ocean

ENVIRONMENTAL/ECONOMIC:

Climate: tropical

Natural Resources: oil, fish, natural gas

Agricultural Products: sugarcane, vegetables, cotton

Major Exports: sugar and molasses, rum, other foods and beverages, chemicals

Natural Hazards: hurricanes, landslides

BELARUS

Country Name: Republic of Belarus
Continent: Europe
Area: 80,153 sq mi / 207,595 sq km
Population: 9,873,000
Population Density: 123 people per sq mi / 48 people per sq km
Capital: Minsk

PHYSICAL:

Highest Point: Dzyarzhynskaya Hara 1,135 ft / 346 m
Lowest Point: Nyoman River 295 ft / 90 m
Swamps:
    Pinsk Marshes: •located in southern Belarus •extend into Ukraine
Rivers:
    Nyoman: •has its source in central Belarus •extends into Lithuania
    Dnyapro (Dnieper): •extends into Russia and Ukraine

POLITICAL:

Independence: August 25, 1991 (from the Soviet Union)
Former Name: Belorussian Soviet Socialist Republic
Bordering Countries: Russia, Ukraine, Lithuania, Poland, Latvia (5)
Administrative Divisions: Brestskaya, Homyelskaya, Hrodzyenskaya,
    Mahilyowskaya, Minskaya, Vitsyebskaya (6 voblasts) •Horad Minsk (1 municipality)

Ethnic/Racial Groups: Belarusian, Russian
Religions: Christianity (Eastern Orthodox, Roman Catholic, Protestant) Judaism, Islam
Languages: Belarusian, Russian
Currency: Belarusian ruble
Current President: Alexander Lukashenko
Cities (capital, largest, or with at least a million people):
>   Minsk: •located in central Belarus •city in the Horad Minsk municipality •capital of Belarus •most populated city in Belarus (1,705,000 people)

ENVIRONMENTAL/ECONOMIC:
Climate: continental/maritime, cold winters/cool summers
Natural Resources: forests, peat deposits, oil, natural gas, granite
Agricultural Products: grain, potatoes, vegetables, sugar beets, beef
Major Exports: machinery and equipment, mineral products, chemicals, metals, textiles
Natural Hazards: floods

BELGIUM
Country Name: Kingdom of Belgium
Continent: Europe
Area: 11,787 sq mi / 30,528 sq km
Population: 10,380,000
Population Density: 873 people per sq mi / 337 people per sq km
Capital: Brussels

PHYSICAL:
Highest Point: Signal de Botrange 2,277 ft / 694 m
Lowest Point: North Sea 0 ft / 0 m (sea level)
Seas:
>   North: •forms the northwestern coast of Belgium •feeds into the Atlantic Ocean

Rivers:
>   Meuse: •forms part of the Belgium-Netherlands border •extends into France and the Netherlands
>   Schelde: •extends into France and the Netherlands

Regions:
>   Ardennes: •forested plateau region in southeastern Belgium •extends into France and Luxembourg

POLITICAL:
Independence: October 4, 1830 (from the Netherlands)
Bordering Countries: France, Netherlands, Germany, Luxembourg (4)
Regions:
>   Flanders: •lowland region in northwestern Belgium •located east of the North Sea

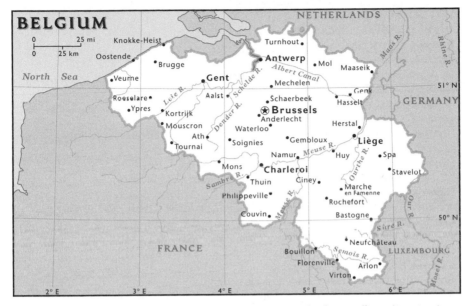

BELGIUM

0 ___ 25 mi
0 ___ 25 km

Administrative Divisions: •Brussels Capital Region, Flanders, Wallonia (3 regions)
Ethnic/Racial Groups: Fleming, Walloon
Religion: Christianity (Roman Catholic, Protestant)
Languages: Flemish (Dutch), French, German
Currency: euro
Current Prime Minister: Guy Verhofstadt
Cities (capital, largest, or with at least a million people):
  Brussels: •located in central Belgium •main city in the Brussels Capital Region
  •capital of Belgium •most populated city in Belgium (998,000 people)

ENVIRONMENTAL/ECONOMIC:
Climate: temperate with mild winters/cool summers
Natural Resources: coal, natural gas, construction materials, silica sand, carbonates
Agricultural Products: sugar beets, fresh vegetables, fruits, grain, beef
Major Exports: machinery and equipment, diamonds, metals and metal products
Natural Hazards: floods

BELIZE
Country Name: Belize
Continent: North America
Area: 8,867 sq mi / 22,965 sq km
Population: 271,000
Population Density: 31 people per sq mi / 12 people per sq km
Capital: Belmopan

PHYSICAL:

Highest Point: Victoria Peak 3,675 ft / 1,120 m
Lowest Point: Caribbean Sea 0 ft / 0 m (sea level)
Mountain Ranges:

Maya: •located in southern Belize •extend into Guatemala

Seas:

Caribbean: •forms most of the eastern coast of Belize •feeds into the Atlantic Ocean

Gulfs:

Gulf of Honduras: •forms the southeastern coast of Belize •feeds into the Caribbean Sea

Bays:

Bay of Chetumal: •forms part of the northern coast of Belize

Rivers:

Hondo: •has its mouth in the Bay of Chetumal •feeds into the Caribbean Sea

POLITICAL:

Independence: September 21, 1981 (from the United Kingdom)
Former Name: British Honduras
Bordering Countries: Guatemala, Mexico (2)
Administrative Divisions: Belize, Cayo, Corozal, Orange Walk, Stann Creek, Toledo (6 districts)
Ethnic/Racial Groups: mestizo, Creole, Maya, Garifuna
Religion: Christianity (Roman Catholic, Protestant)
Languages: English, Spanish, Mayan, Garifuna, Creole

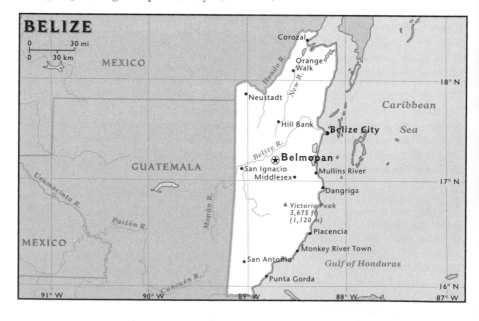

Currency: Belizean dollar
Current Prime Minister: Said Musa
Cities (capital, largest, or with at least a million people):
 Belize City: •located in eastern Belize •city in the Belize district •most populated
  city in Belize (56,000 people) •chief port on the Caribbean Sea
 Belmopan: •located in central Belize •city in the Cayo district •capital of Belize
  (9,000 people)

ENVIRONMENTAL/ECONOMIC:

Climate: tropical, hot and humid
Natural Resources: arable land potential, timber, fish, hydropower
Agricultural Products: bananas, coca, citrus, sugar, fish
Major Exports: sugar, bananas, citrus, clothing, fish products
Natural Hazards: hurricanes, floods

BENIN

Country Name: Republic of Benin
Continent: Africa
Area: 43,484 sq mi / 112,622 sq km
Population: 7,041,000
Population Density: 162 people per sq mi / 63 people per sq km
Capital: Porto-Novo

PHYSICAL:
Highest Point: Mont Sokbaro 2,159 ft / 658 m
Lowest Point: Bight of Benin 0 ft / 0 m (sea level)
Grasslands/Prairies:
   Sahel: •located in northern Benin •extends into Togo, Burkina Faso, Niger, and Nigeria
Bays:
   Bight of Benin: •forms the southern coast of Benin •feeds into the Gulf of Guinea
Rivers:
   Niger: •forms part of the Benin-Niger border •extends into Niger and Nigeria

POLITICAL:
Independence: August 1, 1960 (from France)
Former Name: Dahomey
Bordering Countries: Nigeria, Togo, Burkina Faso, Niger (4)
Administrative Divisions: Alibori, Atakora, Atlantique, Borgou, Collines, Kouffo, Donga, Littoral, Mono, Oueme, Plateau, Zou (12 departments)
Ethnic/Racial Groups: African (mainly Fon, Adja, Yoruba, Bariba)
Religions: indigenous beliefs, Christianity, Islam
Languages: French, Fon, Yoruba, tribal languages
Currency: Communaute Financiere Africaine franc
Current President: Mathieu Kerekou
Cities (capital, largest, or with at least a million people):
   Cotonou: •located in southern Benin •city in the Littoral department •most populated city in Benin (818,100 people) •chief port on the Bight of Benin
   Porto-Novo: •located in southeastern Benin •city in the Oueme department •capital of Benin (238,000 people)

ENVIRONMENTAL/ECONOMIC:
Climate: tropical; hot and humid in the south; semi-arid in the north
Natural Resources: offshore oil deposits, limestone, marble, timber
Agricultural Products: cotton, corn, cassava, yams, livestock
Major Exports: cotton, crude oil, palm products, cacao
Natural Hazards: harmattan winds

BHUTAN
Country Name: Kingdom of Bhutan
Continent: Asia
Area: 17,954 sq mi / 46,500 sq km
Population: 945,000
Population Density: 53 people per sq mi / 20 people per sq km
Capital: Thimphu

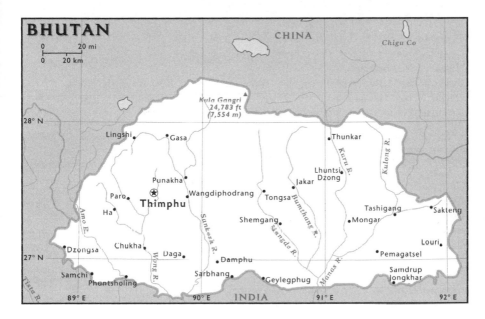

PHYSICAL:
Highest Point: Kula Gangri 24,783 ft / 7,554 m
Lowest Point: Drangme Chhu 318 ft / 97 m
Mountain Ranges:
    Himalaya: •cover most of Bhutan •extend into India and China
Peaks (minimum elevation of 8,000 ft / 2,400 m):
    Kula Gangri: •located in the Himalaya •highest point in Bhutan

POLITICAL:
Independence: August 8, 1949 (from India)
Bordering Countries: India, China (2)
Administrative Divisions: Bumthang, Chhukha, Chirang, Daga, Geylegphug,
    Ha, Lhuntshi, Mongar, Paro, Pemagatsel, Punakha, Samchi, Samdrup Jongkhar,
    Shemgang, Tashigang, Thimphu, Tongsa, Wangdiphodrang (18 districts)
Ethnic/Racial Groups: Bhote, Nepalese, indigenous tribes
Religions: Lamaistic Buddhism, Hinduism
Languages: Dzongkha, Tibetan dialects, Nepalese dialects
Currency: ngultrum, Indian rupee
Current King: Jigme Singye Wangchuck
Cities (capital, largest, or with at least a million people):
    Thimphu: •located in western Bhutan •city in the Thimphu district •capital of
    Bhutan •most populated city in Bhutan (35,000 people) •located in a valley of
    the Himalaya

ENVIRONMENTAL/ECONOMIC:
Climate: tropical in the southern plains; cool winters/hot summers in the central valleys; severe winters/cold summers in the high mountains
Natural Resources: timber, hydropower, gypsum, calcium carbide
Agricultural Products: rice, corn, root crops, citrus, dairy products
Major Exports: electricity, cardamom, gypsum, timber, handicrafts
Natural Hazards: violent storms in the mountains, landslides

BOLIVIA
Country Name: Republic of Bolivia
Continent: South America
Area: 424,164 sq mi / 1,098,581 sq km
Population: 8,595,000
Population Density: 20 people per sq mi / 7.8 people per sq km
Capitals: La Paz (administrative capital), Sucre (judicial capital)

PHYSICAL:
Highest Point: Nevado Sajama 21,463 ft / 6,542 m
Lowest Point: Paraguay River 295 ft / 90 m
Mountain Ranges:
   Andes: •located in western and central Bolivia •extend into Peru, Chile, and Argentina
Peaks (minimum elevation of 8,000 ft / 2,400 m):
   Nevado Sajama: •located in the Andes •highest point in Bolivia

Plateau Regions:
Altiplano: •located in southwestern Bolivia •extends into Peru •basin of the Andes
Swamps:
Pantanal: •located in eastern Bolivia •extends into Brazil and Paraguay
•largest swamp in the world
Lakes:
Poopo: •located in western Bolivia •located on the Altiplano near the slopes of the Andes
Titicaca: •located in western Bolivia •on the Bolivia-Peru border •on the Altiplano near the slopes of the Andes •largest lake in South America
Rivers:
Madeira: •forms part of the Bolivia-Brazil border •extends into Brazil •has its source in the Andes
Mamore: •tributary of the Madeira •forms part of the Bolivia-Brazil border •extends into Brazil •has its source in the Andes

POLITICAL:
Independence: August 6, 1825 (from Spain)
Bordering Countries: Brazil, Peru, Chile, Argentina, Paraguay (5)
Administrative Divisions: Beni, Chuquisaca, Cochabamba, La Paz, Oruro, Pando, Potosi, Santa Cruz, Tarija (9 departments)
Ethnic/Racial Groups: Quechua, mestizo, Aymara, white
Religion: Christianity (primarily Roman Catholic)
Languages: Spanish, Quechua, Aymara
Currency: boliviano
Current President: Carlos Mesa
Cities (capital, largest, or with at least a million people):
La Paz: •located in western Bolivia •city in the La Paz department •administrative capital of Bolivia •most populated city in Bolivia (1,477,000 people)
Santa Cruz: •located in central Bolivia •city in the Santa Cruz department •on the edge of the Andes
Sucre: •located in southern Bolivia •city in the Chuquisaca department •judicial capital of Bolivia (212,000 people)

ENVIRONMENTAL/ECONOMIC:
Climate: humid and tropical in the rain forest; cold and semi-arid in the mountains
Natural Resources: tin, natural gas, petroleum, zinc, tungsten
Agricultural Products: soybeans, coffee, coca, cotton, timber
Major Exports: soybeans, natural gas, zinc, gold, wood
Natural Hazards: floods, earthquakes

BOSNIA AND HERZEGOVINA

Country Name: Republic of Bosnia and Herzegovina
Continent: Europe
Area: 19,741 sq mi / 51,129 sq km
Population: 3,892,000
Population Density: 197 people per sq mi / 76 people per sq km
Capital: Sarajevo

PHYSICAL:
Highest Point: Maglic 7,828 ft / 2,386 m
Lowest Point: Adriatic Sea 0 ft / 0 m (sea level)
Mountain Ranges:
Dinaric Alps: ●located in western Bosnia and Herzegovina ●extend into Croatia and into Serbia and Montenegro
Rivers:
Sava: ●forms part of Bosnia and Herzegovina's border with Croatia and with Serbia and Montenegro ●extends into Croatia and into Serbia and Montenegro

POLITICAL:
Independence: March 1, 1992 (from Yugoslavia)
Former Names: People's Republic of Bosnia and Herzegovina, Socialist Republic of Bosnia and Herzegovina
Bordering Countries: Croatia, Serbia and Montenegro (2)
Administrative Divisions: Bosniak/Croat Federation of Bosnia and Herzegovina,

Republika Srpska (2 first-order administrative divisions) •Brcko (1 internationally supervised district)

Ethnic/Racial Groups: Bosniak, Serbian, Croatian
Religions: Islam, Christianity (Orthodox, Roman Catholic)
Languages: Croatian, Serbian, Bosnian
Currency: marka
Current President: Sulejman Tihic
Cities (capital, largest, or with at least a million people):
Sarajevo: •located in central Bosnia and Herzegovina •city in the Bosniak/Croat Federation of Bosnia and Herzegovina first-order administrative division • capital of Bosnia and Herzegovina •most populated city in Bosnia and Herzegovina (579,000 people) •on the edge of the Dinaric Alps

ENVIRONMENTAL/ECONOMIC:

Climate: hot summers/cold winters in most areas; short and cool summers/long and severe winters in the mountains; mild and rainy winters along the coast
Natural Resources: coal, iron ore, bauxite, copper, lead
Agricultural Products: wheat, corn, fruits, vegetables, livestock
Major Exports: metals, clothing, wood products
Natural Hazards: earthquakes

BOTSWANA

Country Name: Republic of Botswana
Continent: Africa
Area: 224,607 sq mi / 581,730 sq km
Population: 1,573,000
Population Density: 7.0 people per sq mi / 2.7 people per sq km
Capital: Gaborone

PHYSICAL:

Highest Point: point in the Tsodilo Hills 4,885 ft / 1,489 m
Lowest Point: Limpopo/Shashe River Junction 1,683 ft / 513 m
Swamps:
Okavango Delta: •located in northwestern Botswana
Deserts:
Kalahari: •covers most of the country •extends into Namibia and South Africa
Rivers:
Limpopo: •forms part of the Botswana-South Africa border
Okavango: •has its mouth in the Okavango Delta •extends into Namibia
Deltas:
Okavango Delta: •mouth of the Okavango River •feeds into northwestern Botswana

POLITICAL:

Independence: September 30, 1966 (from the United Kingdom)
Former Name: Bechuanaland
Bordering Countries: South Africa, Namibia, Zimbabwe (3)
Administrative Divisions: Central, Ghanzi, Kgalagadi, Kgatleng, Kweneng,
  Northwest, Northeast, Southeast, Southern (9 districts) ●Francistown, Gaborone,
  Lobatse, Selebi-Pikwe (4 town councils)
Ethnic/Racial Groups: Tswana, Kalanga, Basarwa
Religions: indigenous beliefs, Christianity
Languages: English, Setswana
Currency: pula
Current President: Festus Mogae
Cities (capital, largest, or with at least a million people):
  Gaborone: ●located in southern Botswana ●city in the Gaborone town council
    ●capital of Botswana ●most populated city in Botswana (199,000 people)

ENVIRONMENTAL/ECONOMIC:

Climate: semi-arid with warm winters/hot summers
Natural Resources: diamonds, copper, nickel, salt, soda ash
Agricultural Products: sorghum, maize, millet, livestock
Major Exports: diamonds, copper, nickel, soda ash, meat
Natural Hazards: droughts, sandstorms, dust storms

BRAZIL

Country Name: Federative Republic of Brazil
Continent: South America
Area: 3,300,169 sq mi / 8,547,403 sq km (largest in South America)
Population: 176,464,000 (largest in South America)
Population Density: 53 people per sq mi / 21 people per sq km
Capital: Brasilia

PHYSICAL:
Highest Point: Pico da Neblina 9,888 ft / 3,014 m
Lowest Point: Atlantic Ocean 0 ft / 0 m (sea level)
Mountain Ranges:
   Brazilian Highlands: ●cover much of eastern Brazil
   Guiana Highlands: ●located in northern Brazil ●extend into Venezuela, Guyana,
      and Suriname
Peaks (minimum elevation of 8,000 ft / 2,400 m):
   Pico da Neblina: ●on the Brazil-Venezuela border ●highest point in Brazil
Plateau Regions:
   Mato Grosso: ●located in central Brazil ●high region west of the Brazilian Highlands
Rain forests:
   Amazon: ●located in northern Brazil ●extends into Venezuela, Colombia, Peru, and
      Bolivia ●largest rain forest in the world

Swamps:
Pantanal: •located in central Brazil •extends into Bolivia and Paraguay •largest swamp in the world

Oceans:
Atlantic: •forms the northern and eastern coasts of Brazil

Lagoons:
Lagoa dos Patos: •located in southeastern Brazil •feeds into the Atlantic Ocean

Rivers:
Amazon: •has its mouth in the Atlantic Ocean •extends into Peru •longest river in South America •second longest river in the world

Araguaia: •tributary of the Tocantins •has its source in the Brazilian Highlands

Iguacu: •tributary of the Parana River •has its source in southern Brazil •forms part of the Brazil-Argentina border

Japura: •tributary of the Amazon •crosses into Colombia

Jurua: •tributary of the Amazon •has its source in northwestern Brazil

Madeira: •tributary of the Amazon •forms part of the Brazil-Bolivia border

Negro: •tributary of the Amazon

Paraguai (Paraguay): •has its source in the Mato Grosso Plateau •forms part of the Brazil-Paraguay border •extends into Paraguay

Parana: •has its source in the Brazilian Highlands •forms part of the Brazil-Paraguay border •extends into Argentina

Parnaiba: •mouth is in the Atlantic Ocean •source is in the Brazilian Highlands

Purus: •tributary of the Amazon •extends into Peru

Sao Francisco: •mouth is in the Atlantic Ocean •source is in the Brazilian Highlands

Tapajos: •tributary of the Amazon •has its source on the Mato Grosso Plateau

Teles Pires: •tributary of the Tapajos •has its source on the Mato Grosso Plateau

Tocantins: •mouth is in the Atlantic Ocean • source is in the Brazilian Highlands

Uruguai (Uruguay): • source is in southern Brazil •forms part of the Brazil-Argentina border

Xingu: •tributary of the Amazon •has its source on the Mato Grosso Plateau

Deltas:
Amazon River Delta: •mouth of the Amazon River •feeds into the Atlantic Ocean •largest river discharge in the world

Waterfalls:
Iguazu: •located in southwestern Brazil •part of the Iguacu River •on the Brazil-Argentina border

Dams:
Itaipu: •located in southwestern Brazil •crosses the Parana River •on the Brazil-Paraguay border •forms Itaipu Reservoir

Lakes:
Itaipu Reservoir: •located in southwestern Brazil •on the Brazil-Paraguay border •fed by the Parana River •formed by the Itaipu Dam

Islands:
Marajo: •an island in the Amazon River Delta •in northern Brazil •bordered by

the Atlantic Ocean and the Amazon River

POLITICAL:
Independence: September 7, 1822 (from Portugal)
Bordering Countries: Bolivia, Venezuela, Colombia, Peru, Paraguay, Argentina, Guyana, Uruguay, French Guiana (overseas territory of France), Suriname (10)
Administrative Divisions: Acre, Alagoas, Amapa, Amazonas, Bahia, Ceara, Espirito Santo, Goias, Maranhao, Mato Grosso, Mato Grosso do Sul, Minas Gerais, Para, Paraiba, Parana, Pernambuco, Piaui, Rio de Janeiro, Rio Grande do Norte, Rio Grande do Sul, Rondonia, Roraima, Santa Catarina, Sao Paulo, Sergipe, Tocantins (26 states) ●Distrito Federal (1 federal district)
Ethnic/Racial Groups: European (mainly Portuguese, German, Italian, Spanish), black
Religion: Christianity (primarily Roman Catholic)
Languages: Portuguese, Spanish, English, French
Currency: real
Current President: Luiz Inacio "Lula" da Silva
Cities (capital, largest, or with at least a million people):
Sao Paulo: ●located in southern Brazil ●city in the Sao Paulo state ●most populated city in Brazil (19,090,000 people)
Rio de Janeiro: ●located in southeastern Brazil ●city in the Rio de Janeiro state ●chief port on the Atlantic Ocean
Salvador: ●located in eastern Brazil ●city in the Bahia state ●a major port on the Atlantic Ocean
Belo Horizonte: ●located in eastern Brazil ●city in the Minas Gerais state ●located in a valley in the Brazilian Highlands
Fortaleza: ●located in northeastern Brazil ●city in the Ceara state ●a major port on the Atlantic Ocean
Brasilia: ●located in central Brazil ●capital of Brazil (3,099,000 people)●located in the federal district ●in the Brazilian Highlands
Curitiba: ●located in southern Brazil ●city in the Parana state ●chief port on the Iguacu River
Manaus: ●located in northwestern Brazil ●city in the Amazonas state ●chief port on the Amazon River
Recife: ●located in northeastern Brazil ●city in the Pernambuco state ●a major port on the Atlantic Ocean
Belem: ●located in northern Brazil ●city in the Para state ●a major port on the Atlantic Ocean
Porto Alegre: ●located in southwestern Brazil ●city in the Rio Grande do Sul state ●chief port on the Lagoa dos Patos (lagoon)
Goiania: ●located in central Brazil ●city in the Goias state ●in the Brazilian Highlands
Campinas ●located in southern Brazil ●city in the Sao Paulo state

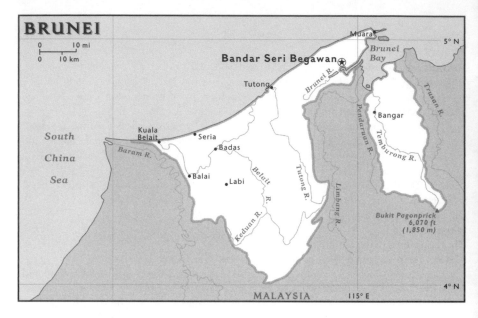

BRUNEI

ENVIRONMENTAL/ECONOMIC:
Climate: mostly tropical; temperate in the south
Natural Resources: bauxite, gold, iron ore, manganese, nickel
Agricultural Products: coffee, soybeans, wheat, rice, beef
Major Exports: transport equipment, iron ore, soybeans, footwear, coffee
Natural Hazards: droughts, floods

BRUNEI
Country Name: Negara Brunei Darussalam
Continent: Asia
Area: 2,226 sq mi / 5,765 sq km
Population: 360,000
Population Density: 162 people per sq mi / 62 people per sq km
Capital: Bandar Seri Begawan

PHYSICAL:
Highest Point: Bukit Pagon 6,070 ft / 1,850 m
Lowest Point: South China Sea 0 ft / 0 m (sea level)
Seas:
  South China: ●forms the northern coast of Brunei ●feeds into the Pacific Ocean
Islands:
  Borneo: ●island where Brunei is located ●bordered by the South China Sea ●also occupied by Malaysia and Indonesia

POLITICAL:
Independence: January 1, 1984 (from the United Kingdom)
Bordering Country: Malaysia (1)
Administrative Divisions: Belait, Brunei and Muara, Temburong, Tutong
    (4 districts)
Ethnic/Racial Groups: Malay, Chinese, indigenous
Religions: Islam, Buddhism, Christianity, indigenous beliefs
Languages: Malay, English, Chinese
Currency: Bruneian dollar
Current Sultan and Prime Minister: Hassanal Bolkiah
Cities (capital, largest, or with at least a million people):
    Bandar Seri Begawan: •located in northern Brunei •city in the Brunei and Muara
        district •capital of Brunei •most populated city in Brunei (61,000 people)
        •chief port on Brunei Bay

ENVIRONMENTAL/ECONOMIC:
Climate: tropical; hot and rainy
Natural Resources: petroleum, natural gas, timber
Agricultural Products: rice, vegetables, fruits, chickens
Major Exports: crude oil, natural gas, refined products
Natural Hazards: typhoons, earthquakes, floods (though rare)

BULGARIA
Country Name: Republic of Bulgaria
Continent: Europe
Area: 42,855 sq mi / 110,994 sq km
Population: 7,519,000
Population Density: 175 people per sq mi / 68 people per sq km
Capital: Sofia

PHYSICAL:
Highest Point: Musala 9,596 ft / 2,925 m
Lowest Point: Black Sea 0 ft / 0 m (sea level)
Mountain Ranges:
    Balkan: •cover central Bulgaria •extend into Serbia and Montenegro
    Pirin: •located in southwestern Bulgaria •extend into Greece
    Rhodope: •located in southern Bulgaria •extend into Greece
    Rila: •located in southwestern Bulgaria
Peaks (minimum elevation of 8,000 ft / 2,400 m):
    Musala: •located in the Rila Mountains •highest point in Bulgaria
Seas:
    Black: •forms the eastern coast of Bulgaria •feeds into the Sea of Marmara

Rivers:

Danube: ●forms most of the Bulgaria-Romania border ●extends into Serbia and Montenegro and into Romania

Regions:

Dobruja: ●lowland region in northeastern Bulgaria ●extends into Romania ●located west of the Black Sea

Macedonia: ●mountainous region in southwestern Bulgaria ●extends into Macedonia and Greece

Thrace: ●lowland region in southern Bulgaria ●extends into Greece and Turkey

POLITICAL:

Independence: March 3, 1878 (from the Ottoman Empire)

Bordering Countries: Romania, Greece, Serbia and Montenegro, Turkey, Macedonia (5)

Administrative Divisions: Blagoevgrad, Burgas, Dobrich, Gabrovo, Khaskovo, Kurdzhali, Kyustendil, Lovech, Montana, Pazardzhik, Pernik, Pleven, Plovdiv, Razgrad, Ruse, Shumen, Silistra, Sliven, Smolyan, Sofia, Sofia-Grad, Stara Zagora, Turgovishte, Varna, Veliko Turnovo, Vidin, Vratsa, Yambol (28 provinces)

Ethnic/Racial Groups: Bulgarian, Turkish

Religions: Christianity (primarily Bulgarian Orthodox), Islam

Language: Bulgarian

Currency: lev

Current President: Georgi Purvanov

Cities (capital, largest, or with at least a million people):
Sofia: •located in western Bulgaria •city in the Sofia province •capital of Bulgaria •most populated city in Bulgaria (1,187,000 people) •on the edge of the Balkan and the Rhodope Mountains

ENVIRONMENTAL/ECONOMIC:
Climate: temperate; cold and damp winters/hot and dry summers
Natural Resources: bauxite, copper, lead, zinc, coal
Agricultural Products: vegetables, fruits, tobacco, livestock
Major Exports: clothing, footwear, iron and steel, machinery and equipment
Natural Hazards: earthquakes, landslides

BURKINA FASO
Country Name: Burkina Faso
Continent: Africa
Area: 105,869 sq mi / 274,200 sq km
Population: 13,228,000
Population Density: 125 people per sq mi / 48 people per sq km
Capital: Ouagadougou

PHYSICAL:
Highest Point: Tena Kourou 2,457 ft / 749 m
Lowest Point: Black Volta River 656 ft / 200 m

Grasslands/Prairies:
Sahel: ●covers most of country ●extends into Mali, Ghana, Togo, Benin, and Niger
Rivers:
Black Volta: ●has its source in southwestern Burkina Faso ●forms part of the
Burkina Faso-Ghana border ●extends into Ghana
White Volta: ●has its source in the Sahel of northern Burkina Faso ●extends
into Ghana

POLITICAL:
Independence: August 5, 1960 (from France)
Former Name: Upper Volta
Bordering Countries: Mali, Niger, Cote d'Ivoire, Ghana, Benin, Togo (6)
Administrative Divisions: Bale, Bam, Banwa, Bazega, Bougouriba, Boulgou,
Boulkiemde, Comoe, Ganzourgou, Gnagna, Gourma, Houet, Ioba, Kadiogo,
Kenedougou, Komondjari, Kompienga, Kossi, Koulpelogo, Kouritenga, Kourweogo,
Leraba, Loroum, Mouhoun, Nahouri, Namentenga, Nayala, Noumbiel, Oubritenga,
Oudalan, Passore, Poni, Sanguie, Sanmatenga, Seno, Sissili, Soum, Sourou, Tapoa,
Tuy, Yagha, Yatenga, Ziro, Zondoma, Zoundweogo (45 provinces)
Ethnic/Racial Groups: Mossi, Gurunsi, Senufo, Lobi, Bobo, Mande, Fulani
Religions: Islam, indigenous beliefs, Christianity (mostly Roman Catholic)
Languages: French, indigenous African languages
Currency: Communaute Financiere Africaine franc
Current President: Blaise Compaore
Cities (capital, largest, or with at least a million people):
Ouagadougou: ●located in central Burkina Faso ●city in the Kadiogo province
●capital of Burkina Faso ●most populated city in Burkina Faso (821,000 people)

ENVIRONMENTAL/ECONOMIC:
Climate: tropical; warm and dry winters/hot and wet summers
Natural Resources: manganese, limestone, marble, gold, antimony
Agricultural Products: cotton, peanuts, shea nuts, sesame, livestock
Major Exports: cotton, livestock, gold
Natural Hazards: droughts

BURUNDI
Country Name: Republic of Burundi
Continent: Africa
Area: 10,747 sq mi / 27,834 sq km
Population: 6,096,000
Population Density: 567 people per sq mi / 219 people per sq km
Capital: Bujumbura

PHYSICAL:
Highest Point: Mount Heha 8,760 ft / 2,670 m
Lowest Point: Lake Tanganyika 2,533 ft / 772 m
Mountain Ranges:
Mitumba: •cover western Burundi •extend into Rwanda, Democratic Republic of the Congo, and Tanzania
Peaks (minimum elevation of 8,000 ft / 2,400 m):
Mount Heha: •located in the Mitumba Mountains •highest point in Burundi
Lakes:
Tanganyika: •located in southwestern Burundi •on the border with Democratic Republic of the Congo and Tanzania

POLITICAL:
Independence: July 1, 1962 (from Belgian administration)
Former Name: Urundi
Bordering Countries: Tanzania, Rwanda, Democratic Republic of the Congo (3)
Administrative Divisions: Bubanza, Bujumbura, Bururi, Cankuzo, Cibitoke, Gitega, Karuzi, Kayanza, Kirundo, Makamba, Muramvya, Muyinga, Mwaro, Ngozi, Rutana, Ruyigi (16 provinces)
Ethnic/Racial Groups: Hutu, Tutsi
Religions: Christianity (Roman Catholic, Protestant), indigenous beliefs, Islam
Languages: Kirundi, French, Swahili
Currency: Burundi franc
Current President: Domitien Ndayizeye

Cities (capital, largest, or with at least a million people):
>Bujumbura: •located in western Burundi •city in the Bujumbura province •capital of Burundi •most populated city in Burundi (378,000 people) •chief port on Lake Tanganyika

ENVIRONMENTAL/ECONOMIC:
Climate: equatorial with wet season and dry season
Natural Resources: nickel, uranium, rare earth oxides, peat, cobalt
Agricultural Products: coffee, cotton, tea, corn, beef
Major Exports: coffee, tea, sugar, cotton, hides
Natural Hazards: flooding, landslides, droughts

CAMBODIA

Country Name: Kingdom of Cambodia
Continent: Asia
Area: 69,898 sq mi / 181,035 sq km
Population: 12,558,000
Population Density: 180 people per sq mi / 69 people per sq km
Capital: Phnom Penh

PHYSICAL:
Highest Point: Phnom Aural, 5,948 ft / 1,813 m
Lowest Point: Gulf of Thailand 0 ft / 0 m (sea level)
Gulfs:
  Gulf of Thailand: •forms the southwestern coast of Cambodia •feeds into the South China Sea
Lakes:
  Tonle Sap: •located in western Cambodia
Rivers:
  Mekong: •extends into Laos and Vietnam

POLITICAL:
Independence: November 9, 1953 (from France)
Former Names: Khmer Republic, Democratic Kampuchea, People's Republic of Kampuchea, State of Cambodia
Bordering Countries: Vietnam, Thailand, Laos (3)
Administrative Divisions: Banteay Mean Cheay, Batdambang, Kampong Cham, Kampong Chhnang, Kampong Spoe, Kampong Thom, Kampot, Kandal, Kaoh Kong, Kracheh, Mondol Kiri, Otdar Mean Cheay, Pouthisat, Preah Vihear, Prey Veng, Rotanah Kiri, Siem Reab, Stoeng Treng, Svay Rieng, Takev (20 provinces) ●Keb, Pailin, Phnom Penh, Preah Sihanouk (4 municipalities)
Ethnic/Racial Groups: Khmer, Vietnamese
Religion: Theravada Buddhism
Languages: Khmer, French, English
Currency: riel
Current Prime Minister: Hun Sen
Cities (capital, largest, or with at least a million people):
Phnom Penh: ●located in southern Cambodia ●city in the Phnom Penh municipality ●capital of Cambodia ●most populated city in Cambodia (1,157,000 people) ●chief port on the Mekong River

ENVIRONMENTAL/ECONOMIC:
Climate: tropical with a rainy monsoon season and a dry season
Natural Resources: oil and gas, timber, gemstones, iron ore, manganese
Agricultural Products: rice, rubber, corn, vegetables
Major Exports: timber, garments, rubber, rice, fish
Natural Hazards: monsoons, floods, droughts

CAMEROON
Country Name: Republic of Cameroon
Continent: Africa
Area: 183,569 sq mi / 475,442 sq km
Population: 15,746,000
Population Density: 86 people per sq mi / 33 people per sq km
Capital: Yaounde

PHYSICAL:
Highest Point: Fako (on Cameroon Mountain) 13,451 ft / 4,100 m
Lowest Point: Gulf of Guinea 0 ft / 0 m (sea level)
Mountain Ranges:
Adamawa: ●covers much of central Cameroon ●extends into Nigeria
Peaks (minimum elevation of 8,000 ft / 2,400 m):
Cameroon Mountain: ●located in southwestern Cameroon ●includes Fako, the highest point in Cameroon

Grasslands/Prairies:
    Sahel: ●located in northern Cameroon ●extends into Nigeria, Chad, and Central African Republic

Bays:
    Bight of Bonny: ●forms the southwestern coast of Cameroon ●feeds into the Gulf of Guinea

Lakes:
    Chad: ●located in northern Cameroon ●on the Cameroon-Chad border● located in the Sahel

Rivers:
    Benoue (Benue): ●has its source in the Adamawa ●extends into Nigeria
    Chari: ●has its mouth in Lake Chad ●forms part of the Cameroon-Chad border ●extends into Chad

POLITICAL:

Independence: January 1, 1960 (for French-ruled areas); October 1, 1961 (for British-ruled areas)

Former Names: French Cameroon, British Cameroon

Bordering Countries: Nigeria, Chad, Central African Republic, Republic of the Congo, Gabon, Equatorial Guinea (6)

Administrative Divisions: Adamaoua, Centre, Est, Extreme-Nord, Littoral, Nord, Nord-Ouest, Ouest, Sud, Sud-Ouest (10 provinces)

Ethnic/Racial Groups: Cameroon Highlanders, Equatorial Bantu, Kirdi, Fulani, Northwestern Bantu, Eastern Nigritic, other African groups

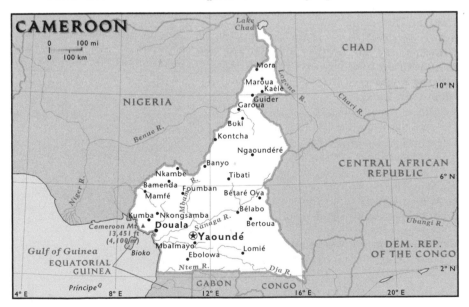

Religions: indigenous beliefs, Christianity, Islam
Languages: French, English, 24 major African language groups
Currency: Communaute Financiere Africaine franc
Current President: Paul Biya
Cities (capital, largest, or with at least a million people):
    Yaounde: •located in southern Cameroon •city in the Centre province •capital of Cameroon (1,616,000 people)
    Douala: •located in southwestern Cameroon •city in the Littoral province •chief port on the Bight of Bonny

ENVIRONMENTAL/ECONOMIC:
Climate: tropical along coast; semi-arid and hot in the north
Natural Resources: petroleum, bauxite, iron ore, timber, hydropower
Agricultural Products: coffee, cacao, cotton, rubber, livestock
Major Exports: crude oil and petroleum products, lumber, cacao, aluminum
Natural Hazards: volcanoes, volcanic gases

CANADA
Country Name: Canada
Continent: North America
Area: 3,855,101 sq mi / 9,984,670 sq km (largest in North America)
Population: 31,630,000
Population Density: 8.2 people per sq mi / 3.2 people per sq km (least dense in North America)
Capital: Ottawa

PHYSICAL:
Highest Point: Mount Logan 19,551 ft / 5,959 m
Lowest Point: Atlantic Ocean 0 ft / 0 m (sea level)
Mountain Ranges:
    Cassiar: •located in western Canada
    Coast: •cover western Canada •extend into the United States
    Columbia: •located in southwestern Canada
    Laurentian: •located in southeastern Canada
    Mackenzie: •located in northwestern Canada
    Notre Dame: •located in southeastern Canada
    Rocky: •cover western Canada •extend into the United States
    Saint Elias: •located in western Canada •extend into the United States
    Selwyn: •located in northwestern Canada
Peaks (minimum elevation of 8,000 ft / 2,400 m):
    Mount Logan: •located in the Saint Elias Mountains •highest point in Canada
    Mount Robson: •located in the Rocky Mountains

Passes:
    Chilkoot: •located in the Coast Mountains •crosses the border into the United
        States (Alaska)
Grasslands/Prairies:
    Great Plains: •located in southern Canada •extend into the United States
Oceans:
    Arctic: •forms part of the northern coast of Canada
    Atlantic: •forms part of the eastern coast of Canada
    Pacific: •forms part of the western coast of Canada
Seas:
    Beaufort: •forms part of the northwestern coast of Canada •feeds into the Arctic Ocean
    Labrador: •forms part of the eastern coast of Canada •feeds into the Atlantic Ocean
Gulfs:
    Amundsen: •forms part of the northwestern coast of Canada •feeds into the
        Beaufort Sea
    Gulf of Boothia: •forms part of the northern coast of Canada
    Gulf of Maine: •forms part of the southeastern coast of Canada •feeds into the
        Atlantic Ocean
    Gulf of Saint Lawrence: •forms part of the southeastern coast of Canada •feeds
        into the Atlantic Ocean
    Queen Maud: •forms part of the northern coast of Canada
Bays:
    Baffin: •forms part of the northern coast of Canada •feeds into the Labrador Sea

Bay of Fundy: ●forms part of the southeastern coast of Canada ●feeds into the Gulf of Maine ●has world's greatest tides

Chaleur: ●forms part of the southeastern coast of Canada ●feeds into the Gulf of Saint Lawrence

Foxe Basin: ●forms part of the northern border of Canada ●feeds into Hudson Bay

Georgian: ●feeds into Lake Huron

Hudson: ●forms part of the central coast of Canada ●feeds into the Labrador Sea

James: ●forms part of the central coast of Canada ●feeds into Hudson Bay

Ungava: ●forms part of the eastern coast of Canada ●feeds into the Labrador Sea

Sounds:

Queen Charlotte: ●forms part of the southwestern coast of Canada ●feeds into the Pacific Ocean

Straits:

Cabot: ●forms part of the southeastern coast of Canada ●separates the Island of Newfoundland from Cape Breton Island ●connects the Gulf of Saint Lawrence and the Atlantic Ocean

Davis: ●forms part of the northeastern coast of Canada ●separates Canada from Greenland (territory of Denmark) ●connects Baffin Bay and the Labrador Sea

Hudson: ●forms part of the eastern coast of Canada ●separates Baffin Island from mainland Canada ●connects Hudson Bay and the Labrador Sea

Strait of Georgia: ●forms part of the southwestern coast of Canada ●separates Vancouver Island from mainland Canada ●connects Queen Charlotte Sound and Puget Sound

Strait of Juan de Fuca: ●forms part of the southwestern coast of Canada ●separates Vancouver Island from the United States ●connects Puget Sound and the Pacific Ocean

Channels:

Foxe: ●forms part of the northern coast of Canada ●separates Baffin Island from Southampton Island ●connects Foxe Basin and Hudson Bay

Parry: ●forms part of the northern coast of Canada ●separates Melville and Devon Islands from Victoria, Prince of Wales, and Baffin Islands ●connects the Arctic Ocean and Baffin Bay

Canals:

Welland: ●connects Lake Erie and Lake Ontario

Lakes:

Great Bear: ●located in northwestern Canada ●largest lake entirely in Canada ●eighth largest lake in the world

Great Slave: ●located in western Canada ●fed by the Slave River ●tenth largest lake in the world

Lake Athabasca: ●located in central Canada

Lake Erie: ●located in southern Canada ●on the Canada-United States border

Lake Huron: ●located in southern Canada ●on the Canada-United States border ●fourth largest lake in the world ●third largest of the Great Lakes in surface area

Lake Manitoba: ●located in southern Canada

Lake Nipigon: •located in southern Canada
Lake Ontario: •located in southern Canada •on the Canada-United States border
Lake Superior: •located in southern Canada •on the Canada-United States border
•westernmost of the Great Lakes •largest lake in North America •second largest lake in the world
Lake Winnipeg: •located in southern Canada
Lake Winnipegosis: •located in southern Canada
Reindeer: •located in central Canada

Rivers:
Columbia: •has its source in the Rocky Mountains •extends into the United States
Fraser: •has its mouth in the Strait of Georgia •has its source in the Rocky Mountains
Mackenzie: •has its mouth in the Beaufort Sea •has its source in the Rocky Mountains
Nelson: •has its mouth in Hudson Bay •has its source in the Rocky Mountains
North Saskatchewan: •tributary of the Saskatchewan River •has its source in the Rocky Mountains
Ottawa: •tributary of the Saint Lawrence River •has its source in southern Canada
Peace: •tributary of the Slave River •has its source in the Rocky Mountains
Saint Lawrence: •has its mouth in the Gulf of Saint Lawrence •forms part of the Canada-United States border
Saskatchewan: •tributary of the Nelson River •has its source in the Rocky Mountains
Slave: •tributary of the Mackenzie River
South Saskatchewan: •tributary of the Saskatchewan River •has its source in the Rocky Mountains
Yukon: •has its source in the Coast Mountains •extends into the United States (Alaska)

Deltas:
Mackenzie River Delta: •mouth of the Mackenzie River •feeds into the Beaufort Sea

Waterfalls:
Niagara: •located in southeastern Canada •part of the Niagara River •on the Canada-United States border (between Ontario and New York)

Peninsulas:
Gaspe: •bordered by the Saint Lawrence River, Chaleur Bay, and Gulf of Saint Lawrence
Nova Scotia: •bordered by the Atlantic Ocean, Gulf of Maine, and Bay of Fundy
Ungava: •bordered by Hudson Bay, Hudson Strait, and Ungava Bay

Islands:
Baffin: •an island off the northern coast of mainland Canada •bordered by Baffin Bay, Parry Channel, Gulf of Boothia, Foxe Basin, Foxe Channel, Hudson Strait, and Davis Strait •fifth largest island in the world
Banks: •an island off the northwestern coast of mainland Canada •bordered by the Arctic Ocean, Beaufort Sea, and Amundsen Gulf
Cape Breton: •an island off the southeastern coast of mainland Canada •bordered by the Gulf of Saint Lawrence, Atlantic Ocean, and Cabot Strait
Devon: •an island in the Queen Elizabeth Islands in northern Canada bordered by Parry Channel and Baffin Bay

Ellesmere: •an island in the Queen Elizabeth Islands in northern Canada bordered by the Arctic Ocean and Baffin Bay •tenth largest island in the world

Melville: •an island in the Queen Elizabeth Islands in northern Canada •bordered by the Parry Channel

Newfoundland: •an island off the eastern coast of mainland Canada •bordered by the Atlantic Ocean, Gulf of Saint Lawrence, and Cabot Strait

Prince Edward: •an island off the southeastern coast of mainland Canada •bordered by the Gulf of Saint Lawrence •also a province

Prince of Wales: •an island off the northern coast of mainland Canada •bordered by Parry Channel

Queen Charlotte: •an island group west of mainland Canada •bordered by the Pacific Ocean and Queen Charlotte Sound

Southampton: •an island off the northern coast of mainland Canada •bordered by the Foxe Channel, Foxe Basin, and Hudson Bay

Vancouver: •an island off the southwestern coast of mainland Canada •bordered by the Pacific Ocean, Queen Charlotte Sound, Strait of Georgia, and Strait of Juan de Fuca

Victoria: •an island off the northern coast of mainland Canada •bordered by the Amundsen Gulf, Parry Channel, and Queen Maud Gulf •ninth largest island in the world

POLITICAL:
Independence: July 1, 1867 (from the United Kingdom); complete legal autonomy 1931

Bordering Country: United States (1)

Administrative Divisions: Alberta, British Columbia, Manitoba, New Brunswick, Newfoundland and Labrador, Nova Scotia, Ontario, Prince Edward Island, Quebec, Saskatchewan (10 provinces) •Northwest Territories, Nunavut, Yukon (3 territories)

Ethnic/Racial Groups: British, French, other European groups, Amerindian

Religion: Christianity (Roman Catholic, Protestant)

Languages: English, French

Currency: Canadian dollar

Current Prime Minister: Paul Martin

Cities (capital, largest, or with at least a million people):

Toronto: •located in southern Canada •city in the Ontario province •most populated city in Canada (5,901,000 people) •chief port on Lake Ontario

Montreal: •located in southeastern Canada •city in the Quebec province •chief port on the Saint Lawrence River

Vancouver: •located in southwestern Canada •city in the British Columbia province •chief port on the Strait of Georgia

Ottawa: •located in southeastern Canada •city in the Ontario province •capital of Canada (1,093,000 people) •chief port on the Ottawa River

ENVIRONMENTAL/ECONOMIC:
Climate: temperate in south, subarctic to arctic in the north

Natural Resources: iron ore, nickel, zinc, copper, gold
Agricultural Products: wheat, barley, oilseed, tobacco, dairy products
Major Exports: motor vehicles and parts, industrial machinery, aircraft, telecommunications equipment, chemicals
Natural Hazards: thunderstorms

CAPE VERDE
Country Name: Republic of Cape Verde
Continent: Africa
Area: 1,558 sq mi / 4,036 sq km
Population: 474,000
Population Density: 304 people per sq mi / 117 people per sq km
Capital: Praia

PHYSICAL:
Highest Point: Mount Fogo 9,281 ft / 2,829 m
Lowest Point: Atlantic Ocean 0 ft / 0 m (sea level)
Peaks (minimum elevation of 8,000 ft / 2,400 m):
   Mount Fogo: ●located on the island of Fogo ●highest point in Cape Verde
Oceans:
   Atlantic: ●forms the entire coast of Cape Verde
Islands:
   Santiago: ●largest island in Cape Verde ●surrounded by the Atlantic Ocean
   Santo Antao: ●second largest island in Cape Verde ●surrounded by the Atlantic Ocean

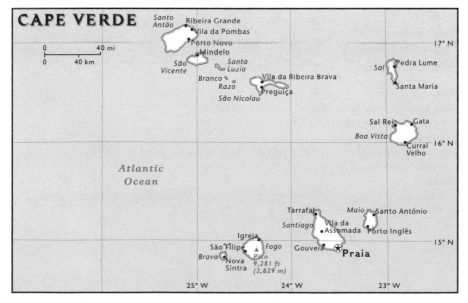

Independence: July 5, 1975 (from Portugal)
Administrative Divisions: Boa Vista, Brava, Maio, Mosteiros, Paul, Porto Novo, Praia, Ribeira Grande, Sal, Santa Catarina, Santa Cruz, Sao Domingos, Sao Filipe, Sao Miguel, Sao Nicolau, Sao Vicente, Tarrafal (17 municipalities)
Ethnic/Racial Groups: Creole, African
Religion: Christianity (Roman Catholic, Protestant)
Languages: Portuguese, Crioulo (Kriolu)
Currency: Cape Verdean escudo
Current President: Pedro Pires
Cities (capital, largest, or with at least a million people):
  Praia: •located on Santiago Island •city in the Praia municipality •capital of Cape Verde •most populated city in Cape Verde (107,000 people) •chief port on the Atlantic Ocean

ENVIRONMENTAL/ECONOMIC:
Climate: temperate, warm and dry summers
Natural Resources: salt, basalt rock, limestone, kaolin, fish
Agricultural Products: bananas, corn, beans, sweet potatoes
Natural Disasters: droughts, harmattan winds, dust storms, volcanoes, earthquakes

CENTRAL AFRICAN REPUBLIC

Country Name: Central African Republic
Continent: Africa
Area: 240,535 sq mi / 622,984 sq km
Population: 3,684,000
Population Density: 15 people per sq mi / 5.9 people per sq km
Capital: Bangui

PHYSICAL:
Highest Point: Mont Ngaoui 4,659 ft / 1,420 m
Lowest Point: Oubangui River 1,099 ft / 335 m
Grasslands/Prairies:
  Sahel: •located in northern Central African Republic •extends into Cameroon, Chad, and Sudan
Rivers:
  Ubangi (Oubangui): •forms part of the Central African Republic-Democratic Republic of the Congo border

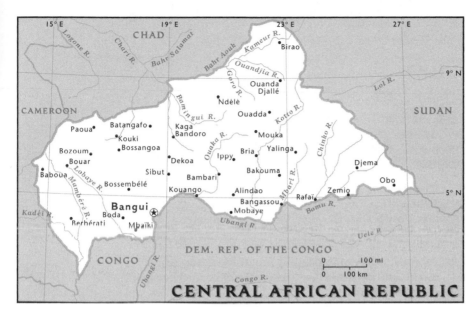

CENTRAL AFRICAN REPUBLIC

POLITICAL:
Independence: August 16, 1960 (from France)
Former Names: Ubangi-Shari, Central African Empire
Bordering Countries: Democratic Republic of the Congo, Chad, Sudan, Cameroon, Republic of the Congo (5)
Regions:
    Dar Rounga: ●located in northern Central African Republic ●extends into Sudan
Administrative Divisions: Bamingui-Bangoran, Basse-Kotto, Haute-Kotto, Haut-Mbomou, Kemo, Lobaye, Mambere-Kadei, Mbomou, Nana-Mambere, Ombella-Mpoko, Ouaka, Ouham, Ouham-Pende, Vakaga (14 prefectures) ●Nana-Grebizi, Sangha-Mbaere (2 economic prefectures) ●Bangui (1 commune)
Ethnic/Racial Groups: Baya, Banda, Mandjia, Sara, Mboum, M'Baka, Yakoma
Religions: indigenous beliefs, Christianity (Protestant, Roman Catholic), Islam
Languages: French, Sangho, Arabic, tribal languages
Currency: Communaute Financiere Africaine franc
Current President: Francois Bozize
Cities (capital, largest, or with at least a million people):
    Bangui: ●located in southwestern Central African Republic ●city in the Bangui commune ●capital of Central African Republic ●most populated city in Central African Republic (698,000 people) ●chief port on the Ubangi River

ENVIRONMENTAL/ECONOMIC:
Climate: tropical with hot and dry winters/mild to hot and wet summers
Natural Resources: diamonds, uranium, timber, gold, oil
Agricultural Products: cotton, coffee, tobacco, manioc (tapioca), timber

Major Exports: diamonds, timber, cotton, coffee, tobacco
Natural Hazards: harmattan winds, floods

CHAD
Country Name: Republic of Chad
Continent: Africa
Area: 495,755 sq mi / 1,284,000 sq km
Population: 9,253,000
Population Density: 19 people per sq mi / 7.2 people per sq km
Capital: N'Djamena

PHYSICAL:
Highest Point: Emi Koussi 11,204 ft / 3,415 m
Lowest Point: Djourab Depression 525 ft / 160 m
Mountain Ranges:
  Tibesti: •located in northwestern Chad •extend into Libya
Peaks (minimum elevation of 8,000 ft / 2,400 m):
  Emi Koussi: •located in the Tibesti Mountains•highest point in Chad
Grasslands/Prairies:
  Sahel: •covers southern and central Chad •extends into Niger, Nigeria, Cameroon,
    Central African Republic, and Sudan
Deserts:
  Sahara: •stretches across northern Chad •extends into neighboring Niger, Libya,
    and Sudan •largest desert in the world

Lakes:
>Lake Chad: ●located in western Chad ●on the Chad-Cameroon border ●located in the Sahel

Rivers:
>Chari: ●has its mouth in Lake Chad ●forms part of the Chad-Cameroon border

Regions:
>Borkou: ●desert region in northern Chad ●located to the south of the Tibesti Mountains in the Sahara

POLITICAL:

Independence: August 11, 1960 (from France)

Bordering Countries: Sudan, Central African Republic, Niger, Cameroon, Libya, Nigeria (6)

Regions:
>Aozou Strip: ●covers much of northern Chad

Administrative Divisions: Batha, Biltine, Borkou-Ennedi-Tibesti, Chari-Baguirmi, Guera, Kanem, Lac, Logone Occidental, Logone Oriental, Mayo-Kebbi, Moyen-Chari, Ouaddai, Salamat, Tandjile (14 prefectures)

Ethnic/Racial Groups: some 200 groups (largest are Arabs and Sara)

Religions: Islam, Christianity, animism

Languages: French, Arabic, Sara, more than 120 different dialects

Currency: Communaute Financiere Africaine franc

Current President: Idriss Deby

Cities (capital, largest, or with at least a million people): .
>N'Djamena: ●located in southwestern Chad ●city in the Chari-Baguirmi prefecture ●capital of Chad ●most populated city in Chad (797,000 people) ●chief port on the Chari River

ENVIRONMENTAL/ECONOMIC:

Climate: tropical in the south; desert in the north

Natural Resources: oil, uranium, natron, kaolin, fish

Agricultural Products: cotton, sorghum, millet, peanuts, cattle

Major Exports: cotton, cattle, gum arabic

Natural Hazards: harmattan winds, droughts, locust plagues

CHILE

Country Name: Republic of Chile

Continent: South America

Area: 291,930 sq mi / 756,096 sq km

Population: 15,774,000

Population Density: 54 people per sq mi / 21 people per sq km

Capital: Santiago

CHILE

0 ——— 300 mi
0 ——— 300 km

20° S
Tropic of Capricorn
·Sala-y-Gomez (Chile)
·Easter Island (Chile)
30° S
40° S

Pacific Ocean

Juan Fernández Is. (Chile)

PERU
Arica•
Iquique•
Antofagasta•
La Serena•
Viña del Mar
Valparaíso•⊛Santiago
Rancagua•
Talcahuano•
Concepción•
Temuco•
Valdivia•
Osorno•
Puerto Montt•
Puerto Aisén•
Punta Arenas•
Tierra del Fuego

BOLIVIA
PARAGUAY
BRAZIL
Salado R.
Paraná R.
Paraná R.
Uruguay R.
ARGENTINA
URUGUAY
Negro R.
Atlantic Ocean
Falkland Islands (U.K.)
Strait of Magellan

90° W   80° W   70° W   50° W   40° W   30° W

PHYSICAL:

Highest Point: Nevado Ojos del Salado 22,572 ft / 6,880 m
Lowest Point: Pacific Ocean 0 ft / 0 m (sea level)
Mountain Ranges:
    Andes: •cover eastern Chile north to south •extend into Argentina
Peaks (minimum elevation of 8,000 ft / 2,400 m):
    Nevado Ojos del Salado: •located in the Andes •on the Chile-Argentina border
      •highest point in Chile
Desert:
    Atacama: •located in northwestern Chile •extends into Peru •driest place in the world
Oceans:
    Pacific: •forms most of the western coast of Chile
Gulfs:
    Gulf of Corcovado: •forms part of the central coast of Chile •feeds into the
      Pacific Ocean
    Gulf of Penas: •forms part of the western coast of Chile •feeds into the Pacific Ocean
Straits:
    Strait of Magellan: •forms part of the southern coast of Chile •separates the island
      of Tierra del Fuego from mainland Chile •connects the Pacific and Atlantic Oceans

Islands:
    Tierra del Fuego: •group of islands south of mainland Chile •also largest island in
      the group •bordered by the Pacific Ocean •eastern half owned by Argentina

POLITICAL:
Independence: September 18, 1810 (from Spain)
Bordering Countries: Argentina, Bolivia, Peru (3)
Administrative Divisions: Aisen del General Carlos Ibanez del Campo,
Antofagasta, Araucania, Atacama, Bio-Bio, Coquimbo, Libertador General Bernardo
O'Higgins, Los Lagos, Magallanes y de la Antartica Chilena, Maule, Region
Metropolitana (Santiago), Tarapaca, Valparaiso (13 regions)
Ethnic/Racial Groups: European, mestizo, Amerindian
Religion: Christianity (Roman Catholic, Protestant)
Language: Spanish
Currency: Chilean peso
Current President: Ricardo Lagos
Cities (capital, largest, or with at least a million people):
Santiago: ●located in central Chile ●city in the Region Metropolitana region ●capital of
Chile ●most populated city in Chile (5,623,000 people) ●on the edge of the Andes

ENVIRONMENTAL/ECONOMIC:
Climate: temperate with desert in the north, Mediterranean climate in the middle,
cool and damp in the south
Natural Resources: copper, timber, iron ore, nitrates, precious metals (gold, silver)
Agricultural Products: wheat, corn, grapes, beans, beef
Major Exports: copper, fish, fruits, paper and pulp, chemicals
Natural Hazards: earthquakes, volcanoes, tsunamis

CHINA
Country Name: People's Republic of China
Continent: Asia
Area: 3,705,405 sq mi / 9,596,960 sq km
Population: 1,288,679,000 (largest in the world)
Population Density: 348 people per sq mi / 134 people per sq km
Capital: Beijing

PHYSICAL:
Highest Point: Mount Everest 29,035 ft / 8,850 m
Lowest Point: Turpan Depression 505 ft / 154 m below sea level
Mountain Ranges:
Altay: ●located in northwestern China ●extend into Kazakhstan, Russia, and Mongolia
Altun Shan: ●located in western China
Bayan Har Shan: ●located in central China
Gangdise Shan: ●located in western China
Hengduan Shan: ●located in southern China
Himalaya: ●cover western China ●extend into Pakistan, India, Nepal, and Bhutan

Hindu Kush: •located in western China •extend into Afghanistan, Tajikistan, and Pakistan

Karakoram: •located in western China •extends into Pakistan and India

Kunlun Shan: •located in western China

Qilian Shan: •located in central China

Tian Shan: •located in northwestern China •extend into Kazakhstan and Kyrgyzstan

Peaks (minimum elevation of 8,000 ft / 2,400 m):

K2: •located in the Karakoram Range •on the China-Pakistan border

Mount Everest: •located in the Himalaya •on the China-Nepal border •highest point in the world

Pobedy Peak: •located in the Tian Shan •on the China-Kyrgyzstan border

Xixabangma Feng: •located in the Himalaya

Passes:

Karakoram: •located in the Karakoram Range •crosses the border into India

Plateau Regions:

Dzungarian Basin: •located in northwestern China •basin between the Altay and Tian Shan

Nei Mongol Plateau: •covers northern China •extends into Mongolia •desert plateau north of the Huang He (Yellow River)

Plateau of Tibet: •located in western China •high plateau between the Himalaya and Kunlun Shan •largest plateau in the world

Tarim Basin: •located in western China •basin between the Tian Shan, Kunlun Shan, and Altun Shan

Depressions:

Turpan Depression: •located in northwestern China •lowest point in China

Deserts:

Gobi: •located in northern China •extends into Mongolia •covers part of the Nei Mongol Plateau

Taklimakan: •located in western China •covers most of the Tarim Basin

Seas:

East China: •forms part of the eastern coast of China •feeds into the Philippine Sea

South China •forms part of the southeastern coast of China •feeds into the Philippine Sea •second largest sea in the world

Yellow: •forms part of the eastern coast of China •feeds into the East China Sea

Gulfs:

Bo Hai: •forms part of the eastern coast of China •feeds into Korea Bay

Gulf of Tonkin: •forms part of the southern coast of China •feeds into the South China Sea

Bays:

Korea: •forms part of the northwestern coast of China •feeds into the Yellow Sea

Straits:

Hainan: •forms part of the southern coast of China •separates the island of Hainan from mainland China •connects the Gulf of Tonkin and the South China Sea

Taiwan: •forms part of the southeastern coast of China •separates the island of Taiwan from mainland China •connects the East China and South China Seas

Canals:

Grand: •connects the Huang (Yellow River) and Chang Jiang (Yangtze River)

Lakes:

Lop Nur: •located in western China •at the eastern end of the Tarim Basin

Qinghai Hu: •located in central China •near the Qilian Shan

Rivers:

Amur: •forms part of the China-Russia border •extends into Russia •eighth longest river in the world

Brahmaputra: •has its source in the Gangdise Shan •extends into India

Chang Jiang (Yangtze): •has its mouth in the East China Sea •has its source in the Kunlun Shan •third longest river in the world •longest river in Asia

Huang (Yellow): •has its mouth in Bo Hai •has its source in the Bayan Har Shan •sixth longest river in the world

Ertix (Irtysh): •located in northwestern China •extends into Kazakhstan and Russia

Mekong: •has its source on the Plateau of Tibet •extends into Laos and Vietnam

Red: •has its source in the Hengduan Shan •forms part of the China-Vietnam border •extends into Vietnam

Salween: •has its source on the Plateau of Tibet •extends into Myanmar

Xi: •has its mouth in the South China Sea •has its source in southern China

Deltas:

Mouth of the Chang Jiang (Yangtze River): •feeds into the East China Sea

Dams:
   Three Gorges Dam: ●located in central China ●spans the Chang Jiang (Yangtze River) ●world's largest hydroelectric dam
Peninsulas:
   Shandong: ●bordered by Bo Hai, Korea Bay, and the Yellow Sea
Islands:
   Hainan: ●island off the southern coast of mainland China ●bordered by the Gulf of Tonkin, Hainan Strait, and the South China Sea
Regions:
   Manchuria: ●plains region in northeastern China ●located to the west of the Nei Mongol Plateau

POLITICAL:
Independence: 221 B.C.(unification under the Qin or Chin Dynasty)
Bordering Countries: Mongolia, Russia, India, Myanmar, Kazakhstan, North Korea, Vietnam, Nepal, Kyrgyzstan, Pakistan, Bhutan, Laos, Tajikistan, Afghanistan (14)
Administrative Divisions: Anhui, Fujian, Gansu, Guangdong, Guizhou, Hainan, Hebei, Heilongjiang, Henan, Hubei, Hunan, Jiangsu, Jiangxi, Jilin, Liaoning, Qinghai, Shaanxi, Shandong, Shanxi, Sichuan, Taiwan (claimed by China), Tianjin, Yunnan, Zhejiang (24 provinces) ●Guangxi, Nei Mongol, Ningxia, Xinjiang, Xizang (5 autonomous regions) ●Beijing, Chongqing, Shanghai, Tianjin (4 municipalities)
Special Administrative Regions: Hong Kong, Macau
Ethnic/Racial Groups: Han, and 55 other groups, including Tibetan and Mongol
Religions: officially atheist; Taoism, Buddhism, Islam
Languages: Mandarin, Yue (Cantonese), other dialects and minority languages
Currency: yuan
Current President: Hu Jintao
Cities (capital, largest, or with at least a million people):
   Shanghai: ●located in eastern China ●city in the Shanghai municipality ●most populated city in China (13,972,000 people)
   Beijing: ●located in eastern China ●city in the Beijing municipality ●capital of China (10,849,000 people)
   Wuhan: ●located in eastern China ●city in the Hubei province ●a major port on the Chang Jiang (Yangtze River)
   Chengdu: ●located in central China ●city in the Sichuan province
   Tianjin: ●located in eastern China ●city in the Tianjin municipality
   Shenyang: ●located in northeastern China ●city in the Liaoning province
   Chongqing: ●located in southern China ●city in the Chongqing municipality ●a major port on the Chang Jiang (Yangtze River)
   Guangzhou: ●located in southeastern China ●city in the Guangdong province
   Harbin: ●located in northeastern China ●city in the Heilongjiang province
   Xian: ●located in central China ●city in the Shanxi province
   Nanjing: ●located in eastern China ●city in the Jiangsu province ●a major port on the Chang Jiang (Yangtze River)

Taiyuan: •located in central China city in the Shanxi province
Changchun: •located in northeastern China •city in the Jilin province
Zhengzhou: •located in eastern China •city in the Henan province
Jiulong: •located in southeastern China •city in Hong Kong
Jinan: •located in eastern China •city in the Shandong province
Dalian: •located in northeastern China •city in the Liaoning province
Changsha: •located in central China •city inthe Hunan province

ENVIRONMENTAL/ECONOMIC:
Climate: tropical in the south; subarctic in the north
Natural Resources: coal, iron ore, petroleum, natural gas, mercury
Agricultural Products: rice, wheat, potatoes, sorghum, pork
Major Exports: machinery and equipment, textiles and clothing, footwear, toys and sporting goods, mineral fuels
Natural Hazards: typhoons, floods, tsunamis, earthquakes, droughts, land subsidence

COLOMBIA
Country Name: Republic of Colombia
Continent: South America
Area: 440,831 sq mi / 1,141,748 sq km
Population: 44,172,000
Population Density: 110 people per sq mi / 39 people per sq km
Capital: Bogota

PHYSICAL:
Highest Points:
Pico Cristobal Colon 18,947 ft / 5,775 m
Pico Simon Bolivar 18,947 ft / 5,775 m
Lowest Point: Pacific Ocean 0 ft / 0 m (sea level)
Mountain Ranges:
Andes: •cover much of western and central Colombia •extend into Ecuador
Sierra Nevada de Santa Marta: •located in northern Colombia
Peaks (minimum elevation of 8,000 ft / 2,400 m):
Pico Cristobal Colon: •located in the Sierra Nevada de Santa Marta •one of the highest points in Colombia
Pico Simon Bolivar: •located in the Sierra Nevada de Santa Marta •one of the highest points in Colombia
Grasslands/Prairies:
Llanos: •located in eastern Colombia •extend into Venezuela
Rain forests:
Amazon: •located in southeastern Colombia •extends into Ecuador, Peru, Brazil, and Venezuela •largest rain forest in the world

Oceans:
  Pacific: • forms part of the western coast of Colombia
Seas:
  Caribbean: • forms most of the northern coast of Colombia • feeds into the
    Atlantic Ocean
Gulfs:
  Gulf of Venezuela: • forms part of the northeastern coast of Colombia • feeds into
    the Caribbean Sea
Rivers:
  Cauca: • tributary of the Magdalena River • has its source in the Andes
  Guaviare: • tributary of the Orinoco River • has its source in the Andes
  Magdalena: • has its mouth in the Caribbean Sea • has its source in the Andes
  Meta: • tributary of the Orinoco River • has its source in the Andes • forms part of
    the Colombia-Venezuela border
  Negro: • forms part of the Colombia-Venezuela border • extends into Brazil
  Orinoco: • forms part of the Colombia-Venezuela border • extends into Venezuela
  Putumayo: • has its source in the Andes • forms most of the Colombia-Peru border
    • forms part of the Colombia-Ecuador border
Peninsulas:
  Guajira: • bordered by the Caribbean Sea and the Gulf of Venezuela • shares the
    border with Venezuela

POLITICAL:
Independence: July 20, 1810 (from Spain)

Bordering Countries: Venezuela, Brazil, Peru, Ecuador, Panama (5)
Administrative Divisions: Amazonas, Antioquia, Arauca, Atlantico, Bolivar,
   Boyaca, Caldas, Caqueta, Casanare, Cauca, Cesar, Choco, Cordoba, Cundinamarca,
   Guainia, Guaviare, Huila, La Guajira, Magdalena, Meta, Narino, Norte de
   Santander, Putumayo, Quindio, Risaralda, San Andres y Providencia, Santander,
   Sucre, Tolima, Valle del Cauca, Vaupes, Vichada (32 departments) •Distrito Capital
   de Bogota (1 capital district)
Ethnic/Racial Groups: mestizo, European, Creole, black, Amerindian
Religion: Christianity (mainly Roman Catholic)
Language: Spanish
Currency: Colombian peso
Current President: Alvaro Uribe Velez
Cities (capital, largest, or with at least a million people):
   Bogota. •located in central Colombia •city in the Distrito Capital (capital district)
       •capital of Colombia •most populated city in Colombia (7,594,000 people)
       •located in a valley in the Andes
   Cali: •located in western Colombia •city in the Valle de Cauca department •located
       in a valley in the Andes •chief port on the Cauca River
   Medellin: •located in western Colombia •city in the Antioquia department •located
       in a valley in the Andes
   Barranquilla: •located in northern Colombia •city in the Atlantico department
       •a major port on the Magdalena River and the Caribbean Sea

ENVIRONMENTAL/ECONOMIC:
Climate: tropical along the coast and eastern plains; cooler in highlands
Natural Resources: petroleum, natural gas, coal, iron ore, nickel
Agricultural Products: coffee, cut flowers, bananas, rice, forest products
Major Exports: petroleum, coffee, coal, apparel, bananas
Natural Hazards: volcanoes, earthquakes, droughts

COMOROS
Country Name: Union of the Comoros
Continent: Africa
Area: 719 sq mi / 1,862 sq km
Population: 633,000
Population Density: 880 people per sq mi / 340 people per sq km
Capital: Moroni

PHYSICAL:
Highest Point: Kartala 7,746 ft / 2,361 m
Lowest Point: Indian Ocean 0 ft / 0 m (sea level)
Oceans:
   Indian: •forms part of the coast of Comoros

Channels:
　　Mozambique: ●forms part of the coast of Comoros ●separates Madagascar and
　　Comoros from mainland Africa
Islands:
　　Grande Comore: ●largest island in Comoros ●bordered by the Indian Ocean and
　　the Mozambique Channel

POLITICAL:
Independence: July 6, 1975 (from France)
Administrative Divisions: Anjouan, Grande Comore, and Moheli (3 islands)
Ethnic/Racial Groups: Antalote, Cafre, Makoa, Oimatsaha, Sakalava
Religions: Islam (predominantly Sunni), Christianity (mainly Roman Catholic)
Languages: Arabic, French, Shikomoro
Currency: Comoran franc
Current President: Azali Assoumani
Cities (capital, largest, or with at least a million people):
　　Moroni: ●located on Grande Comore Island ●city in the Grande Comore Island
　　division ●capital of Comoros ●most populated city in Comoros (53,000 people)
　　●chief port on the Mozambique Channel

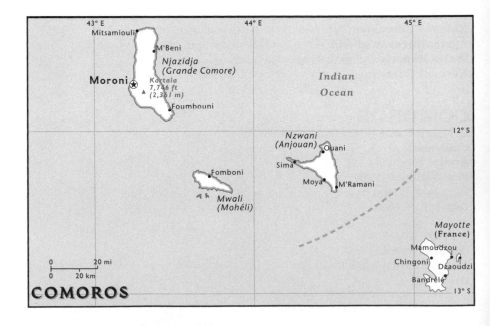

Climate: tropical marine with a rainy season
Agricultural Products: vanilla, cloves, perfume essences, copra
Major Exports: vanilla, ylang-ylang, cloves, perfume oil, copra
Natural Hazards: cyclones, volcanoes

CONGO, REPUBLIC OF THE

Country Name: Republic of the Congo
Continent: Africa
Area: 132,047 sq mi / 342,000 sq km
Population: 3,723,000
Population Density: 28 people per sq mi / 11 people per sq km
Capital: Brazzaville

PHYSICAL:

Highest Point: Mount Berongou 2,963 ft / 903 m
Lowest Point: Atlantic Ocean 0 ft / 0 m (sea level)
Rain forests:

Congo: •covers much of northern and central Republic of the Congo •extends into Democratic Republic of the Congo and Gabon

Oceans:

Atlantic: •forms the southwestern coast of the Republic of the Congo

Rivers:

Congo: •forms part of the Republic of the Congo-Democratic Republic of the Congo border •extends into Democratic Republic of the Congo •tenth longest river in the world

Ubangi (Oubangui): •tributary of the Congo River •forms part of the Republic of the Congo-Democratic Republic of the Congo border

POLITICAL:

Independence: August 15, 1960 (from France)

Former Names: Middle Congo, Congo/Brazzaville, Congo

Bordering Countries: Gabon, Cameroon, Central African Republic, Democratic Republic of the Congo, Angola (5)

States/Provinces: Bouenza, Cuvette, Cuvette-Ouest, Kouilou, Lekoumou, Likouala, Niari, Plateaux, Pool, Sangha (10 regions) •Brazzaville (1 commune)

Ethnic/Racial Groups: Kongo, Sangha, Teke, M'Bochi

Religions: Christianity, animism, Islam

Languages: French, Lingala, Monokutuba, many local dialects

Currency: Communaute Finaciere Africaine franc

Current President: Denis Sassou-Nguesso

Cities (capital, largest, or with at least a million people):

Brazzaville: •located in southeastern Republic of the Congo •city in the Pool region •Brazzaville commune is located in center of the city •capital of Republic of the Congo •most populated city in Republic of the Congo (1,080,000)•chief port on the Congo River

ENVIRONMENTAL/ECONOMIC:

Climate: tropical with rainy/dry seasons; hot and humid

Natural Resources: petroleum, timber, potash, lead, zinc

Agricultural Products: cassava (tapioca), sugar, rice, corn, forest products

Major Exports: petroleum, lumber, plywood, sugar, cacao

Natural Disasters: floods

CONGO, DEMOCRATIC REPUBLIC OF THE

Country Name: Democratic Republic of the Congo
Continent: Africa
Area: 905,365 sq mi / 2,344,885 sq km
Population: 56,625,000
Population Density: 63 people per sq mi / 24 people per sq km
Capital: Kinshasa

PHYSICAL:

Highest Point: Margherita Peak (on Mount Stanley) 16,763 ft / 5,109 m
Lowest Point: Atlantic Ocean 0 ft / 0 m (sea level)

Mountain Ranges:

Bleus: ●located in northeastern Democratic Republic of the Congo ●extend into Uganda

Mitumba: ●cover much of eastern Democratic Republic of the Congo ●extend into Uganda, Rwanda, Burundi, and Tanzania

Peaks (minimum elevation of 8,000 ft / 2,400 m):

Mount Stanley: ●located in the Bleus Mountains ●on the Democratic Republic of the Congo-Uganda border ●includes Margherita Peak, the highest point in Democratic Republic of the Congo

Valleys:

Great Rift: ●located in eastern Democratic Republic of the Congo ●extends into Uganda, Rwanda, Burundi, Tanzania, and Zambia

Rain forests:

Congo: ●covers most of the Democratic Republic of the Congo ●extends into the Republic of the Congo

Oceans:

Atlantic: ●forms the western coast of Democratic Republic of the Congo

Lakes:

Lake Albert: ●located in northeastern Democratic Republic of the Congo ●fed by the Victoria Nile River ●on the Democratic Republic of the Congo-Uganda border ●located on the edge of the Bleus Mountains in the Great Rift Valley

Lake Edward: ●located in northeastern Democratic Republic of the Congo ●on the Democratic Republic of the Congo-Uganda border ●located on the edge of the Bleus Mountains in the Great Rift Valley

Lake Kivu: ●located in eastern Democratic Republic of the Congo ●on the Democratic

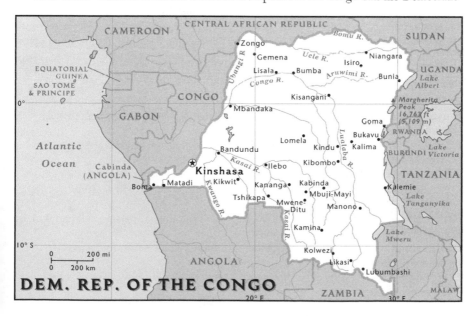

Republic of the Congo-Rwanda border with •located on the edge of the Mitumba
Mountains in the Great Rift Valley

Lake Mweru: •located in southeastern Democratic Republic of the Congo •on the
Democratic Republic of the Congo-Zambia border •located on the edge of the
Mitumba Mountains

Lake Tanganyika: •located in southeastern Democratic Republic of the Congo •on
the border with Burundi, Tanzania, and Zambia •located on the edge of the
Mitumba Mountains in the Great Rift Valley •sixth largest lake in the world

Rivers:

Congo: •has its mouth in the Atlantic Ocean •has its source in the Mitumba
Mountains •forms part of Democratic Republic of the Congo's border with
the Republic of the Congo and Angola •tenth longest river in the world

Kasai: •tributary of the Kwa River •forms part of the Democratic Republic of the
Congo-Angola border•extends into Angola

Kwa: •tributary of the Congo River

Kwango: •tributary of the Kwa River •forms part of the Democratic Republic of
the Congo-Angola border •extends into Angola

Kwilu: •tributary of the Kwango River •extends into Angola

Lualaba: •tributary of the Congo River •has its source in the Mitumba Mountains

Ubangi: •tributary of the Congo River •has its source in the Bleus Mountains •forms
part of the Democratic Republic of the Congo's border with the Republic of the
Congo and Central African Republic

Deltas:

Congo River Delta: •mouth of the Congo River •feeds into the Atlantic Ocean
•borders Democratic Republic of the Congo and Angola

Waterfalls:

Stanley (or Boyoma): •located in northern Democratic Republic of the Congo •part
of the Lualaba River

POLITICAL:

Independence: June 30, 1960 (from Belgium)

Former Names: Congo Free State, Belgian Congo, Katanga, Congo/Leopoldville,
Congo/Kinshasa, Zaire

Bordering Countries: Angola, Republic of the Congo, Zambia, Central African
Republic, Uganda, Sudan, Tanzania, Burundi, Rwanda (9)

Administrative Divisions: Bandundu, Bas-Congo, Equateur, Kasai-Occidental,
Kasai-Oriental, Katanga, Maniema, Nord-Kivu, Orientale, Sud-Kivu (10 provinces)
•Kinshasa (1 city)

Ethnic/Racial Groups: more than 200 African groups, mainly Bantu (Mongo, Luba,
Kongo) and Hamitic (Mangbetu-Azande)

Religions: Christianity (Roman Catholic, Protestant) Kimbanguist (indigenous),
Islam, traditional

Languages: French, Lingala, Kingwana, Kikongo, Tshiluba

Currency: Congolese franc

Current President: Joseph Kabila
Cities (capital, largest, or with at least a million people):
> Kinshasa: ●located in western Democratic Republic of the Congo ●city in the Kinshasa city division ●capital of the Democratic Republic of the Congo ●most populated city in Democratic Republic of the Congo (5,717,000 people) ●chief port on the Congo River
> Lubumbashi: ●located in southeastern Democratic Republic of the Congo ●city in the Katanga province

ENVIRONMENTAL/ECONOMIC:
Climate: tropical; hot and humid in the equatorial basin; cooler and drier in the southern highlands; cooler and wetter in the eastern highlands; wet/dry seasons
Natural Resources: cobalt, copper, cadmium, petroleum, industrial and gem diamonds
Agricultural Products: coffee, sugar, palm oil, rubber, wood products
Major Exports: diamonds, copper, crude oil, coffee, cobalt
Natural Hazards: droughts, floods, volcanoes

COSTA RICA
Country Name: Republic of Costa Rica
Continent: North America
Area: 19,730 sq mi / 51,100 sq km
Population: 4,171,000
Population Density: 211 people per sq mi / 82 people per sq km
Capital: San Jose

PHYSICAL:
Highest Point: Cerro Chirripo 12,500 ft / 3,810 m
Lowest Point: Pacific Ocean 0 ft / 0 m (sea level)
Mountain Ranges:
> Cordillera de Talamanca: ●covers much of northwestern and southeastern Costa Rica ●extends from Costa Rica into Panama
Peaks (minimum elevation of 8,000 ft / 2,400 m):
> Cerro Chirripo: ●located in the Cordillera de Talamanca ●highest point in Costa Rica
Oceans:
> Pacific: ●forms most of the western and southern coasts of Costa Rica
Seas:
> Caribbean: ●forms part of the eastern coast of Costa Rica ●feeds into the Atlantic Ocean

POLITICAL:
Independence: September 15, 1821 (from Spain)
Bordering Countries: Panama, Nicaragua (2)
Administrative Divisions: Alajuela, Cartago, Guanacaste, Heredia, Limon, Puntarenas, San Jose (7 provinces)

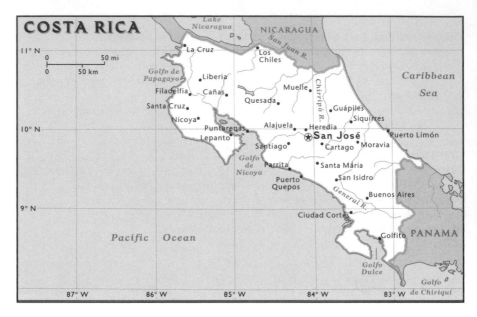

Ethnic/Racial Groups: European, mestizo, black, Amerindian, Chinese
Religion: Christianity (Roman Catholic, Evangelical)
Languages: Spanish, English
Currency: Costa Rican colon
Current President: Abel Pacheco
Cities (capital, largest, or with at least a million people):
San Jose: •located in central Costa Rica •city in the San Jose province •capital of Costa Rica •most populated city in Costa Rica (1,085,000 people) •located in a valley near the Cordillera de Talamanca

ENVIRONMENTAL/ECONOMIC:
Climate: tropical to subtropical with rainy/dry seasons; cooler in the highlands
Natural Resources: hydropower
Agricultural Products: coffee, pineapples, bananas, sugar, beef, timber
Major Exports: coffee, bananas, sugar, pineapples, textiles
Natural Hazards: earthquakes, hurricanes, floods, landslides, volcanoes

COTE D'IVOIRE
Country Name: Republic of Cote d'Ivoire
Continent: Africa
Area: 124,503 sq mi / 322,462 sq km
Population: 16,962,000
Population Density: 136 people per sq mi / 53 people per sq km
Capitals: Abidjan (administrative capital), Yamoussoukro (legislative capital)

PHYSICAL:
Highest Point: Mont Nimba 5,748 ft / 1,752 m
Lowest Point: Gulf of Guinea 0 ft / 0 m (sea level)
Gulfs:
> Gulf of Guinea: •forms the southern coast of Cote d'Ivoire •feeds into the Atlantic Ocean

Lakes:
> Lake Kossou: •located in central Cote d'Ivoire

POLITICAL:
Independence: August 7, 1960 (from France)
Bordering Countries: Liberia, Ghana, Guinea, Burkina Faso, Mali (5)
Administrative Divisions: Abengourou, Abidjan, Aboisso, Adiake, Adzope, Agboville, Agnibilekrou, Alepe, Bangolo, Beoumi, Biankouma, Bocanda, Bondoukou, Bongouanou, Bouafle, Bouake, Bouna, Boundiali, Dabakala, Dabou, Daloa, Danane, Daoukro, Dimbokro, Divo, Duekoue, Ferkessedougou, Gagnoa, Grand-Bassam, Grand-Lahou, Guiglo, Issia, Jacqueville, Katiola, Korhogo, Lakota, Man, Mankono, Mbahiakro, Odienne, Oume, Sakassou, San-Pedro, Sassandra, Seguela, Sinfra, Soubre, Tabou, Tanda, Tiebissou, Tingrela, Tiassale, Touba, Toulepleu, Toumodi, Vavoua, Yamoussoukro, Zuenoula (58 departments)
Ethnic/Racial Groups: Akan, Gur, Northern Mandes, Krous, Southern Mandes
Religions: Christianity, Islam, indigenous beliefs
Languages: French, Dioula, 60 native dialects
Currency: Communaute Finaciere Africaine franc

Current President: Laurent Gbagbo
Cities (capital, largest, or with at least a million people):
   Abidjan: ●located in southeastern Cote d'Ivoire ●city in the Abidjan department
      ●administrative capital of Cote d' Ivoire ●most populated city in Cote d' Ivoire
      (3,516,000 people) ●chief port on the Gulf of Guinea
   Yamoussoukro: ●located in central Cote d'Ivoire ●legislative capital of Cote d'Ivoire
      (416,000 people)

ENVIRONMENTAL/ECONOMIC:
Climate: tropical along the coast, semi-arid in the far north
Natural Resources: petroleum, natural gas, diamonds, manganese, iron ore
Agricultural Products: coffee, cacao, bananas, palm kernels, timber
Major Exports: cacao, coffee, timber, petroleum, cotton
Natural Hazards: tall waves, flooding

CROATIA
Country Name: Republic of Croatia
Continent: Europe
Area: 21,831 sq mi / 56,542 sq km
Population: 4,287,000
Population Density: 196 people per sq mi / 76 people per sq km
Capital: Zagreb

PHYSICAL:
Highest Point: Dinara 6,007 ft / 1,831 m
Lowest Point: Adriatic Sea 0 ft / 0 m (sea level)
Mountain Ranges:
   Dinaric Alps: ●cover much of western Croatia ●extend into Bosnia and Herzegovina
      and into Serbia and Montenegro
Grasslands/Prairies:
   Great Alfold: ●located in northeastern Croatia ●extends into Serbia and
      Montenegro and into Hungary
Seas:
   Adriatic: ●forms most of the western and southern coasts of Croatia ●feeds into the
      Ionian Sea
Rivers:
   Danube: ●forms part of the Croatia-Serbia and Montenegro border ●extends into
      Hungary and into Serbia and Montenegro
   Drava: ●tributary of the Danube River ●forms part of the Croatia-Hungary border
      ●extends into Slovenia
   Sava: ●forms part of the Croatia-Bosnia and Herzegovina border ●extends into
      Slovenia and into Serbia and Montenegro

Regions:

Dalmatia: ●mountainous coastal region in southern Croatia ●located east of the Adriatic Sea in the Dinaric Alps

POLITICAL:

Independence: June 25, 1991 (from Yugoslavia)

Former Names: People's Republic of Croatia, Socialist Republic of Croatia

Bordering Countries: Bosnia and Herzegovina, Slovenia, Hungary, Serbia and Montenegro (4)

Administrative Divisions: Bjelovarsko-Bilogorska, Brodsko-Posavska, Dubrovacko-Neretvanska, Istarska, Karlovacka, Koprivnicko-Krizevacka, Krapinsko-Zagorska, Licko-Senjska, Medimurska Zupanija, Osjecko-Baranjska, Pozesko-Slavonska, Primorsko-Goranska, Sibensko-Kninska, Sisacko-Moslavacka, Splitsko-Dalmatinska, Varazdinska, Viroviticko-Podravska, Vukovarsko-Srijemska, Zadarska, Zagrebacka (20 counties) ●Zagreb (1 city)

Regions:

Slavonia: ●region located in central and eastern Croatia

Ethnic/Racial Groups: Croat, Serb, Bosniak

Religion: Christianity (Roman Catholic, Orthodox)

Language: Croatian

Currency: kuna

Current President: Stjepan Mesic

Cities (capital, largest, or with at least a million people):

Zagreb: ●located in northern Croatia ●city in the Zagreb city division ●capital of Croatia ●most populated city in Croatia (688,000 people) ●chief port on the Sava River

ENVIRONMENTAL/ECONOMIC:
Climate: Mediterranean and continental with hot summers/cold winters
Natural Resources: oil, coal, bauxite, low-grade iron ore, calcium
Agricultural Products: wheat, corn, sugar beets, sunflower seed, livestock
Major Exports: transport equipment, textiles, chemicals, foodstuffs, fuels
Natural Hazards: earthquakes

CUBA
Country Name: Republic of Cuba
Continent: North America
Area: 42,803 sq mi / 110,860 sq km
Population: 11,279,000
Population Density: 264 people per sq mi / 102 people per sq km
Capital: Havana

PHYSICAL:
Highest Point: Pico Turquino 6,476 ft / 1,974 m
Lowest Point: Caribbean Sea 0 ft / 0 m (sea level)
Oceans:
   Atlantic: •forms part of the northern coast of Cuba
Seas:
   Caribbean: •forms most of the southern coast of Cuba •feeds into the Atlantic Ocean
Gulfs:
   Gulf of Mexico: •forms part of the northwestern coast of Cuba •feeds into the
      Atlantic Ocean
Straits:
   Straits of Florida: •forms part of the northern coast of Cuba •separates Cuba from
      the United States •connects the Gulf of Mexico and the Atlantic Ocean
Channels:
   Yucatan: •forms part of the western coast of Cuba •separates Cuba from
   Mexico •connects the Gulf of Mexico and the Caribbean Sea
Passages:
   Windward: •forms part of the southeastern coast of Cuba •separates Cuba from the
      island of Hispaniola

POLITICAL:
Independence: May 20, 1902 (from Spain)
Administrative Divisions: Camaguey, Ciego de Avila, Cienfuegos, Ciudad de La
   Habana, Granma, Guantanamo, Holguin, La Habana, Las Tunas, Matanzas, Pinar
   del Rio, Sancti Spiritus, Santiago de Cuba, Villa Clara (14 provinces) •Isla de la
   Juventud (1 special municipality)
Ethnic/Racial Groups: Creole, white, black

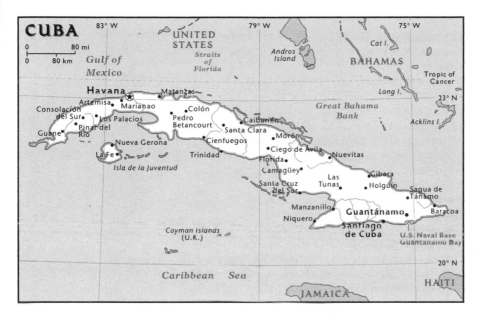

Religions: Christianity (Roman Catholic, Protestant, Jehovah's Witness), Judaism, Santeria

Language: Spanish

Currency: Cuban peso

Current President: Fidel Castro

Cities (capital, largest, or with at least a million people):
Havana: •located in northwestern Cuba •city in the La Habana province •capital of Cuba •most populated city in Cuba (2,189,000 people) •chief port on the Gulf of Mexico

ENVIRONMENTAL/ECONOMIC:

Climate: tropical, moderated by trade winds; dry/rainy season

Natural Resources: cobalt, nickel, iron ore, chromium, copper

Agricultural Products: sugar, tobacco, citrus, coffee, livestock

Major Exports: sugar, nickel, tobacco, fish, medical products

Natural Hazards: hurricanes, droughts

CYPRUS

Country Name: Republic of Cyprus

Continent: Europe

Area: 3,572 sq mi / 9,251 sq km

Population: 934,000

Population Density: 261 people per sq mi / 101 people per sq km

Capital: Nicosia

PHYSICAL:
Highest Point: Mount Olympus 6,401 ft / 1,951 m
Lowest Point: Mediterranean Sea 0 ft / 0 m
Seas:
  Mediterranean: •forms the entire coast of Cyprus •feeds into the Atlantic Ocean

POLITICAL:
Independence: August 16, 1960 (from the United Kingdom)
Administrative Divisions: Famagusta, Kyrenia, Larnaca, Limassol, Nicosia,
  Paphos (6 districts)
Regions: Northern Cyprus (occupied by Turkey since 1974)
Ethnic/Racial Groups: Greek, Turkish
Religions: Christianity (primarily Greek Orthodox), Islam
Languages: Greek, Turkish, English
Currency: Cypriot pound, Turkish lira
Current President: Tassos Papadopoulos
Cities (capital, largest, or with at least a million people):
  Nicosia: •located in central Cyprus •city in the Nicosia district •capital of Cyprus
  •most populated city in Cyprus (205,000 people)

ENVIRONMENTAL/ECONOMIC:
Climate: temperate, Mediterranean; hot and dry summers/cool winters
Natural Resources: copper, pyrites, asbestos, gypsum, timber
Agricultural Products: potatoes, citrus, vegetables, barley

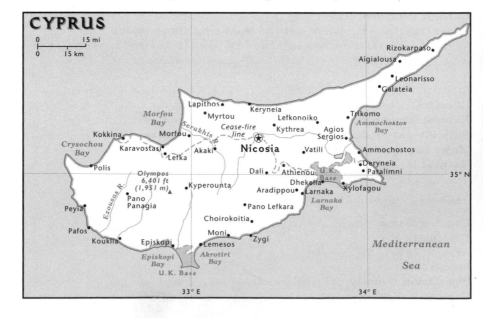

Major Exports: citrus, potatoes, pharmaceuticals, cement (Greek area); citrus, potatoes, textiles (Turkish area)
Natural Hazards: earthquakes, droughts

CZECH REPUBLIC
Country Name: Czech Republic
Continent: Europe
Area: 30,450 sq mi / 78,866 sq km
Population: 10,177,000
Population Density: 334 people per sq mi / 129 people per sq km
Capital: Prague

PHYSICAL:
Highest Point: Snezka 5,256 ft / 1,602 m
Lowest Point: Elbe River 377 ft / 115 m
Mountain Ranges:
Carpathian: •located in southeastern Czech Republic •extend into Slovakia and Poland
Erzgebirge: •located in northwestern Czech Republic •extend into Germany
Sudeten: •cover much of northern Czech Republic •extend into Poland
Rivers:
Elbe: •has its source in the Sudeten Mountains •extends into Germany
Morava: •has its source in the Sudeten Mountains •forms part of the Czech Republic-Slovakia border
Oder: •has its source in the Sudeten Mountains •extends into Poland
Vltava: •tributary of the Elbe River •has its source in southwestern Czech Republic

POLITICAL:
Independence: January 1, 1993 (from Czechoslovakia)
Bordering Countries: Poland, Germany, Austria, Slovakia (4)
Administrative Divisions: Jihocesky, Jihomoravsky, Karlovarsky, Kralovehradecky, Liberecky, Moravskoslezsky, Olomoucky, Pardubicky, Plzensky, Stredocesky, Ustecky, Vysocina, Zlinsky (13 regions) •Praha (1 capital city)
Ethnic/Racial Groups: Czech, Moravian, Slovak
Religion: Christianity (Roman Catholic, Protestant), largest percent is atheist
Language: Czech
Currency: Czech Koruna
Current President: Vaclav Klaus
Cities (capital, largest, or with at least a million people):
Prague: •located in central Czech Republic •city in the Praha capital city division •capital of the Czech Republic •most populated city in the Czech Republic (1,170,000 people) •chief port on the Vltava River

ENVIRONMENTAL/ECONOMIC:

Climate: temperate with cool summers/cold winters

Natural Resources: hard coal, soft coal, kaolin, clay, graphite

Agricultural Products: wheat, potatoes, sugar beets, hops, pigs

Major Exports: machinery and equipment, intermediate manufactures, chemicals, raw materials, fuel

Natural Hazards: floods

DENMARK

Country Name: Kingdom of Denmark
Continent: Europe
Area: 16,640 sq mi / 43,098 sq km
Population: 5,395,000
Population Density: 324 people per sq mi / 125 people per sq km
Capital: Copenhagen

PHYSICAL:
Highest Point: Yding Skovhoej 568 ft / 173 m
Lowest Point: Lammefjord 23 ft / 7 m below sea level
Seas:
> North: •forms most of the western coast of Denmark •feeds into the Atlantic Ocean
> Baltic: •forms part of the southeastern coast of Denmark •feeds into the Kattegat

Gulfs:
> Kattegat: •forms part of the eastern and northern coasts of Denmark •feeds into the North Sea

Bays:
> Alborg: •forms part of the northeastern coast of Denmark •feeds into the Kattegat
> Kieler (Kiel): •forms part of the southern coast of Denmark •feeds into the Kattegat
> Mecklenburger: •forms part of the southeastern coast of Denmark •feeds into the Baltic Sea

Straits:
> Store Baelt: •forms part of the southern coast of Denmark •separates the island of Fyn from the island of Sjaelland •connects Kiel Bay and the Kattegat

Channels:
> Skagerrak: •forms part of the northern coast of Denmark •separates the Jutland Peninsula from Norway •connects the Kattegat and the North Sea

Passages:
> Oresund: •forms part of the eastern coast of Denmark •separates the island of Sjaelland from Sweden •connects the Kattegat and the Baltic Sea

Peninsulas:
> Jutland: •bordered by the North Sea, the Skagerrak, and the Kattegat

Islands:
> Bornholm: •island off the southern coast of Sweden •surrounded by the Baltic Sea
> Fyn: •island off of the southeastern coast of Jutland Peninsula •bordered by the Store Baelt and Kiel Bay

D

DENMARK

0 ──── 50 mi
0 ──── 50 km

57° N

55° N

Skagerrak

Skagen
Hirtshals
Hjørring
Brønderslev
Dronninglund
Frederikshavn
Vesterø Havn
Læsø

Hanstholm

Thisted
Nykøbing
Thyborøn

Ålborg
Lønfjorden
Ålborg Bugt
Hadsund

Anholt

North Sea

Holstebro
Skive
Viborg
Randers
Grenå

Kattegat

SWEDEN

Herning
Ringkøbing Fjord
Skjern R.

Århus
Ebeltoft
Samsø

Helsingør

Store å
Gudenå R.
Varde R.
Flads R
Vejle
Kolding
Horsens

Sjælland
Slagelse
Korsør

Copenhagen
Køge Bugt

Esbjerg
Ribe
Rømø
Åbenrå
Sønderborg

Fyn
Odense
Nyborg
Næstved

Fakse Bugt
Møn
Stege

Bornholm
Rønne
Allinge

North Frisian Islands

GERMANY
Kieler Bucht

Nakskov
Rudkøbing
Lolland
Nykøbing
Falster
Gedser

Baltic Sea

9° E   11° E   13° E   15° E

Lolland: ●island located south of Sjaelland ●bordered by Kiel Bay, Mecklenburger Bay, and the Baltic Sea

Sjaelland: ●island located east of Fyn ●bordered by the Kattegat, Store Baelt, Oresund, and the Baltic Sea

POLITICAL:

Independence: organized in the 10th century; constitution established on June 5, 1849

Bordering Country: Germany (1)

Administrative Divisions: Arhus, Bornholm, Frederiksborg, Fyn, Kobenhavn, Nordjylland, Ribe, Ringkobing, Roskilde, Sonderjylland, Storstrom, Vejle, Vestsjalland, Viborg (14 counties) ●Fredericksberg, Kobenhavns (2 boroughs)

External Territories: Faroe Islands, Greenland (2)

Ethnic/Racial Groups: Danish, German

Religion: Christianity (primarily Evangelical Lutheran)

Languages: Danish, Faroese, Greenlandic, German

Currency: Danish krone

Current Prime Minister: Anders Fogh Rasmussen

Cities (capital, largest, or with at least a million people):

Copenhagen: ●located in eastern Denmark ●city in Kobenhavn county ●Kobenhavns borough is located in the center of the city ●capital of Denmark ●most populated city in Denmark (1,066,000 people) ●chief port on the Oresund and the Baltic Sea

ENVIRONMENTAL/ECONOMIC:
Climate: temperate with mild winters/cool summers
Natural Resources: petroleum, natural gas, fish, salt, limestone
Agricultural Products: barley, wheat, potatoes, sugar beets, pork
Major Exports: machinery and instruments, meat and meat products, dairy products, fish, chemicals
Natural Hazards: floods

DJIBOUTI
Country Name: Republic of Djibouti
Continent: Africa
Area: 8,958 sq mi / 23,200 sq km
Population: 658,000
Population Density: 73 people per sq mi / 28 people per sq km
Capital: Djibouti

PHYSICAL:
Highest Point: Mous alli 6,631 ft / 2,021 m
Lowest Point: Lake Assal 512 ft / 156 m below sea level
Valleys:
    Great Rift: •covers an area from southwest to northeast Djibouti •extends into Ethiopia
Depressions:
    Lake Assal: •located in the Great Rift Valley •lowest point in Africa
Gulfs:
    Gulf of Aden: •forms part of the eastern coast of Djibouti •feeds into the Arabian Sea
    Gulf of Tadjoura: •inlet of the Gulf of Aden between Tadjoura and Djibouti city
Straits:
    Bab al Mandab: •forms the northeastern coast of Djibouti •separates Djibouti from Yemen •connects the Red Sea and the Gulf of Aden
Regions:
    Denakil: •lowland, geothermal region that covers much of western Djibouti •extends into Ethiopia and Eritrea •located north of the Great Rift Valley

POLITICAL:
Independence: June 27, 1977 (from France)
Former Names: French Territory of the Afars and Issas, French Somaliland
Bordering Countries: Ethiopia, Eritrea, Somalia (3)
Administrative Divisions: 'Ali Sabih, Dikhil, Djibouti, Obock, Tadjoura (5 districts)
Ethnic/Racial Groups: Somali, Afar
Religions: Islam, Christianity
Languages: French, Arabic, Somali, Afar
Currency: Djiboutian franc

DJIBOUTI

Mousâ'alli 6,631 ft (2,021 m)

ERITREA

Red Sea · YEMEN

Moulhouli

Bāb al Mandab

Khor Angar

Dorra

Balho

12° N

Obock

ETHIOPIA

Randa

Tadjoura

Gulf of Aden

Lake Gemeri

Lake Assal

Sâgallou

Gulf of Tadjoura

Djibouti

Lake Abhe

Yoboki

'Arta

Loyada

Awash R.

Holhol

Dikhil

'Ali Sabîh

SOMALIA

As Ela

11° N

42° E

ETHIOPIA

43° E

Current President: Ismail Omar Guelleh
Cities (capital, largest, or with at least a million people):
Djibouti: •located in eastern Djibouti •city in the Djibouti district •capital of Djibouti •most populated city in Djibouti (502,000 people) •chief port on the Gulf of Aden

ENVIRONMENTAL/ECONOMIC:
Climate: desert, dry
Natural Resources: geothermal areas
Agricultural Products: fruits, vegetables, goats
Major Exports: re-exports, hides and skins, coffee (in transit)
Natural Disasters: earthquakes, droughts, cyclones, flash floods

DOMINICA
Country Name: Commonwealth of Dominica
Continent: North America
Area: 290 sq mi / 751 sq km
Population: 70,000
Population Density: 241 people per sq mi / 93 people per sq km
Capital: Roseau

PHYSICAL:
Highest Point: Morne Diablotins 4,747 ft / 1,447 m
Lowest Point: Caribbean Sea 0 ft / 0 m (sea level)
Oceans:
   Atlantic: •forms the eastern coast of Dominica
Seas:
   Caribbean: •forms the western coast of Dominica •feeds into the Atlantic Ocean

POLITICAL:
Independence: November 3, 1978 (from the United Kingdom)
Administrative Divisions: Saint Andrew, Saint David, Saint George, Saint John,
   Saint Joseph, Saint Luke, Saint Mark, Saint Patrick, Saint Paul, Saint Peter (10 parishes)
Ethnic/Racial Groups: black, Creole, white, Carib Amerindian
Religion: Christianity (Roman Catholic, Protestant)
Languages: English, French patois
Currency: East Caribbean dollar
Current President: Nicholas Liverpool
Cities (capital, largest, or with at least a million people):
   Roseau: •located in southwestern Dominica •city in the Saint George parish •capital
   of Dominica •most populated city in Dominica (27,000 people) •chief port on
   the Caribbean Sea

ENVIRONMENTAL/ECONOMIC:
Climate: tropical, moderated by trade winds; heavy rains
Natural Resources: timber, hydropower, arable land
Agricultural Products: bananas, citrus, mangoes, root crops
Major Exports: bananas, soap, bay oil, vegetables, grapefruit
Natural Hazards: flash floods, hurricanes

DOMINICAN REPUBLIC

Country Name: Dominican Republic
Continent: North America
Area: 18,704 sq mi / 48,442 sq km
Population: 8,716,000
Population Density: 466 people per sq mi / 180 people per sq km
Capital: Santo Domingo

PHYSICAL:
Highest Point: Pico Duarte 10,417 ft / 3,175 m
Lowest Point: Lake Enriquillo 151 ft / 46 m below sea level
Peaks (minimum elevation of 8,000 ft / 2,400 m):
  Pico Duarte: •located in western Dominican Republic •highest point in
    Dominican Republic •highest point in the Caribbean
Oceans:
  Atlantic: •forms the northern coast of Dominican Republic
Seas:
  Caribbean: •forms the southern coast of Dominican Republic •feeds into the
    Atlantic Ocean
Passages:
  Mona: •forms part of the eastern coast of Dominican Republic •separates the
    island of Hispaniola from Puerto Rico (U.S. commonwealth) •connects the
    Caribbean Sea and the Atlantic Ocean
Islands:
  Hispaniola: •Dominican Republic takes up the eastern portion of this island
    •bordered by the Atlantic Ocean and the Caribbean Sea •Haiti takes up the
    western portion of the island

POLITICAL:
Independence: February 27, 1844 (from Haiti)
Bordering Countries: Haiti (1)
Administrative Divisions: Azua, Baoruco, Barahona, Dajabon, Duarte, Elias Pina,
  El Seibo, Espaillat, Hato Mayor, Independencia, La Altagracia, La Romana, La
  Vega, Maria Trinidad Sanchez, Monsenor Nouel, Monte Cristi, Monte Plata,
  Pedernales, Peravia, Puerto Plata, Salcedo, Samana, Sanchez Ramirez, San Cristobal,
  San Jose de Ocoa, San Juan, San Pedro de Macoris, Santiago, Santiago Rodriguez,
  Santo Domingo, Valverde (31 provinces) •Distrito Nacional (1 district)

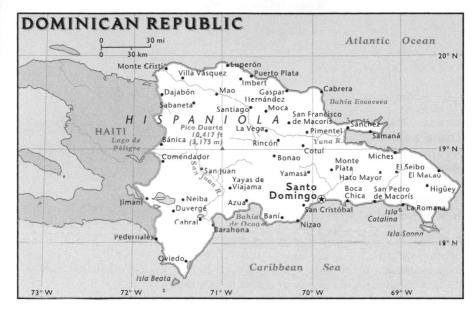

DOMINICAN REPUBLIC

Ethnic/Racial Groups: Creole, white, black
Religion: Christianity (primarily Roman Catholic)
Language: Spanish
Currency: Dominican peso
Current President: Leonel Fernandez
Cities (capital, largest, or with at least a million people):
    Santo Domingo: •located in southern Dominican Republic •city in the Distrito
        Nacional (district) •capital of Dominican Republic •most populated city in
    Dominican Republic (1,865,000 people) •chief port on the Caribbean Sea

ENVIRONMENTAL/ECONOMIC:
Climate: tropical maritime with little temperature change
Natural Resources: nickel, bauxite, gold, silver
Agricultural Products: sugarcane, coffee, cotton, cacao, cattle
Major Exports: ferronickel, sugar, gold, silver, coffee
Natural Hazards: hurricanes, floods, droughts

EAST TIMOR

Country Name: Democratic Republic of Timor-Leste
Other Names: Timor-Leste
Continent: Asia
Area: 5,640 sq mi / 14,609 sq km
Population: 778,000
Population Density: 138 people per sq mi / 53 people per sq km
Capital: Dili

PHYSICAL:

Highest Point: Foho Tatamailau 9,721 ft / 2,976 m
Lowest Point: Timor Sea 0 ft / 0 m (sea level)
Peaks (minimum elevation of 8,000 ft /2,400 m):
    Foho Tatamailau: •located in western East Timor •highest point in East Timor
Seas:
    Savu: •forms most of the northern coast of East Timor •feeds into the Indian Ocean
    Timor: •forms most of the southern coast of East Timor •feeds into the Indian Ocean

TIMOR-LESTE
(EAST TIMOR)

Straits:
    Wetar: •forms most of the northern coast of East Timor •separates East
        Timor from the island of Wetar
Islands:
    Timor: •main island of East Timor •bordered by the Savu Sea, Timor Sea, and
        Wetar Strait •western half belongs to Indonesia

POLITICAL:
Independence: May 20, 2002 (from Indonesia)
Former Name: Portuguese Timor
Bordering Country: Indonesia (1)
Administrative Divisions: Aileu, Ainaro, Baucau, Bobonaro (Maliana), Cova-Lima
    (Suai), Dili, Ermera, Lautem (Los Palos), Liquica, Manatuto, Manufahi (Same),
    Oecussi (Ambeno), Viqueque (13 administrative districts)
Ethnic/Racial Groups: Austronesian, Papuan
Religion: Christianity (primarily Roman Catholic)
Languages: Tetum, Portuguese, Bahasa Indonesian, English
Currency: U.S. dollar and Indonesian rupiah
Current President: Xanana Gusmao
Cities:
    Dili: •located in northern East Timor •city in the Dili administrative district •capital
    of East Timor •most populated city in East Timor (49,000 people) •chief port on
    the Wetar Strait

ENVIRONMENTAL/ECONOMIC:
Climate: tropical, hot and humid with rainy/dry seasons
Natural Resources: gold, petroleum, natural gas, manganese, marble
Agricultural Products: coffee, rice, maize, cassava, sweet potatoes
Major Exports: coffee, sandalwood, marble
Natural Hazards: floods, landslides, earthquakes, tsunamis, tropical cyclones

ECUADOR

Country Name: Republic of Ecuador
Continent: South America
Area: 109,483 sq mi / 283,560 sq km
Population: 12,558,000
Population Density: 115 people per sq mi / 44 people per sq km (most dense in
    South America)
Capital: Quito

PHYSICAL:
Highest Point: Chimborazo 20,702 ft / 6,310 m
Lowest Point: Pacific Ocean 0 ft / 0 m (sea level)

E

Mountain Ranges:
Andes: •cover much of Ecuador •extend into Colombia and Peru
Peaks (minimum elevation of 8,000 ft /2,400 m):
Chimborazo: •located in the Andes •highest point in Ecuador
Rain forests:
Amazon: •located in eastern Ecuador •extends into Colombia and Peru •largest rain forest in the world
Oceans:
Pacific: •forms most of the western coast of Ecuador
Gulfs:
Gulf of Guayaquil: •forms the southwestern coast of Ecuador •feeds into the Pacific Ocean
Rivers:
Pastaza: •has its source in the Andes •extends into Peru
Putumayo: •forms part of the Ecuador-Colombia border •extends into Colombia

POLITICAL:
Independence: May 24, 1822 (from Spain)
Bordering Countries: Peru, Colombia (2)
Administrative Divisions: Azuay, Bolivar, Canar, Carchi, Chimborazo, Cotopaxi, El Oro, Esmeraldas, Galapagos, Guayas, Imbabura, Loja, Los Rios, Manabi, Morona-Santiago, Napo, Orellana, Pastaza, Pichincha, Sucumbios, Tungurahua, Zamora-Chinchipe (22 provinces)

Ethnic/Racial Groups: mestizo, Amerindian, black
Religion: Christianity (Roman Catholic)
Languages: Spanish, Quechua
Currency: U.S. dollar
Current President: Lucio Gutierrez
Cities (capital, largest, or with at least a million people):
  Guayaquil: •located in western Ecuador •city in the Guayas province of Ecuador •most populated city in Ecuador (2,636,000 people) •chief port on the Gulf of Guayaquil
  Quito: •located in northern Ecuador •city in the Pichincha province of Ecuador •capital of Ecuador (1,451,00 people) •located in a valley in the Andes

ENVIRONMENTAL/ECONOMIC:
Climate: tropical along the coasts and in the rain forest; cooler in the highlands
Natural Resources: petroleum, fish, timber, hydropower
Agricultural Products: bananas, coffee, cacao, rice, cattle
Major Exports: petroleum, bananas, shrimp, coffee, cacao
Natural Hazards: earthquakes, landslides, volcanoes, floods, droughts

EGYPT
Country Name: Arab Republic of Egypt
Continent: Africa
Area: 386,874 sq mi / 1,002,000 sq km

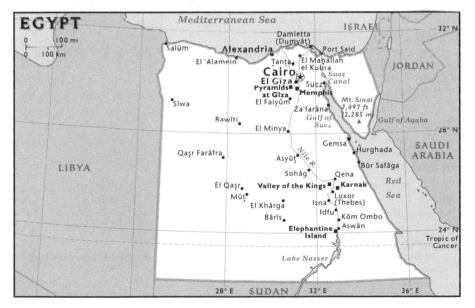

Population: 72,062,000
Population Density: 186 people per sq mi / 72 people per sq km
Capital: Cairo

PHYSICAL:
Highest Point: Mount Catherine 8,652 ft / 2,637 m
Lowest Point: Qattara Depression 436 ft / 133 m below sea level
Peaks (minimum elevation of 8,000 ft /2,400 m):
Mount Catherine: •located on the Sinai Peninsula •highest point in Egypt
Plateau Regions:
Libyan Plateau: •located in northwestern Egypt •extends into Libya
Depressions:
Qattara Depression: •located in northwestern Egypt •lowest point in Egypt
Deserts:
Eastern: •located in eastern Eqypt •extends into Sudan
Libyan: •located in southwestern Egypt •extends into Libya and Sudan
Sahara: •covers most of the country •extends into Libya and Sudan •largest desert
in the world
Western: •located in central Egypt •extends into Libya
Seas:
Mediterranean: •forms most of the northern coast of Egypt •feeds into the
Atlantic Ocean
Red: •forms much of the eastern coast of Egypt •feeds into the Gulf of Aden
Gulfs:
Gulf of Suez: •forms part of the northeastern coast of Egypt •feeds into the Red Sea
Gulf of Aqaba: •forms part of the northeastern coast of Egypt •feeds into the Red Sea
Canals:
Suez: •connects the Mediterranean and Red Seas •separates the Sinai Peninsula
from the rest of Egypt
Lakes:
Lake Nasser: •located in southeastern Egypt •on the border with Sudan •fed by the
Nile River •formed by the Aswan High Dam
Rivers:
Nile: •has its mouth in the Mediterranean Sea •extends into Sudan •longest river
in the world
Deltas:
Nile River Delta: •mouth of the Nile River •feeds into the Mediterranean Sea
Dams:
Aswan High Dam: •located in southeastern Egypt •part of the Nile River •forms
Lake Nasser
Peninsulas:
Sinai: •bordered by the Red Sea, Gulf of Suez, Gulf of Aqaba, and Mediterranean Sea

POLITICAL:
Independence: February 28, 1922 (from the United Kingdom)
Former Name: United Arab Republic (with Syria)
Bordering Countries: Sudan, Libya, Israel (3)
Administrative Divisions: Ad Daqahliyah, Al Bahr al Ahmar, Al Buhayrah,
Al Fayyum, Al Gharbiyah, Al Iskandariyah, Al Ismailiyah, Al Jizah, Al Minufiyah,
Al Minya, Al Qahirah, Al Qalyubiyah, Al Uqsor, Al Wadi al Jadid, Ash Sharqiyah,
As Suways, Aswan, Asyut, Bani Suwayf, Bur Said, Dumyat, Janub Sina, Kafr ash
Shaykh, Matruh, Qina, Shamal Sina, Suhaj (27 governorates)
Ethnic/Racial Groups: Egyptian Arab
Religions: Islam (primarily Sunni), Christianity (primarily Coptic)
Languages: Arabic, English, French
Currency: Egyptian pound
Current President: Hosni Mubarak
Cities (capital, largest, or with at least a million people):
Cairo: •located in northern Egypt •city in the Al Qahirah governorate •capital of
Egypt •most populated city in Egypt (11,146,000 people) •chief port on the
Nile River
Alexandria: •located in northern Egypt •city in the Al Iskandariyah governorate
•chief port on the Mediterranean Sea
Al Jizah (Giza): •located in northern Egypt •city in the Al Jizah governorate
Shubra al Khaymah: •located in northern Egypt •city in the Al Qalyubiyah governorate

ENVIRONMENTAL/ECONOMIC:
Climate: desert; hot and dry summers/moderate winters
Natural Resources: petroleum, natural gas, iron ore, phosphates, manganese
Agricultural Products: cotton, rice, corn, wheat, cattle
Major Exports: crude oil and petroleum products, cotton, textiles, metal products, chemicals
Natural Hazards: droughts, earthquakes, flash floods, landslides, khamsin
(windstorms), dust storms, sandstorms

EL SALVADOR
Country Name: Republic of El Salvador
Continent: North America
Area: 8,124 sq mi / 21,041 sq km
Population: 6,640,000
Population Density: 817 people per sq mi / 316 people per sq km
Capital: San Salvador

PHYSICAL:
Highest Point: Cerro El Pital 8,957 ft / 2,730 m
Lowest Point: Pacific Ocean 0 ft / 0 m (sea level)

EL SALVADOR

Peaks (minimum elevation of 8,000 ft /2,400 m):
    Cerro El Pital: ●located in northwestern El Salvador ●on the El Salvador-Honduras border ●highest point in El Salvador
    Santa Ana Volcano: ●located in western El Salvador

Oceans:
    Pacific: ●forms most of the southern coast of El Salvador

Gulfs:
    Gulf of Fonseca: ●forms part of the southeastern coast of El Salvador ●feeds into the Pacific Ocean

POLITICAL:

Independence: September 15, 1821 (from Spain)

Bordering Countries: Honduras, Guatemala (2)

Administrative Divisions: Ahuachapan, Cabanas, Chalatenango, Cuscatlan, La Libertad, La Paz, La Union, Morazan, San Miguel, San Salvador, Santa Ana, San Vicente, Sonsonate, Usulutan (14 departments)

Ethnic/Racial Groups: mestizo, white, Amerindian

Religion: Christianity (Roman Catholic, Evangelical)

Languages: Spanish, Nahua

Currency: U.S. dollar

Current President: Elias Antonio Saca

Cities (capital, largest, or with at least a million people):
    San Salvador: ●located in central El Salvador ●city in the San Salvador department ●capital of El Salvador ●most populated city in El Salvador (1,424,000 people)

ENVIRONMENTAL/ECONOMIC:
Climate: tropical; temperate in the uplands with rainy/dry seasons
Natural Resources: hydropower, geothermal power, petroleum, arable land
Agricultural Products: coffee, sugar, corn, rice, shrimp
Major Exports: offshore-assembly exports, coffee, sugar, shrimp, textiles
Natural Hazards: earthquakes, volcanoes, hurricanes

EQUATORIAL GUINEA
Country Name: Republic of Equatorial Guinea
Continent: Africa
Area: 10,831 sq mi / 28,051 sq km
Population: 510,000
Population Density: 47 people per sq mi / 18 people per sq km
Capital: Malabo

PHYSICAL:
Highest Point: Pico de Santa Isabel 9,869 ft / 3,008 m
Lowest Point: Gulf of Guinea 0 ft / 0 m (sea level)
Mountain Ranges:
   Monts de Cristal: •located in southern Equatorial Guinea •extend into Gabon
Peaks (minimum elevation of 8,000 ft /2,400 m):
   Pico de Santa Isabel: •located on the island of Bioko •highest point in Equatorial Guinea
Gulfs:
   Gulf of Guinea: •forms most of the western coast of Equatorial Guinea •feeds into the Atlantic Ocean
Bays:
   Bight of Bonny: •forms part of the western coast of Equatorial Guinea •feeds into the Gulf of Guinea
Islands:
   Bioko: •an island off the coast of Cameroon •bordered by the Gulf of Guinea and the Bight of Bonny

POLITICAL:
Independence: October 12, 1968 (from Spain)
Former Name: Spanish Guinea
Bordering Countries: Gabon, Cameroon (2)
Regions:
   Rio Muni: •includes all of mainland Equatorial Guinea
Administrative Divisions: Annobon, Bioko Norte, Bioko Sur, Centro Sur, Kie-Ntem, Litoral, Wele-Nzas (7 provinces)
Ethnic/Racial Groups: Fang, Bubi
Religions: Christianity (predominantly Roman Catholic), pagan practices
Languages: Spanish, French, pidgin English, Fang, Bubi, Ibo

Currency: Communaute Financiere Africaine franc
Current President: Teodoro Obiang Nguema Mbasogo
Cities (capital, largest, or with at least a million people):
Malabo: •located on the island of Bioko •city in the Bioko Norte province •capital of Equatorial Guinea •most populated city in Equatorial Guinea (95,000 people) •chief port on the Bight of Bonny

ENVIRONMENTAL/ECONOMIC:
Climate: tropical, hot and humid
Natural Resources: oil, petroleum, timber, gold, manganese
Agricultural Products: coffee, cocoa, rice, yarns, livestock
Major Exports: petroleum, methanol, timber, cacao
Natural Hazards: windstorms, flash floods

ERITREA

Country Name: State of Eritrea
Continent: Africa
Area: 46,774 sq mi / 121,144 sq km
Population: 4,362,000
Population Density: 93 people per sq mi / 36 people per sq km
Capital: Asmara

PHYSICAL:
Highest Point: Soira 9,902 ft / 3,018 m
Lowest Point: Denakil Depression 381 ft / 116 m below sea level
Mountain Ranges:
  Ethiopian Highlands: •stretch across western and central Eritrea •extend into Ethiopia
Peaks (minimum elevation of 8,000 ft /2,400 m):
  Soira: •located in the Ethiopian Highlands •highest point in Eritrea
Depressions:
  Denakil: •extends into Ethiopia •lowest point in Eritrea
Seas:
  Red: •forms most of the coast of Eritrea •feeds into the Gulf of Aden
Straits:
  Bab al Mandab: •forms part of the southeastern coast of Eritrea •separates Eritrea
    from Yemen •connects the Red Sea and the Gulf of Aden
Regions:
  Denakil: •lowland, geothermal region in central and eastern Eritrea •extends into
    Ethiopia and Djibouti •located to the east of the Ethiopian Highlands

POLITICAL:
Independence: May 24, 1993 (from Ethiopia)
Former Name: Eritrea Autonomous Region in Ethiopia
Bordering Countries: Ethiopia, Sudan, Djibouti (3)
Administrative Divisions: Anelba, Central, Gash-Barka, Northern Red Sea,
  Southern, Southern Red Sea (6 regions)

Ethnic/Racial Groups: Tigrinya, Tigre, Kunama, Afar, Saho
Religions: Islam, Christianity (Coptic, Roman Catholic, Protestant)
Languages: Afar, Arabic, Tigre, Kunama, Tigrinya
Currency: nafka
Current President: Isaias Afwerki
Cities (capital, largest, or with at least a million people):
    Asmara: ●located in central Eritrea ●city in the Central region ●capital of Eritrea
        ●most populated city in Eritrea (556,000 people)

ENVIRONMENTAL/ECONOMIC:
Climate: arid to semiarid; hot and dry in the desert along the Red Sea; cooler and
    wetter in the highlands
Natural Resources: gold, potash, zinc, copper, salt
Agricultural Products: sorghum, lentils, vegetables, corn, livestock
Major Exports: livestock, sorghum, textiles, food, small manufactures
Natural Hazards: droughts, locust swarms

ESTONIA
Country Name: Republic of Estonia
Continent: Europe
Area: 17,462 sq mi / 45,227 sq km
Population: 1,353,000
Population Density: 77 people per sq mi / 30 people per sq km
Capital: Tallinn

PHYSICAL:
Highest Point: Suur Munamagi 1,043 ft / 318 m
Lowest Point: Baltic Sea 0 ft / 0 m (sea level)
Seas:
    Baltic: ●forms part of the western coast of Estonia ●feeds into the Kattegat
Gulfs:
    Gulf of Finland: ●forms the northern coast of Estonia ●feeds into the Baltic Sea
    Gulf of Riga: ●forms the southwestern coast of Estonia ●forms part of the western
        coast of Estonia ●feeds into the Baltic Sea
Lakes:
    Lake Peipus: ●located in eastern Estonia ●on the Estonia-Russia border
    Lake Pskov: ●southern part of Lake Peipus ●on the Estonia-Russia border
    Vorts: ●located in central Estonia
Islands:
    Hiiumaa: ●located off the western coast of Estonia ●bordered by the Baltic Sea
    Saaremaa: ●located off the southwestern coast of Estonia ●bordered by the Baltic
        Sea and Gulf of Riga

POLITICAL:
Independence: August 20, 1991 (from Soviet Union)
Former Name: Estonian Soviet Socialist Republic
Bordering Countries: Latvia, Russia (2)
Administrative Divisions: Harjumaa, Hiiumaa, Ida-Virumaa, Jarvamaa,
   Jogevamaa, Laanemaa, Laane-Virumaa, Parnumaa, Polvamaa, Raplamaa, Saaremaa,
   Tartumaa, Valgamaa, Viljandimaa, Vorumaa (15 counties)
Ethnic/Racial Groups: Estonian, Russian
Religion: Christianity (Evangelical Lutheran, Russian Orthodox, Eastern Orthodox)
Languages: Estonian, Russian, Ukrainian
Currency: Estonian kroon
Current President: Arnold Ruutel
Cities (capital, largest, or with at least a million people):
   Tallinn: ●located in northern Estonia ●city in the Harjumaa county ●capital of
      Estonia ●most populated city in Estonia (391,000 people) ●chief port on the
      Gulf of Finland

ENVIRONMENTAL/ECONOMIC:
Climate: maritime, wet and moderate winters /cool summers
Natural Resources: oil shale, peat, phosphorite, clay, limestone
Agricultural Products: potatoes, vegetables, livestock and dairy products, fish
Major Exports: machinery and equipment, wood and paper, textiles, food products,
   furniture
Natural Hazards: floods

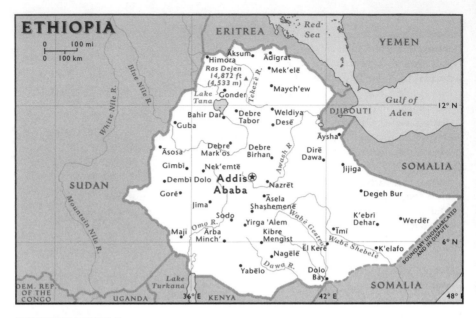

ETHIOPIA

Country Name: Federal Democratic Republic of Ethiopia
Continent: Africa
Area: 437,600 sq. mi / 1,133,380 sq. km
Population: 70,677,000
Population Density: 162 people per sq mi / 62 people per sq km
Capital: Addis Ababa

PHYSICAL:
Highest Point: Ras Dejen 14,872 ft / 4,533 m
Lowest Point: Denakil Depression 410 ft / 125 m below sea level
Mountain Ranges:
   Ethiopian Highlands: ●cover most of western and central Ethiopia ●extend into Eritrea
Peaks (minimum elevation of 8,000 ft /2,400 m):
   Ras Dejen: ●located in the Ethiopian Highlands ●highest point in Ethiopia
Valleys:
   Great Rift: ●covers an area from northeastern to southwestern Ethiopia ●surrounded by the Ethiopian Highlands ●extends from Ethiopia into Djibouti and Kenya
Depressions:
Denakil Depression: ●located in northern Ethiopia ●extends into Eritrea ●contains the lowest point in Ethiopia ●location of Dalol, the world's hottest place

Lakes:

Lake Tana: •located in northwestern Ethiopia •located high in the Ethiopian Highlands •source of the Blue Nile

Lake Turkana: •located in southwestern Ethiopia •lake in the Great Rift Valley on the edge of the Ethiopian Highlands •fed by the Omo River •extends into Kenya

Rivers:

Awash: •has its mouth in Lake Abbe •in the Great Rift Valley •has its source in the Ethiopian Highlands

Blue Nile: •has its source in Lake Tana •in the Ethiopian Highlands •extends into Sudan

Omo: •has its mouth in Lake Turkana •has its source in the Ethiopian Highlands

Wabe Shebele: •has its source in the Ethiopian Highlands •extends into Somalia

Regions:

Denakil: •lowland, geothermal region in northeastern Africa •east of the Ethiopian Highlands •extends into Eritrea and Djibouti •location of Dalol, the world's hottest place

Haud: •lowland, desert region in eastern Ethiopia •east of the Ethiopian Highlands •extends into Somalia

Ogaden: •lowland, desert region in southeastern Ethiopia •east of the Ethiopian Highlands

POLITICAL:

Independence: the oldest independent country in Africa (since the early 1800s) and one of the oldest in the world

Former Names: Abyssinia, Italian East Africa

Bordering Countries: Sudan, Somalia, Eritrea, Kenya, Djibouti (5)

Regions:

Afar: •region in northeastern Ethiopia •located in the lowland region of Denakil

Amhara: •region in western and central Ethiopia •located in the Ethiopian Highlands

Boran: •region in southern Ethiopia •located to the south of the Ethiopian Highlands •extends into Kenya

Oromia: •region in central Ethiopia •located in the Ethiopian Highlands and the Great Rift Valley

Somali: •region in eastern Ethiopia •located in the lowland regions of Haud and Ogaden •located east of the Ethiopian Highlands

Tigray: •region in northern Ethiopia •located in the Ethiopian Highlands and the Denakil region

Administrative Divisions: Afar, Amara (Amhara), Binshangul Gumuz, Gambela Hizboch (Gambela Peoples), Hareri Hizb (Harari People), Oromiya (Oromia), Sumale (Somali), Tigray, Ye Debub Biheroch Bihereseboch na Hizboch (Southern Nations, Nationalities, and Peoples) (9 ethnically based states) •Addis Ababa, Dire Dawa (2 self-governing administrations)

Ethnic/Racial Groups: Oromo, Amhara, Tigre, Sidamo, Shankella, Somali, Afar, Gurage

Religions: Islam, Christianity (Ethiopian Orthodox), animism

Languages: Amharic, Tigrinya, Orominga, Guaraginga, Somali, Arabic
Currency: birr
Current President: Girma Woldegiorgis
Cities (capital, largest, or with at least a million people):
    Addis Ababa: ●located in central Ethiopia ●city in the Addis Ababa self-governing
        administration ●capital of Ethiopia ●most populated city in Ethiopia
        (2,723,000 people) ●in the Ethiopian Highlands

ENVIRONMENTAL/ECONOMIC:
Climate: tropical monsoon; variance in climates
Natural Resources: gold, platinum, copper, potash, natural gas
Agricultural Products: cereals, pulses, coffee, oilseed, cattle
Major Exports: coffee, qat, gold, leather products, live animals
Natural Hazards: earthquakes, volcanoes, droughts

FIJI

Country Name: Republic of the Fiji Islands
Continent: Australia/Oceania
Area: 7,095 sq mi / 18,376 sq km
Population: 865,000
Population Density: 122 people per sq mi / 47 people per sq km
Capital: Suva

PHYSICAL:

Highest Point: Tomanivi 4,341 ft / 1,323 m
Lowest Point: Pacific Ocean 0 ft / 0 m (sea level)
Oceans:
  Pacific: •forms most of the coast of the Fiji Islands
Islands:
  Vanua Levu: •second largest island in the Fiji Islands •bordered by the
    Pacific Ocean
  Viti Levu: •largest island in the Fiji Islands •bordered by the Pacific Ocean

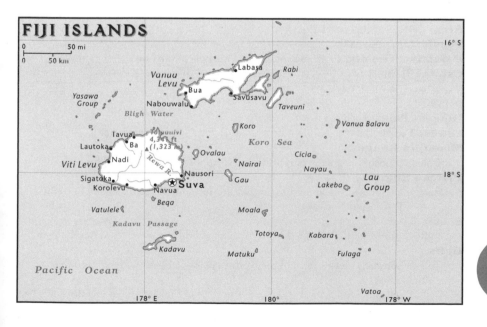

FIJI ISLANDS

Independence: October 10, 1970 (from the United Kingdom)
Administrative Divisions: Central, Eastern, Northern, Western (4 divisions)
Rotuma (1 dependency)
Ethnic/Racial Groups: Fijian, Indian
Religions: Christianity, Hinduism, Islam
Languages: English, Fijian, Hindustani
Currency: Fijian dollar
Current President: Ratu Josefa Iloilovatu
Cities: (capital, largest, or with at least a million people):
Suva: • located on the island of Viti Levu • city in the Central division • capital of the
Fiji Islands • most populated city in the Fiji Islands (210,000 people) • chief port
on the Pacific Ocean

ENVIRONMENTAL/ECONOMIC:
Climate: tropical marine, little temperature variation
Natural Resources: timber, fish, gold, copper, offshore oil potential
Agricultural Products: sugarcane, coconuts, cassava (tapioca), rice
Major Exports: sugar, garments, gold, timber, fish
Natural Hazards: cyclones

FINLAND
Country Name: Republic of Finland
Continent: Europe
Area: 130,558 sq mi / 338,145 sq km
Population: 5,212,000
Population Density: 40 people per sq mi / 15 people per sq km
Capital: Helsinki

PHYSICAL:
Highest Point: Halti 4,357 ft / 1,328 m
Lowest Point: Baltic Sea 0 ft / 0 m (sea level)
Mountain Ranges:
Kjolen: • located in northwestern Finland • extend into Norway and Sweden
Plateau Regions:
Maanselka: • covers an area from northeastern to southeastern Finland • extends
into Russia and Norway
Seas:
Baltic: • forms part of the southwestern coast of Finland • feeds into the Kattegat
Gulfs:
Gulf of Bothnia: • forms most of the western coast of Finland • feeds into the
Baltic Sea
Gulf of Finland: • forms most of the southern coast of Finland • feeds into the Baltic Sea

Islands:
   Aland •located off the coast of southwestern Finland •bordered by the Baltic Sea
   and Gulf of Bothnia

POLITICAL:
Independence: December 6, 1917 (from Russia)
Bordering Countries: Russia, Norway, Sweden (3)
Regions:
   Lapland: •region in northern Finland •southeast of Kjolen •extends into Norway,
   Sweden, and Russia
Administrative Divisions: Aland, Etela-Suomen Laani, Ita-Suomen Laani, Lansi-
   Suomen Laani, Lappi, Oulun Laani (6 provinces)
Ethnic/Racial Groups: Finnish, Swedish
Religion: Christianity (primarily Evangelical Lutheran)
Languages: Finnish, Swedish
Currency: euro
Current President: Tarja Halonen
Cities (capital, largest, or with at least a million people): :
   Helsinki: •located in southern Finland •city in the Etela-Suomen Laani province
   •capital of Finland •most populated city in Finland (1,075,000 people) •chief
   port on the Gulf of Finland

Climate: cold temperate, potentially subarctic, moderated by the North Atlantic Current, the Baltic Sea, and many lakes
Natural Resources: timber, iron ore, copper, lead, zinc
Agricultural Products: barley, wheat, sugar beets, potatoes, dairy cattle
Major Exports: machinery and equipment, chemicals, metals, timber, paper
Natural Hazards: snowstorms

FRANCE

Country Name: French Republic
Continent: Europe
Area: 210,026 sq mi / 543,965 sq km
Population: 59,771,000
Population Density: 285 people per sq mi / 110 people per sq km
Capital: Paris

PHYSICAL:
Highest Point: Mont Blanc 15,781 ft / 4,810 m
Lowest Point: Rhone River Delta 7 ft / 2 m below sea level
Mountain Ranges:
   Alps: • located in southeastern France • extend into Switzerland and Italy
   Cevennes: • located in southern France
   Jura: • located in eastern France • extend into Switzerland
   Massif Central: • located in southern France
   Pyrenees: • located in southwestern France • extend into Spain
   Vosges: • located in northeastern France
Peaks (minimum elevation of 8,000 ft /2,400 m):
   Mont Blanc: • located in the Alps • highest point in France
Plateau Regions:
   Plateau de Langres: • located in eastern France
Oceans:
   Atlantic: • forms part of the western coast of France
Seas:
   Ligurian: • forms part of the southeastern coast of France • feeds into the Mediterranean Sea
   Mediterranean: • forms part of the southeastern coast of France • feeds into the Atlantic Ocean
   North: • forms part of the northern coast of France • feeds into the Atlantic Ocean
   Tyrrhenian: • forms most of the eastern coast of the island of Corsica
Gulfs:
   Gulf of Lion: • forms part of the southern coast of France • feeds into the Mediterranean Sea
   Gulf of Saint-Malo: • forms part of the northwestern coast of France • feeds into the English Channel

Bays:

    Bay of Biscay: •forms part of the western coast of France •feeds into the Atlantic Ocean

    Bay of the Seine: •forms part of the northwestern coast of France • feeds into the
        English Channel

Straits:

    Strait of Bonifacio: •forms part of the southern coast of the island of Corsica
        •separates Corsica from the island of Sardinia (Italy) •connects the Mediterranean
        and Tyrrhenian Seas

    Strait of Dover: •forms part of the northern coast of France •separates France from
        the United Kingdom •connects the North Sea and the English Channel

Channels:

    English: •forms most of the northern coast of France •separates France
        from the United Kingdom •connects the North Sea and the Atlantic Ocean

Lakes:

    Lake Geneva: •located in eastern France •on the France-Switzerland border
        •surrounded by the Jura Mountains and the Alps

Rivers:

    Allier: •tributary of the Loire River •has its source in Massif Central

    Durance: •tributary of the Rhone River •has its source in the Alps

    Garonne: •has its mouth in the Gironde estuary •has its source in the Pyrenees

    Loire: •has its mouth in the Bay of Biscay •has its source in Massif Central

    Meuse: •has its source in northeastern France •extends into Belgium

    Moselle: •has its source in the Vosges •extends into Germany

Rhine: •forms part of the France-Germany border •extends into Germany and Switzerland

Rhone: •has its mouth in the Gulf of Lion •extends into Switzerland

Saone: •tributary of the Rhone River •has its source in northeastern France

Seine: •has its mouth in the Bay of the Seine •has its source on the Plateau de Langres

Deltas:

Gironde Estuary: •mouth of the Garonne River •feeds into the Bay of Biscay

Rhone River Delta: •mouth of the Rhone River •feeds into the Gulf of Lion

Peninsulas:

Cotentin: •bordered by the English Channel, Gulf of Saint-Malo, and Bay of the Seine

Islands:

Corsica: •in the Mediterranean Sea •off the southeastern coast of France •region of France •separated from the Italian island of Sardinia by the Strait of Bonifacio

Regions:

Landes: •lowland region in southwestern France •east of the Bay of Biscay

POLITICAL:

Independence: 486 (unified by Clovis)

Bordering Countries: Spain, Belgium, Switzerland, Italy, Germany, Luxembourg, Andorra, Monaco (8)

Regions:

Alsace: •region in northeastern France •east of the Vosges •west of the Rhine River •north of the Jura Mountains

Angoumois: •region in western France

Anjou: •region in western France

Ardennes: •region in northeastern France •extends into Belgium

Artois: •region in northern France •east of the English Channel

Auvergne: •region in central France •located in the Massif Central

Bearn: •region in southwestern France •southern half is in the Pyrenees

Berry: •region in central France

Bourbonnais: •region in central France •north of the Massif Central

Brittany: •region in northwestern France •south of the English Channel •east of the Atlantic Ocean •north of the Bay of Biscay

Burgundy: •region in eastern France •south of the Plateau de Langres •northeast of the Massif Central •west of the Jura Mountains and the Alps

Champagne: •region in northern France

Dauphine: •region in southeastern France •located in the Alps

Flanders: •region in northern France •south of the North Sea •extends into Belgium

Foix: •region in southern France •north of the Pyrenees

Franche: •region in eastern France •west of the Jura Mountains

Gascony: •region in southwestern France •east of the Bay of Biscay •north of the Pyrenees

Guienne: • region that stretches across southern France • east of the Bay of Biscay • eastern part is in the Massif Central

Ile-de-France: • region in northern France • Paris is located here

Languedoc: • region in southern France • includes the Cevennes • southeast of the Massif Central

Limousin: • region in central France • west of the Massif Central

Lorraine: • region in northeastern France • west of the Vosges

Lyonnais: • region in eastern France • northeast of the Massif Central

Maine: • region in northwestern France

Marche: • region in central France • north of the Massif Central

Nivernais: • region in central France

Normandy: • region in northwestern France • south of the English Channel • east of the Gulf of Saint-Malo • includes the Cotentin Peninsula

Orleanais: • region in central France

Perche: • region in northern France

Picardy: • region in northern France • east of the English Channel

Poitou: • region in western France • east of the Bay of Biscay

Provence: • region in southeastern France • eastern part is located in the Alps • north of the Mediterranean Sea • northeast of the Gulf of Lion • northwest of the Ligurian Sea

Roussillon: • region in southern France • western part is in the Pyrenees • west of the Mediterranean Sea

Saintonge: • region in western France • east of the Bay of Biscay

Savoy: • region in eastern France • located in the Alps

Administrative Divisions: Alsace, Aquitaine, Auvergne, Basse-Normandie, Bourgogne, Bretagne, Centre, Champagne-Ardenne, Corse (Corsica), Franche-Comte, Haute-Normandie, Ile-de-France, Languedoc-Roussillon, Limousin, Lorraine, Midi-Pyrenees, Nord-Pas-de-Calais, Pays de la Loire, Picardie, Poitou-Charentes, Provence-Alpes-Cote d'Azur, Rhone-Alpes (22 regions)

External Territories: French Guiana, French Polynesia, French Southern and Antarctic Territories, Guadeloupe, Martinique, Mayotte, New Caledonia, Reunion, Saint-Pierre and Miquelon, Wallis and Futuna (10)

Ethnic/Racial Groups: French, with Slavic, North African, Indochinese, and Basque minorities

Religion: Christianity (primarily Roman Catholic)

Language: French

Currency: euro

Current President: Jacques Chirac

Cities (capital, largest, or with at least a million people):

Paris: • located in northern France • city in the Ile-de-France region • capital of France • most populated city in France (9,854,000 people) • chief port on the Seine River

Lyon • located in eastern France city in the Rhone-Alpes region • located at the junction of the Rhone and Saone Rivers

Marseille: •located in southeastern France •city in the Provence-Alpes-Cote d'Azur region •chief port on the Gulf of Lion

ENVIRONMENTAL/ECONOMIC:

Climate: Cool winters/mild summers with mild winters/hot summers along the Mediterranean; occasional mistral winds

Natural Resources: coal, iron ore, bauxite, zinc, uranium

Agricultural Products: wheat, cereals, sugar beets, potatoes, beef

Major Exports: machinery and transportation equipment, aircraft, plastics, chemicals, pharmaceuticals

Natural Hazards: floods, avalanches, windstorms, droughts, forest fires

GABON

Country Name: Gabonese Republic
Continent: Africa
Area: 103,347 sq mi / 267,667 sq km
Population: 1,327,000
Population Density: 13 people per sq mi / 5.0 people per sq km
Capital: Libreville

PHYSICAL:

Highest Point: Mount Iboundji 3,189 ft / 972 m
Lowest Point: Atlantic Ocean 0 ft / 0 m (sea level)
Mountain Ranges:
   Monts de Cristal: •cover much of Gabon •extend into Equatorial Guinea and
      Republic of the Congo
Oceans:
   Atlantic: •forms part of the western coast of Gabon
Gulfs:
   Gulf of Guinea: •forms part of the western coast of Gabon •feeds into the Atlantic Ocean

POLITICAL:
Independence: August 17, 1960 (from France)
Bordering Countries: Republic of the Congo, Equatorial Guinea, Cameroon (3)
Administrative Divisions: Estuaire, Haut-Ogooue, Moyen-Ogooue, Ngounie, Nyanga, Ogooue-Ivindo, Ogooue-Lolo, Ogooue-Maritime, Woleu-Ntem (9 provinces)
Ethnic/Racial Groups: Fang, Bapounou, Nzebi, Obama, European
Religions: Christianity, indigenous beliefs
Languages: French, Fang, Myene, Nzebi, Bapounou/Eschira, Bandjabi
Currency: Communaute Financiere Africaine franc
Current President: Omar Bongo
Cities (capital, largest, or with at least a million people):
Libreville: • located in northwestern Gabon • city in the Estuaire province • capital of Gabon • most populated city in Gabon (611,000 people) • chief port on the Gulf of Guinea

ENVIRONMENTAL/ECONOMIC:
Climate: tropical, hot and humid
Natural Resources: petroleum, manganese, uranium, gold, timber
Agricultural Products: cacao, coffee, sugar, palm oil, cattle
Major Exports: crude oil, timber, manganese, uranium
Natural Hazards: floods, thunderstorms

GAMBIA
Country Name: Republic of the Gambia
Continent: Africa
Area: 4,361 sq mi / 11,295 sq km
Population: 1,501,000
Population Density: 344 people per sq mi / 133 people per sq km
Capital: Banjul

PHYSICAL:
Highest Point: unnamed location 174 ft / 53 m
Lowest Point: Atlantic Ocean 0 ft / 0 m (sea level)
Oceans:
Atlantic: • forms the western coast of the Gambia
Rivers:
Gambia: • has its mouth in the Atlantic Ocean • extends into Senegal

POLITICAL:
Independence: February 18, 1965 (from the United Kingdom)
Bordering Country: Senegal (1)

GAMBIA

Administrative Divisions: Central River, Lower River, North Bank, Upper River, Western (5 divisions) •Banjul (1 city)
Ethnic/Racial Groups: Mandinka, Fula, Wolof, Jola, Serahuli
Religions: Islam, Christianity
Languages: English, Mandinka, Wolof, Fula
Currency: dalasi
Current President: Yahya A.J.J. Jammeh
Cities (capital, largest, or with at least a million people):
  Banjul: •located in western Gambia •city in the Banjul city division •capital of Gambia •most populated city in Gambia (372,000 people) •chief port on the Gambia River and the Gulf of Guinea

ENVIRONMENTAL/ECONOMIC:
Climate: tropical with rainy/dry seasons
Natural Resources: fish
Agricultural Products: rice, millet, sorghum, peanuts, cattle
Major Exports: peanut products, fish, palm kernels, re-exports
Natural Hazards: droughts

GEORGIA
Country Name: Republic of Georgia
Continent: Asia

Area: 26,911 sq mi / 69,700 sq km
Population: 4,660,000
Population Density: 173 people per sq mi / 67 people per sq km
Capital: Tbilisi

PHYSICAL:
Highest Point: Mta Shkhara 17,064 ft / 5,201 m
Lowest Point: Black Sea 0 ft / 0 m (sea level)
Mountain Ranges:
Caucasus: •cover much of northern Georgia •extend into Russia and Azerbaijan
Lesser Caucasus: •cover much of southern Georgia •extend into Turkey, Armenia, and Azerbaijan
Peaks (minimum elevation 8,000 ft / 2,400 m):
Mta Shkhara: •located in the Caucasus •on the Georgia-Russia border •highest point in Georgia
Seas:
Black: •forms the western coast of Georgia •feeds into the Mediterranean Sea

POLITICAL:
Independence: April 9, 1991 (from Soviet Union)
Former Name: Georgian Soviet Socialist Republic
Bordering Countries: Russia, Azerbaijan, Turkey, Armenia (4)
Administrative Divisions: Guria, Imereti, Kakheti, Kvemo Kartli, Mtskheta-Mtianeti, Racha-Lechkhumi and Kvemo Svaneti, Samegrelo and Zemo Svaneti,

Samtskhe-Javakheti, Shida Kartli (9 regions) ●Chiatura, Gori, Kutaisi, Poti, Rustavi, Tbilisi, Tqibuli, Tsqaltubo, Zugdidi (9 cities) ●Abkhazia, Ajaria (2 autonomous republics)
Ethnic/Racial Groups: Georgian, Armenian, Russian, Azeri
Religions: Christianity (Georgian Orthodox, Russian Orthodox), Islam
Languages: Georgian, Russian, Armenian, Azeri
Currency: lari
Current President: Mikheil Saakashvili
Cities (capital, largest, or with at least a million people):
Tbilisi: ●located in southeastern Georgia ●city in the Tbilisi city division ●capital of Georgia ●most populated city in Georgia (1,064,000 people) ●between the Caucasus and Lesser Caucasus

ENVIRONMENTAL/ECONOMIC:
Climate: mild; Mediterranean-like along the Black Sea coast
Natural Resources: forests, hydropower, manganese deposits, iron ore, copper
Agricultural Products: citrus, grapes, tea, hazelnuts, livestock
Major Exports: scrap metal, machinery, chemicals, fuel re-exports, citrus fruits, tea
Natural Hazards: earthquakes

GERMANY
Country Name: Federal Republic of Germany
Continent: Europe
Area: 137,847 sq mi / 357,022 sq km
Population: 82,621,000 (largest of any country entirely in Europe)
Population Density: 599 people per sq mi / 231 people per sq km
Capital: Berlin

PHYSICAL:
Highest Point: Zugspitze 9,721 ft / 2,963 m
Lowest Point: Neuendorf bei Wilster 12 ft / 3.54 m below sea level
Mountain Ranges:
Alps: ●located in southern Germany ●extend into Austria and Switzerland
Erzgebirge: ●located in eastern Germany ●extend into the Czech Republic
Harz: ●located in central Germany
Schwabische Alb: ●located in southern Germany
Schwarzwald: ●located in southwestern Germany
Thuringer Wald: ●located in central Germany
Peaks (minimum elevation 8,000 ft / 2,400 m):
Zugspitze: ●located in the Alps ●on the Germany-Austria border
Seas:
Baltic: ●forms part of the northeastern coast of Germany ●feeds into the Kattegat
North: ●forms part of the northwestern coast of Germany ●feeds into the Atlantic Ocean

Bays:

Helgolander: • forms part of the northwestern coast of Germany • feeds into the North Sea

Kiel: • forms part of the northern coast of Germany • feeds into Mecklenburger Bay

Mecklenburger: • forms part of the northern coast of Germany • feeds into the Baltic Sea

Pomeranian : • forms part of the northeastern coast of Germany • feeds into the Baltic Sea

Lakes:

Lake Constance: • located in southern Germany • on the border with Switzerland and Austria • fed by the Rhine River

Rivers:

Danube: • has its source in the Schwabische Alb • forms part of the Germany-Austria border • extends into Austria

Elbe: • has its mouth in Helgolander Bay • extends into the Czech Republic

Main: • tributary of the Rhine River • has its source in southern Germany

Mosel: • tributary of the Rhine River • forms part of the Germany-Luxembourg border • extends into France

Oder: • forms part of the Germany-Poland border • extends into Poland

Rhine: • forms part of Germany's border with France and Switzerland • extends into the Netherlands and Switzerland

Ruhr: • tributary of the Rhine River • has its source in western Germany

Weser: • has its mouth in Helgolander Bay • has its source in central Germany

Lagoons:
    Stettiner Haff: ●feeds into the Baltic Sea ●extends into Poland
Islands:
    East Frisian: ●island group off the northwestern coast of Germany ●bordered by the
        North Sea and Helgolander Bay
    North Frisian: ●island group off the northwestern coast of Germany ●bordered by
        the North Sea and Helgolander Bay ●northern islands in this group belong to
        Denmark
    Rugen: ●island off the northeastern coast of Germany ●bordered by the Baltic Sea
Regions:
    Eifel: ●mountainous region in western Germany
    Black Forest: ●mountainous region in southwestern Germany

POLITICAL:
Independence: January 18, 1871 (German Empire unification)
Former Names: German Empire, German Republic, German Reich
Bordering Countries: Austria, Czech Republic, Netherlands, Poland, France,
    Switzerland, Belgium, Luxembourg, Denmark (9)
Regions:
    Franconia: ●region in southern Germany ●north of the Schwabische Alb
    Friesland: ●region in northwestern Germany ●south of the North Sea and
        Helgolander Bay: ●extends into the Netherlands
    Pomerania: ●region in northeastern Germany ●south of the Baltic Sea and
        Pomeranian Bay: ●extends into Poland
Administrative Divisions: Baden-Wurttemberg, Bavaria, Berlin, Brandenburg,
    Bremen, Hamburg, Hessen, Lower Saxony, Mecklenburg-West Pomerania, North
    Rhine-Westphalia, Rhineland-Palatinate, Saarland, Saxony, Saxony-Anhalt,
    Schleswig-Holstein, Thuringia (16 states)
Ethnic/Racial Groups: German, Turkish
Religion: Christianity (Protestant, Roman Catholic)
Language: German
Currency: euro
Current President: Johannes Rau
Cities (capital, largest, or with at least a million people):
    Berlin: ●located in northeastern Germany ●city in the Berlin state ●capital of
        Germany ●most populated city in Germany (3,327,000 people)
    Hamburg: ●located in northern Germany ●city in the Hamburg state ●chief port on
        the Elbe River
    Munich: ●located in southern Germany ●city in the Bavaria state
    Cologne: ●located in western Germany ●city in the North Rhine-Westphalia state
        ●chief port on the Rhine River

ENVIRONMENTAL/ECONOMIC:
Climate: temperate and marine; cool and wet; occasional foehn winds

Natural Resources: coal, lignite, natural gas, iron ore, copper
Agricultural Products: potatoes, wheat, barley, sugar beets, cattle
Major Exports: machinery, vehicles, chemicals, metals and manufactures, foodstuffs
Natural Hazards: floods

GHANA

Country Name: Republic of Ghana
Continent: Africa
Area: 92,100 sq mi / 238,537 sq km
Population: 20,468,000
Population Density: 222 people per sq mi / 86 people per sq km
Capital: Accra

PHYSICAL:

Highest Point: Mount Afadjato 2,887 ft / 880 m
Lowest Point: Gulf of Guinea 0 ft / 0 m (sea level)
Gulfs:
Gulf of Guinea: •forms part of the southwestern coast of Ghana •feeds into the Atlantic Ocean
Bays:
Bight of Benin: •forms most of the southern coast •feeds into the Gulf of Guinea
Lakes:
Lake Volta: •covers parts of central and eastern Ghana •fed by the White Volta and Black Volta Rivers •dammed by the Akosombo Dam
Rivers:
Black Volta: •tributary of the Volta River •forms part of Ghana's border with Cote d'Ivoire and Burkina Faso •extends into Burkina Faso
Red Volta: •tributary of the White Volta River •extends into Burkina Faso
Volta: •has its mouth in the Bight of Benin
White Volta: •tributary of the Volta River •extends into Burkina Faso
Dams:
Akosombo: •located in southeastern Ghana •on the Volta River •forms Lake Volta

POLITICAL:

Independence: March 6, 1957 (from the United Kingdom)
Former Name: Gold Coast
Bordering Countries: Togo, Cote d'Ivoire, Burkina Faso (3)
Administrative Divisions: Ashanti, Brong-Ahafo, Central, Eastern, Greater Accra, Northern, Upper East, Upper West, Volta, Western (10 regions)
Ethnic/Racial Groups: Akan, Moshi-Dagomba, Ewe, Ga, Gurma, Yoruba
Religions: Christian, indigenous beliefs, Islam
Languages: English, Akan, Moshi-Dagomba, Ewe, Ga
Currency: cedi

GHANA

Current President: John Agyekum Kufuor

Cities (capital, largest, or with at least a million people):
Accra: •located in southern Ghana •city in the Greater Accra region •capital of Ghana •most populated city in Ghana (1,847,000 people) •chief port on the Bight of Benin

ENVIRONMENTAL/ECONOMIC:

Climate: tropical; warm and dry along the southeastern coast; hot and humid in the southwest; hot and dry in the north

Natural Resources: gold, timber, industrial diamonds, bauxite, manganese

Agricultural Products: cacao, rice, coffee, cassava (tapioca), timber

Major Exports: gold, cacao, timber, tuna, bauxite

Natural Hazards: harmattan winds, droughts

GREECE

Name: Hellenic Republic
Continent: Europe
Area: 50,949 sq mi / 131,957 sq km
Population: 10,988,000
Population Density: 216 people per sq mi / 83 people per sq km
Capital: Athens

GREECE

0   70 mi
0   70 km

ITALY

ALBANIA

MACEDONIA

BULGARIA

Orestiáda

Black Sea

Bosporus

Kilkís•

Kaválа• •Xánthi

Nestos R.

Véria• Alexandroúpoli

Kozáni, **Thessaloníki**

Aliákmona R.

40° N

Sea of Marmara

Límnos

Kérkira •Kérkira Lárissa

(Corfu) Ioánina• •Vólos *Aegean Sea*

Árta• *Pinjós R.*

Acheloos

Mitilíni•

Lamía• •Istiéa *Lesvós (Lesbos)*

Ionian Agrínio• •Skíros

Náfpaktos Halkída

Pátra• (Chalkís) Híos•

Corinth• Marathónas

Sea Zákinthos• Salamína★**Athína (Athens)**

Tripoli Piréas •Ándros

Megalópoli• (Piraeus)

Gargaliánol• (Sparta) Páros• •Náxos

Kalamáta Kos•

Areópoli• Mílos•

•Neápoli *Kikládes* Ródos (Rhodes)

Kíthira Ródos (Rhodes)

Kárpathos

Mediterranean Sea *Sea of Crete* Kárpathos

Haniá• •Iráklio •Sitía

Kríti (Crete)

TURKEY

38° N

36° N

18° E   20° E   22° E   24° E   26° E   28° E

PHYSICAL:
Highest Point: Mount Olympus 9,570 ft / 2,917 m
Lowest Point: Mediterranean Sea 0 ft / 0 m (sea level)
Mountain Ranges:
    Pindus: •cover much of western Greece •extend into Albania
    Pirin: •located in northern Greece •extend into Bulgaria
    Rhodope: •located in northeastern Greece •extend into Bulgaria
Peaks (minimum elevation 8,000 ft / 2,400 m):
    Mount Olympus: •located in northern Greece •highest point in Greece
Seas:
    Aegean: •forms much of the eastern coast of Greece •feeds into the Sea of Crete
    Ionian: •forms much of the western coast of Greece •feeds into the Mediterranean Sea
    Mediterranean: •forms part of the western and southern coasts of Greece •feeds
        into the Atlantic Ocean
    Sea of Crete: •forms much of the southern coast of Greece •feeds into the
        Mediterranean Sea
Gulfs:
    Gulf of Corinth: •forms part of the western coast of Greece •feeds into the Gulf
        of Patrai
    Gulf of Euboea: •forms part of the central coast of Greece •feeds into the Aegean Sea
    Gulf of Patrai: •forms part of the western coast of Greece •feeds into the Ionian Sea
    Saronic: •forms part of the central coast of Greece •feeds into the Sea of Crete
    Thermaic: •forms part of the northern coast of Greece •feeds into the Aegean Sea

Lakes:

    Lake Prespa: ●located in northwestern Greece ●on the border with Albania and Macedonia ●on the edge of the Pindus Mountains

Rivers:

    Evros: ●has its mouth in the Aegean Sea ●forms the Greece-Turkey border

Peninsulas:

    Peloponnesus: ●bordered by the Gulf of Corinth, Gulf of Patrai, Mediterranean Sea, Sea of Crete, and Saronic Gulf

Islands:

    Cephalonia: ●island off the western coast of Greece ●bordered by the Ionian and Mediterranean Seas

    Chios: ●island off the coast of Turkey ●surrounded by the Aegean Sea

    Corfu: ●island off the northwestern coast of Greece ●surrounded by the Ionian Sea

    Crete: ●island between the Mediterranean Sea and the Sea of Crete

    Kiklades (Cyclades): ●island group bordered by the Aegean Sea and the Sea of Crete

    Euboea: ●island off the coast of central Greece ●bordered by the Aegean Sea and the Gulf of Euboea

    Lesvos: ●island off the coast of Turkey ●surrounded by the Aegean Sea

    Limnos: ●island off the coast of Turkey ●surrounded by the Aegean Sea

    Rhodes: ●island off the coast of Turkey ●bordered by the Sea of Crete and the Mediterranean Sea

    Samos: ●island off the coast of Turkey ●bordered by the Aegean Sea

    Thassos: ●island off the northeastern coast of Greece ●surrounded by the Aegean Sea

POLITICAL:

Independence: 1829 (from the Ottoman Empire)

Former Name: Kingdom of Greece

Bordering Countries: Bulgaria, Albania, Macedonia, Turkey (4)

Regions:

    Macedonia: ●region in northern Greece ●extends into Macedonia and Bulgaria ●east of the Pindus Mountains ●south of the Pirin Mountains ●north of the Thermaic Gulf and the Aegean Sea

    Thessaly: ●region in central Greece ●east of the Pindus Mountains ●west of the Thermaic Gulf and the Aegean Sea

    Thrace: ●region in northeastern Greece ●extends into Bulgaria and Turkey ●south of the Rhodope Mountains ●north of the Aegean Sea

Administrative Divisions: Achaia, Aitolia kai Akarmania, Argolis, Arkadia, Arta, Attiki, Chalkidiki, Chanion, Chios, Dodekanisos, Drama, Evros, Evrytania, Evvoia, Florina, Fokidos, Fthiotis, Grevena, Ileia, Imathia, Ioannina, Irakleion, Karditsa, Kastoria, Kavala, Kefallinia, Kerkyra, Kilkis, Korinthia, Kozani, Kyklades, Lakonia, Larisa, Lasithi, Lefkas, Lesvos, Magnisia, Messinia, Pella, Pieria, Preveza, Rethynnis, Rodopi, Samos, Serrai, Thesprotia, Thessaloniki, Trikala, Voiotia, Xanthi, Zakynthos (51 prefectures) ●Agion Oros (1 autonomous region)

Ethnic/Racial Groups: predominantly Greek
Religion: Christianity (predominantly Greek Orthodox)
Language: predominantly Greek
Currency: euro
Current President: Constantinos Stephanopoulos
Cities (capital, largest, or with at least a million people):
>   Athens: •located in central Greece •city in the Attiki prefecture •capital of Greece •most populated city in Greece (3,238,000 people) •chief port on the Saronic Gulf

ENVIRONMENTAL/ECONOMIC:
Climate: temperate, mild and wet winters/hot and dry summers
Natural Resources: lignite, petroleum, iron ore, bauxite, lead
Agricultural Products: wheat, corn, barley, sugar beets, beef
Major Exports: food and beverages, manufactured goods, petroleum products, chemicals
Natural Hazards: earthquakes

GRENADA
Country Name: Grenada
Continent: North America
Area: 133 sq mi / 344 sq km
Population: 105,000
Population Density: 789 people per sq mi / 305 people per sq km
Capital: Saint George's

PHYSICAL:
Highest Point: Mount Saint Catherine 2,756 ft / 840 m
Lowest Point: Caribbean Sea 0 ft / 0 m (sea level)
Oceans:
>   Atlantic: •forms the eastern coast of Grenada

Seas:
>   Caribbean: •forms the western coast of Grenada •feeds into the Atlantic Ocean

Islands:
>   Grenada: •largest island in Grenada •bordered by the Atlantic Ocean and the Caribbean Sea

POLITICAL:
Independence: February 7, 1974 (from the United Kingdom)
Administrative Divisions: Saint Andrew, Saint David, Saint George, Saint John, Saint Mark, Saint Patrick (6 parishes) •Carriacou and Petit Martinique (1 dependency)
Ethnic/Racial Groups: black, Creole
Religion: Christianity (mainly Roman Catholic, Anglican, other Protestant)

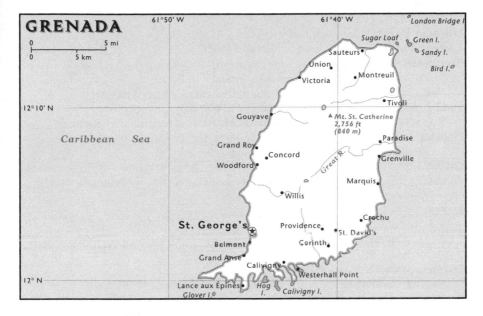

GRENADA

61°50' W   61°40' W   °London Bridge I

0   5 mi
0   5 km

Sugar Loaf   Green I.
Sauteurs•   ◊ Sandy I.
Union•   Bird I.°
•Victoria   •Montreuil

12°10' N   •Tivoli

Gouyave•   ▲ Mt. St. Catherine
          2,756 ft
          (840 m)

Caribbean   Sea   •Paradise

Grand Roy•   Great R.
    •Concord   •Grenville
Woodford•

       Marquis•

   •Willis

            •Crochu
St. George's⊛   Providence•   •St. David's
Belmont•   Corinth•
Grand Anse•
   Calivigny•
      •Westerhall Point
12° N   Lance aux Épines•   Hog
      Glover I.°   I.   Calivigny I.

Languages: English, French patois
Currency: East Caribbean dollar
Major Exports: bananas, cacao, nutmeg, fruits and vegetables
Current Prime Minister: Keith Mitchell
Cities (capital, largest, or with at least a million people):
    Saint George's: •located on the island of Grenada •city in the Saint George parish
      •capital of Grenada •most populated city in Grenada (33,000 people) •chief
      port on the Caribbean Sea

ENVIRONMENTAL/ECONOMIC:
Climate: tropical, moderated by trade winds
Natural Resources: timber, tropical fruit, deepwater harbors
Agricultural Products: bananas, cacao, nutmeg, mace
Natural Hazards: hurricanes

GUATEMALA
Country Name: Republic of Guatemala
Continent: North America
Area: 42,042 sq mi / 108,889 sq km
Population: 12,360,000
Population Density: 294 people per sq mi / 114 people per sq km
Capital: Guatemala City

PHYSICAL:

Highest Point: Volcan Tajumulco 13,845 ft / 4,220 m
Lowest Point: Pacific Ocean 0 ft / 0 m (sea level)
Mountain Ranges:
  Maya: ●located in eastern Guatemala ●extend into Belize
  Sierra Madre: ●covers much of southern Guatemala ●extends into Mexico
Peaks (minimum elevation 8,000 ft / 2,400 m):
  Volcan Tajumulco: ●located in the Sierra Madre ●highest point in Guatemala
Oceans:
  Pacific: ●forms the southern coast of Guatemala
Gulfs:
  Gulf of Honduras: ●forms the eastern coast of Guatemala ●feeds into the
    Caribbean Sea
Lakes:
  Lake Izabal: ●located in eastern Guatemala

POLITICAL:

Independence: September 15, 1821 (from Spain)
Bordering Countries: Mexico, Belize, Honduras, El Salvador (4)
Administrative Divisions: Alta Verapaz, Baja Verapaz, Chimaltenango,
  Chiquimula, El Progreso, Escuintla, Guatemala, Huehuetenango, Izabal, Jalapa,
  Jutiapa, Peten, Quetzaltenango, Quiche, Retalhuleu, Sacatepequez, San Marcos,
  Santa Rosa, Solola, Suchitepequez, Totonicapan, Zacapa (22 departments)
Ethnic/Racial Groups: mestizo, Amerindian

Religions: Christianity (Roman Catholic, Protestant), indigenous Mayan beliefs
Languages: Spanish, Amerindian languages
Currency: quetzal, U.S. dollar, others allowed
Current President: Oscar Berger Perdomo
Cities (capital, largest, or with at least a million people):
 Guatemala City: •located in southern Guatemala •city in the Guatemala department •capital of Guatemala •most populated city in Guatemala (951,000 people) •located in a valley in the Sierra Madre

ENVIRONMENTAL/ECONOMIC:
Climate: tropical; hot and humid in the lowlands, cooler in the highlands
Natural Resources: petroleum, nickel, rare woods, fish, chicle
Agricultural Products: sugarcane, corn, bananas, coffee, cattle
Major Exports: coffee, sugar, bananas, fruits and vegetables, cardamom
Natural Hazards: volcanoes, earthquakes, hurricanes

GUINEA
Country Name: Republic of Guinea
Continent: Africa
Area: 94,926 sq mi / 245,857 sq km
Population: 9,030,000
Population Density: 95 people per sq mi / 37 people per sq km
Capital: Conakry

PHYSICAL:
Highest Point: Mont Nimba 5,748 ft / 1,752 m
Lowest Point: Atlantic Ocean 0 ft / 0 m (sea level)
Grasslands/Prairies:
 Sahel: •covers much of northern Guinea •extends into Guinea-Bissau, Senegal, Mali, and Cote d'Ivoire
Oceans:
 Atlantic: •forms the western coast of Guinea
Rivers:
 Bafing: •has its source in central Guinea •forms part of the Guinea-Mali border •extends into Mali
 Gambie (Gambia): •has its source in northern Guinea •extends into Senegal
 Niger: •has its source in southern Guinea •extends into Mali
Regions:
 Fouta Djallon: •highland region that covers parts of northern and central Guinea •south of the Sahel

POLITICAL:
Independence: October 2, 1958 (from France)

Former Name: French Guinea

Bordering Countries: Mali, Sierra Leone, Cote d'Ivoire, Liberia, Guinea-Bissau, Senegal (6)

Administrative Divisions: Beyla, Boffa, Boke, Coyah, Dabola, Dalaba, Dinguiraye, Dubreka, Faranah, Forecariah, Fria, Gaoual, Gueckedou, Kankan, Kerouane, Kindia, Kissidougou, Koubia, Koundara, Kouroussa, Labe, Lelouma, Lola, Macenta, Mali, Mamou, Mandiana, Nzerekore, Pita, Siguiri, Telimele, Tougue, Yomou (33 prefectures) ●Conakry (1 special zone)

Ethnic/Racial Groups: Peuhl, Malinke, Soussou

Religions: Islam, Christianity, indigenous beliefs

Languages: French, local languages

Currency: Guinean franc

Current President: Lansana Conte

Cities (capital, largest, or with at least a million people):
Conakry: ●located in western Guinea ●city in the Conakry special zone ●capital of Guinea ●most populated city in Guinea (1,366,000 people) ●chief port on the Atlantic Ocean

ENVIRONMENTAL/ECONOMIC:

Climate: hot and humid with rainy/dry seasons; harmattan winds

Natural Resources: bauxite, iron ore, diamonds, gold, uranium

Agricultural Products: rice, coffee, pineapples, palm kernels

Major Exports: bauxite, alumina, gold, diamonds, coffee

Natural Disasters: harmattan haze

GUINEA-BISSAU

Country Name: Republic of Guinea-Bissau
Continent: Africa
Area: 13,948 sq mi / 36,125 sq km
Population: 1,288,000
Population Density: 92 people per sq mi / 36 people per sq km
Capital: Bissau

PHYSICAL:
Highest Point: unnamed location 984 ft / 300 m
Lowest Point: Atlantic Ocean 0 ft / 0 m (sea level)
Grasslands/Prairies:
    Sahel: •covers most of the country •extends into Senegal and Guinea
Oceans:
    Atlantic: •forms the western coast of Guinea-Bissau

POLITICAL:
Independence: September 24, 1973 (from Portugal)
Former Name: Portuguese Guinea
Bordering Countries: Senegal, Guinea (2)
Administrative Divisions: Bafata, Biombo, Bissau, Bolama, Cacheu, Gabu, Oio,
    Quinara, Tombali (9 regions)
Ethnic/Racial Groups: Balanta, Fula, Manjaca, Mandinga, Papel

Religions: indigenous beliefs, Islam, Christianity
Languages: Portuguese, Crioulo, African languages
Currency: Communaute Financiere Africaine franc
Current President: Henrique Rosa
Cities (capital, largest, or with at least a million people):
>   Bissau: •located in western Guinea-Bissau •city in the Bissau region •capital of
>   Guinea-Bissau •most populated city in Guinea-Bissau (336,000 people) •chief port
>   on the Atlantic Ocean

ENVIRONMENTAL/ECONOMIC:
Climate: tropical, hot and humid, rainy/dry seasons, harmattan winds
Natural Resources: fish, timber, phosphates, bauxite, petroleum
Agricultural Products: rice, corn, beans, cassava (tapioca), timber
Major Exports: cashew nuts, shrimp, peanuts, palm kernels, sawn lumber
Natural Hazards: harmattan haze, brush fires

GUYANA
Country Name: Co-operative Republic of Guyana
Continent: South America
Area: 83,000 sq mi / 214,969 sq km
Population: 765,000
Population Density: 9.2 people per sq mi / 3.6 people per sq km
Capital: Georgetown

PHYSICAL:
Highest Point: Mount Roraima 9,094 ft / 2,772 m
Lowest Point: Atlantic Ocean 0 ft / 0 m (sea level)
Mountain Ranges:
>   Guiana Highlands: •cover much of central and southern Guyana •extend into
>   Venezuela, Brazil, and Suriname
Peaks (minimum elevation 8,000 ft / 2,400 m):
>   Mount Roraima: •located in the Guiana Highlands •on the border with Venezuela
>   and Brazil •highest point in Guyana
Oceans:
>   Atlantic: •forms the northern coast of Guyana
Rivers:
>   Essequibo: •has its mouth in the Atlantic Ocean •has its source in the Guiana
>   Highlands

POLITICAL:
Independence: May 26, 1966 (from the United Kingdom)
Former Name: British Guiana
Bordering Countries: Brazil, Venezuela, Suriname (3)

Administrative Divisions: Barima-Waini, Cuyuni-Mazaruni, Demerara-Mahaica, East Berbice-Corentyne, Essequibo Islands-West Demerara, Mahaica-Berbice, Pomeroon-Supenaam, Potaro-Siparuni, Upper Demerara-Berbice, Upper Takutu-Upper Essequibo (10 regions)

Ethnic/Racial Groups: East Indian, black, Amerindian

Religions: Christianity, Hinduism, Islam

Languages: English, Amerindian dialects, Creole, Hindi, Urdu

Currency: Guyanese dollar

Current President: Bharrat Jagdeo

Cities (capital, largest, or with at least a million people):
   Georgetown: ●located in northeastern Guyana ●city in the Demerara-Mahaica region ●capital of Guyana ●most populated city in Guyana (231,000 people) ●chief port on the Atlantic Ocean

ENVIRONMENTAL/ECONOMIC:

Climate: tropical; hot and humid with two rainy seasons; moderated by trade winds

Natural Resources: bauxite, gold, diamonds, hardwood timber, shrimp

Agricultural Products: sugar, rice, wheat, vegetable oils, beef

Major Exports: sugar, gold, bauxite/alumina, rice, shrimp

Natural Hazards: flash floods

HAITI

Country Name: Republic of Haiti
Continent: North America
Area: 10,714 sq mi / 27,750 sq km
Population: 7,528,000
Population Density: 703 people per sq mi / 271 people per sq km
Capital: Port-au-Prince

PHYSICAL:

Highest Point: Chaine de la Selle 8,773 ft / 2,674 m
Lowest Point: Caribbean Sea 0 ft / 0 m (sea level)
Peaks (minimum elevation of 8,000 ft / 2,400 m):
   Chaine de la Selle: •located in southeastern Haiti •highest point in Haiti
Oceans:
   Atlantic: •forms much of the northern coast of Haiti
Seas:
   Caribbean: •forms the southern coast of Haiti •feeds into the Atlantic Ocean

Gulfs:
Golfe de la Gonave: •forms the west coast of Haiti
Passages:
Windward: •forms part of the northwestern coast of Haiti •separates Haiti from Cuba •connects the Atlantic Ocean and the Caribbean Sea
Islands:
Hispaniola: •Haiti takes up the western portion of this island •bordered by the Atlantic Ocean, Caribbean Sea, Golfe de la Gonave, and Windward Passage •the Dominican Republic takes up the eastern portion of the island
Ile de la Gonave: •island off the west coast of Hispaniola •surrounded by the Golfe de la Gonave

POLITICAL:
Independence: January 1, 1804 (from France)
Bordering Country: Dominican Republic (1)
Administrative Divisions: Artibonite, Centre, Grand Anse, Nord, Nord-Est, Nord-Ouest, Ouest, Sud, Sud-Est (9 departments)
Ethnic/Racial Groups: black, Creole and other
Religions: Christianity (Roman Catholic, Protestant), voodoo traditions
Languages: French, Creole
Currency: gourde
Current President: Jean-Bertrand Aristide
Cities (capital, largest, or with at least a million people):
Port-au-Prince: •located on the island of Hispaniola •city in the Ouest department •capital of Haiti •most populated city in Haiti (1,961,000 people) •chief port on the Golfe de la Gonave

ENVIRONMENTAL/ECONOMIC:
Climate: tropical; semi-arid in the eastern mountains
Natural Resources: bauxite, copper, calcium carbonate, gold, marble
Agricultural Products: coffee, mangoes, sugarcane, rice, wood
Major Exports: manufactures, coffee, oils, cocoa
Natural Hazards: hurricanes, floods, earthquakes, droughts

HONDURAS
Country Name: Republic of Honduras
Continent: North America
Area: 43,433 sq mi / 112,492 sq km
Population: 6,876,000
Population Density: 158 people per sq mi / 61 people per sq km
Capital: Tegucigalpa

PHYSICAL:
Highest Point: Las Minas, 9,347 ft / 2,849 m
Lowest Point: Caribbean Sea 0 ft / 0 m (sea level)
Peaks (minimum elevation of 8,000 ft / 2,400 m):
    Las Minas: ●located in western Honduras ●highest point in Honduras
Seas:
    Caribbean: ●forms most of the northern coast of Honduras ●feeds into the
       Atlantic Ocean
Gulfs:
    Golfo de Fonseca: ●forms the southern coast of Honduras ●feeds into the
       Pacific Ocean
    Gulf of Honduras: ●forms part of the northwestern coast of Honduras ●feeds into
       the Caribbean Sea
Islands:
    Islas de la Bahia: ●island group off the northern coast of Honduras ●surrounded by
       the Caribbean Sea

POLITICAL:
Independence: September 15, 1821 (from Spain)
Bordering Countries: Nicaragua, El Salvador, Guatemala (3)
Administrative Divisions: Atlantida, Choluteca, Colon, Comayagua, Copan,
    Cortes, El Paraiso, Francisco Morazan, Gracias a Dios, Intibuca, Islas de la Bahia,
    La Paz, Lempira, Ocotepeque, Olancho, Santa Barbara, Valle, Yoro (18 departments)
Ethnic/Racial Groups: mestizo, Amerindian, black, white

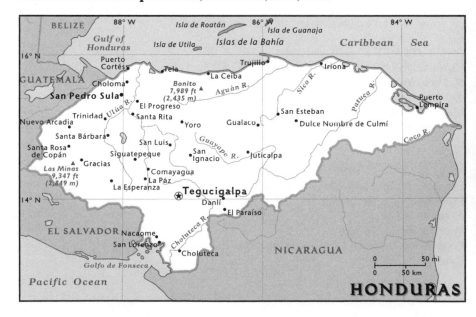

Religion: Christianity (predominantly Roman Catholic)
Languages: Spanish, Amerindian dialects
Currency: lempira
Current President: Ricardo Maduro
Cities (capital, largest, or with at least a million people):
Tegucigalpa: ●located in central Honduras ●city in the Francisco Morazan department ●capital of Honduras ● most populated city in Honduras (1,007,000 people)

ENVIRONMENTAL/ECONOMIC:
Climate: subtropical in the lowlands; temperate in the mountains
Natural Resources: timber, gold, silver, copper, lead
Agricultural Products: bananas, coffee, citrus, beef, timber
Major Exports: coffee, bananas, shrimp, lobster, meat
Natural Hazards: earthquakes, hurricanes, floods

HUNGARY
Country Name: Republic of Hungary
Continent: Europe
Area: 35,919 sq mi / 93,030 sq km
Population: 10,141,000
Population Density: 282 people per sq mi / 109 people per sq km
Capital: Budapest

PHYSICAL:
Highest Point: Kekes, 3,330 ft / 1,015 m
Lowest Point: Tisza River 256 ft / 78 m
Grasslands/Prairies:
Great Alfold: ●covers an area from southern to northeastern Hungary ●extends into
Croatia, Serbia and Montenegro, Romania, Slovakia, and Ukraine
Lakes:
Balaton: ●located in western Hungary
Rivers:
Danube: ●forms part of the Hungary-Slovakia border ●extends into Austria, Serbia
and Montenegro, and Romania
Drava: ●forms part of the Hungary-Croatia border ●extends into Croatia and Slovenia
Tisza: ●extends into Ukraine and into Serbia and Montenegro

POLITICAL:
Independence: 1001
Bordering Countries: Slovakia, Romania, Austria, Croatia, Serbia and Montenegro,
Ukraine, Slovenia (7)
Administrative Divisions: Bacs-Kiskun, Baranya, Bekes, Borsod-Abauj-Zemplen,
Csongrad, Fejer, Gyor-Moson-Sopron, Hajdu-Bihar, Heves, Jasz-Nagykun-Szolnok,
Komarom-Esztergom, Nograd, Pest, Somogy, Szabolcs-Szatmar-Bereg, Tolna, Vas,
Veszprem, Zala (19 counties) ●Bekescsaba, Debrecen, Dunaujvaros, Eger, Gyor,
Hodmezovasarhely, Kaposvar, Kecskemet, Miskolc, Nagykanizsa, Nyiregyhaza, Pecs,
Sopron, Szeged, Szekesfehervar, Szolnok, Szombathely, Tatabanya, Veszprem,
Zalaegerszeg (20 urban counties) ●Budapest (1 capital city division)
Ethnic/Racial Groups: Hungarian, Roma, German, Serb
Religion: Christianity (Roman Catholic, Calvinist, Lutheran)
Language: Hungarian
Currency: forint
Current President: Ferenc Madl
Cities (capital, largest, or with at least a million people):
Budapest: ●located in northern Hungary ●city in the Budapest capital city division
●capital of Hungary ●most populated city in Hungary (1,708,000 people) ●chief
port on the Danube River

ENVIRONMENTAL/ECONOMIC:
Climate: temperate, cold and humid winters/warm summers
Natural Resources: bauxite, coal, natural gas, fertile soils, arable land
Agricultural Products: wheat, corn, sunflower seed, potatoes, sugar beets
Major Exports: machinery and equipment, other manufactures, food products,
raw materials
Natural Hazards: floods, thunderstorms

ICELAND

Country Name: Republic of Iceland
Continent: Europe
Area: 39,769 sq mi / 103,000 sq km
Population: 289,000
Population Density: 7.3 people per sq mi / 2.8 people per sq km (least dense in Europe)
Capital: Reykjavik

PHYSICAL:
Highest Point: Hvannadalshnukur 6,952 ft / 2,119 m
Lowest Point: Atlantic Ocean 0 ft / 0 m (sea level)
Oceans:
   Atlantic: •forms most of the southern and eastern coasts of Iceland •forms part of
      the western coast of Iceland
Seas:
   Greenland: •forms most of the northern coast of Iceland •feeds into the
      Atlantic and Arctic Oceans

I

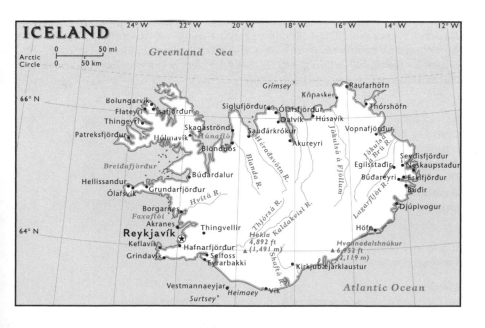

Straits:
  Denmark: •forms part of the northwestern coast of Iceland •separates Iceland
    from Greenland (territory of Denmark) •connects the Atlantic Ocean and the
    Greenland Sea
Islands:
  Iceland: •main island in Iceland •bordered by the Atlantic Ocean, Greenland Sea,
    and Denmark Strait
  Surtsey: •island off southern coast of Iceland •formed by volcanic activity from
    1963 to 1967

POLITICAL:
Independence: June 17, 1944 (from Denmark)
Administrative Divisions: Austurland, Hofudhborgarsvaedhi, Nordhurland
  Eystra, Nordhurland Vestra, Sudhurland, Sudhurnes, Vestfirdhir, Vesturland (8 regions)
Ethnic/Racial Groups: Icelandic
Religion: Christianity (primarily Evangelical Lutheran)
Languages: Icelandic, English, Nordic languages, German
Currency: Icelandic krona
Current President: Olafur Ragnar Grimsson
Cities (capital, largest, or with at least a million people):
  Reykjavik: •located in southwestern Iceland •city in the Hofudhborgarsvaedhi region
    •capital of Iceland •most populated city in Iceland (184,000 people) •chief port
    on the Atlantic Ocean

ENVIRONMENTAL/ECONOMIC:
Climate: temperate; moderated by the North Atlantic Current; mild winters/cool summers
Natural Resources: fish, hydropower, geothermal power, diatomite
Agricultural Products: potatoes, green vegetables, chicken, pork, fish
Major Exports: fish and fish products, animal products, aluminum, diatomite, ferrosilicon
Natural Hazards: earthquakes, volcanoes

INDIA
Country Name: Republic of India
Continent: Asia
Area: 1,269,221 sq mi / 3,287,270 sq km
Population: 1,068,572,000
Population Density: 842 people per sq mi / 325 people per sq km
Capital: New Delhi

PHYSICAL:
Highest Point: Kanchenjunga 28,209 ft / 8,598 m
Lowest Point: Indian Ocean 0 ft / 0 m (sea level)

Mountain Ranges:
  Eastern Ghats: •border the eastern edge of the Deccan Plateau

Himalaya: •located in northern India •extend into Pakistan, China, Nepal, and Bhutan
Karakoram Range: •located in northwestern India •extends into Pakistan and China
Satpura Range: •located in central India •north of the Deccan Plateau
Western Ghats: •border the western edge of the Deccan Plateau

Peaks:
Kamet: •located in the Himalaya •on the India-China border
Kanchenjunga: •located in the Himalaya •on the India-Nepal border •highest
   point in India
Nanda Devi: •located in the Himalaya

Passes:
Karakoram: •located in the Karakoram Range •on the India-China border

Grasslands/Prairies:
Sundarbans: •located in eastern India •north of the Bay of Bengal •extend into
   Bangladesh

Plateau Regions:
Chota Nagpur Plateau: •located in central India •plateau at the eastern end of the
   Satpura Range
Deccan Plateau: •covers much of southern India and part of central India •basin
   between the Satpura Range, Eastern Ghats, and Western Ghats

Deserts:
Great Indian: •located in northwestern India •extends into Pakistan

Oceans:
Indian: •forms most of the southern coast of India

Seas:
    Andaman: •forms part of the southeastern coast of India •feeds into the Indian Ocean
    Arabian: •forms part of the western coast of India •feeds into the Indian Ocean
    Laccadive: •forms part of the southwestern coast of India •feeds into the Indian Ocean
Gulfs:
    Gulf of Khambhat: •forms part of the western coast of India •feeds into the Arabian Sea
    Gulf of Kutch: •forms part of the western coast of India •feeds into the Arabian Sea
    Gulf of Mannar: •forms part of the southern coast of India •feeds into the Indian Ocean
Bays:
    Bay of Bengal: •forms most of the eastern coast of India •feeds into the Indian Ocean
Straits:
    Palk: •forms part of the southern coast of India •separates India from Sri Lanka
    •connects the Bay of Bengal and the Gulf of Mannar
Rivers:
    Brahmaputra: •located in northeastern India •extends into China and Bangladesh
    Ganges: •has its source in the Himalaya •extends into Bangladesh
    Godavari: •has its mouth in the Bay of Bengal •has its source in the Western Ghats
    Indus: •extends into Pakistan and China
    Narmada: •has its mouth in the Gulf of Khambhat •has its source in the
    Satpura Range
    Yamuna: •tributary of the Ganges River •has its source in the Himalaya
Deltas:
    Mouths of the Ganges: •mouth of the Ganges River •feeds into the Bay of Bengal
    •extends into Bangladesh
Peninsulas:
    Kathiawar: •bordered by the Arabian Sea, Gulf of Kutch, and Gulf of Khambhat
Islands:
    Andaman: •island group between the Andaman Sea and the Bay of Bengal
    Lakshadweep: •island group between the Laccadive Sea and the Indian Ocean
    Nicobar: •island group between the Andaman Sea and the Indian Ocean

POLITICAL:
Independence: August 15, 1947 (from the United Kingdom)
Bordering Countries: Bangladesh, China, Pakistan, Nepal, Myanmar, Bhutan (6)
Administrative Divisions: Andhra Pradesh, Arunachal Pradesh, Assam, Bihar,
    Chhattisgarh, Goa, Gujarat, Haryana, Himachal Pradesh, Jammu and Kashmir,
    Jharkhand, Karnataka, Kerala, Madhya Pradesh, Maharashtra, Manipur, Meghalaya,
    Mizoram, Nagaland, Orissa, Punjab, Rajasthan, Sikkim, Tamil Nadu, Tripura,
    Uttaranchal, Uttar Pradesh, West Bengal (28 states) •Andaman and Nicobar Islands,
    Chandigarh, Dadra and Nagar Haveli, Daman and Diu, Delhi, Lakshadweep,
    Pondicherry (7 union territories)
Ethnic/Racial Groups: Indo-Aryan, Dravidian
Religions: Hinduism, Islam, Christianity, Sikh, Buddhism, Jain, Parsi
Languages: Hindi, English, 14 other official languages

Currency: Indian rupee

Current President: Doctor A.P.J. Abdul Kalam

Cities (capital, largest, or with at least a million people):

Delhi: •located in northwestern India •city in the Delhi union territory •most populated city in India (17,341,000 people) •chief port on the Yamuna River

Mumbai (Bombay): •located in western India •city in the Maharashtra state •chief port on the Arabian Sea

Kolkata (Calcutta): •located in eastern India •city in the West Bengal state •north of the Sundarbans •on the edge of the Mouths of the Ganges

Bangalore: •located in southwestern India •city in the Karnataka state •on the edge of the Eastern Ghats on the Deccan Plateau

Chennai (Madras): •located in southern India •city in the Tamil Nadu state •chief port on the Bay of Bengal

Ahmadabad: •located in western India •city in the Gujarat state

Hyderabad: •located in central India •city in the Andhra Pradesh state •on the Deccan Plateau

Pune: •located in western India •city in the Maharashtra state •on the edge of the Western Ghats

Kanpur: •located in central India •city in the Uttar Pradesh state •chief port on the Ganges River

Nagpur: •located in central India •city in the Maharashtra state •on the edge of the Satpura Range on the Deccan Plateau

Surat: •located in western India •city in the Gujarat state •chief port on the Gulf of Khambhat

Jaipur: •located in northwestern India •city in the Rajasthan state

Lucknow: •located in northern India •city in the Uttar Pradesh state

Indore: •located in central India •city in the Madhya Pradesh state

Bhophal: •located in central India •city in the Madhya Pradesh state

Ludhiana: •located in northern India •city in the Punjab state

Patna: • located in northern India •city in the Bihar state

Vadodara: •located in western India •city in the Gujarat state

Thana: •located in western India •city in the Maharashtra state

Agra: •located in northern India •city in the Uttar Pradesh state

New Delhi: •located in northwestern India •city in the Delhi union territory •on Yamuna River •capital of India (295,000 people)

ENVIRONMENTAL/ECONOMIC:

Climate: tropical monsoon in south; temperate in north

Natural Resources: coal, iron ore, manganese, mica, bauxite

Agricultural Products: rice, wheat, oilseed, cotton, cattle

Major Exports: textile goods, gems and jewelry, engineering goods, chemicals, leather manufactures

Natural Hazards: droughts, flash floods, monsoonal floods, severe thunderstorms, earthquakes

INDONESIA

Country Name: Republic of Indonesia
Continent: Asia
Area: 742,308 sq mi / 1,922,570 sq km
Population: 220,483,000
Population Density: 297 people per sq mi / 115 people per sq km
Capital: Jakarta

PHYSICAL:
Highest Point: Puncak Jaya 16,503 ft / 5,030 m
Lowest Point: Indian Ocean 0 ft / 0 m (sea level)
Mountain Ranges:
   Maoke: •located on the island of New Guinea •extend into Papua New Guinea
Peaks:
   Puncak Jaya: •located in the Maoke Mountains •highest point in Indonesia
Oceans:
   Indian: •forms part of the western and southern coasts of Indonesia
   Pacific: •forms part of the northern coast of New Guinea
Seas:
   Andaman: •forms part of the northern coast of Sumatra •feeds into the Indian Ocean
   Arafura: •forms part of the southeastern coast of Indonesia •feeds into the Timor
      and Coral Seas
   Bali: •forms part of the inner coast of Indonesia •feeds into the Java Sea
   Banda: •forms part of the inner coast of Indonesia •feeds into the Timor Sea

Celebes: •forms part of the northern coast of Indonesia •feeds into the Philippine Sea
Ceram: •forms part of the inner coast of Indonesia •feeds into the Halmahera Sea
Flores: •forms part of the inner coast of Indonesia •feeds into the Banda Sea
Halmahera: •forms part of the inner coast of Indonesia •feeds into the Pacific Ocean
Java: •forms part of the inner coast of Indonesia •feeds into the Indian Ocean
Molucca: •forms part of the inner coast of Indonesia •feeds into the Pacific Ocean
Philippine: •forms part of the northeastern coast of Indonesia •feeds into the
    Pacific Ocean
Savu: •forms part of the southern coast of Indonesia •feeds into the Indian Ocean
South China: •forms part of the western coast of Indonesia •feeds into the Java and
    Philippine Seas
Timor: •forms part of the southern coast of Indonesia •feeds into the Indian Ocean

Gulfs:

Gulf of Bone: •forms part of the inner coast of Celebes •feeds into the Flores Sea
Gulf of Tomini: •forms part of the inner coast of Celebes •feeds into the Molucca Sea

Straits:

Makassar: •forms part of the inner coast of Indonesia •separates the island of
    Borneo from the island of Celebes •connects the Celebes and Java Seas
Strait of Malacca: •forms part of the northern coast of Sumatra •separates the island
    of Sumatra from Thailand and Malaysia •connects the South China and
    Andaman Seas
Sumba: •forms part of the southern coast of Indonesia •separates the islands of
    Sumbawa and Flores from the island of Sumba •connects the Indian Ocean and
    the Savu Sea
Sunda: •forms part of the southwestern coast of Indonesia •separates the island of
    Sumatra from the island of Java •connects the Indian Ocean and the Java Sea

Peninsulas:

Minahasa: •bordered by the Celebes Sea, Molucca Sea, and Gulf of Tomimi
    •located on the island of Celebes
Doberai: •bordered by the Pacific Ocean and Ceram Sea •located on the north-
    western part of the island of New Guinea

Islands:

Bali: •westernmost of the Lesser Sunda Islands •bordered by the Bali Sea and
    Indian Ocean
Borneo: •second largest island in Indonesia •bordered by the South China Sea,
    Java Sea, Celebes Sea, and Makassar Strait •parts of the island belong to
    Malaysia and Brunei
Buru: •one of the Moluccas •bordered by the Ceram and Banda Seas
Sulawesi (Celebes): •easternmost of the Greater Sunda Islands •bordered by the
    Celebes Sea, Flores Sea, Molucca Sea, Banda Sea, Gulf of Tomimi, Gulf of
    Bone, and Makassar Strait
Ceram: •one of the Moluccas •bordered by the Ceram and Banda Seas
Flores: •one of the Lesser Sunda Islands •bordered by the Flores and Savu Seas
Halmahera: •northernmost of the Moluccas •bordered by the Pacific Ocean,
    the Molucca Sea, and the Halmahera Sea

Java: •southernmost of the Greater Sunda Islands •bordered by the Indian Ocean, Java Sea, and Sunda Strait

Lombok: •one of the Lesser Sunda Islands •bordered by the Bali Sea and Indian Ocean

New Guinea: •largest island in Indonesia •bordered by the Pacific Ocean, Ceram Sea, and Arafura Sea •the country of Papua New Guinea makes up the eastern half

Sumatra: •westernmost of the Greater Sunda Islands •bordered by the Indian Ocean, Andaman Sea, South China Sea, Java Sea, Strait of Malacca, and Sunda Strait

Sumba: •one of the Lesser Sunda Islands •bordered by the Indian Ocean, Savu Sea, and Sumba Strait

Sumbawa: •one of the Lesser Sunda Islands •bordered by the Flores Sea and Indian Ocean

Timor: •easternmost of the Lesser Sunda Islands •bordered by the Savu and Timor Seas •the country of East Timor makes up the northern half of the island

POLITICAL:

Independence: August 17, 1945 (from the Netherlands)

Former Names: Netherlands East Indies, Dutch East Indies

Bordering Countries: Malaysia, Papua New Guinea, East Timor (Timor-Leste) (3)

Regions:

Irian Jaya: •region covering the western end of New Guinea •west of Papua New Guinea •south of the Pacific Ocean •east of the Ceram Sea •north of the Arafura Sea

Administrative Divisions: Bali, Banten, Bengkulu, Gorontalo, Jambi, Jawa Barat, Jawa Tengah, Jawa Timur, Kalimantan Barat, Kalimantan Selatan, Kalimantan Tengah, Kalimantan Timur, Kepulauan Bangka Belitung, Lampung, Maluku, Maluku Utara, Nusa Tenggara Barat, Nusa Tenggara Timur, Papua, Riau, Sulawesi Selatan, Sulawesi Tengah, Sulawesi Tenggara, Sulawesi Utara, Sumatera Barat, Sumatera Selatan, Sumatera Utara (27 provinces) •Yogyakarta (1 special region) •Jakarta Raya (1 special capital city district)

Ethnic/Racial Groups: Javanese, Sundanese, Madurese, Malay

Religions: Islam, Christianity (Protestant, Roman Catholic), Hinduism, Buddhism

Languages: Bahasa Indonesia, English, Dutch, Javanese, other local dialects

Currency: Indonesian rupiah

Current President: Susilo Bambang Yudhoyono

Cities (capital, largest, or with at least a million people):

Jakarta: •located on the island of Java •city in the Jakarta Raya special capital city district •capital of Indonesia •most populated city in Indonesia (13,194,000 people) •chief port on the Java Sea

Surabaya: •located on the island of Java •city in the Jawa Timur province •chief port on the Bali Sea

Bandung: •located on the island of Java •city in the Jawa Barat province

Medan: •located on the island of Sumatra •city in the Sumatera Utara province

Semarang: •located on the island of Java •city in the Jawa Tengah province

Palembang: •located on the island of Sumatra •city in the Sumatera Selatan province

Tangerang: •located on the island of Java •city in the Banten province
Makasar: •located on the island of Sulawesi •city in the Sulawesi Selatan province

ENVIRONMENTAL/ECONOMIC:
Climate: tropical; hot and humid; moderate in the highlands
Natural Resources: petroleum, tin, natural gas, nickel, timber
Agricultural Products: rice, cassava (tapioca), peanuts, rubber, poultry
Major Exports: oil and gas, electrical appliances, plywood, textiles, rubber
Natural Hazards: floods, droughts, tsunamis, earthquakes, volcanoes, forest fires

IRAN
Country Name: Islamic Republic of Iran
Continent: Asia
Area: 636,296 sq mi / 1,648,000 sq km
Population: 66,582,000
Population Density: 105 people per sq mi / 40 people per sq km
Capital: Tehran

PHYSICAL:
Highest Point: Qolleh-ye Damavand 18,606 ft / 5,671 m
Lowest Point: Caspian Sea 92 ft / 28 m below sea level

Mountain Ranges:
Elburz: •located in northern Iran

Zagros: •cover an area from northwestern to southeastern Iran •extend into Turkey and Iraq

Peaks:
Qolleh-ye Damavand: •located in the Elburz Mountains •highest point in Iran

Depressions:
Caspian Sea: •located in northern Iran •lowest point in Iran

Deserts:
Dasht-e Kavir: •located in northern Iran

Dasht-e Lut: •covers much of eastern Iran

Gulfs:
Gulf of Oman: •forms the southeastern coast of Iran •feeds into the Arabian Sea

Persian: •forms the southwestern coast of Iran •feeds into the Gulf of Oman

Straits:
Strait of Hormuz: •forms part of the southern coast of Iran •separates Iran from Oman •connects the Persian Gulf and Gulf of Oman

Lakes:
Caspian Sea: •forms the northern coast of Iran •also borders Azerbaijan and Turkmenistan •largest lake in the world

Lake Urmia: •located in northwestern Iran •surrounded by the Zagros Mountains

Rivers:
Aras: •forms part of Iran's border with Azerbaijan and Armenia •extends into Turkey and Azerbaijan

POLITICAL:
Independence: April 1, 1979

Former Name: Persia

Bordering Countries: Iraq, Afghanistan, Turkmenistan, Pakistan, Azerbaijan, Turkey, Armenia (7)

Regions:
Baluchistan: •region in southeastern Iran •located north of the Gulf of Oman •extends into Pakistan

Fars: •region in southern Iran •located in the southern Zagros Mountains •north of the Persian Gulf

Khorasan: •region in northeastern Iran •located south of the Elburz Mountains in the Dasht-e Kavir

Kurdistan: •region in northwestern Iran •located in the Zagros Mountains •extends into Turkey and Iraq

Administrative Divisions: Ardabil, Azarbayjan-e Gharbi, Azarbayjan-e Sharqi, Bushehr, Chahar Mahall va Bakhtiari, Esfahan, Fars, Gilan, Golestan, Hamadan, Hormozgan, Ilam, Kerman, Kermanshah, Khorasan, Khuzestan, Kohkiluyeh va Buyer Ahmad, Kordestan, Lorestan, Markazi, Mazandaran, Qazvin, Qom, Semnan, Sistan va Baluchestan, Tehran, Yazd, Zanjan (28 provinces)

Ethnic/Racial Groups: Persian, Azeri, Gilaki/Mazandarani, Kurd, Arab, Lur, Balochi, Turkmen
Religion: Islam (primarily Shiite and Sunni)
Languages: Persian (Farsi), Turkic, Kurdish, various local dialects
Currency: Iranian rial
Current President: Mohammad Khatami
Cities (capital, largest, or with at least a million people):
  Tehran: •located in northern Iran •city in the Tehran province •capital of Iran •most populated city in Iran (7,352,000 people) •on the edge of the Elburz Mountains
  Mashhad: •located in northeastern Iran •city in the Khorasan province •located in a valley in the Elburz Mountains
  Esfahan: •located in central Iran •city in the Esfahan province •on the edge of the Zagros Mountains
  Tabriz: •located in northwestern Iran •city in the Azarbayjan-e Gharbi province •located in a valley in the Zagros Mountains
  Shiraz: •located in southwestern Iran •city in the Fars province •located in a valley in the Zagros Mountains
  Karaj: •located in northern Iran •city in the Tehran province
  Qom: •located in northern Iran •city in the Qom province •located in the Dasht-e Kavir on the edge of the Zagros Mountains

ENVIRONMENTAL/ECONOMIC:
Climate: arid to semi-arid; subtropical along the Caspian coast
Natural Resources: petroleum, natural gas, coal, chromium, copper
Agricultural Products: wheat, rice, other grains, sugar beets, dairy products
Major Exports: petroleum, carpets, fruits and nuts, iron and steel, chemicals
Natural Hazards: droughts, floods, dust storms, sandstorms, earthquakes

IRAQ
Country Name: Republic of Iraq
Continent: Asia
Area: 168,754 sq mi / 437,072 sq km
Population: 24,205,000
Population Density: 143 people per sq mi / 55 people per sq km
Capital: Baghdad

PHYSICAL:
Highest Point: unnamed peak 11,847 ft / 3,611 m
Lowest Point: Persian Gulf 0 ft / 0 m (sea level)
Mountain Ranges:
  Zagros: •located in northeastern Iraq •extend into Turkey and Iran
Deserts: Syrian: •covers most of western Iraq •extends into Syria, Jordan, and Saudi Arabia

Gulfs:
Persian: ●forms the southern coast of Iraq ●feeds into the Gulf of Oman
Lakes:
Razzaza: ●located in central Iraq ●on the edge of the Syrian Desert
Tharthar: ●located in central Iraq ●on the edge of the Syrian Desert
Rivers:
Euphrates: ●tributary of the Shatt al Arab ●extends into Syria and Turkey
Shatt al Arab: ●has its mouth in the Persian Gulf ●forms part of the Iraq-Iran border
Tigris: ●tributary of the Shatt al Arab ●extends into Turkey

POLITICAL:
Independence: October 3, 1932 (from British administration)
Bordering Countries: Iran, Saudi Arabia, Syria, Turkey, Kuwait, Jordan (6)
Regions:
Kurdistan: ●region in northern Iraq ●located in the Zagros Mountains ●extends into Turkey and Iran
Mesopotamia: ●ancient region that covers an area from northwestern to southeastern Iraq ●southwest of the Zagros Mountains
Administrative Divisions: Al Anbar, Al Basrah, Al Muthanna, Al Qadisiyah, An Najaf, Arbil, As Sulaymaniyah, At Tamim, Babil, Baghdad, Dahuk, Dhi Qar, Diyala, Karbala, Maysan, Ninawa, Salah ad Din, Wasit (18 governorates)
Ethnic/Racial Groups: Arab, Kurdish
Religion: Islam (primarily Shiite and Sunni)
Languages: Arabic, Kurdish, Assyrian, Armenian

Currency: Iraqi dinar
Current President (interim government): Ghazi al-Yawer
Cities (capital, largest, or with at least a million people):
    Baghdad: •located in central Iraq •city in the Baghdad governorate •capital of Iraq
      •most populated city in Iraq (5,620,000 people) •chief port on the Tigris River
    Al Mawsil (Mosul): •located in northern Iraq •city in the Ninawa governorate •a
      major port on the Tigris River
    Al Basrah (Basra): •located in southeastern Iraq •city in the Al Basrah governorate
      •chief port on the Shatt al Arab

ENVIRONMENTAL/ECONOMIC:
Climate: desert; mild to cool winters/hot summers; cold winters in northern mountains
Natural Resources: petroleum, natural gas, phosphates, sulfur
Agricultural Products: wheat, barley, rice, vegetables, cattle
Major Exports: crude oil
Natural Hazards: dust storms, sandstorms, floods

IRELAND
Country Name: Ireland
Continent: Europe
Area: 27,133 sq mi / 70,273 sq km
Population: 3,990,000
Population Density: 147 people per sq mi / 57 people per sq km
Capital: Dublin

PHYSICAL:
Highest Point: Carrantuohill 3,415 ft / 1,041 m
Lowest Point: Atlantic Ocean 0 ft / 0 m (sea level)
Mountain Ranges:
    Wicklow: •located in eastern Ireland
Oceans:
    Atlantic: •forms most of the western coast of Ireland
Seas:
    Celtic: •forms most of the southern coast of Ireland •feeds into the Atlantic Ocean
    Irish: •forms part of the eastern coast of Ireland •feeds into the Celtic Sea and the
      Atlantic Ocean
Bays:
    Clew: •forms part of western coast of Ireland •feeds into the Atlantic Ocean
    Dingle: •forms part of the southwestern coast of Ireland •feeds into the
      Atlantic Ocean
    Donegal: •forms part of the northern coast of Ireland •feeds into the Atlantic Ocean
    Dundalk: •forms part of the northeastern coast of Ireland •feeds into the Irish Sea
    Galway: •forms part of the western coast of Ireland •feeds into the Atlantic Ocean

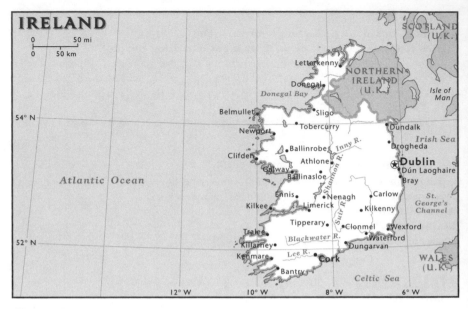

IRELAND

0   50 mi

0   50 km

Channels:

Saint George's: ● forms part of the southeastern coast of Ireland ● separates Ireland from the United Kingdom ● connects the Irish and Celtic Seas

Lakes:

Lough Corrib: ● located in western Ireland

Lough Derg: ● located in central Ireland ● fed by the Shannon River

Lough Foyle: ● located in northeastern Ireland ● on the Ireland-United Kingdom border

Rivers:

Shannon: ● has its mouth in the Atlantic Ocean ● has its source in northern Ireland

Regions:

Connemara: ● lowland region in western Ireland ● north of the Atlantic Ocean and Galway Bay ● west of Lough Corrib

POLITICAL:

Independence: December 6, 1921 (from the United Kingdom)

Bordering Country: United Kingdom (1)

Regions:

Connacht: ● region in western Ireland ● east of the Atlantic Ocean

Leinster: ● located in eastern Ireland ● includes the Wicklow Mountains ● west of the Irish Sea

Munster: ● located in southern Ireland ● north of the Celtic Sea ● east of the Atlantic Ocean

Ulster: ● located in northern Ireland ● east of the Atlantic Ocean ● extends into the United Kingdom

Administrative Divisions: Carlow, Cavan, Clare, Cork, Donegal, Dublin, Galway, Kerry, Kildare, Kilkenny, Laois, Leitrim, Limerick, Longford, Louth, Mayo, Meath, Monaghan, Offaly, Roscommon, Sligo, Tipperary, Waterford, Westmeath, Wexford, Wicklow (26 counties)

Ethnic/Racial Groups: Celtic, English

Religion: Christianity (primarily Roman Catholic)

Languages: English, Irish (Gaelic)

Currency: euro

Current President: Mary McAleese

Cities (capital, largest, or with at least a million people):
Dublin: •located in eastern Ireland •city in Dublin county •capital of Ireland •most populated city in Ireland (1,015,000 people) •chief port on the Irish Sea

ENVIRONMENTAL/ECONOMIC:

Climate: temperate maritime; moderated by the North Atlantic Current; mild winters/cool summers; humid

Natural Resources: natural gas, peat, copper, lead, zinc

Agricultural Products: turnips, barley, potatoes, sugar beets, beef

Major Exports: machinery and equipment, computers, chemicals, pharmaceuticals, live animals

Natural Hazards: floods, thunderstorms

ISRAEL

Country Name: State of Israel

Continent: Asia

Area: 8,550 sq mi / 22,145 sq km

Population: 6,707,000

Population Density: 784 people per sq mi / 303 people per sq km

Capital: Jerusalem

PHYSICAL:

Highest Point: Har Meron 3,963 ft / 1,208 m

Lowest Point: Dead Sea 1,365 ft / 416 m below sea level

Depressions:
Dead Sea: •located in eastern Israel •on the Israel-Jordan border •lowest point on land in the world

Deserts:
Negev: •covers most of southern Israel •extends into Egypt

Seas:
Mediterranean: •forms the western coast of Israel •feeds into the Atlantic Ocean

Gulfs:
Gulf of Aqaba: •forms the southern coast of Israel •feeds into the Red Sea

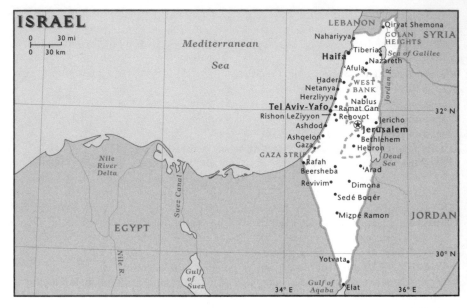

ISRAEL

0   30 mi
0   30 km

Mediterranean

Sea

LEBANON   Qiryat Shemona
Nahariyya   GOLAN   SYRIA
     HEIGHTS
Haifa   Tiberias   *Sea of Galilee*
      Nazareth
   'Afula
Hadera   WEST
Netanya   BANK
Herzliyya
Tel Aviv-Yafo   Nablus
Rishon LeZiyyon   Ramat Gan
     Rehovot   Jericho
Ashdod   **Jerusalem**
Ashqelon   Bethlehem
Gaza   Hebron
GAZA STRIP
   Rafah   'Arad
Beersheba   *Dead*
Revivim   *Sea*
    Dimona
   Sedé Boqér

*Nile
River
Delta*

Suez Canal

EGYPT

Nile R.

*Gulf
of
Suez*

   Mizpé Ramon   JORDAN

Yotvata

*Gulf of
Aqaba*   Elat

32° N

30° N

34° E   36° E

Jordan R.

Lakes:
    Sea of Galilee: located in northeastern Israel
    Dead Sea: located on the Israel-Jordan border lowest point on land in the world
Rivers:
    Jordan: has its mouth in the Dead Sea forms part of the Israel-Jordan border

POLITICAL:
Independence: May 14, 1948 (from British administration)
Bordering Countries: Egypt, Jordan, Lebanon, Syria (4)
Regions:
    Golan Heights: located in northeastern Israel northeast of the Sea of Galilee
Administrative Divisions: Central, Haifa, Jerusalem, Northern, Southern, Tel Aviv
    (6 districts)
Palestinian Areas: Gaza Strip, West Bank (2)
Ethnic/Racial Groups: Jewish, Arab
Religions: Judaism, Islam, Christianity
Languages: Hebrew, Arabic, English
Currency: new Israeli shekel
Current Prime Minister: Ariel Sharon
Cities (capital, largest, or with at least a million people):
    Tel Aviv-Yafo: located in western Israel city in the Tel Aviv district most
        populated city in Israel (3,004,000 people) a major port on the Mediterranean Sea
    Jerusalem: located in central Israel city in the Jerusalem district capital of Israel
        (692,300 people)

ENVIRONMENTAL/ECONOMIC:

Climate: temperate to desert

Natural Resources: timber, potash, copper ore, natural gas, phosphate rock

Agricultural Products: citrus, vegetables, cotton, beef

Major Exports: machinery and equipment, software, cut diamonds, agricultural products, chemicals

Natural Hazards: sandstorms, droughts, earthquakes

ITALY

Country Name: Italian Republic
Continent: Europe
Area: 116,345 sq mi / 301,333 sq km
Population: 57,166,000
Population Density: 491 people per sq mi / 190 people per sq km
Capital: Rome

PHYSICAL:

Highest Point: Mont Blanc de Coumayeur 15,477 ft / 4,748 m
Lowest Point: Mediterranean Sea 0 ft / 0 m (sea level)
Mountain Ranges:

Alps: •cover much of northern Italy •extend into France, Switzerland, Austria, and Slovenia

Apennines: •cover an area from northwestern to southeastern Italy •extend into
    San Marino
Dolomites: •located in northeastern Italy
Peaks (minimum elevation 8,000 ft / 2,400 m):
Dufourspitze: •located in the Alps •on the Italy-Switzerland border
Mont Blanc de Coumayeur: •located in the Alps •on the Italy-France border
    •highest point in Italy
Mount Etna: •located on the island of Sicily
Passes:
Brenner Pass: •located in the Alps •connects Italy and Austria
Great Saint Bernard: •located in the Alps •connects Italy and Switzerland
Valleys:
Po: •covers much of northern Italy •between the Alps and the Apennines •eastern
    end borders the Gulf of Venice and the Adriatic Sea
Seas:
Adriatic: •forms part of the eastern coast of Italy •feeds into the Ionian Sea
Ionian: •forms part of the southeastern coast of Italy •feeds into the Mediterranean Sea
Ligurian: •forms part of the northwestern coast of Italy •feeds into the Mediterranean Sea
Mediterranean: •forms most of the western coast of Sardinia •forms most of the
    southern and eastern coasts of Sicily •feeds into the Atlantic Ocean
Tyrrhenian: •forms most of the inner coast of Italy •feeds into the Mediterranean Sea
Gulfs:
Gulf of Gaeta: •forms part of the western coast of Italy •feeds into the Tyrrhenian Sea
Gulf of Genova: •forms part of the northwestern coast of Italy •feeds into the
    Ligurian Sea
Gulf of Taranto: •forms part of the southeastern coast of Italy •feeds into the Ionian Sea
Gulf of Trieste: •forms part of the northeastern coast of Italy •feeds into the Gulf of Venice
Gulf of Venice: •forms part of the northeastern coast of Italy •feeds into the Adriatic Sea
Straits:
Strait of Bonifacio: •forms part of the northern coast of Sardinia •separates the
    island of Sardinia from the French island of Corsica •connects the Mediterranean
    and Tyrrhenian Seas
Strait of Messina: •forms part of the southern border of Italy •separates the island of
    Sicily from mainland Italy •connects the Tyrrhenian and Mediterranean Seas
Strait of Otranto: •forms part of the southeastern coast of Italy •separates Italy
    from Albania •connects the Adriatic and Ionian Seas
Strait of Sicily: •forms part of the western coast of Sicily •separates the island of
    Sicily from Tunisia
Channels:
Malta: •forms part of the southern coast of Italy •separates Italy from Malta

Lakes:
Lake Como: •located in northern Italy •in a valley of the Alps
Lake Garda: •located in northern Italy •on the edge of the Alps

Lake Maggiore: •located in northwestern Italy •in a valley of the Alps •extends
into Switzerland

Rivers:

Adige: •has its mouth in the Gulf of Venice •has its source in the Alps

Po: •has its mouth in the Adriatic Sea •has its source in the Alps

Tiber: •has its mouth in the Tyrrhenian Sea •has its source in the Appenines

Deltas:

Mouths of the Po: •mouth of the Po River •feeds into the Adriatic Sea

Islands:

Sardinia: •island off the western coast of mainland Italy •bordered by the
Mediterranean Sea, Tyrrhenian Sea, and Strait of Bonifacio

Sicily: •island off the southern coast of mainland Italy •bordered by the Mediterranean
Sea, Tyrrhenian Sea, Strait of Sicily, Strait of Messina, and Malta Channel

POLITICAL:

Independence: March 17, 1861 (kingdom of Italy proclaimed; Italy was not finally
unified until 1870)

Former Name: Kingdom of Italy

Bordering Countries: Switzerland, France, Austria, Slovenia, San Marino,
Vatican City (6)

Administrative Divisions: Abruzzi, Apulia, Basilicata, Calabria, Campania,
Emilia-Romagna, Friuli-Venezia Giulia, Latium, Liguria, Lombardy, Marches,
Molise, Piedmont, Sardinia, Sicily, Tuscany, Trentino-Alto Adige, Umbria, Valle
d'Aosta, Veneto (20 regions)

Ethnic/Racial Groups: predominantly Italian

Religion: Christianity (predominantly Roman Catholic)

Languages: Italian, German, French, Slovene

Currency: euro

Current President: Carlo Azeglio Ciampi

Cities (capital, largest, or with at least a million people):

Rome: •located in central Italy •city in the Latium region •capital of Italy •most
populated city in Italy (2,628,000 people) •chief port on the Tiber River

Milan: •located in northern Italy •city in the Lombardy region

ENVIRONMENTAL/ECONOMIC:

Climate: Mediterranean; alpine in the far north; hot and dry in the south

Natural Resources: coal, mercury, zinc, potash, marble

Agricultural Products: fruits, vegetables, grapes, potatoes, beef

Major Exports: engineering products, textiles and clothing, production machinery,
motor vehicles, transport equipment

Natural Hazards: landslides, mudflows, avalanches, earthquakes, volcanoes, floods,
land subsidence in Venice

COUNTRIES

JAMAICA

Country Name: Jamaica
Continent: North America
Area: 4,244 sq mi / 10,991 sq km
Population: 2,646,000
Population Density: 623 people per sq mi / 241 people per sq km
Capital: Kingston

PHYSICAL:

Highest Point: Blue Mountain Peak 7,402 ft / 2,256 m
Lowest Point: Caribbean Sea 0 ft / 0 m (sea level)
Seas:
   Caribbean: •surrounds Jamaica •feeds into the Atlantic Ocean
Islands:
   Jamaica: •main island in Jamaica •surrounded by the Caribbean Sea

POLITICAL:

Independence: August 6, 1962 (from the United Kingdom)

Administrative Divisions: Clarendon, Hanover, Kingston, Manchester, Portland, Saint Andrew, Saint Ann, Saint Catherine, Saint Elizabeth, Saint James, Saint Mary, Saint Thomas, Trelawny, Westmoreland (14 parishes)

Ethnic/Racial Groups: black, mixed, East Indian

Religions: Christianity (Protestant, Roman Catholic), other spiritual beliefs

Languages: English, patois English

Currency: Jamaican dollar

Current Prime Minister: Percival James Patterson

Cities (capital, largest, or with at least a million people):
Kingston: ●located in eastern Jamaica ●city in the Kingston parish ●capital of Jamaica ●most populated city in Jamaica (575,000 people) ●chief port on the Caribbean Sea

ENVIRONMENTAL/ECONOMIC:

Climate: tropical; hot and humid with temperate interior

Natural Resources: bauxite, gypsum, limestone

Agricultural Products: sugarcane, bananas, coffee, citrus, poultry

Major Exports: alumina, bauxite, sugar, bananas, rum

Natural Hazards: hurricanes

JAPAN

Country Name: Japan

Continent: Asia

Area: 145, 902 sq mi / 377,887 sq km

Population: 127,508,000

Population Density: 873 people per sq mi / 337 people per sq km

Capital: Tokyo

J

PHYSICAL:

Highest Point: Mount Fuji 12,388 ft / 3,776 m

Lowest Point: Hachiro-gata 13 ft / 4 m below sea level

Peaks (minimum elevation of 8,000 ft / 2,400 m):
Mount Fuji: ●located on the island of Honshu ●highest point in Japan

Oceans:
Pacific: ●forms most of the eastern and southern coasts of Japan

Seas:
East China: ●forms most of the western coast of the island of Kyushu ●feeds into the Pacific Ocean

Inland: ●forms part of the inner coast of Japan ●feeds into the Pacific Ocean

Sea of Japan: ●forms most of the western coast of Japan ●feeds into the Sea of Okhotsk, Pacific Ocean, and East China Sea

Sea of Okhotsk: ●forms most of the northern coast of the island of Hokkaido ●feeds into the Pacific Ocean

JAPAN

0 ————— 250 mi
0 ————— 250 km

CHINA
RUSSIA
Wakkanai
Sea of Okhotsk
Kuril Islands
44° N
Asahikawa
Otaru
Sapporo
Nemuro
Kushiro
Hokkaidō
Hakodate

NORTH KOREA
Korea Bay
CHINA
Aomori
Hirosaki
Hachinohe
40° N

Sea of Japan
(East Sea)
Akita
Morioka
Honshū

Yamagata
Niigata
Sendai
Fukushima

SOUTH KOREA
Yellow Sea
Toyama
Kanazawa
Nagano
Tokyo
Utsunomiya
36° N

Matsue
Kyōto
Nagoya
Chiba
Yokohama

Hiroshima
Kobe
Osaka
Shizuoka
Hamamatsu
Pacific

Kitakyūshū
Fukuoka
Matsuyama
Izu
Islands
Ocean

Nagasaki
Ōita
Shikoku
Kumamoto
Kyūshū
Kagoshima
Miyazaki

East China Sea
32° N

124° E   128° E   132° E   136° E   140° E   144° E

Bays:

   Toyama: •forms part of the northern coast of Japan •feeds into the Sea of Japan
Straits:

   Korea: •forms part of the southwestern coast of Japan •separates Japan from South Korea •connects the East China Sea and Sea of Japan

   La Perouse: •forms part of the northwestern coast of Hokkaido •separates the island of Hokkaido from Russia •connects the Sea of Japan and Sea of Okhotsk

   Tsugaru: •forms part of the northern coast of Japan •separates the island of Hokkaido from the island of Honshu •connects the Sea of Japan and Pacific Ocean
Lakes:

   Lake Biwa: •located on the island of Honshu
Islands:

   Hokkaido: •northernmost of the four main islands of Japan •bordered by the Pacific Ocean, Sea of Okhotsk, Sea of Japan, La Perouse Strait, and Tsugaru Strait

   Honshu: •largest of the four main islands of Japan •bordered by the Pacific Ocean, Sea of Japan, Inland Sea, Toyama Bay, Tsugaru Strait, and Korea Strait

   Kyushu: •southernmost of the four main islands of Japan •bordered by the Pacific Ocean, East China Sea, and Korea Strait

   Ryukyu: •island group located south of Kyushu •bordered by the East China Sea and the Pacific Ocean

   Shikoku: •smallest of the four main islands of Japan •bordered by the Pacific Ocean and Inland Sea

POLITICAL:

Independence: 660 B.C. (traditional founding by Emperor Jimmu)

Administrative Divisions: Aichi, Akita, Aomori, Chiba, Ehime, Fukui, Fukuoka, Fukushima, Gifu, Gumma, Hiroshima, Hokkaido, Hyogo, Ibaraki, Ishikawa, Iwate, Kagawa, Kagoshima, Kanagawa, Kochi, Kumamoto, Kyoto, Mie, Miyagi, Miyazaki, Nagano, Nagasaki, Nara, Niigata, Oita, Okayama, Okinawa, Osaka, Saga, Saitama, Shiga, Shimane, Shizuoka, Tochigi, Tokushima, Tokyo, Tottori, Toyama, Wakayama, Yamagata, Yamaguchi, Yamanashi (47 prefectures)

Ethnic/Racial Groups: predominantly Japanese

Religions: Shinto, Buddhism

Language: predominantly Japanese

Currency: yen

Current Prime Minister: Junichiro Koizumi

Cities (capital, largest, or with at least a million people):

Tokyo-Yokohama: ●located on the island of Honshu ●cities in the Tokyo, Saitama, Kanagawa, and Chiba prefectures ●Tokyo is the capital of Japan ●most populated metropolitan area in the world (35,327,000 people) ●Yokohama is a major port on the Pacific Ocean

Osaka-Kobe-Kyoto: ●located on the island of Honshu ●cities in the Osaka, Hyogo, Kyoto, and Nara prefectures ●a major port on the Pacific Ocean and Lake Biwa

Nagoya: ●located on the island of Honshu ●city in the Aichi and Gifu prefectures ●a major port on the Pacific Ocean

Sapporo: ●located on the island of Hokkaido ●city in the Hokkaido prefecture

Fukuoka: ●located on the island of Kyushu ●city in the Fukuoka prefecture

Hiroshima: ●located on the island of Honshu ●city in the Hiroshima prefecture ●chief port on the Inland Sea

Kitakyushu: ●located on the island of Kyushu ●city in the Fukuoka prefecture

Sendai: ●located on the island of Honshu ●city in the Miyagi prefecture

ENVIRONMENTAL/ECONOMIC:

Climate: tropical in the south; cool temperate in the north

Natural Resources: negligible mineral resources, fish

Agricultural Products: rice, sugar beets, vegetables, fruits, pork

Major Exports: motor vehicles, semiconductors, office machinery, chemicals

Natural Hazards: volcanoes, earthquakes, tsunamis, typhoons

JORDAN

Country Name: Hashemite Kingdom of Jordan

Continent: Asia

Area: 34,495 sq mi / 89,342 sq km

Population: 5,480,000

Population Density: 159 people per sq mi / 61 people per sq km

Capital: Amman

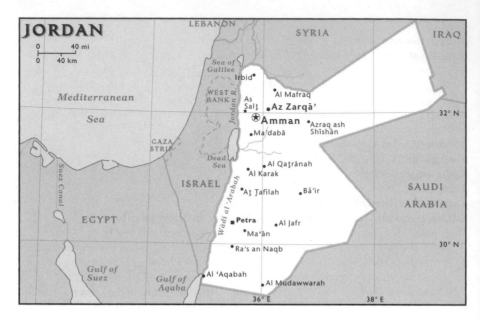

PHYSICAL:

Highest Point: Jabal Ram 5,689 ft / 1,734 m
Lowest Point: Dead Sea 1,365 ft / 416 m below sea level
Depressions:

  Dead Sea: •located in western Jordan •on the Jordan-Israel border •lowest point on land in the world

Deserts:

  Syrian: •covers much of central and eastern Jordan •extends into Syria, Iraq, and Saudi Arabia

Gulfs:

  Gulf of Aqaba: •forms the southern coast of Jordan •feeds into the Red Sea

Lakes:

  Dead Sea: •on the Jordan-Israel border •lowest point on land in the world

Rivers:

  Jordan: •has its mouth in the Dead Sea •forms part of the Jordan-Israel border

POLITICAL:

Independence: May 25, 1946 (from British administration)
Former Name: Transjordan
Bordering Countries: Saudi Arabia, Syria, Israel, Iraq (4)
Administrative Divisions: Ajlun, Al Aqabah, Al Balqa, Al Karak, Al Mafraq, Amman, At Tafilah, Az Zarqa, Irbid, Jarash, Maan, Madaba (12 governorates)
Ethnic/Racial Groups: predominantly Arab
Religions: Islam (primarily Sunni), Christianity

Languages: Arabic, English
Currency: Jordanian dinar
Current King: Abdullah II
Cities (capital, largest, or with at least a million people):
    Amman: ●located in northwestern Jordan ●city in the Amman governorate ●capital of Jordan ●most populated city in Jordan (1,237,000 people) ●on the edge of the Syrian Desert

ENVIRONMENTAL/ECONOMIC:
Climate: mostly arid desert with rainy/dry seasons in the west
Natural Resources: phosphates, potash, shale oil
Agricultural Products: wheat, barley, citrus, tomatoes, sheep
Major Exports: phosphates, fertilizers, potash, agricultural products, manufactures
Natural Hazards: droughts, earthquakes

KAZAKHSTAN

Country Name: Republic of Kazakhstan
Continent: Asia
Area: 1,049,155 sq mi / 2,717,300 sq km
Population: 14,787,000
Population Density: 14 people per sq mi / 5.4 people per sq km
Capital: Astana

PHYSICAL:

Highest Point: Khan Tangiri 22,949 ft / 6,995 m
Lowest Point: Vpadina Kaundy (in the Caspian Depression) 433 ft / 132 m
    below sea level
Mountain Ranges:
    Altay: ●located in eastern Kazakhstan ●extend into Russia and China
    Tian Shan: ●located in southeastern Kazakhstan ●extend into Kyrgyzstan and China
Peaks (minimum elevation of 8,000 ft / 2,400 m):
    Khan Tangiri: ●located in the Tian Shan ●on Kazakhstan's border with China and
    Kyrgyzstan ●highest point in Kazakhstan

Depressions:
    Caspian Depression: •located in western Kazakhstan •north of the Caspian Sea
        •extends into Russia •includes the lowest point in Kazakhstan
Plateau Regions:
    Kazakh Uplands: •uplands in central Kazakhstan
    Ustyurt Plateau: •basin in southwestern Kazakhstan •extends into Uzbekistan
Deserts:
    Qizilqum: •located in southern Kazakhstan •extends into Uzbekistan
Lakes:
    Aral Sea: •located in southwestern Kazakhstan •on the Kazakhstan-Uzbekistan border
    Caspian Sea: •forms the western coast of Kazakhstan •also borders Russia and
        Turkmenistan •largest lake in the world
    Lake Balkhash: •located in eastern Kazakhstan
Rivers:
    Ertis (Irtysh): •located in northeastern Kazakhstan •extends into Russia and China
    Syr Darya: •has its mouth in the Aral Sea •extends into Uzbekistan

POLITICAL:
Independence: December 16, 1991 (from the Soviet Union)
Former Name: Kazakh Soviet Socialist Republic
Bordering Countries: Russia, Uzbekistan, China, Kyrgyzstan, Turkmenistan (5)
Administrative Divisions: Almaty, Aqmola, Aqtobe, Atyrau, Batys Qazaqstan,
    Mangghystau, Ongtustik Qazaqstan, Pavlodar, Qaraghandy, Qostanay, Qyzylorda,
    Shyghys Qazaqstan, Soltustik Qazaqstan, Zhambyl (14 provinces) •Almaty, Astana,
    Bayqongyr (3 cities)
Ethnic/Racial Groups: Kazakh, Russian, Ukrainian, Uzbek
Religions: Islam, Christianity (primarily Russian Orthodox)
Languages: Kazakh, Russian
Currency: tenge
Current President: Nursultan Nazarbayev
Cities (capital, largest, or with at least a million people):
    Almaty: •located in southeastern Kazakhstan •city in the Almaty city division •most
        populated city in Kazakhstan (1,275,000 people) •on the edge of the Tian Shan
    Astana: •located in northern Kazakhstan •city in the Astana city division •capital
    of Kazakhstan (332,000 people)

K

ENVIRONMENTAL/ECONOMIC:
Climate: continental; cold winters/hot summers; arid to semi-arid
Natural Resources: petroleum, natural gas, coal, iron ore, manganese
Agricultural Products: grain, cotton, livestock
Major Exports: oil and oil products, ferrous metals, chemicals, machinery, grain
Natural Hazards: earthquakes, mudslides

KENYA

Country Name: Republic of Kenya
Continent: Africa
Area: 224,081 sq mi / 580,367 sq km
Population: 31,639,000
Population Density: 141 people per sq mi / 55 people per sq km
Capital: Nairobi

PHYSICAL:
Highest Point: Mount Kenya 17,057 ft / 5,199 m
Lowest Point: Indian Ocean 0 ft / 0 m (sea level)
Mountain Ranges:
Kenya Highlands: •covers much of central Kenya
Peaks (minimum elevation of 8,000 ft / 2,400 m):
Mount Kenya: •located in the Kenya Highlands •highest point in Kenya
Valleys:
Great Rift: •covers an area from northwestern to southwestern Kenya •cuts
   through the Kenya Highlands •extends into Ethiopia, Uganda, and Tanzania
Grasslands/Prairies:
Serengeti Plain: •located in southwestern Kenya •extends into Tanzania
Deserts:
Chalbi: •located in northern Kenya

Oceans:
    Indian: • forms the southern coast of Kenya
Lakes:
    Lake Turkana: •located in northwestern Kenya •in the Great Rift Valley •extends
        into Ethiopia
    Lake Victoria: •located in southwestern Kenya •extends into Uganda and Tanzania
        •largest lake in Africa •third largest lake in the world
Rivers:
    Tana: •has its mouth in the Indian Ocean •has its source in the Kenya Highlands

POLITICAL:
Independence: December 12, 1963 (from the United Kingdom)
Former Name: British East Africa
Bordering Countries: Uganda, Ethiopia, Tanzania, Somalia, Sudan (5)
Administrative Divisions: Central, Coast, Eastern, North Eastern, Nyanza,
    Rift Valley, Western (7 provinces) •Nairobi Area (1 area)
Ethnic/Racial Groups: Kikuyu, Luhya, Luo, Kalenjin, Kamba, Kisii, Meru
Religions: Christianity (Protestant, Roman Catholic), indigenous beliefs, Islam
Languages: English, Kiswahili, numerous indigenous languages
Currency: Kenyan shilling
Current President: Mwai Kibaki
Cities (capital, largest, or with at least a million people):
    Nairobi; •located in southern Kenya •city in the Nairobi Area •capital of Kenya
        •most populated city in Kenya (2,818,000 people) •on the edge of the Kenya
        Highlands

ENVIRONMENTAL/ECONOMIC:
Climate: tropical along the coast; arid in the interior
Natural Resources: gold, limestone, soda ash, salt, rubies
Agricultural Products: tea, coffee, corn, wheat, dairy products
Major Exports: tea, horticultural products, coffee, petroleum products, fish
Natural Hazards: droughts, floods

KIRIBATI
Country Name: Republic of Kiribati
Continent: Australia/Oceania
Area: 313 sq mi / 811 sq km
Population: 98,000
Population Density: 313 people per sq mi / 121 people per sq km
Capital: Tarawa

PHYSICAL:
Highest Point: unnamed location 266 ft / 81 m
Lowest Point: Pacific Ocean 0 ft / 0 m (sea level)
Oceans:
  Pacific: •forms the entire coast of Kiribati
Islands:
  Gilbert: •island group in western Kiribati •surrounded by the Pacific Ocean
  Line: •island group in eastern Kiribati •surrounded by the Pacific Ocean
  Phoenix: •island group in central Kiribati •surrounded by the Pacific Ocean

POLITICAL:
Independence: July 12, 1979 (from the United Kingdom)
Former Name: Gilbert Islands
Administrative Divisions: Gilbert Islands (includes Tarawa district), Line Islands,
  Phoenix Islands (3 units)
Ethnic/Racial Groups: predominantly Micronesian
Religion: Christianity (Roman Catholic, Protestant)
Languages: English, I-Kiribati
Currency: Australian dollar
Current President: Anote Tong
Cities (capital, largest, or with at least a million people):
  Tarawa (district): •located in the Gilbert island chain •city in the Gilbert Islands unit
    •capital of Kiribati •most populated city in Kiribati (42,000 people) •chief port
    on the Pacific Ocean

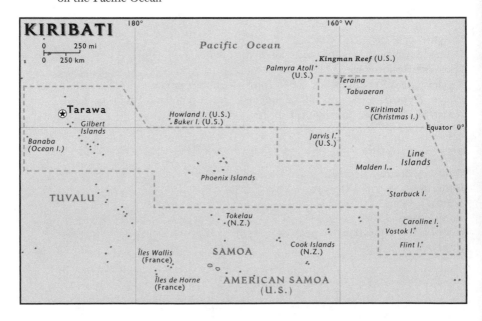

ENVIRONMENTAL/ECONOMIC:
Climate: tropical marine; hot and humid, moderated by trade winds
Natural Resources: phosphate
Agricultural Products: copra, taro, breadfruit, sweet potatoes, fish
Major Exports: copra, coconuts, seaweed, fish
Natural Hazards: typhoons, tornadoes

KOREA, NORTH
Country Name: Democratic People's Republic of Korea
Continent: Asia
Area: 46,540 sq mi / 120,538 sq km
Population: 22,661,000
Population Density: 487 people per sq mi / 188 people per sq km
Capital: Pyongyang

PHYSICAL:
Highest Point: Paektu-san 9,003 ft / 2,744 m
Lowest Point: Sea of Japan 0 ft / 0 m (sea level)
Peaks (minimum elevation of 8,000 ft / 2,400 m):
   Paektu-san: ●located in northern North Korea ●on the North Korea-China border ●highest point in North Korea
Seas:
   Sea of Japan: ●forms most of the eastern coast of North Korea ●feeds into the East China Sea, Sea of Okhotsk, and Pacific Ocean

Yellow: ● forms part of the southwestern coast of North Korea ● feeds into the East China Sea

Bays:
Korea: ● forms part of the western coast of North Korea ● feeds into the Yellow Sea
Tonghan: ● forms part of the eastern coast of North Korea ● feeds into the Sea of Japan

POLITICAL:
Independence: August 15, 1945 (from Japan)
Bordering Countries: China, South Korea (2)
Administrative Divisions: Chagang, North Hamgyong, South Hamgyong, North Hwanghae, South Hwanghae, Kangwon, North Pyongan, South Pyongan, Yanggang (9 provinces) ● Kaesong, Najin Sonbong, Nampo, Pyongyang (4 special cities)
Ethnic/Racial Groups: Korean
Religions: Buddhism, Confucianism
Language: Korean
Currency: North Korean won
Current President: Kim Il-sung
Cities (capital, largest, or with at least a million people):
Pyongyang: ● located in southwestern North Korea ● city in the Pyongyang special city ● capital of North Korea ● most populated city in North Korea (3,228,000 people)

ENVIRONMENTAL/ECONOMIC:
Climate: temperate with rainy summers
Natural Resources: coal, lead, tungsten, zinc, graphite
Agricultural Products: rice, corn, potatoes, soybeans, cattle
Major Exports: minerals, metallurgical products, manufactures, textiles
Natural Hazards: droughts, floods, typhoons

KOREA, SOUTH
Country Name: Republic of Korea
Continent: Asia
Area: 38,321 sq mi / 99,250 sq km
Population: 47,939,000
Population Density: 1,251 people per sq mi / 483 people per sq km
Capital: Seoul

PHYSICAL:
Highest Point: Hallasan 6,398 ft / 1,950 m
Lowest Point: Sea of Japan 0 ft / 0 m (sea level)
Seas:
East China: ● forms the southern coast of the island of Jeju ● feeds into the South China Sea and Pacific Ocean

SOUTH KOREA

Sea of Japan: •forms most of the eastern coast of South Korea •feeds into the East
China Sea, Sea of Okhotsk, and Pacific Ocean •known as the East Sea to Koreans
Yellow: •forms most of the western coast of South Korea •feeds into the East China Sea
Straits:
Jeju: •forms part of the southwestern coast of South Korea •separates the island of
Jeju from mainland South Korea
Korea: •forms part of the southern coast of South Korea •separates South
Korea from Japan •connects the East China Sea and the Sea of Japan (East Sea)
Islands:
Jeju: •separated from mainland South Korea by the Jeju Strait •bordered by the
Yellow Sea, the East China Sea, and the Jeju Strait

POLITICAL:
Independence: August 15, 1945 (from Japan)
Bordering Country: North Korea (1)
Administrative Divisions: Chungcheongbuk-do, Chungcheongnam-do,
Gangwon, Gyeonggi, Gyeongsangbuk-do, Gyeongsangnam-do, Jeju-do, Jeollabuk-do,
Jeollanam-do (9 provinces) •Busan, Daegu, Daejeon, Gwangju, Incheon, Seoul,
Ulsan (7 metropolitan cities)
Ethnic/Racial Groups: Korean
Religions: Christianity, Buddhism
Languages: Korean, English
Currency: South Korean won

Current President: Roh Moo-hyun
Cities (capital, largest, or with at least a million people):
> Seoul: • located in northwestern South Korea • city in the Seoul metropolitan city division • capital of South Korea • most populated city in South Korea (9,592,000 people)
> Busan: • located in southeastern South Korea • city in the Busan metropolitan city division • chief port on the Korea Strait
> Daegu: • located in central South Korea • city in the Daegu metropolitan city division
> Incheon: • located in northwestern South Korea • city in the Incheon metropolitan city division • chief port on the Yellow Sea
> Daejeon: • located in western South Korea • city in the Daejeon metropolitan city division

ENVIRONMENTAL/ECONOMIC:
Climate: temperate, heavier rain in summer than in winter
Natural Resources: coal, tungsten, graphite, molybdenum, lead
Agricultural Products: rice, root crops, barley, vegetables, cattle
Major Exports: electronic products, machinery and equipment, motor vehicles, steel, ships, textiles
Natural Hazards: typhoons, minor earthquakes

KUWAIT
Country Name: State of Kuwait
Continent: Asia
Area: 6,880 sq mi / 17,818 sq km
Population: 2,384,000
Population Density: 347 people per sq mi / 134 people per sq km
Capital: Kuwait City

PHYSICAL:
Highest Point: unnamed location 1,004 ft / 306 m
Lowest Point: Persian Gulf 0 ft / 0 m (sea level)
Gulfs:
> Persian Gulf: • forms most of the eastern coast of Kuwait • feeds into the Gulf of Oman

POLITICAL:
Independence: June 19, 1961 (from the United Kingdom)
Bordering Countries: Iraq, Saudi Arabia (2)
Administrative Divisions: Al Ahmadi, Al 'Asimah, Al Farwaniyah, Al Jahra', Hawalli (5 governorates)

KUWAIT

0   10 mi
0   10 km

IRAQ

IRAN

30° N

Khawr 'Abd Allāh

Būbiyān

Qaṣr aş Şabīyah

Jūn al Kuwayt

⊛ **Kuwait**   *Faylakah*

Al Jehrā.   As Sālimīyah

Ḩawalli

Al Aḩmadī
Mīnā' 'abd Allah

29° N

Persian

SAUDI ARABIA

Gulf

Mina' Su'ūd.
Al Wafra.   Az Zawr
Al Khīrān

47° E   48° E

Ethnic/Racial Groups: Arab, South Asian, Iranian
Religions: Islam (Sunni and Shiite), Christianity, Hinduism, Parsi
Languages: Arabic, English
Currency: Kuwaiti dinar
Current Amir: Sheikh Jabir al-Ahmad al-Jabir Al Sabah
Cities (capital, largest, or with at least a million people):
Kuwait City: •located in eastern Kuwait •city in Al 'Asimah governorate •capital of Kuwait •most populated city in Kuwait (1,222,000 people) •chief port on the Persian Gulf

ENVIRONMENTAL/ECONOMIC:
Climate: dry desert with intensely hot summers/short and cool winters
Natural Resources: petroleum, fish, shrimp, natural gas
Agricultural Products: few crops, fish
Major Exports: oil and refined products, fertilizers
Natural Hazards: sudden rainstorms, sandstorms, dust storms

KYRGYZSTAN
Country Name: Kyrgyz Republic
Continent: Asia
Area: 77,182 sq mi / 199,900 sq km
Population: 5,033,000

KYRGYZSTAN

Population Density: 65 people per sq mi / 25 people per sq km
Capital: Bishkek

PHYSICAL:
Highest Point: Jengish Chokusu (Pobedy Peak) 24,406 ft / 7,439 m
Lowest Point: Kara-Daryya 433 ft / 132 m
Mountain Ranges:
Tian Shan: •cover an area from southwest to northeast Kyrgyzstan •extend into China
Peaks (minimum elevation of 8,000 ft / 2,400 m):
Jengish Chokusu (Pobedy Peak): •located in the Tian Shan •on the Kyrgyzstan-China border
Lakes:
Ysyk Kol: •located in northeastern Kyrgyzstan •on the edge of the Tian Shan

POLITICAL:
Independence: August 31, 1991 (from the Soviet Union)
Former Name: Kirghiz Soviet Socialist Republic
Bordering Countries: Uzbekistan, Kazakhstan, Tajikistan, China (4)
Administrative Divisions: Batken, Chuy, Jalal-Abad, Naryn, Osh, Talas, Ysyk-Kol (7 provinces) •Bishkek (1 city)
Ethnic/Racial Groups: Kyrgyz, Russian, Uzbek, Ukrainian
Religions: Islam, Christianity (primarily Russian Orthodox)

Languages: Kyrgyz, Russian
Currency: Kyrgyzstani som
Current President: Askar Akayev
Cities (capital, largest, or with at least a million people):
   Bishkek: •located in northern Kyrgyzstan •city in the Bishkek city division •capital of Kyrgyzstan •most populated city in Kyrgyzstan (806,000 people) •on the edge of the Tian Shan

ENVIRONMENTAL/ECONOMIC:

Climate: dry continental to polar in mountains; subtropical in southwest; temperate in northern foothills
Natural Resources: hydropower, gold and rare earth metals, coal, oil, natural gas
Agricultural Products: tobacco, cotton, potatoes, vegetables, sheep
Major Exports: cotton, wool, meat, tobacco, gold
Natural Hazards: floods, droughts

LAOS

Country Name: Lao People's Democratic Republic
Continent: Asia
Area: 91,429 sq mi / 236,800 sq km
Population: 5,593,000
Population Density: 61 people per sq mi / 24 people per sq km
Capital: Vientiane

PHYSICAL:
Highest Point: Phou Bia 9,245 ft / 2,818 m
Lowest Point: Mekong River 223 ft / 70 m
Mountain Ranges:
   Annam Cordillera: •covers most of eastern Laos •extends into Vietnam
Peaks (minimum elevation of 8,000 ft / 2,400 m):
   Phou Bia: •located on the Xiangkhoang Plateau •highest point in Laos
Plateau Regions:
   Plateau of Xiangkhoang: •mountainous plateau that covers much of northern Laos

Rivers:
> Mekong: •forms part of Laos' border with Myanmar and Thailand •extends into China, Cambodia, and Vietnam

POLITICAL:
Independence: July 19, 1949 (from France)
Bordering Countries: Vietnam, Thailand, Cambodia, China, Myanmar (5)
Administrative Divisions: Attapu, Bokeo, Bolikhamxai, Champasak, Houaphan, Khammouan, Louangnamtha, Louangphrabang, Oudomxai, Phongsali, Salavan, Savannakhet, Viangchan, Xaignabouri, Xekong, Xiangkhoang (16 provinces) •Viangchan (1 municipality) •Xiasomboun (1 special zone)
Ethnic/Racial Groups: Lao Loum, Lao Theung, Lao Soung
Religions: Buddhism, animism, other
Languages: Lao, French, English, various ethnic languages
Currency: kip
Current President: Khamtai Siphandon
Cities (capital, largest, or with at least a million people):
> Vientiane: • located in western Laos •city in the Viangchan municipality •capital of Laos •most populated city in Laos (716,000 people) •chief port on Mekong River

ENVIRONMENTAL/ECONOMIC:
Climate: tropical monsoon with rainy/dry seasons
Natural Resources: timber, hydropower, gypsum, tin, gold
Agricultural Products: sweet potatoes, vegetables, corn, coffee, water buffalo
Major Exports: wood products, garments, electricity, coffee, tin
Natural Hazards: floods, droughts

LATVIA
Country Name: Republic of Latvia
Continent: Europe
Area: 24,938 sq mi / 64,589 sq km
Population: 2,320,000
Population Density: 93 people per sq mi / 36 people per sq km
Capital: Riga

PHYSICAL:
Highest Point: Gaizina Kalns 1,024 ft / 312 m
Lowest Point: Baltic Sea 0 ft / 0 m (sea level)
Seas:
> Baltic: •forms part of the western coast of Latvia •feeds into the Kattegat

Gulfs:
> Gulf of Riga: • forms part of the northern and central coasts of Latvia •feeds into the Baltic Sea

L

Rivers:

Daugava: ●has its mouth in the Gulf of Riga ●extends into Belarus

POLITICAL:

Independence: August 21, 1991 (from the Soviet Union)

Former Name: Latvian Soviet Socialist Republic

Bordering Countries: Lithuania, Estonia, Russia, Belarus (4)

Administrative Divisions: Aizkraukles, Aluksnes, Balvu, Bauskas, Cesu, Daugavpils, Dobeles, Gulbenes, Jekabpils, Jelgavas, Kraslavas, Kuldigas, Liepajas, Limbazu, Ludzas, Madonas, Ogres, Preilu, Rezeknes, Rigas, Saldus, Talsu, Tukuma, Valkas, Valmieras, Ventspils (26 counties) ●Daugavpils, Jelgava, Jurmala, Liepaja, Rezekne, Riga, Ventspils (7 municipalities)

Ethnic/Racial Groups: Latvian, Russian, Belarusian, Ukrainian, Polish

Religion: Christianity (Lutheran, Roman Catholic, Russian Orthodox)

Languages: Latvian, Lithuanian, Russian

Currency: Latvian lat

Current President: Vaira Vike-Freiberga

Cities (capital, largest, or with at least a million people):

Riga: ●located in central Latvia ●city in the Riga municipality ●capital of Latvia ●most populated city in Latvia (733,000 people) ●chief port on the Daugava River

ENVIRONMENTAL/ECONOMIC:

Climate: maritime, wet and moderate winters

Natural Resources: peat, limestone, dolomite, amber, hydropower
Agricultural Products: grain, sugar beets, potatoes, vegetables, beef
Major Exports: wood and wood products, machinery and equipment, metals, textiles
Natural Hazards: floods, snowstorms, thunderstorms

LEBANON
Country Name: Lebanese Republic
Continent: Asia
Area: 4,036 sq mi / 10,452 sq km
Population: 4,198,000
Population Density: 1,040 people per sq mi / 402 people per sq km
Capital: Beirut

PHYSICAL:
Highest Point: Qurnat as Sawda 10,131 ft / 3,088 m
Lowest Point: Mediterranean Sea 0 ft / 0 m (sea level)
Mountain Ranges:
Anti-Lebanon : •located in eastern Lebanon •extend into Syria
Lebanon: •located in central Lebanon
Peaks (minimum elevation of 8,000 ft / 2,400 m):
Qurnat as Sawda: •located in the Lebanon Mountains •highest point in Lebanon
Valleys:
Bekaa: •located between the Lebanon and Anti-Lebanon Mountains

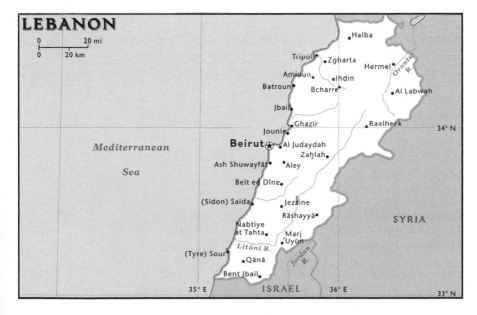

Seas:
Mediterranean: ●forms the western coast of Lebanon ●feeds into the Atlantic Ocean
Rivers:
Orontes: ●has its source in the Anti-Lebanon Mountains ●extends into Syria

POLITICAL:
Independence: November 22, 1943 (from French administration)
Bordering Countries: Syria, Israel (2)
Administrative Divisions: Beqaa, Beyrouth, Liban-Nord, Liban-Sud, Mont-Liban, Nabatiye (6 governorates)
Ethnic/Racial Groups: Arab, Armenian
Religions: Islam, Christianity
Languages: Arabic, French, English, Armenian
Currency: Lebanese pound
Current President: Emile Lahoud
Cities (capital, largest, or with at least a million people):
Beirut: ●located in western Lebanon ●city in the Beyrouth governorate ●capital of Lebanon ●most populated city in Lebanon (1,792,000 people) ●chief port on the Mediterranean Sea

ENVIRONMENTAL/ECONOMIC:
Climate: Mediterranean; mild to cool and wet winters/hot and dry summers, heavy winter snows in the mountains
Natural Resources: limestone, iron ore, salt, water-surplus, arable land
Agricultural Products: citrus, grapes, tomatoes, apples, sheep
Major Exports: foodstuffs and tobacco, textiles, chemicals, precious stones, metal products
Natural Hazards: dust storms, sandstorms

LESOTHO
Country Name: Kingdom of Lesotho
Continent: Africa
Area: 11,720 sq mi / 30,355 sq km
Population: 1,800,000
Population Density: 154 people per sq mi / 59 people per sq km
Capital: Maseru

PHYSICAL:
Highest Point: Thabana-Ntlenyana 11,424 ft / 3,482 m
Lowest Point: Orange/Makhaleng River junction 4,593 ft / 1,400 m
Mountain Ranges:
Drakensberg: ●cover most of the country ●extend into South Africa
Peaks (minimum elevation of 8,000 ft / 2,400 m):
Thabana-Ntlenyana: ●located in the Drakensberg ●highest point in Lesotho

Rivers:
    Orange: •has its source in the Drakensberg •extends into South Africa

POLITICAL:
Independence: October 4, 1966 (from the United Kingdom)
Former Name: Basutoland
Bordering Country: South Africa (1)
Administrative Divisions: Berea, Butha-Buthe, Leribe, Mafeteng, Maseru, Mohales Hoek, Mokhotlong, Qacha's Nek, Quthing, Thaba-Tseka (10 districts)
Ethnic/Racial Groups: predominantly Sotho
Religions: Christianity, indigenous beliefs
Languages: Sesotho, English, Zulu, Xhosa
Currency: loti, South African rand
Current Prime Minister: Pakalitha Mosisili
Cities (capital, largest, or with at least a million people):
    Maseru: • located in western Lesotho •city in the Maseru district •capital of Lesotho •most populated city in Lesotho (170,000 people) •on the edge of the Drakensberg

ENVIRONMENTAL/ECONOMIC:
Climate: temperate; cool to cold with dry winters/hot and wet summers
Natural Resources: water, agricultural and grazing lands, some diamonds and other minerals

Agricultural Products: corn, wheat, pulses, sorghum, livestock
Major Exports: manufactures, wool, mohair
Natural Hazards: droughts

LIBERIA
Country Name: Republic of Liberia
Continent: Africa
Area: 43,000 sq mi / 111,370 sq km
Population: 3,317,000
Population Density: 77 people per sq mi / 30 people per sq km
Capital: Monrovia

PHYSICAL:
Highest Point: Mount Wuteve 4,528 ft / 1,380 m
Lowest Point: Atlantic Ocean 0 ft / 0 m (sea level)
Oceans:
   Atlantic: •forms the southern coast of Liberia

POLITICAL:
Independence: July 26, 1847 (established as an independent republic)
Bordering Countries: Cote d'Ivoire, Guinea, Sierra Leone (3)
Administrative Divisions: Bomi, Bong, Gbarpolu, Grand Bassa, Grand Cape
   Mount, Grand Gedeh, Grand Kru, Lofa, Margibi, Maryland, Montserrado, Nimba,
   River Cess, River Gee, Sinoe (15 counties)

Ethnic/Racial Groups: Kpelle, Bassa, Dey, and other indigenous tribes
Religions: indigenous beliefs, Christianity, Islam
Languages: English, 20 ethnic languages
Currency: Liberian dollar
Current President: Gyude Bryant
Cities (capital, largest, or with at least a million people):
    Monrovia: •located in western Liberia •city in Montserrado county •capital of
        Liberia •most populated city in Liberia (572,000 people) •chief port on the
        Atlantic Ocean

ENVIRONMENTAL/ECONOMIC:
Climate: tropical; hot and humid with dry and moderate winters/wet summers
Natural Resources: iron ore, timber, diamonds, gold, hydropower
Agricultural Products: rubber, coffee, cacao, rice, sheep
Major Exports: rubber, timber, iron, diamonds, cacao
Natural Hazards: harmattan winds

LIBYA
Country Name: Great Socialist People's Libyan Arab Jamahiriya
Continent: Africa
Area: 679,362 sq mi / 1,759,540 sq km
Population: 5,499,000
Population Density: 8.1 people per sq mi / 3.1 people per sq km
Capital: Tripoli

PHYSICAL:
Highest Point: Bette 7,434 ft / 2,266 m
Lowest Point: Sabkhat Ghuzayyil 154 ft / 47 m below sea level
Mountain Ranges:
    Tibesti: •located in southern Libya •extend into Chad
Plateau Regions:
    Libyan Plateau: •located in northeastern Libya •extends into Egypt •arid plateau
        north of the Sahara
Depressions:
    Sabkhat Ghuzayyil: •located in northern Libya •lowest point in Libya
Deserts:
    Libyan: •covers much of eastern Libya •extends into Egypt and Sudan
    Sahara: •covers most of central and southern Libya •extends into Tunisia, Algeria,
        Niger, Chad, Sudan, and Egypt •largest desert in the world
Seas:
    Mediterranean: •forms part of the northern coast of Libya •feeds into the
        Atlantic Ocean

Gulfs:

Gulf of Sidra: •forms part of the northern coast of Libya •feeds into the Mediterranean Sea

POLITICAL:

Independence: December 24, 1951 (from Italy)

Bordering Countries: Egypt, Chad, Algeria, Tunisia, Sudan, Niger (6)

Regions:

Cyrenaica: •region in eastern Libya •includes part of the Sahara and the Libyan Desert

Fezzan: •region in southwestern Libya •includes part of the Sahara

Tripolitania: •region in northwestern Libya •south of the Mediterranean Sea •includes part of the Sahara

Administrative Divisions: Ajdabiya, Al Aziziyah, Al Fatih, Al Jabal al Akhdar, Al Jufrah, Al Khums, Al Kufrah, An Nuqat al Khams, Ash Shati, Awbari, Az Zawiyah, Banghazi, Darnah, Ghadamis, Gharyan, Misratah, Murzuq, Sabha, Sawfajjin, Surt, Tarabulus, Tarhunah, Tubruq, Yafran, Zlitan (25 municipalities)

Ethnic/Racial Groups: predominantly Arab-Berber

Religion: Islam (predominantly Sunni)

Languages: Arabic, Italian, English

Currency: Libyan dinar

Current President: Muammar Qaddafi

Cities (capital, largest, or with at least a million people):

Tripoli: • located in northwestern Libya •city in the Tarabulas municipality •capital

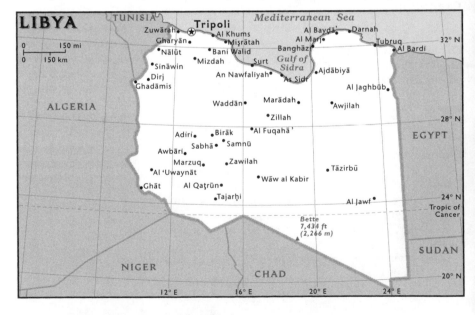

of Libya •most populated city in Libya (2,006,000 people) •chief port on the Mediterranean Sea

ENVIRONMENTAL/ECONOMIC:
Climate: Mediterranean along the coast; dry desert in the interior
Natural Resources: petroleum, natural gas, gypsum
Agricultural Products: wheat, barley, olives, dates, cattle
Major Exports: crude oil, refined petroleum products
Natural Disasters: ghibli winds, dust storms, sandstorms

LIECHTENSTEIN
Country Name: Principality of Liechtenstein
Continent: Europe
Area: 62 sq mi / 160 sq km
Population: 35,000
Population Density: 565 people per sq mi / 219 people per sq km
Capital: Vaduz

PHYSICAL:
Highest Point: Grauspitz 8,527 ft / 2,599 m
Lowest Point: Ruggeller Riet 1,411 ft / 430 m
Mountain Ranges:
    Alps: •cover most of Liechtenstein •extend into Switzerland and Austria

Peaks (minimum elevation of 8,000 ft / 2,400 m):
   Grauspitz: •located in the Alps •on the Liechtenstein-Switzerland border •highest point in Liechtenstein
Rivers:
   Rhine: • forms most of the Liechtenstein-Switzerland border •extends into Switzerland and Austria

POLITICAL:
Independence: January 23, 1719 (from the Holy Roman Empire)
Bordering Countries: Switzerland, Austria (2)
Administrative Divisions: Balzers, Eschen, Gamprin, Mauren, Planken, Ruggell, Schaan, Schellenberg, Triesen, Triesenberg, Vaduz (11 communes)
Ethnic/Racial Groups: Alemannic, Italian, Turkish
Religion: Christianity (Roman Catholic, Lutheran, Russian Orthodox, Protestant)
Languages: German, Alemannic dialect
Currency: Swiss franc
Current Prince: Hans Adam II
Cities (capital, largest, or with at least a million people):
   Vaduz: •located in western Liechtenstein •city in the Vaduz commune •capital of Liechtenstein •most populated city in Liechtenstein (5,000 people) •on the edge of the Alps •chief port on the Rhine River

ENVIRONMENTAL/ECONOMIC:
Climate: continental; cold winters/cool to moderate summers
Natural Resources: hydroelectric potential, arable land
Agricultural Products: wheat, barley, corn, potatoes, livestock
Major Exports: small specialty machinery, connectors for audio and video, parts for motor vehicles, dental products

LITHUANIA
Country Name: Republic of Lithuania
Continent: Europe
Area: 25,212 sq mi / 65,300 sq km
Population: 3,458,000
Population Density: 137 people per sq mi / 53 people per sq km
Capital: Vilnius

PHYSICAL:
Highest Point: Juozapines/Kalnas 958 ft / 292 m
Lowest Point: Baltic Sea 0 ft / 0 m (sea level)
Seas:
   Baltic: •forms the western coast of Lithuania •feeds into the Kattegat

Rivers:
    Nemunas: ●has its mouth in the Baltic Sea ●forms part of the Lithuania-
    Russia (Kaliningrad province) border ●extends into Belarus

POLITICAL:
Independence: March 11, 1990 (from the Soviet Union)
Former Name: Lithuanian Soviet Socialist Republic
Bordering Countries: Belarus, Latvia, Russia (Kaliningrad province), Poland (4)
Administrative Divisions: Alytaus, Kauno, Klaipedos, Marijampoles, Panevezio,
    Siauliu, Taurages, Telsiu, Utenos, Vilniaus (10 counties)
Ethnic/Racial Groups: Lithuanian, Russian, Polish, Belarusian
Religion: Christianity (Roman Catholic, Lutheran, Russian Orthodox, Protestant)
Languages: Lithuanian, Polish, Russian
Currency: litas
Current President: Valdas Adamkus
Cities (capital, largest, or with at least a million people):
    Vilnius: ●located in southeastern Lithuania ●city in Vilniaus county ●capital of
    Lithuania ●most populated city in Lithuania (549,000 people)

ENVIRONMENTAL/ECONOMIC:
Climate: transitional; maritime to continental; wet and moderate
Natural Resources: peat, arable land
Agricultural Products: grain, potatoes, sugar beets, flax, beef
Major Exports: mineral products, textiles and clothing, machinery and equipment, chemicals

LUXEMBOURG

Country Name: Grand Duchy of Luxembourg
Continent: Europe
Area: 998 sq mi / 2,586 sq km
Population: 452,000
Population Density: 453 people per sq mi / 175 people per sq km
Capital: Luxembourg

PHYSICAL:
Highest Point: Buurgplaatz 1,834 ft / 559 m
Lowest Point: Moselle (Mosel) River 436 ft / 133 m
Rivers:
 Moselle (Mosel): ●forms part of the Luxembourg-Germany border ●extends into
 Germany and France

POLITICAL:
Independence: 1839 (from the Netherlands)
Bordering Countries: Belgium, Germany, France (3)
Regions:
 Ardennes: ●forested plateau region in northern Luxembourg ●extends into Belgium
Administrative Divisions: Diekirch, Grevenmacher, Luxembourg (3 districts)
Ethnic/Racial Groups: mixture of French and German
Religion: Christianity (Roman Catholic)
Languages: Luxembourgish, German, French

Currency: euro
Current Prime Minister: Jean-Claude Juncker
Cities (capital, largest, or with at least a million people):
    Luxembourg: •located in southern Luxembourg •city in the Luxembourg district
        •capital of Luxembourg •most populated city in Luxembourg (77,000 people)

ENVIRONMENTAL/ECONOMIC:
Climate: modified continental; mild winters/cool summers
Natural Resources: iron ore, arable land
Agricultural Products: barley, oats, potatoes, wheat, livestock
Major Exports: machinery and equipment, steel products, chemicals, rubber
    products, glass
Natural Hazards: floods, thunderstorms

MACEDONIA

Country Name: Republic of Macedonia
Continent: Europe
Area: 9,928 sq mi / 25,713 sq km
Population: 2,059,000
Population Density: 207 people per sq mi / 80 people per sq km
Capital: Skopje

PHYSICAL:

Highest Point: Golem Korab 9,068 ft / 2,764 m
Lowest Point: Vardar River 164 ft / 50 m
Mountain Ranges:
   Pindus: •cover much of western Macedonia •extend into Albania and Greece
Peaks (minimum elevation of 8,000 ft / 2,400 m):
   Golem Korab: •located in the Pindus Mountains •on the Macedonia-Albania border
      •highest point in Macedonia
Lakes:
   Lake Ohrid: •located in southwestern Macedonia •on the edge of the Pindus
      Mountains •on the Macedonia-Albania border
   Lake Prespa: •located in southwestern Macedonia •surrounded by the Pindus
      Mountains •on the border with Albania and Greece

POLITICAL:

Independence: September 8, 1991 (from Yugoslavia)
Former Names: People's Republic of Macedonia, Socialist Republic of Macedonia
Bordering Countries: Greece, Serbia and Montenegro, Albania, Bulgaria (4)
Regions:
   Macedonia: •region that stretches across southern Macedonia •includes part of the
      Pindus Mountains •extends into Greece and Bulgaria
Administrative Divisions: Aracinovo, Bac, Belcista, Berovo, Bistrica, Bitola, Blatec,
   Bogdanci, Bogomila, Bogovinje, Bosilovo, Brvenica, Cair (Skopje), Capari, Caska,
   Cegrane, Centar (Skopje), Centar Zupa, Cesinovo, Cucer-Sandevo, Debar, Delcevo,
   Delogozdi, Demir Hisar, Demir Kapija, Dobrusevo, Dolna Banjica, Dolneni, Dorce
   Petrov (Skopje), Drugovo, Dzepciste, Gazi Baba (Skopje), Gevgelija, Gostivar, Gradsko,
   Ilinden, Izvor, Jegunovce, Kamenjane, Karbinci, Karpos (Skopje), Kavadarci, Kicevo,
   Kisela Voda (Skopje), Klecevce, Kocani, Konce, Kondovo, Konopiste, Kosel, Kratovo,
   Kriva Palanka, Krivogastani, Krusevo, Kuklis, Kukurecani, Kumanovo, Labunista,
   Lipkovo, Lozovo, Lukovo, Makedonska Kamenica, Makedonski Brod, Mavrovi Anovi,
   Meseista, Miravci, Mogila, Murtino, Negotino, Negotino-Polosko, Novaci, Novo Selo,

Oblesevo, Ohrid, Orasac, Orizari, Oslomej, Pehcevo, Petrovec, Plasnica, Podares, Prilep, Probistip, Radovis, Rankovce, Resen, Rosoman, Rostusa, Samokov, Saraj, Sipkovica, Sopiste, Sopotnica, Srbinovo, Star Dojran, Staravina, Staro Nagoricane, Stip, Struga, Strumica, Studenicani, Suto Orizari (Skopje), Sveti Nikole, Tearce, Tetovo, Topolcani, Valandovo, Vasilevo, Velesta, Veles, Vevcani, Vinica, Vitoliste, Vranestica, Vrapciste, Vratnica, Vrutok, Zajas, Zelenikovo, Zeleno, Zitose, Zletovo, Zrnovci (123 municipalities)

Ethnic/Racial Groups: Macedonian, Albanian, Turkish
Religions: Christianity (primarily Macedonian Orthodox), Islam
Languages: Macedonian, Albanian, Turkish
Currency: Macedonian denar
Current President: Branko Crvenkovski
Cities (capital, largest, or with at least a million people):
Skopje: •located in northern Macedonia •city encompasses 7 different municipalities •capital of Macedonia •most populated city in Macedonia (447,000 people)

ENVIRONMENTAL/ECONOMIC:

Climate: warm and dry summers/cold and snowy winters
Natural Resources: iron ore, copper, lead, zinc, chromite
Agricultural Products: rice, tobacco, wheat, corn, beef
Major Exports: food, beverages, tobacco, miscellaneous manufactures, iron and steel
Natural Hazards: earthquakes

MADAGASCAR

Country Name: Republic of Madagascar
Continent: Africa
Area: 226,658 sq mi / 587,041 sq km
Population: 16,980,000
Population Density: 75 people per sq mi / 29 people per sq km
Capital: Antananarivo

PHYSICAL:

Highest Point: Maromokotro 9,436 ft / 2,876 m
Lowest Point: Indian Ocean 0 ft / 0 m (sea level)
Peaks (minimum elevation of 8,000 ft / 2,400 m):
Maromokotro: •located in northeastern Madagascar •highest point in Madagascar
Oceans:
Indian: •forms the eastern coast of Madagascar
Channels:
Mozambique: •forms the western coast of Madagascar •separates the island of
Madagascar from mainland Africa
Islands:
Madagascar: •main island in Madagascar •bordered by the Indian Ocean and
Mozambique Channel

POLITICAL:

Independence: June 26, 1960 (from France)
Former Name: Malagasy Republic
Administrative Divisions: Antananarivo, Antsiranana, Fianarantsoa, Mahajanga, Toamasina, Toliara (6 provinces)
Ethnic/Racial Groups: Malagasy, Cotiers, French, Indian, Chinese
Religions: indigenous beliefs, Christianity, Islam
Languages: French, Malagasy
Currency: Malagasy franc
Current President: Marc Ravalomanana
Cities (capital, largest, or with at least a million people):
　Antananarivo: •located in central Madagascar •city in the Antananarivo province
　　•capital of Madagascar •most populated city in Madagascar (1,678,000 people)

ENVIRONMENTAL/ECONOMIC:

Climate: tropical along the coast; temperate inland; and in south
Natural Resources: graphite, chromite, coal, bauxite, salt
Agricultural Products: coffee, vanilla, sugarcane, cloves, livestock products
Major Exports: coffee, vanilla, shellfish, sugar, cotton cloth
Natural Hazards: cyclones, droughts, locust swarms

MALAWI

Country Name: Republic of Malawi
Continent: Africa
Area: 45,747 sq mi / 118,484 sq km
Population: 11,651,000
Population Density: 255 people per sq mi / 98 people per sq km
Capital: Lilongwe

PHYSICAL:

Highest Point: Sapitwa 9,843 ft / 3,000 m
Lowest Point: Shire River 121 ft / 37 m
Peaks (minimum elevation of 8,000 ft / 2,400 m):
　Sapitwa: •located in southeastern Malawi •highest point in Malawi
Valleys:
　Great Rift: •covers much of Malawi •extends into Zambia, Tanzania, and
　　Mozambique
Lakes:
　Lake Malawi: •covers most of eastern Malawi •located in the Great Rift Valley
　　•on the border with Tanzania and Mozambique •ninth largest lake in the world
Rivers:
　Shire: •has its source in Lake Malawi •extends into Mozambique

POLITICAL:
Independence: July 6, 1964 (from the United Kingdom)
Former Names: British Central African Protectorate, Nyasaland Protectorate, Nyasaland
Bordering Countries: Mozambique, Zambia, Tanzania (3)
Administrative Divisions: Balaka, Blantyre, Chikwawa, Chiradzulu, Chitipa, Dedza, Dowa, Karonga, Kasungu, Likoma, Lilongwe, Machinga (Kasupe), Mangochi, Mchinji, Mulanje, Mwanza, Mzimba, Nkhata Bay, Nkhotakota, Nsanje, Ntcheu, Ntchisi, Phalombe, Rumphi, Salima, Thyolo, Zomba (27 districts)
Ethnic/Racial Groups: Chewa, Nyanja, Tumbuka, Yao, Lomwe, Sena, Tonga, Ngoni, Ngonde
Religions: Christianity (Protestant, Roman Catholic), Islam
Languages: English, Chichewa
Currency: Malawian kwacha
Current President: Bingu wa Mutharika
Cities (capital, largest, or with at least a million people):
Lilongwe: •located in western Malawi •city in the Lilongwe district •capital of Malawi •most populated city in Malawi (587,000 people)

ENVIRONMENTAL/ECONOMIC:
Climate: subtropical, rainy/dry seasons
Natural Resources: limestone, arable land, hydropower, uranium, coal
Agricultural Products: tobacco, sugarcane, cotton, tea, groundnuts
Major Exports: tobacco, tea, sugar, cotton, coffee

MALAYSIA

Country Name: Malaysia
Continent: Asia
Area: 127,355 sq mi / 329,847 sq km
Population: 25,061,000
Population Density: 197 people per sq mi / 76 people per sq km
Capital: Kuala Lumpur

PHYSICAL:

Highest Point: Kinabalu 13,455 ft / 4,101 m
Lowest Point: South China Sea 0 ft / 0 m (sea level)
Peaks (minimum elevation of 8,000 ft / 2,400 m):
 Kinabalu: •located on the island of Borneo •highest point in Malaysia
Seas:
 Celebes: •forms part of the northeastern coast of the island of Borneo •feeds into
  the Philippine Sea
 South China: •forms the eastern coast of the Malay Peninsula and the northern
  coast of the island of Borneo •feeds into the Java and Philippine Seas
 Sulu: •forms part of the northeastern coast of the island of Borneo •feeds into the
  Celebes and South China Seas
Straits:
 Strait of Malacca: •forms the western coast of the Malay Peninsula •separates the
  Malay Peninsula from Indonesia •connects the Andaman and South China Seas

Singapore: •forms part of the southern coast of the Malay Peninsula •separates the
Malay Peninsula from Indonesia •connects the Strait of Malacca and the South
China Sea

Peninsulas:
Malay: •bordered by the Strait of Malacca, South China Sea, and Singapore Strait
•Thailand and Myanmar are located on the northern half

Islands:
Borneo: •largest of the Greater Sunda Islands •bordered by the South China, Sulu,
and Celebes Seas •parts of the island also belong to Brunei and Indonesia

POLITICAL:
Independence: August 31, 1957 (from the United Kingdom)
Former Name: Federation of Malaysia
Bordering Countries: Indonesia, Thailand, Brunei (3)
Regions:
Sabah: •region on the island of Borneo •east of the South China Sea •west of the Sulu Sea
Sarawak: •region on the island of Borneo •south of the South China Sea
Administrative Divisions: Johor, Kedah, Kelantan, Melaka, Negeri Sembilan,
Pahang, Perak, Perlis, Pulau Pinang, Sabah, Sarawak, Selangor, Terengganu (13 states)
•Labuan, Putrajaya, Wilayah Persekutuan (3 federal territories)
Ethnic/Racial Groups: Malay and other indigenous people, Chinese, East Indian
Religions: Islam, Buddhism, Daoism, Hinduism, Christianity, Sikh, Shamanism
Languages: Bahasa Melayu, English, Chinese dialects, other regional dialects and
indigenous languages
Currency: ringgit
Current Prime Minister: Abdullah bin Ahmad Badawi
Cities (capital, largest, or with at least a million people):
Kuala Lumpur: •located on the western side of the Malay Peninsula •city in
Wilayah Persekutuan federal territory •capital of Malaysia •most populated city
in Malaysia (1,352,000 people)

ENVIRONMENTAL/ECONOMIC:
Climate: tropical, annual monsoons
Natural Resources: tin, petroleum, timber, copper, iron ore
Agricultural Products: rubber, palm oil, cacao, rice
Major Exports: electronic equipment, petroleum and liquefied natural gas, wood and
wood products, palm oil
Natural Hazards: floods, landslides, forest fires

MALDIVES
Country Name: Republic of Maldives
Continent: Asia
Area: 115 sq mi / 298 sq km (smallest in Asia)

Population: 285,000 (smallest in Asia)
Population Density: 2,478 people per sq mi / 956 people per sq km
Capital: Male

PHYSICAL:
Highest Point: unnamed location 8 ft / 2.4 m
Lowest Point: Indian Ocean 0 ft / 0 m (sea level)
Oceans:
    Indian: •forms most of the southern coast of the Maldives
Seas:
    Arabian: •forms the northwestern coast of the Maldives •feeds into the Indian Ocean
    Laccadive: •forms much of the eastern coast of the Maldives •feeds into the
        Indian Ocean
Islands:
    Maldives: •main island group of the Maldives •bordered by the Indian Ocean,
        Arabian Sea, and Laccadive Sea •consists of many coral reefs and atolls

POLITICAL:
Independence: July 26, 1965 (from the United Kingdom)
Administrative Divisions: Alifu, Baa, Dhaalu, Faafu, Gaafu Alifu, Gaafu Dhaalu,
    Gnaviyani, Haa Alifu, Haa Dhaalu, Kaafu, Laamu, Lhaviyani, Meemu, Noonu, Raa,
    Seenu, Shaviyani, Thaa, Vaavu (19 atolls) •Male (1 first-order administrative division)
Ethnic/Racial Groups: Dravidian, Sinhalese, Arab
Religion: Islam (primarily Sunni)

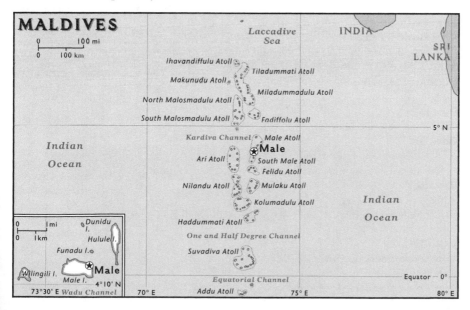

Languages: Maldivian Dhivehi, English
Currency: rufiyaa
Current President: Maumoon Abdul Gayoom
Cities (capital, largest, or with at least a million people):
Male: •located in central Maldives •city in the Maale first-order administrative division •capital of the Maldives •most populated city in the Maldives (83,000 people) •chief port on the Indian Ocean

ENVIRONMENTAL/ECONOMIC:
Climate: tropical hot and humid with dry/rainy seasons
Natural Resources: fish
Agricultural Products: coconuts, corn, sweet potatoes, fish
Major Exports: fish, clothing
Natural Hazards: rising tides (flood lowland islands)

MALI
Country Name: Republic of Mali
Continent: Africa
Area: 478,841 sq mi / 1,240,192 sq km
Population: 11,626,000
Population Density: 24 people per sq mi / 9.4 people per sq km
Capital: Bamako

PHYSICAL:
Highest Point: Hombori Tondo 3,789 ft / 1,155 m
Lowest Point: Senegal River 75 ft / 23 m
Grasslands/Prairies:
Sahel: •covers much of southern and central Mali •extends into Senegal, Guinea, Cote d'Ivoire, Burkina Faso, and Niger
Plateau Regions:
Adrar des Iforas: •located in the Sahara in northeastern Mali •extends into Algeria
Swamps:
Macina: •located in central Mali
Deserts:
Sahara: •covers most of northern Mali and parts of central Mali •extends into Mauritania, Algeria, and Niger •largest desert in the world
Rivers:
Niger: •extends into Guinea and Niger
Senegal: •extends into Guinea •flows across the Mali-Senegal-Mauritania border

POLITICAL:
Independence: September 22, 1960 (from France)
Former Names: French Sudan, Sudanese Republic
Bordering Countries: Mauritania, Algeria, Burkina Faso, Guinea, Niger, Cote d'Ivoire, Senegal (7)

MALI

Administrative Divisions: Gao, Kayes, Kidal, Koulikoro, Mopti, Segou, Sikasso, Tombouctou (8 regions)
Ethnic/Racial Groups: Mande, Peul, Voltaic, Tuareg and Moor, Songhai
Religions: Islam, indigenous beliefs
Languages: French, Bambara, numerous African languages
Currency: Communaute Financiere Africaine franc
Current President: Amadou Toure
Cities (capital, largest, or with at least a million people):
  Bamako: •located in southern Mali •city in the Koulikoro region •capital of Mali
    •most populated city in Mali (1,264,000 people) •chief port on the Niger River

ENVIRONMENTAL/ECONOMIC:
Climate: subtropical to arid with hot summers/cool winters
Natural Resources: gold, phosphates, kaolin, salt, limestone
Agricultural Products: cotton, millet, rice, corn, cattle
Major Exports: cotton, gold, livestock
Natural Hazards: harmattan haze, droughts, floods

MALTA
Country Name: Republic of Malta
Continent: Europe
Area: 122 sq mi / 316 sq km

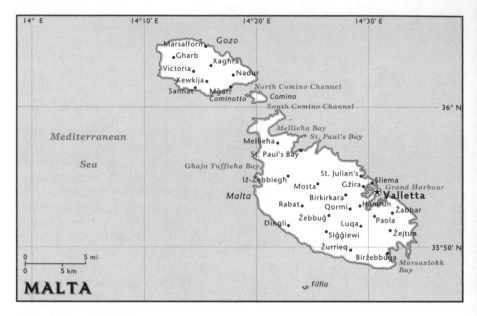

Population: 396,000
Population Density: 3,246 people per sq mi / 1,253 people per sq km
Capital: Valletta

PHYSICAL:
Highest Point: Ta'Dmejrek 830 ft / 253 m
Lowest Point: Mediterranean Sea 0 ft / 0 m (sea level)
Seas:
   Mediterranean: •forms most of the coast of Malta •feeds into the Atlantic Ocean
Channels:
   Malta: •forms the northern coast of Malta •separates Malta from Sicily
Islands:
   Gozo: •second largest island in Malta •borders the Mediterranean Sea and Malta
      Channel
   Malta: •largest island in Malta •borders the Mediterranean Sea and Malta Channel

POLITICAL:
Independence: September 21, 1964 (from the United Kingdom)
Ethnic/Racial Groups: predominantly Maltese
Religion: Christianity (primarily Roman Catholic)
Languages: Maltese, English
Currency: Maltese lira
Current President: Eddie Fenech Adami

Cities (capital, largest, or with at least a million people):
    Valletta: •located on the island of Malta •capital of Malta •most populated city in
        Malta (83,000 people) •chief port on the Malta Channel

ENVIRONMENTAL/ECONOMIC:
Climate: Mediterranean with mild and rainy winters/hot and dry summers
Natural Resources: limestone, salt, arable land
Agricultural Products: potatoes, cauliflower, grapes, wheat, pork
Major Exports: machinery and transport equipment, manufactures
Natural Hazards: droughts

MARSHALL ISLANDS
Country Name: Republic of the Marshall Islands
Continent: Australia/Oceania
Area: 70 sq mi / 181 sq km
Population: 55,000
Population Density: 786 people per sq mi / 304 people per sq km
Capital: Majuro

PHYSICAL:
Highest Point: unnamed location 33 ft / 10 m
Lowest Point: Pacific Ocean 0 ft / 0 m (sea level)
Oceans:
    Pacific: •surrounds the Marshall Islands
Islands:
    Ralik Chain: •western chain of atolls and coral islands in the Marshall Islands
        •surrounded by the Pacific Ocean
    Ratak Chain: •eastern chain of atolls and coral islands in the Marshall Islands
        •surrounded by the Pacific Ocean

POLITICAL:
Independence: October 21, 1986 (from United States administration)
Former Name: Marshall Islands District (part of the Trust Territory of the Pacific Islands)
Administrative Divisions: Ailinginae, Ailinglaplap, Ailuk, Arno, Aur, Bikar, Bikini,
    Bokak, Ebon, Enewetak, Erikub, Jabat, Jaluit, Jemo, Kili, Kwajalein, Lae, Lib,
    Likiep, Majuro, Maloelap, Mejit, Mili, Namorik, Namu, Rongelap, Rongrik, Toke,
    Ujae, Ujelang, Utirik, Wotho, Wotje (33 municipalities)
Ethnic/Racial Groups: Micronesian
Religion: Christianity (primarily Protestant)
Languages: English, Marshallese, Japanese
Currency: U.S. dollar
Current President: Kessai Note

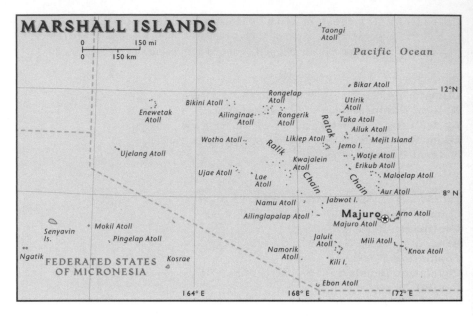

MARSHALL ISLANDS

0 ___ 150 mi
0 ___ 150 km

Pacific Ocean

Taongi Atoll

Bikar Atoll

12°N

Rongelap Atoll

Bikini Atoll

Enewetak Atoll

Ailinginae Atoll

Rongerik Atoll

Utirik Atoll

Taka Atoll

Ailuk Atoll

Ralik Chain

Ratak Chain

Wotho Atoll

Likiep Atoll

Jemo I.

Mejit Island

Ujelang Atoll

Kwajalein Atoll

Wotje Atoll

Erikub Atoll

Ujae Atoll

Lae Atoll

Maloelap Atoll

Aur Atoll

8° N

Namu Atoll

Jabwot I.

Ailinglapalap Atoll

Majuro

Majuro Atoll

Arno Atoll

Senyavin Is.

Mokil Atoll

Pingelap Atoll

Jaluit Atoll

Mili Atoll

Knox Atoll

Ngatik

FEDERATED STATES
OF MICRONESIA

Kosrae

Namorik Atoll

Kili I.

Ebon Atoll

164° E

168° E

172° E

Cities (capital, largest, or with at least a million people):
Majuro: •located in the Ratak Chain •city in the Majuro municipality •capital of the
Marshall Islands •most populated city in the Marshall Islands (25,000 people)
•chief port on the Pacific Ocean

ENVIRONMENTAL/ECONOMIC:
Climate: tropical; hot and humid
Natural Resources: coconut products, marine products, deep seabed minerals
Agricultural Products: coconuts, tomatoes, melons, taro, pigs
Major Exports: copra cake, coconut oil, handicrafts, fish
Natural Hazards: typhoons

MAURITANIA
Country Name: Islamic Republic of Mauritania
Continent: Africa
Area: 397,955 sq mi / 1,030,700 sq km
Population: 2,914,000
Population Density: 7.3 people per sq mi / 2.8 people per sq km
Capital: Nouakchott

PHYSICAL:
Highest Point: Kediet ej Jill 3,002 ft / 915 m
Lowest Point: Sebkha de Ndrhamcha 10 ft / 5 m below sea level

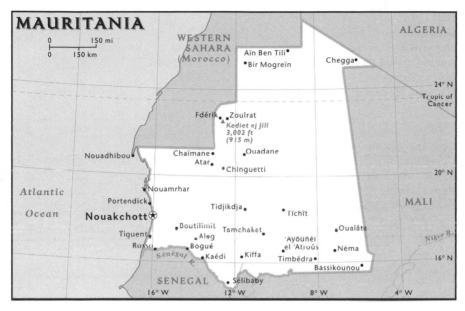

MAURITANIA

Deserts:
Sahara: •covers most of the country •extends into Algeria, Mali, and Western Sahara (claimed by Morocco) •largest desert in the world

Oceans:
Atlantic: •forms the western coast of Mauritania

Rivers:
Senegal: •has its mouth in the Atlantic Ocean •forms all of the Mauritania-Senegal border •extends into Mali

POLITICAL:
Independence: November 28, 1960 (from France)
Bordering Countries: Mali, Senegal, Algeria, Western Sahara (claimed by Morocco) (4)
Administrative Divisions: Adrar, Assaba, Brakna, Dakhlet Nouadhibou, Gorgol, Guidimaka, Hodh Ech Chargui, Hodh El Gharbi, Inchiri, Tagant, Tiris Zemmour, Trarza (12 regions) •Nouakchott (1 capital district)
Ethnic/Racial Groups: mixed Maur/black, Maur, black
Religion: predominantly Islam
Languages: Hassaniya Arabic, Wolof, Pulaar, Soninke, French
Currency: ouguiya
Current President: Maaouya Ould Sid Ahmed Taya
Cities (capital, largest, or with at least a million people):
Nouakchott: •located in southwestern Mauritania •city in the Nouakchott capital district •capital of Mauritania •most populated city in Mauritania (600,000 people) •chief port on the Atlantic Ocean

ENVIRONMENTAL/ECONOMIC:
Climate: desert; hot and dry
Natural Resources: iron ore, gypsum, copper, phosphate, diamonds
Agricultural Products: dates, millet, sorghum, rice, cattle
Major Exports: iron ore, fish and fish products, gold
Natural Hazards: sirocco winds, droughts

MAURITIUS
Country Name: Republic of Mauritius
Continent: Africa
Area: 788 sq mi / 2,040 sq km
Population: 1,221,000
Population Density: 1,549 people per sq mi / 599 people per sq km (most dense in Africa)
Capital: Port Louis

PHYSICAL:
Highest Point: Piton de la Riviere Noire, 2,710 ft / 826 m
Lowest Point: Indian Ocean 0 ft / 0 m (sea level)
Oceans:
   Indian: •surrounds Mauritius
Islands:
   Mauritius: •main island in Mauritius •surrounded by the Indian Ocean

POLITICAL:
Independence: March 12, 1968 (from the United Kingdom)
Administrative Divisions: Black River, Flacq, Grand Port, Moka, Pamplemousses, Plaines Wilhems, Port Louis, Riviere du Rempart, Savanne (9 districts) •Agalega Islands, Cargados Carajos Shoals, Rodrigues (3 dependencies north and east of Mauritius)
Ethnic/Racial Groups: Indo-Mauritian, Creole, Sino-Mauritian, Franco-Mauritian
Religions: Hinduism, Christianity (primarily Roman Catholic), Islam
Languages: English, French, Creole, Hindi, Urdu, Hakka, Bhojpuri
Currency: Mauritian rupee
Current President: Anerood Jugnauth
Cities (capital, largest, or with at least a million people):
   Port Louis: •located in northwestern Mauritius •city in the Port Louis district •capital of Mauritius •most populated city in Mauritius (143,000 people) •chief port on the Indian Ocean

ENVIRONMENTAL/ECONOMIC:
Climate: tropical, moderated by southeast trade winds; dry winters/hot and rainy summers
Natural Resources: arable land, fish
Agricultural Products: sugarcane, tea, corn, potatoes, bananas

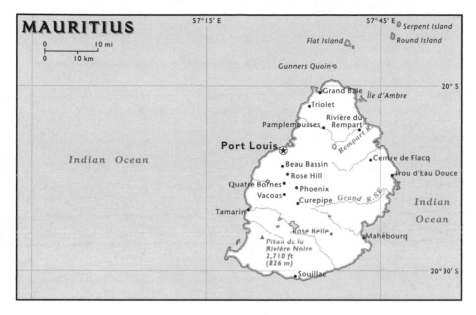

MAURITIUS

57°15' E   57°45' E   Serpent Island

0   10 mi
0   10 km

Flat Island   Round Island

Gunners Quoin

20° S

Grand Baie   Île d'Ambre
Triolet
Rivière du
Pamplemousses   Rempart

Port Louis

Rempart R.

Centre de Flacq
Beau Bassin
Rose Hill   Trou d'Eau Douce
Quatre Bornes
Phoenix
Vacoas
Curepipe   Grand R.S.E.

Indian Ocean

Indian
Ocean

Tamarin

Rose Belle
Piton de la
Rivière Noire
2,710 ft
(826 m)

Mahébourg

20° 30' S

Souillac

Major Exports: clothing and textiles, sugar, cut flowers, molasses
Natural Hazards: cyclones, maritime hazards

MEXICO
Country Name: United Mexican States
Continent: North America
Area: 758,449 sq mi / 1,964,375 sq km
Population: 104,878,000
Population Density: 138 people per sq mi / 53 people per sq km
Capital: Mexico City

PHYSICAL:
Highest Point: Pico de Orizaba 18,878 ft / 5,754 m
Lowest Point: Laguna Salada 33 ft / 10 m below sea level
Mountain Ranges:
    Sierra Madre: •located in southeastern Mexico •extend into Guatemala
    Sierra Madre del Sur: •located in southern Mexico
    Sierra Madre Occidental: •cover much of western Mexico
    Sierra Madre Oriental: •cover much of eastern Mexico
Peaks (minimum elevation of 8,000 ft / 2,400 m):
    Pico de Orizaba: •located in the Sierra Madre Oriental •highest point in Mexico
    Volcan Popocatepetl: •located in the Sierra Madre Oriental •active volcano

Deserts:
    Chihuahuan: •located in northern Mexico •east of the Sierra Madre Occidental •extends into the United States
    Sonoran: •located in northwestern Mexico •west of the Sierra Madre Occidental •extends into the United States

Oceans:
    Pacific: •forms most of the western coast of Mexico •forms part of the southern coast of Mexico

Seas:
    Caribbean: •forms most of the southeastern coast of Mexico •feeds into the Atlantic Ocean

Gulfs:
    Gulf of California: •forms part of the northwestern coast of Mexico •feeds into the Pacific Ocean
    Gulf of Mexico: •forms most of the eastern coast of Mexico •feeds into the Caribbean Sea and Atlantic Ocean
    Gulf of Tehuantepec: •forms part of the southern coast of Mexico •feeds into the Pacific Ocean

Lagoons:
    Laguna Madre: •located in northeastern Mexico •feeds into the Gulf of Mexico

Channels:
    Yucatan: •forms part of the eastern coast of Mexico •separates the Yucatan Peninsula from Cuba •connects the Gulf of Mexico and Caribbean Sea

Lakes:
    Lake Chapala: •located in southwestern Mexico •on the edge of Sierra Madre Occidental

Rivers:
    Balsas: •has its mouth in the Pacific Ocean •has its source in the Sierra Madre Oriental
    Rio Grande: •has its mouth in the Gulf of Mexico •forms much of the Mexico-United States border •extends into the United States

Peninsulas:
    Baja California: •bordered by the Pacific Ocean and Gulf of California
    Yucatan: •bordered by the Caribbean Sea, Gulf of Mexico, and Yucatan Channel

POLITICAL:
Independence: September 16, 1810 (from Spain)
Bordering Countries: United States, Guatemala, Belize (3)
Administrative Divisions: Aguascalientes, Baja California, Baja California Sur, Campeche, Chiapas, Chihuahua, Coahuila de Zaragoza, Colima, Durango, Guanajuato, Guerrero, Hidalgo, Jalisco, Mexico, Michoacan de Ocampo, Morelos, Nayarit, Nuevo Leon, Oaxaca, Puebla, Queretaro de Arteaga, Quintana Roo, San Luis Potosi, Sinaloa, Sonora, Tabasco, Tamaulipas, Tlaxcala, Veracruz-Llave, Yucatan, Zacatecas (31 states) •Distrito Federal (1 federal district)

Ethnic/Racial Groups: mestizo, Amerindian, white
Religion: Christianity (Roman Catholic, Protestant)
Languages: Spanish, Mayan, Nahuatl, other indigenous languages
Currency: Mexican peso
Current President: Vicente Fox Quesada
Cities (capital, largest, or with at least a million people):

Mexico City: •located in southern Mexico •city in the Distrito Federal and the Mexico state •capital of Mexico •most populated city in Mexico (19,013,000 people) •on the edge of the Sierra Madre Oriental

Guadalajara: •located in central Mexico •city in the Jalisco state •on the edge of the Sierra Madre Occidental

Puebla: •located in southern Mexico •city in the Puebla state •on the edge of the Sierra Madre Oriental

Ciudad Juarez: •located in northern Mexico •city in the Chihuahua state •chief port on the Rio Grande

Netzahualcoyotl: •located in southern Mexico •city in the Mexico state •on the edge of the Sierra Madre Oriental

Monterrey: •located in central Mexico •city in the Nuevo Leon state •on the edge of the Sierra Madre Oriental

Tijuana: •located in northwestern Mexico •city in the Baja California state •a major port on the Pacific Ocean

Leon: •located in central Mexico •city in the Guanajuato state •on the edge of the Sierra Madre Occidental

Climate: tropical to desert
Natural Resources: petroleum, silver, copper, gold, lead
Agricultural Products: corn, wheat, soybeans, rice, beef
Major Exports: manufactured goods, oil and oil products, silver, fruits, vegetables
Natural Hazards: tsunamis, volcanoes, earthquakes, hurricanes

MICRONESIA
Country Name: Federated States of Micronesia
Continent: Australia/Oceania
Area: 271 sq mi / 702 sq km
Population: 115,000
Population Density: 424 people per sq mi / 164 people per sq km
Capital: Palikir

PHYSICAL:
Highest Point: Dolohmwar 2,595 ft / 791 m
Lowest Point: Pacific Ocean 0 ft / 0 m (sea level)
Oceans:
Pacific: •surrounds Micronesia
Islands:
Caroline: •main island group in Micronesia •surrounded by the Pacific Ocean

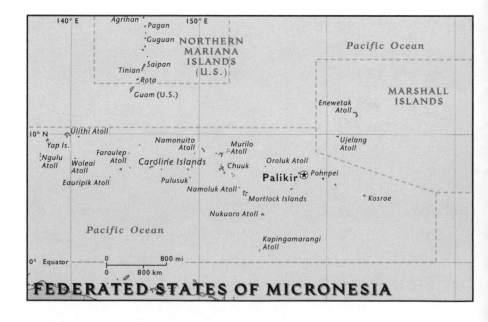

POLITICAL:

Independence: November 3, 1986 (from United States administration)
Former Names: Pnape, Truk, and Yap Districts (part of the Trust Territory of the Pacific Islands)
Administrative Divisions: Chuuk, Kosrae, Pohnpei, Yap (4 states)
Ethnic/Racial Groups: Micronesian, Polynesian
Religion: Christianity (Roman Catholic, Protestant)
Languages: English, Trukese, Pohnpeian, Yapese, Kosrean, Ulithian
Currency: U.S. dollar
Current President: Joseph Urusemal
Cities (capital, largest, or with at least a million people):
    Palikir: •located in eastern Micronesia •city in the Pohnpei state •capital of Micronesia •most populated city in Micronesia (7,000 people) •chief port on the Pacific Ocean

ENVIRONMENTAL/ECONOMIC:

Climate: tropical wet
Natural Resources: forests, marine products, deep-seabed minerals
Agricultural Products: black pepper, tropical fruits and vegetables, coconuts, cassava (tapioca), pigs
Major Exports: fish, garments, bananas, black pepper
Natural Hazards: typhoons

MOLDOVA

Country Name: Republic of Moldova
Continent: Europe
Area: 13,050 sq mi / 33,800 sq km
Population: 4,253,000
Population Density: 326 people per sq mi / 126 people per sq km
Capital: Chisinau

PHYSICAL:

Highest Point: Dealul Balanesti 1,411 ft / 430 m
Lowest Point: Nistru (Dniester) River 7 ft / 2 m
Grasslands/Prairies:
    Black Sea Lowland: •covers much of southern Moldova •extends into Ukraine and Romania
Rivers:
    Nistru (Dniester): •forms part of the Moldova-Ukraine border •extends into Ukraine
    Prut: •forms all of the Moldova-Romania border •extends into Ukraine •tributary of the Danube

MOLDOVA

0 ————— 50 mi
0 ————— 50 km

Briceni
Edineţ
Rîşcani
Soroca
Drochia
Camenca
Bălţi
Floreşti
Rezina
Ribniţa
Făleşti
Corneşti
Orhei
Călăraşi
Dubăsari
Grigoriopol
Chişinău ⊛
Tiraspol
Hînceşti
Bender
Slobozia
Cimişlia
Leova
Căuşeni
Iargara
Comrat
Basarabeasca
Congaz
Ceadir-Lunga
Cahul
Taraclia
Vulcăneşti

ROMANIA
UKRAINE
Dniester Bay
Black Sea

Dniester R.
Prut R.
Siret R.
Răut R.
Siret R.
Danube R.

48° N
46° N
26° E
28° E
30° E
32° E

POLITICAL:

Independence: August 27, 1991 (from the Soviet Union)

Former Names: Soviet Socialist Republic of Moldova, Moldavia

Bordering Countries: Ukraine, Romania (2)

Regions:

   Bessarabia: •region that covers most of the country •includes part of the Black Sea Lowland •extends into Ukraine

Administrative Divisions: Balti, Cahul, Chisinau, Edinet, Lapusna, Orhei, Soroca, Tighina, Ungheni (9 counties) •Chisinau (1 municipality) •Gagauzia (1 autonomous territorial unit) •Stinga Nistrului, also known as Transdniestria (1 territorial unit)

Ethnic/Racial Groups: Moldovan/Romanian, Ukrainian, Russian

Religion: Christianity (predominantly Eastern Orthodox)

Languages: Moldovan, Russian, Gagauz

Currency: Moldovan leu

Current President: Vladimir Voronin

Cities (capital, largest, or with at least a million people):

   Chisinau: •located in central Moldova •city in the Chisinau municipality •capital of Moldova •most populated city in Moldova (662,000 people)

ENVIRONMENTAL/ECONOMIC:

Climate: moderate winters/warm summers

Natural Resources: lignite, phosphorites, gypsum, arable land, limestone

Agricultural Products: vegetables, fruits, wine, grain, beef

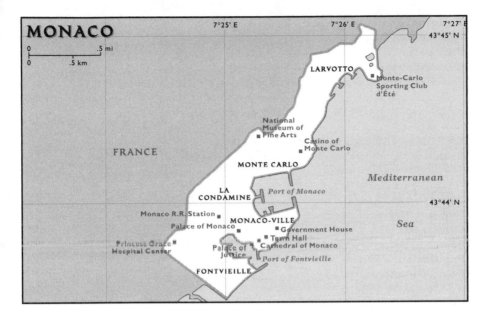

MONACO

0 .5 mi
0 .5 km

7°25' E 7°26' E 7°27' E
43°45' N

LARVOTTO

Monte-Carlo
Sporting Club
d'Été

FRANCE

National
Museum of
Fine Arts

Casino of
Monte Carlo

MONTE CARLO

Mediterranean

LA
CONDAMINE

Port of Monaco

43°44' N

Monaco R.R. Station
Palace of Monaco

MONACO-VILLE

Government House

Sea

Princess Grace
Hospital Center

Palace of
Justice

Town Hall

Cathedral of Monaco

Port of Fontvieille

FONTVIEILLE

Major Exports: foodstuffs, textiles, machinery
Natural Hazards: landslides

MONACO
Country Name: Principality of Monaco
Continent: Europe
Area: 1 sq mi / 2 sq km
Population: 34,000
Population Density: 34,000 people per sq mi / 17,000 people per sq km (most
dense in Europe and the world)
Capital: Monaco

PHYSICAL:
Highest Point: Mont Agel 459 ft / 140 m
Lowest Point: Mediterranean Sea 0 ft / 0 m (sea level)
Seas:
Mediterranean: •forms the coast of Monaco •feeds into the Atlantic Ocean

POLITICAL:
Independence: 1419 (beginning of rule by the House of Grimaldi)
Bordering Country: France (1)
Ethnic/Racial Groups: French, Monegasque, Italian

Religion: Christianity (primarily Roman Catholic)
Languages: French, English, Italian, Monegasque
Currency: euro
Current Prince: Rainier III
Cities (capital, largest, or with at least a million people):
  Monaco: •makes up the whole country •capital of Monaco •most populated city in Monaco (34,000 people) •chief port on the Mediterranean Sea

ENVIRONMENTAL/ECONOMIC:
Climate: Mediterranean with mild and wet winters/hot and dry summers

MONGOLIA
Country Name: Mongolia
Continent: Asia
Area: 603,909 sq mi / 1,564,116 sq km
Population: 2,500,000
Population Density: 4.1 people per sq mi / 1.6 people per sq km (least dense in Asia and the world)
Capital: Ulaanbaatar

PHYSICAL:
Highest Point: Nayramadlin Orgil 14,350 ft / 4,374 m
Lowest Point: Hoh Nuur 1,699 ft / 518 m

Mountain Ranges:
 Altay: ● cover an area from northwestern to southern Mongolia ● extend into China
   and Russia
 Eastern Sayans: ● located in northern Mongolia ● extend into Russia
 Hangayn: ● located in central Mongolia
Peaks (minimum elevation of 8,000 ft / 2,400 m):
 Nayramadlin Orgil: ● located in the Altay Mountains ● on the Mongolia-Russia border
   ● highest point in Mongolia
Plateau Regions:
 Mongolian Plateau: ● covers much of eastern Mongolia ● extends into China
Deserts:
 Gobi: ● covers much of southern Mongolia ● extends into China

POLITICAL:
Independence: July 11, 1921 (from China)
Former Name: Outer Mongolia
Bordering Countries: China, Russia (2)
Administrative Divisions: Arhangay, Bayanhongor, Bayan-Olgiy, Bulgan, Darhan
 Uul, Dornod, Dornogovi, Dundgovi, Dzavhan, Govi-Altay, Govi-Sumber, Hentiy,
 Hovd, Hovsgol, Omnogovi, Orhon, Ovorhangay, Selenge, Suhbaatar, Tov, Uvs
 (21 provinces) ● Ulaanbataar (1 municipality)
Ethnic/Racial Groups: Mongol, Turkic
Religions: Tibetan Buddhism, Lamaism
Languages: Khalkha Mongol, Turkic, Russian
Currency: togrog (tugrik)
Current President: Natsagiyn Bagabandi
Cities (capital, largest, or with at least a million people):
 Ulaanbaatar: ● located in northern Mongolia ● city in the Ulaanbataar municipality
   ● capital of Mongolia ● most populated city in Mongolia (812,000 people)

ENVIRONMENTAL/ECONOMIC:
Climate: desert; continental
Natural Resources: oil, coal, copper, molybdenum, tungsten
Agricultural Products: wheat, barley, potatoes, forage crops, sheep
Major Exports: copper, gold, livestock, animal products, cashmere, wool, hides
Natural Hazards: dust storms, grassland and forest fires, droughts, *zud* (harsh
 winter conditions)

MOROCCO
Country Name: Kingdom of Morocco
Continent: Africa
Area: 274,461 sq mi / 710,850 sq km
Population: 30,366,000

Population Density: 111 people per sq mi / 43 people per sq km
Capital: Rabat

PHYSICAL:
Highest Point: Jebel Toubkal 13,665 ft / 4,165 m
Lowest Point: Sebkha Tah 180 ft / 55 m below sea level
Mountain Ranges:
    Atlas: ●cover an area from southwestern to northeastern Morocco ●extend into
        Algeria
Peaks (minimum elevation of 8,000 ft / 2,400 m):
    Jebel Toubkal: ●located in the Atlas Mountains ●highest point in Morocco
Plateau Regions:
    Hauts Plateaux: ●located in northeastern Morocco ●extend into Algeria ●high
        basin surrounded by the Atlas Mountains
Oceans:
    Atlantic: ●forms the western coast of Morocco
Seas:
    Alboran (sometimes labeled as part of the Mediterranean): ●forms the northeastern
        coast of Morocco ●feeds into the Atlantic Ocean
Straits:
    Strait of Gibraltar: ●forms part of the northern coast of Morocco ●separates
        Morocco from Spain ●connects the Alboran Sea and Atlantic Ocean

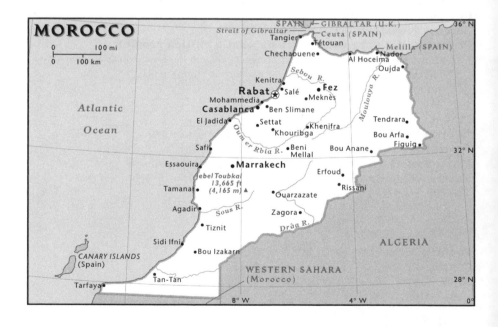

POLITICAL:
Independence: March 2, 1956 (from France)
Bordering Countries: Algeria, Western Sahara (claimed by Morocco) (2)
Administrative Divisions: Agadir, Al Hoceima, Azilal, Beni Mellal, Ben Slimane,
Boulemane, Chaouen, El Jadida, El Kelaa des Sraghna, Er Rachidia, Essaouira, Fez,
Figuig, Guelmim, Ifrane, Kenitra, Khemisset, Khenifra, Khouribga, Laayoune,
Larache, Marrakech, Meknes, Nador, Ouarzazate, Oujda, Safi, Settat, Sidi Kacem,
Tangier, Tan-Tan, Taounate, Taroudannt, Tata, Taza, Tetouan, Tiznit (37 provinces)
●Casablanca, Rabat-Sale (2 wilayas)
Ethnic/Racial Groups: predominantly Arab-Berber
Religion: predominantly Islam
Languages: Arabic, Berber dialects, French
Currency: Moroccan dirham
Current King: Mohammed VI
Cities (capital, largest, or with at least a million people):
Casablanca: ●located in northwestern Morocco ●city in the Casablanca wilaya ●most
populated city in Morocco (3,673,000 people) ●a major port on the Atlantic Ocean
Rabat: ●located in northwestern Morocco ●city in the Rabat-Sale wilaya ●capital of
Morocco (1,759,000 people)
Fez: ●located in northern Morocco ●city in the Fez province ●on the edge of the
Atlas Mountains

ENVIRONMENTAL/ECONOMIC:
Climate: Mediterranean; more extreme in the mountains
Natural Resources: phosphates, iron ore, manganese, lead, zinc
Agricultural Products: barley, wheat, citrus, wine, livestock
Major Exports: clothing, fish, inorganic chemicals, transistors, crude materials
Natural Hazards: earthquakes, droughts

MOZAMBIQUE
Country Name: Republic of Mozambique
Continent: Africa
Area: 308,642 sq mi / 799,380 sq km
Population: 17,479,000
Population Density: 57 people per sq mi / 22 people per sq km
Capital: Maputo

PHYSICAL:
Highest Point: Monte Binga 7,992 ft / 2,436 m
Lowest Point: Indian Ocean 0 ft / 0 m (sea level)
Valleys:
Great Rift: ●located in central Mozambique ●extends into Malawi and Tanzania

MOZAMBIQUE

Oceans:
  Indian: •forms part of the northeastern coast of Mozambique •forms much of the southern coast of Mozambique
Channels:
  Mozambique: •forms most of the eastern coast of Mozambique •separates Mozambique and Madagascar
Lakes:
  Lake Cahora Bassa: •located in northwestern Mozambique •fed by the Zambezi River •formed by the Cahora Bassa Dam
  Lake Malawi: •located in northern Mozambique •located in the Great Rift Valley •on the border with Malawi •extends into Tanzania
Rivers:
  Chire (Shire): •tributary of the Zambezi River •extends into Malawi
  Limpopo: •has its mouth in the Indian Ocean •extends into South Africa and Zimbabwe
  Luangwa: •tributary of the Zambezi River •forms part of the Mozambique-Zambia border •extends into Zambia
  Save: •has its mouth in the Mozambique Channel •extends into Zimbabwe
  Zambeze (Zambezi): •has its mouth in the Mozambique Channel •extends into Zambia

POLITICAL:
Independence: June 25, 1975 (from Portugal)
Former Name: Portuguese East Africa
Bordering Countries: Malawi, Zimbabwe, Tanzania, South Africa, Zambia, Swaziland (6)

Administrative Divisions: Cabo Delgado, Gaza, Inhambane, Manica, Maputo, Nampula, Niassa, Sofala, Tete, Zambezia (10 provinces) ●Maputo (1 city)
Ethnic/Racial Groups: Shangaan, Chockwe, Manyika, Sena, Makua
Religions: indigenous beliefs, Christianity, Islam
Languages: Portuguese, indigenous dialects
Currency: metical
Current President: Joaquim Alberto Chissano
Cities (capital, largest, or with at least a million people):
  Maputo: ●located in southern Mozambique ●city in the Maputo province
    ●capital of Mozambique ●most populated city in Mozambique (1,221,000 people)
    ●chief port on the Indian Ocean

ENVIRONMENTAL/ECONOMIC:
Climate: tropical to subtropical
Natural Resources: coal, titanium, natural gas, hydropower, tantalum
Agricultural Products: cotton, cashew nuts, sugarcane, tea, beef
Major Exports: aluminum, prawns, cashews, cotton, sugar
Natural Hazards: droughts, cyclones, floods

MYANMAR
Country Name: Union of Myanmar
Continent: Asia
Area: 261,218 sq mi / 676,552 sq km

Population: 49,481,000
Population Density: 189 people per sq mi / 73 people per sq km
Capital: Yangon (Rangoon)

PHYSICAL:
Highest Point: Hkakabo Razi 19,295 ft / 5,881 m
Lowest Point: Andaman Sea 0 ft / 0 m (sea level)
Mountain Ranges:
Hengduan Shan: •located in northern Myanmar •extend into China
Peaks (minimum elevation of 8,000 ft / 2,400 m):
Hkakabo Razi: •located in the Hengduan Shan •on the Myanmar-China border •highest point in Myanmar
Plateau Regions:
Shan Plateau: •located in eastern Myanmar
Seas:
Andaman: •forms most of the southern coast of Myanmar •feeds into the Bay of Bengal and Indian Ocean
Bays:
Bay of Bengal: •forms most of the western coast of Myanmar •feeds into the Indian Ocean
Rivers:
Ayeyarwady: •has its mouth in the Andaman Sea
Mekong: •forms all of the Myanmar-Laos border •extends into China and Laos
Salween (Thanlwin): •has its mouth in the Andaman Sea •forms part of the Myanmar-Thailand border •extends into China
Deltas:
Mouths of the Ayeyarwady: •mouth of the Ayeyarwady River •feeds into the Andaman Sea

POLITICAL:
Independence: January 4, 1948 (from the United Kingdom)
Former Names: Burma, Socialist Republic of the Union of Burma
Bordering Countries: China, Thailand, India, Laos, Bangladesh (5)
Administrative Divisions: Chin, Kachin, Kayin, Kayah, Mon, Rakhine, Shan (7 states) •Ayeyarwady, Bago, Magway, Mandalay, Sagaing, Tanintharyi, Yangon (7 districts)
Ethnic/Racial Groups: Burman, Shan, Karen, Rahkine, Chinese
Religions: Buddhism, Christianity, Islam
Languages: Burmese, minor languages
Currency: kyat
Current Chairman: Than Shwe

Cities (capital, largest, or with at least a million people):
   Yangon: •located in central Myanmar •city in the Yangon district •capital of Myanmar
      •most populated city in Myanmar (3,874,000 people) •chief port on the Andaman Sea
   Mandalay: •located in central Myanmar •city in the Mandalay district •chief port
      on the Ayeyarwady River

ENVIRONMENTAL/ECONOMIC:
Climate: tropical monsoon with hot and rainy summers/mild winters
Natural Resources: petroleum, timber, tin, antimony, zinc
Agricultural Products: rice, pulses, beans, sesame, hardwood (teak)
Major Exports: natural gas, wood products, pulses, beans, fish
Natural Hazards: earthquakes, cyclones, floods, landslides, droughts

NAMIBIA

Country Name: Republic of Namibia
Continent: Africa
Area: 318,261 sq mi / 824,292 sq km
Population: 1,927,000
Population Density: 6.1 people per sq mi / 2.3 people per sq km (least dense in Africa)
Capital: Windhoek

PHYSICAL:
Highest Point: Brandberg 8,441 ft / 2,573 m
Lowest Point: Atlantic Ocean 0 ft / 0 m (sea level)
Mountain Ranges:
    Kaokoveld: •located in northwestern Namibia
Peaks (minimum elevation of 8,000 ft / 2,400 m):
    Brandberg: •located in the Kaokoveld •highest point in Namibia
Deserts:
    Kalahari: •covers much of eastern Namibia •extends into Botswana and South Africa
    Namib: •located along the western coast of Namibia

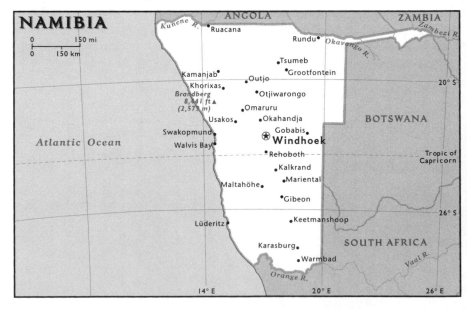

Oceans:
    Atlantic: •forms the western coast of Namibia
Rivers:
    Okavango: •forms part of the Namibia-Angola border •extends into Angola
        and Botswana
    Orange: •has its mouth in the Atlantic Ocean •forms part of the Namibia-South
        Africa border •extends into South Africa
Regions:
    Kaukau Veld: •lowland region in northeastern Namibia •extends into Botswana
        •north of the Kalahari Desert
    Skeleton Coast: •region in western Namibia •includes part of the Atlantic coast
        •west of the Namib Desert

POLITICAL:
Independence: March 21, 1990 (from South African administration)
Former Names: German Southwest Africa, South-West Africa
Bordering Countries: Angola, Botswana, South Africa, Zambia (4)
Regions:
    Caprivi Strip: •region in northeastern Namibia •panhandle bordered on the north
        by Angola and Zambia and on the south by Botwana •extends as far east as
        Zimbabwe
    Damaraland: •region that covers much of central Namibia •includes part of the
        Kaokoveld and the Namib Desert
    Great Namaland: •region that covers much of southern Namibia •includes part of
        the Namib Desert
    Ovamboland: •region in northern Namibia •includes part of the Kaokoveld
Administrative Divisions: Caprivi, Erongo, Hardap, Karas, Khomas, Kunene,
    Ohangwena, Okavango, Omaheke, Omusati, Oshana, Oshikoto, Otjozondjupa (13 regions)
Ethnic/Racial Groups: Ovambo, Kavangos, Herero, Damara, white
Religions: Christianity, indigenous beliefs
Languages: English, Afrikaans, German, indigenous languages
Currency: Namibian dollar, South African rand
Current President: Sam Nujoma
Cities (capital, largest, or with at least a million people):
    Windhoek: •located in central Namibia •city in the Khomas region •capital of
        Namibia •most populated city in Namibia (237,000 people)

ENVIRONMENTAL/ECONOMIC:
Climate: desert, hot and dry
Natural Resources: diamonds, copper, uranium, gold, lead
Agricultural Products: millet, sorghum, peanuts, livestock, fish
Major Exports: diamonds, copper, gold, zinc, lead
Natural Hazards: droughts

NAURU

Country Name: Republic of Nauru
Continent: Australia/Oceania
Area: 8 sq mi / 21 sq km (smallest in Australia/Oceania)
Population: 12,000
Population Density: 1,500 people per sq mi / 571 people per sq km (most dense in Australia/Oceania)
Capital: Yaren

PHYSICAL:

Highest Point: unnamed location 229 ft / 70 m
Lowest Point: Pacific Ocean 0 ft / 0 m (sea level)
Oceans:
 Pacific: •surrounds Nauru

POLITICAL:

Independence: January 31, 1968 (from Australia/New Zealand/United Kingdom administered UN trusteeship)
Former Name: Pleasant Island
Administrative Divisions: Aiwo, Anabar, Anetan, Anibare, Baiti, Boe, Buada, Denigomodu, Ewa, Ijuw, Meneng, Nibok, Uaboe, Yaren (14 districts)
Ethnic/Racial Groups: Nauruan, other Pacific Islander, Chinese, European
Religion: Christianity (Protestant, Roman Catholic)
Languages: Nauruan, English

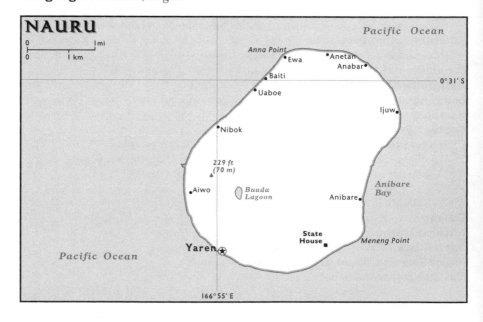

Currency: Australian dollar
Current President: Ludwig Scotty
Cities (capital, largest, or with at least a million people):
    Yaren: ●located in southern Nauru ●city in the Yaren district ●capital of Nauru
       ●most populated city in Nauru (11,300 people) ●chief port on the Pacific Ocean

ENVIRONMENTAL/ECONOMIC:

Climate: tropical; monsoonal with rainy/dry seasons
Natural Resources: phosphates, fish
Agricultural Products: coconuts
Major Exports: phosphates
Natural Hazards: droughts

NEPAL

Country Name: Kingdom of Nepal
Continent: Asia
Area: 56,827 sq mi / 147,181 sq km
Population: 25,164,000
Population Density: 443 people per sq mi / 171 people per sq km
Capital: Kathmandu

PHYSICAL:

Highest Point: Mount Everest 29,035 ft / 8,850 m

Lowest Point: Kanchan Kalan 230 ft / 70 m
Mountain Ranges:
Himalaya: •cover much of northern Nepal •extend into China and India
Peaks (minimum elevation of 8,000 ft / 2,400 m):
Annapurna: •located in the Himalaya
Cho Oyu: •located in the Himalaya •on the Nepal-China border
Dhaulagiri: •located in the Himalaya
Everest: •located in the Himalaya •on the Nepal-China border •highest point in the world
Kanchenjunga: • located in the Himalaya •on the Nepal-India border
Lhotse: •located in the Himalaya
Makalu • located in the Himalaya •on the Nepal-China border
Manaslu: •located in the Himalaya

POLITICAL:
Independence: 1768 (unified by Prithvi Narayan Shah)
Bordering Countries: India, China (2)
Administrative Divisions: Bagmati, Bheri, Dhawalagiri, Gandaki, Janakpur, Karnali, Kosi, Lumbini, Mahakali, Mechi, Narayani, Rapti, Sagarmatha, Seti (14 zones)
Ethnic/Racial Groups: Brahman, Chetri, Newar, Gurung, Magar, Tamang, Rai, Limbu, Sherpa, Tharu
Religions: Hinduism, Buddhism, Islam
Languages: Nepali, English, many other languages and dialects
Currency: Nepalese rupee
Current King: Gyanendra
Cities (capital, largest, or with at least a million people):
Kathmandu: •located in central Nepal •city in the Bagmati zone •capital of Nepal •most populated city in Nepal (741,000 people) •on the edge of the Himalaya

ENVIRONMENTAL/ECONOMIC:
Climate: mountainous with cool summers and harsh winters in the north; subtropical with mild winters in the south
Natural Resources: quartz, water, timber, hydropower, scenic beauty
Agricultural Products: rice, corn, wheat, sugarcane, milk
Major Exports: carpets, clothing, leather goods, jute goods, grain
Natural Hazards: severe thunderstorms, floods, landslides, drought, long monsoon seasons

NETHERLANDS
Country Name: Kingdom of the Netherlands
Continent: Europe
Area: 16,034 sq mi / 41,528 sq km
Population: 16,237,000
Population Density: 1,013 people per sq mi / 341 people per sq km
Capital: Amsterdam

PHYSICAL:
Highest Point: Vaalserberg 1,056 ft / 322 m
Lowest Point: Zuidplaspolder 23 ft / 7 m below sea level
Seas:

North: •forms much of the western and northern coasts of the Netherlands •feeds into the Atlantic Ocean

Wadden: •forms part of the northern coast of the Netherlands •feeds into the North Sea

Lakes:

IJsselmeer: •located in northwestern Netherlands

Rivers:

Maas: •has its mouth in the North Sea •forms part of the Netherlands-Belgium border •extends into Belgium

Rhine: •has its mouth in the North Sea •extends into Germany

Schelde: •has its mouth in the Westerschelde estuary •extends into Belgium

Deltas:

Westerschelde estuary: •mouth of the Schelde River •feeds into the North Sea

Islands:

Flevoland: •island in IJsselmeer Lake

West Frisian: •island chain off the northern coast of the Netherlands •bordered by the North and Wadden Seas

POLITICAL:
Independence: 1579 (from Spain)
Bordering Countries: Germany, Belgium (2)
Administrative Divisions: Drenthe, Flevoland, Friesland, Gelderland, Groningen, Limburg, Noord-Brabant, Noord-Holland, Overijssel, Utrecht, Zeeland, Zuid-Holland (12 provinces)
Ethnic/Racial Groups: predominantly Dutch
Religions: Christianity (Roman Catholic, Protestant), Islam
Languages: Dutch, Frisian
Currency: euro
Current Queen: Beatrix
Cities (capital, largest, or with at least a million people):
   Amsterdam: ●located in western Netherlands ●city in the Noord-Holland province ●capital of the Netherlands ●most populated city in the Netherlands (1,145,000 people) ●chief port on IJsselmeer Lake

ENVIRONMENTAL/ECONOMIC:
Climate: temperate marine with cool summers/mild winters
Natural Resources: natural gas, petroleum, peat, limestone, salt
Agricultural Products: grains, potatoes, sugar beets, fruits, livestock
Major Exports: machinery and equipment, chemicals, fuels, foodstuffs
Natural Hazards: floods

NEW ZEALAND
Country Name: New Zealand
Continent: Australia/Oceania
Area: 104,454 sq mi / 270,534 sq km
Population: 4,008,000
Population Density: 38 people per sq mi / 15 people per sq km
Capital: Wellington

PHYSICAL:
Highest Point: Mount Cook 12,316 ft / 3,754 m
Lowest Point: Pacific Ocean 0 ft / 0 m (sea level)
Mountain Ranges:
   Southern Alps: ●cover much of New Zealand ●located on South Island
Peaks (minimum elevation of 8,000 ft / 2,400 m):
   Mount Cook: ●located in the Southern Alps ●highest point in New Zealand
   Mount Ruapehu: ●located in the Southern Alps
Oceans:
   Pacific: ●forms most of the eastern coast of New Zealand
Seas:
   Tasman: ●forms most of the western coast of New Zealand ●feeds into the Pacific Ocean

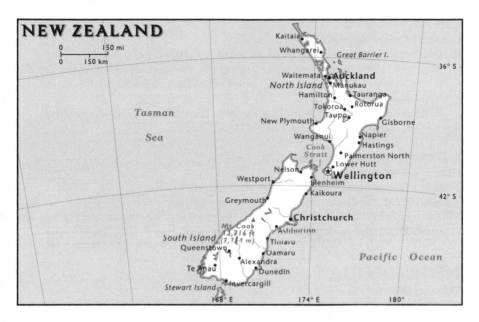

NEW ZEALAND

0 —————— 150 mi
0 —————— 150 km

Tasman

Sea

Kaitaia
Whangarei
Great Barrier I.
36° S

Waitemata ●Auckland
North Island ●Manukau
Hamilton ●Tauranga
Tokoroa ●Rotorua
Taupo
New Plymouth ●Gisborne
Wanganui ●Napier
Cook ●Hastings
Strait ● Palmerston North
Nelson ●Lower Hutt
Westport ⊕Wellington
Blenheim
Greymouth ●Kaikoura
42° S

●Christchurch

Mt. Cook ●Ashburton
13,316 ft
South Island (3,764 m) ●Timaru
Queenstown ●Oamaru
●Alexandra
Te Anau ●Dunedin
Stewart Island ●Invercargill
168° E   174° E   180°

Pacific   Ocean

Bays:
> Bay of Plenty: •forms part of the northern coast of North Island •feeds into the Pacific Ocean
> Canterbury Bight: •forms part of the eastern coast of South Island •feeds into the Pacific Ocean

Straits:
> Cook: •forms much of the inner coast of New Zealand •separates North and South Islands •connects the Tasman Sea and Pacific Ocean

Islands:
> North: •second largest island in New Zealand •bordered by the Pacific Ocean, Tasman Sea, Bay of Plenty, and Cook Strait
> South: •largest island in New Zealand •bordered by the Pacific Ocean, Tasman Sea, Canterbury Bight, and Cook Strait

POLITICAL:

Independence: September 26, 1907 (from the United Kingdom)

Administrative Divisions: Auckland, Bay of Plenty, Canterbury, Gisborne, Hawke's Bay, Manawatu-Wanganui, Marlborough, Nelson, Northland, Otago, Southland, Taranaki, Tasman, Waikato, Wellington, West Coast (16 regions)

Ethnic/Racial Groups: New Zealand European (Kiwi), Maori (indigenous), other European, Pacific Islander

Religion: Christianity (Protestant, Roman Catholic)

Languages: English, Maori

Currency: New Zealand dollar
Current Prime Minister: Helen Clark
Cities (capital, largest, or with at least a million people):
> Auckland: •located on North Island •city in the Auckland region •most populated city in New Zealand (1,102,000 people) •chief port on the Pacific Ocean and Tasman Sea
> Wellington: •located on North Island •city in the Wellington region •capital city (343,000 people) •chief port on the Cook Strait

ENVIRONMENTAL/ECONOMIC:
Climate: temperate
Natural Resources: natural gas, iron ore, sand, coal, timber
Agricultural Products: wheat, barley, potatoes, pulses, wool
Major Exports: dairy products, meat, wood and wood products, fish, chemicals
Natural Hazards: earthquakes, volcanoes

NICARAGUA

Country Name: Republic of Nicaragua
Continent: North America
Area: 50,193 sq mi / 130,000 sq km
Population: 5,482,000
Population Density: 109 people per sq mi / 42 people per sq km
Capital: Managua

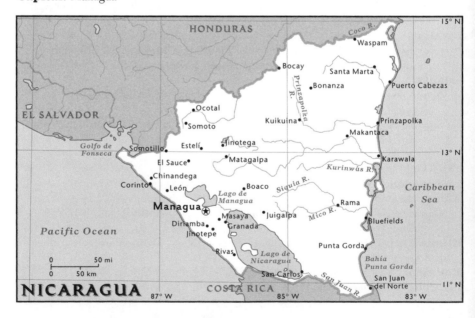

PHYSICAL:

Highest Point: Pico Mogotan 7,999 ft / 2,438 m
Lowest Point: Pacific Ocean 0 ft / 0 m (sea level)
Oceans:
  Pacific: •forms most of the western coast of Nicaragua
Seas:
  Caribbean: •forms the eastern coast of Nicaragua •feeds into the Atlantic Ocean
Gulfs:
  Gulf of Fonseca: •forms part of the northwestern coast of Nicaragua •feeds into the Pacific Ocean
Lakes:
  Lake Managua: •located in western Nicaragua
  Lake Nicaragua: •located in southwestern Nicaragua •largest lake in Central America
Regions:
  Mosquito Coast: • lowland region in eastern Nicaragua •borders the Caribbean coast •extends into Honduras

POLITICAL:

Independence: September 15, 1821 (from Spain)
Bordering Countries: Honduras, Costa Rica (2)
Administrative Divisions: Boaco, Carazo, Chinandega, Chontales, Esteli, Granada, Jinotega, Leon, Madriz, Managua, Masaya, Matagalpa, Nueva Segovia, Rio San Juan, Rivas (15 departments) •Atlantico Norte, Atlantico Sur (2 autonomous regions)
Ethnic/Racial Groups: mestizo, white, black, Amerindian
Religion: Christianity (Roman Catholic, Protestant)
Languages: Spanish, English, indigenous languages
Currency: gold cordoba
Current President: Enrique Bolanos
Cities (capital, largest, or with at least a million people):
  Managua: •located in western Nicaragua •city in the Managua department •capital of Nicaragua •most populated city in Nicaragua (1,098,000 people) •chief port on Lake Managua

ENVIRONMENTAL/ECONOMIC:

Climate: tropical in the lowlands; cooler in the highlands
Natural Resources: gold, silver, copper, tungsten, lead
Agricultural Products: coffee, bananas, sugarcane, cotton, beef
Major Exports: coffee, shrimp and lobster, cotton, tobacco, bananas
Natural Hazards: earthquakes, volcanoes, landslides, hurricanes

NIGER

Country Name: Republic of Niger
Continent: Africa
Area: 489,191 sq mi / 1,267,000 sq km
Population: 12,073,000
Population Density: 25 people per sq mi / 9.5 people per sq km
Capital: Niamey

PHYSICAL:
Highest Point: Monts Bagzane 6,634 ft / 2,022 m
Lowest Point: Niger River 656 ft / 200 m
Mountain Ranges:
   Air: •located in central Niger
Grasslands/Prairies:
   Sahel: •covers much of southern Niger •extends into Mali, Burkina Faso, Benin, Nigeria, and Chad
Plateau Regions:
   Plateau of Djado: •located in northeastern Niger •desert basin in the Sahara
Deserts:
   Sahara: •covers much of northern and central Niger •extends into Mali, Algeria, Libya, and Chad •largest desert in the world
   Talak: •located in western Niger •extends into Mali and Algeria
   Tenere: •covers an area from northern to southeastern Niger •extends into Algeria

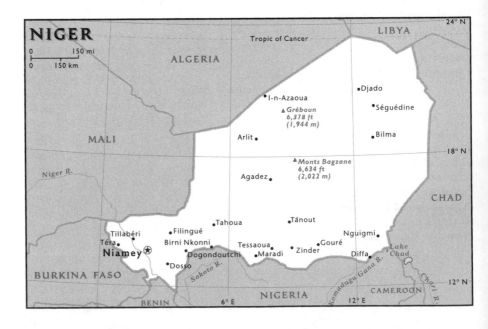

Rivers:
Niger: •forms part of the Niger-Benin border •extends into Mali and Nigeria

POLITICAL:
Independence: August 3, 1960 (from France)
Bordering Countries: Nigeria, Chad, Algeria, Mali, Burkina Faso, Libya, Benin (7)
Administrative Divisions: Agadez, Diffa, Dosso, Maradi, Tahoua, Tillaberi,
    Zinder (7 departments) •Niamey (1 capital district)
Ethnic/Racial Groups: Hausa, Djerma, Fula, Tuareg, Beri Beri (Kanouri)
Religions: Islam, indigenous beliefs, Christianity
Languages: French, Hausa, Djerma
Currency: Communaute Financiere Africaine franc
Current President: Tandja Mamadou
Cities (capital, largest, or with at least a million people):
Niamey: •located in southwestern Niger •city in the Niamey capital district •capital of
    Niger •most populated city in Niger (890,000 people) •chief port on the Niger River

ENVIRONMENTAL/ECONOMIC:
Climate: desert, hot and dry; tropical in the far south
Natural Resources: uranium, coal, iron ore, tin, phosphates
Agricultural Products: cowpeas, cotton, peanuts, millet, cattle
Major Exports: uranium ore, livestock, cowpeas, onions
Natural Hazards: droughts

NIGERIA
Country Name: Federal Republic of Nigeria
Continent: Africa
Area: 356,669 sq mi / 923,768 sq km
Population: 133,882,000 (largest in Africa)
Population Density: 375 people per sq mi / 145 people per sq km
Capital: Abuja

PHYSICAL:
Highest Point: Chappal Wadi 7,936 ft / 2,419 m
Lowest Point: Gulf of Guinea 0 ft / 0 m (sea level)
Mountain Ranges:
Adamawa: •located in southeastern Nigeria •extends into Cameroon
Grasslands/Prairies:
Sahel: •covers much of northern Nigeria •extends into Benin, Niger, Chad, and
    Cameroon
Sokoto Plains: •located in northwestern Nigeria
Plateau Regions:
Jos: •located in central Nigeria
Plateau of Yorubaland: •located in western Nigeria

Gulfs:
  Gulf of Guinea: • forms part of the southern coast of Nigeria • feeds into the Atlantic Ocean
Bays:
  Bight of Benin: • forms the southwestern coast of Nigeria • feeds into the Gulf of Guinea
  Bight of Bonny: • forms the southeastern coast of Nigeria • feeds into the Gulf of Guinea
Lakes:
  Kainji Reservoir: • located in western Nigeria • formed by the Kainji Dam • fed by the Niger River
Rivers:
  Benue: • tributary of the Niger River • extends into Cameroon
  Niger: • has its mouth in the Gulf of Guinea • extends into Niger
Deltas:
  Niger Delta: • mouth of the Niger River • ends in the Gulf of Guinea, the Bight of Benin, and the Bight of Bonny
Dams:
  Kainji: • on the Niger River • forms Kainji Reservoir • in western Nigeria

POLITICAL:
Independence: October 1, 1960 (from the United Kingdom)
Bordering Countries: Cameroon, Niger, Benin, Chad (4)
Administrative Divisions: Abia, Adamawa, Akwa Ibom, Anambra, Bauchi, Bayelsa, Benue, Borno, Cross River, Delta, Ebonyi, Edo, Ekiti, Enugu, Gombe, Imo, Jigawa,

Kaduna, Kano, Katsina, Kebbi, Kogi, Kwara, Lagos, Nassarawa, Niger, Ogun, Ondo, Osun, Oyo, Plateau, Rivers, Sokoto, Taraba, Yobe, Zamfara (36 states) •Abuja Federal Capital Territory (1 territory)
Ethnic/Racial Groups: more than 250 native African groups
Religions: Islam, Christianity, indigenous beliefs
Languages: English, Hausa, Yoruba, Igbo, Fulani
Currency: naira
Current President: Olusegun Obasanjo
Cities (capital, largest, or with at least a million people):
  Lagos: •located in southwestern Nigeria •city in the Lagos state •most populated city in Nigeria (9,954,000 people) •chief port on the Bight of Benin
  Ibadan: •located in southwestern Nigeria •city in the Oyo state •on the edge of the Plateau of Yorubaland
  Kano: •located in northern Nigeria •city in the Kano state • located in the Sahel
  Kaduna: •located in central Nigeria •city in the Kaduna state
  Port Harcourt: •located in southern Nigeria •city in the Rivers state
  Benin: •located in southwestern Nigeria •city in the Edo state
  Maiduguri: •located in northeastern Nigeria •city in the Borno state
  Abuja: •located in central Nigeria •city in the Abuja Federal Capital Territory •capital of Nigeria (452,000 people)

ENVIRONMENTAL/ECONOMIC:
Climate: equatorial in the south; tropical in the center; arid in the north
Natural Resources: natural gas, petroleum, tin, columbite, iron ore
Agricultural Products: cacao, peanuts, palm oil, corn, cattle
Major Exports: petroleum and petroleum products, cacao, rubber
Natural Hazards: droughts, floods

NORWAY
Country Name: Kingdom of Norway
Continent: Europe
Area: 125,004 sq mi / 323,758 sq km
Population: 4,568,000
Population Density: 37 people per sq mi / 14 people per sq km
Capital: Oslo

PHYSICAL:
Highest Point: Galdhopiggen 8,100 ft / 2,469 m
Lowest Point: Norwegian Sea 0 ft / 0 m (sea level)
Mountain Ranges:
  Kjolen: •cover much of Norway •extend into Sweden and Finland
Peaks (minimum elevation of 8,000 ft / 2,400 m):
  Galdhopiggen: •located in the Kjolen •highest point in Norway

Plateau Regions:
   Maanselka: •located in northeastern Norway •extends into Sweden and Finland •large basin west of the Kjolen
Seas:
   Barents: •forms part of the northeastern coast of Norway •feeds into the Arctic Ocean
   North: •forms much of the southwestern coast of Norway •feeds into the Atlantic Ocean
   Norwegian: •forms most of the western coast of Norway •feeds into the Atlantic and Arctic Oceans
Channels:
   Skagerrak: •forms much of the southern coast of Norway •separates Norway from Denmark •connects the Kattegat and North Sea

POLITICAL:
Independence: June 7, 1905 (from Sweden)
Bordering Countries: Sweden, Finland, Russia (3)
Regions:
   Lapland: •region in northern Norway •includes part of the Kjolen •extends into Sweden and Finland
Administrative Divisions: Akershus, Aust-Agder, Buskerud, Finnmark, Hedmark, Hordaland, More og Romsdal, Nordland, Nord-Trondelag, Oppland, Oslo, Ostfold, Rogaland, Sogn og Fjordane, Sor-Trondelag, Telemark, Troms, Vest-Agder, Vestfold (19 counties)
External Territories: Bouvet Island, Jan Mayen, Svalbard

Ethnic/Racial Groups: Norwegian, Sami
Religion: Christianity (Evangelical Lutheran)
Languages: Norwegian
Currency: Norwegian krone
Current President: King Harald V
Cities (capital, largest, or with at least a million people):
  Oslo: •located in southeastern Norway •city in the Oslo province •capital of
  Norway •most populated city in Norway (795,000 people) •southeast of the
  Kjolen •chief port on the Skagerrak

ENVIRONMENTAL/ECONOMIC:
Climate: temperate along the coast, moderated by North Atlantic Current; cooler and
  rainier in the interior
Natural Resources: petroleum, natural gas, iron ore, copper, lead
Agricultural Products: barley, wheat, potatoes, pork, fish
Major Exports: petroleum and petroleum products, machinery and equipment,
  metals, chemicals, ships
Natural Hazards: rockslides, avalanches

OMAN

Country Name: Sultanate of Oman
Continent: Asia
Area: 119,500 sq mi / 309,500 sq km
Population: 2,637,000
Population Density: 22 people per sq mi / 8.5 people per sq km
Capital: Muscat

PHYSICAL:

Highest Point: Jabal Shams 9,777 ft / 2,980 m
Lowest Point: Arabian Sea 0 ft / 0 m (sea level)
Peaks (minimum elevation of 8,000 ft / 2,400 m):
   Jabal Shams: •located in northern Oman •highest point in Oman
Deserts:
   Rub al Khali: •located in western Oman •extends into Saudi Arabia, Yemen, and
      United Arab Emirates
Seas:
   Arabian: •forms most of the southern and eastern coasts of Oman •feeds into
      the Indian Ocean
Gulfs:
   Gulf of Oman: •forms most of the northern coast of Oman •feeds into the Arabian Sea
   Persian: •forms part of the northwestern coast of Oman •feeds into the Gulf
      of Oman
Straits:
   Strait of Hormuz: •forms part of the northwestern coast of Oman •separates Oman
      from Iran •connects the Persian Gulf and Gulf of Oman

POLITICAL:

Independence: 1650 (from Portugal)
Former Name: Muscat and Oman
Bordering Countries: Saudi Arabia, United Arab Emirates, Yemen (3)
Administrative Divisions: Ad Dakhiliyah, Al Batinah, Al Wusta, Ash Sharqiyah,
   Az Zahirah, Masqat (Muscat) (6 regions) •Musandam, Zufar (2 governorates)
Ethnic/Racial Groups: Arab, Baluchi, South Asian, African
Religions: Islam (Ibadhi, Sunni, Shiite), Hinduism
Languages: Arabic, English, Baluchi, Urdu, Indian dialects
Currency: Omani rial
Current Sultan: Qaboos bin Said Al Said

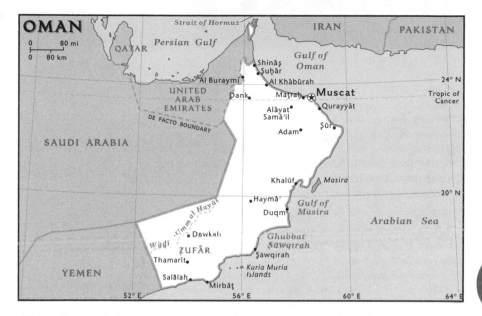

OMAN

0 ——— 80 mi
0 ——— 80 km

Strait of Hormuz
Persian Gulf
QATAR
Gulf of Oman
IRAN
PAKISTAN
Shinās
Şuḥār
Al Buraymī
Al Khābūrah
24° N
UNITED ARAB EMIRATES
Dank
Maṭraḥ
Muscat
Tropic of Cancer
Alāyat
Samā'il
Qurayyāt
DE FACTO BOUNDARY
Adam
Şūr
SAUDI ARABIA
Khalūf
Masira
20° N
Haymā'
Gulf of Masira
Duqm
Arabian Sea
Umm al Hayal
Dawkah
Ghubbat Şawqirah
Wādī
ZUFĀR
Şawqirah
Thamarīt
Kuria Muria Islands
YEMEN
Salālah
Mirbāṭ
52° E
56° E
60° E
64° E

Cities (capital, largest, or with at least a million people):

Muscat: ●located in northeastern Oman ●city in the Masqaṭ region ●capital of Oman ●most populated city in Oman (638,000 people) ●chief port on the Gulf of Oman

ENVIRONMENTAL/ECONOMIC:

Climate: dry desert; hot and humid along the coast, hot and dry in the interior; summer monsoon in the far south

Natural Resources: petroleum, copper, asbestos, marble, limestone

Agricultural Products: dates, limes, bananas, alfalfa, camels

Major Exports: petroleum, re-exports, fish, metals, textiles

Natural Hazards: sandstorms, dust storms, droughts

PAKISTAN

Country Name: Islamic Republic of Pakistan
Continent: Asia
Area: 307,374 sq mi / 796,095 sq km
Population: 149,147,000
Population Density: 485 people per sq mi / 187 people per sq km
Capital: Islamabad

PHYSICAL:

Highest Point: K2 28,251 ft / 8,611 m
Lowest Point: Arabian Sea 0 ft / 0 m (sea level)
Mountain Ranges:

Central Makran: ●located in southwestern Pakistan
Himalaya: ●located in northeastern Pakistan ●extend into China and India
Hindu Kush: ●cover parts of northern Pakistan ●extend into Afghanistan
Karakoram: ●located in northeastern Pakistan ●extend into China and India

Peaks (minimum elevation of 8,000 ft / 2,400 m):

Broad Peak: ●located in the Karakoram Range
Gasherbrum I: ●located in the Karakoram Range

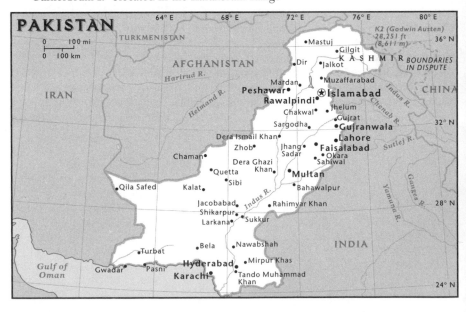

Gasherbrum II: ●located in the Karakoram Range

K2: ●located in the Karakoram Range ●on the Pakistan-China border ●highest point in Pakistan ●also called Godwin Austen

Nanga Parbat: ●located in the Himalaya

Passes:

Khyber: ●located in the Safed Koh Range in the Hindu Kush ●crosses from Pakistan into Afghanistan

Grasslands/Prairies:

Punjab Plains: ●located in eastern Pakistan ●extend into India

Deserts:

Thar: ●covers much of eastern Pakistan ●extends into India

Seas:

Arabian: ●forms most of the southern coast of Pakistan ●feeds into the Indian Ocean

Rivers:

Indus: ●has its mouth in the Arabian Sea ●extends into India and China

Deltas:

Mouths of the Indus: ●mouth of the Indus River ●feeds into the Arabian Sea

POLITICAL:

Independence: August 14, 1947 (from the United Kingdom)

Former Name: West Pakistan

Bordering Countries: India, Afghanistan, Iran, China (4)

Regions:

Kashmir: ●located in northeastern Pakistan ●includes parts of the Himalaya, the Hindu Kush, and the Karakoram Range ●extends into India

Baluchistan: ●located in southwestern Pakistan ●includes most of the Central Makran Range ●extends into Iran

Administrative Divisions: Balochistan, North-West Frontier, Punjab, Sindh (4 provinces) ●Federally Administered Tribal Areas (1 territory) ●Islamabad Capital Territory (1 capital territory)

Ethnic/Racial Groups: Punjabi, Sindhi, Pashtun, Baloch

Religions: Islam, Christianity, Hinduism

Languages: Punjabi, Sindhi, Siraiki, Pashtu, Urdu, English

Currency: Pakistani rupee

Current President: Pervez Musharraf

Cities (capital, largest, or with at least a million people):

Karachi: ●located in southern Pakistan ●city in the Sindh province ●most populated city in Pakistan (10,889,000 people) ●chief port on the Arabian Sea

Lahore: ●located in eastern Pakistan ●city in the Punjab province ●in the center of the Punjab Plains

Faisalabad: ●located in eastern Pakistan ●city in the Punjab province ●in the center of the Punjab Plains

Rawalpindi: ●located in eastern Pakistan ●city in the Punjab province● in the center of the Punjab Plains

Multan: ●located in eastern Pakistan ●city in the Punjab province ●in the southwestern part of the Punjab Plains
Hyderabad: ●located in southeastern Pakistan ●city in the Sindh province ●chief port on the Indus River
Gujranwala: ●located in eastern Pakistan ●city in the Punjab province ●in the northern part of the Punjab Plains
Peshawar: ●located in northwestern Pakistan ●city in the North-West Frontier province
Islamabad: ●located in northern Pakistan ●city in the Punjab province ●capital city of Pakistan (698,000 people)

ENVIRONMENTAL/ECONOMIC:
Climate: mostly desert; temperate in the northwest; arctic at high elevations
Natural Resources: land, natural gas, petroleum, coal, iron ore
Agricultural Products: cotton, wheat, rice, sugarcane, milk
Major Exports: textiles, rice, leather, sporting goods, carpets and rugs
Natural Hazards: earthquakes, floods

PALAU
Country Name: Republic of Palau
Continent: Australia/Oceania
Area: 189 sq mi / 489 sq km
Population: 20,000
Population Density: 106 people per sq mi / 41 people per sq km
Capital: Koror

PHYSICAL:
Highest Point: Mount Ngerchelchuus 794 ft / 242 m
Lowest Point: Pacific Ocean 0 ft / 0 m (sea level)
Oceans:
Pacific: ●forms the eastern coast of Palau
Seas:
Philippine: ●forms the western coast of Palau ●feeds into the Pacific Ocean
Islands:
Babelthuap: ●largest island in Palau ●bordered by the Pacific Ocean and Philippine Sea

POLITICAL:
Independence: October 1, 1994 (from United States administration)
Former Name: Palau District (part of the Trust Territory of Pacific Islands)
Administrative Divisions: Aimeliik, Airai, Angaur, Hatobohei, Kayangel, Koror, Melekeiok, Ngaraard, Ngarchelong, Ngardmau, Ngatpang, Ngchesar, Ngeremlengui, Ngiwal, Peleliu, Sonsoral (16 states)
Ethnic/Racial Groups: Palauan, Asian, white
Religions: Christianity (Roman Catholic, Protestant), Modekngei (indigenous)

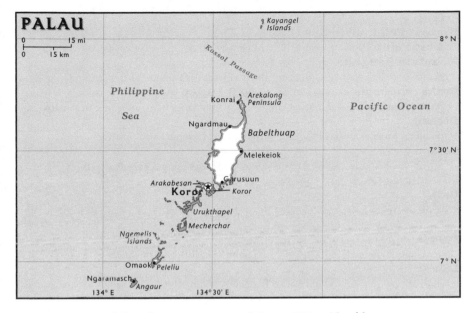

Kayangel
Islands

8° N

Kossol Passage

Philippine

Konrai
Arekalong
Peninsula

Pacific Ocean

Sea

Ngardmau

Babelthuap

7° 30' N

Melekeiok

Arakabesan
Garusuun

Koror
Koror

7° 30' N

Urukthapel

Mecherchar

Ngemelis
islands

7° N

Omaok Peleliu

Ngaramasch
Angaur

134° E
134° 30' E

Languages: English, Palauan, Japanese, and three additional local languages
Currency: U.S. dollar
Current President: Kuniwo Nakamura
Cities (capital, largest, or with at least a million people):
Koror: •located on a small island south of Babelthuap •city in the Koror state •capital of Palau •most populated city in Palau (14,000 people) •chief port on the Philippine Sea and Pacific Ocean

ENVIRONMENTAL/ECONOMIC:
Climate: tropical; hot and humid with rainy/dry seasons
Natural Resources: forests, minerals, marine products, deep-seabed minerals
Agricultural Products: coconuts, copra, cassava (tapioca), sweet potatoes
Major Exports: shellfish, tuna, copra, garments
Natural Hazards: typhoons

PANAMA
Country Name: Republic of Panama
Continent: North America
Area: 29,157 sq mi / 75,517 sq km
Population: 2,981,000
Population Density: 102 people per sq mi / 39 people per sq km
Capital: Panama City

PHYSICAL:

Highest Point: Volcan Baru 11,400 ft / 3,475 m
Lowest Point: Pacific Ocean 0 ft / 0 m (sea level)
Mountain Ranges:

Cordillera de Talamanca: ●covers much of western Panama ●extends into Costa Rica
Peaks (minimum elevation of 8,000 ft / 2,400 m):

Volcan Baru: ●located in the Cordillera de Talamanca ●highest point in Panama
Oceans:

Pacific: ●forms much of the southern coast of Panama
Seas:

Caribbean: ●forms most of the northern coast of Panama ●feeds into the
Atlantic Ocean
Gulfs:

Gulf of Panama: ●forms much of the southern coast of Panama ●feeds into the
Pacific Ocean
Canals:

Panama: ●connects the Gulf of Panama and Caribbean Sea
Lakes:

Lake Bayano: ●located in eastern Panama
Lake Gatun: ●located in central Panama ●near the end of the Panama Canal

POLITICAL:

Independence: November 3, 1903 (from Colombia)
Bordering Countries: Costa Rica, Colombia (2)

Administrative Divisions: Bocas del Toro, Chiriqui, Cocle, Colon, Darien, Herrera, Los Santos, Panama, Veraguas (9 provinces) • San Blas (1 territory)
Ethnic/Racial Groups: mestizo, Amerindian-West Indian, white, Amerindian
Religion: Christianity (Roman Catholic, Protestant)
Languages: Spanish, English
Currency: balboa, U.S. dollar
Current President: Mireya Elisa Moscoso Rodriguez
Cities (capital, largest, or with at least a million people):
Panama City: • located in central Panama • city in the Panama province • capital of Panama • most populated city in Panama (930,000 people)

ENVIRONMENTAL/ECONOMIC:
Climate: tropical marine; hot and humid with rainy/dry seasons
Natural Resources: copper, mahogany forests, shrimp, hydropower
Agricultural Products: bananas, rice, corn, coffee, livestock
Major Exports: bananas, shrimp, sugar, coffee, clothing
Natural Hazards: severe storms, forest fires

PAPUA NEW GUINEA
Country Name: Independent State of Papua New Guinea
Continent: Australia/Oceania
Area: 178,703 sq mi / 462,840 sq km
Population: 5,525,000
Population Density: 31 people per sq mi / 12 people per sq km
Capital: Port Moresby

PHYSICAL:
Highest Point: Mount Wilhelm 14,793 ft / 4,509 m
Lowest Point: Pacific Ocean 0 ft / 0 m
Mountain Ranges:
Bismarck: • located on the island of New Guinea
Maoke: • located on the island of New Guinea • extend into Indonesia
Owen Stanley: • located on the island of New Guinea
Peaks (minimum elevation of 8,000 ft / 2,400 m):
Mount Wilhelm: • located in the Bismarck Range • highest point in Australia/Oceania
Oceans:
Pacific: • forms much of the northern coast of Papua New Guinea
Seas:
Bismarck: • forms much of the northern coast of Papua New Guinea • feeds into the Pacific Ocean
Coral: • forms much of the southern coast of Papua New Guinea • feeds into the Pacific Ocean

PAPUA NEW GUINEA

Solomon: ●forms much of the eastern coast of Papua New Guinea ●feeds into the Pacific Ocean

Gulfs:

Gulf of Papua: ●forms part of the southern coast of Papua New Guinea ●feeds into the Coral Sea

Straits:

Torres: ●forms part of the southwestern coast of Papua New Guinea ●separates the island of New Guinea from Australia ●connects the Coral and Arafura Seas

Islands:

Bougainville: ●island bordered by the Pacific Ocean and Solomon Sea

New Britain: ●second largest island in Papua New Guinea ●bordered by the Bismarck and Solomon Seas

New Guinea: ●largest island in Papua New Guinea ●bordered by the Bismarck Sea, Solomon Sea, Coral Sea, Gulf of Papua, and Torres Strait ●western half belongs to Indonesia

New Ireland: ●island bordered by the Pacific Ocean and Bismarck Sea

POLITICAL:

Independence: September 16, 1975 (from Australian administration)

Former Name: Territory of Papua New Guinea

Bordering Country: Indonesia (1)

Administrative Divisions: Bougainville, Central, Chimbu, Eastern Highlands, East New Britain, East Sepik, Enga, Gulf, Madang, Manus, Milne Bay, Morobe, National Capital, New Ireland, Northern, Sandaun, Southern Highlands, Western, Western Highlands, West New Britain (20 provinces)

Ethnic/Racial Groups: Melanesian, Papuan, Negrito, Micronesian, Polynesian
Religions: Christianity (Protestant, Roman Catholic), indigenous beliefs
Languages: 715 indigenous languages
Currency: kina
Current President: Silas Atopare
Cities (capital, largest, or with at least a million people):
　　　Port Moresby:　●located on the island of New Guinea ●city in the National Capital province ●capital of Papua New Guinea ●most populated city in Papua New Guinea (275,000 people) ●chief port on the Gulf of Papua

ENVIRONMENTAL/ECONOMIC:
Climate: tropical; monsoons with little temperature variation
Natural Resources: gold, copper, silver, natural gas, timber
Agricultural Products: coffee, cacao, coconuts, palm kernels, poultry
Major Exports: oil, gold, copper ore, logs
Natural Hazards: volcanoes, earthquakes, mudslides, tsunamis

PARAGUAY

Country Name: Republic of Paraguay
Continent: South America
Area: 157,048 sq mi / 406,752 sq km
Population: 6,188,000
Population Density: 39 people per sq mi / 15 people per sq km
Capital: Asuncion

PHYSICAL:
Highest Point: Cerro Pero 2,762 ft / 842 m
Lowest Point: Paraguay/Parana River junction 151 ft / 46 m
Grasslands/Prairies:
　　　Gran Chaco:　●covers much of Paraguay ●extends into Argentina
Swamps:
　　　Pantanal:　●located in northeastern Paraguay ●extends into Bolivia and Brazil ●largest swamp in the world
Rivers:
　　　Paraguay:　●tributary of the Parana River ●forms part of Paraguay's border with Brazil and Argentina ●extends into Brazil
　　　Parana:　●forms part of Paraguay's border with Argentina and Brazil ●extends into Brazil
　　　Pilcomayo:　●tributary of the Paraguay River ●forms part of the Paraguay-Argentina border ●extends into Bolivia
Lakes:
　　　Itaipu Reservoir:　●located in southeastern Paraguay ●on the Paraguay-Brazil border ●fed by the Parana River ●formed by the Itaipu Dam

PARAGUAY

0   80 mi
0   80 km

BOLIVIA

BRAZIL

Cap. Pablo
Lagerenza

Puerto
Bahía Negra

Gral.
Eugenio A. Garay

Fuerte
Olimpo

20° S

Dr. Pedro P. Peña

Puerto
Pinasco

Pedro Juan
Caballero

22° S

Concepción

Tropic of
Capricorn

Verde R.

Monte Lindo R.

Colorado

San Pedro

Salto del
Guairá

24° S

Rosario

Itaipu
Res.

Asunción

San Lorenzo

Villarrica

Ciudad
del Este

Iguaçu R.

Caazapá

26° S

Pilar

San Juan Bautista

Paraná R.

Coronel Bogado
Encarnación

ARGENTINA

Pilcomayo

Pilcomayo R.

Bermejo R.

Paraguay R.

Paraná R.

66° W   64° W   62° W   60° W   58° W   56° W   54° W   52° W

Dams:
    Itaipu: •located in southeastern Paraguay •on the Paraguay-Brazil border •crosses the Parana River •forms Itaipu Reservoir

POLITICAL:

Independence: May 14, 1811 (from Spain)

Bordering Countries: Argentina, Brazil, Bolivia (3)

Administrative Divisions: Alto Paraguay, Alto Parana, Amambay, Boqueron, Caaguazu, Caazapa, Canindeyu, Central, Concepcion, Cordillera, Guaira, Itapua, Misiones, Neembucu, Paraguari, Presidente Hayes, San Pedro (17 departments) •Asuncion (1 capital city)

Ethnic/Racial Groups: mestizo

Religion: Christianity (primarily Roman Catholic)

Languages: Spanish, Guarani

Currency: guarani

Current President: Nicanor Duarte Frutos

Cities (capital, largest, or with at least a million people):
    Asuncion: •located in southwestern Paraguay •city in the Asuncion capital city division •capital of Paraguay •most populated city in Paraguay (1,639,000 people) •chief port on the Paraguay River

ENVIRONMENTAL/ECONOMIC:

Climate: subtropical to temperate; rainy in the east; semi-arid in the far west

Natural Resources: hydropower, timber, iron ore, manganese, limestone

Agricultural Products: cotton, sugarcane, soybeans, corn, beef
Major Exports: soybeans, feed, cotton, meat, edible oils
Natural Hazards: floods

PERU

Country Name: Republic of Peru
Continent: South America
Area: 496,224 sq mi / 1,285,216 sq km
Population: 27,126,000
Population Density: 55 people per sq mi / 21 people per sq km
Capital: Lima

PHYSICAL:
Highest Point: Mt. Huascaran 22,205 ft / 6,768 m
Lowest Point: Pacific Ocean 0 ft / 0 m (sea level)
Mountain Ranges:
    Andes: ●cover much of Peru ●extend into Ecuador, Bolivia, and Chile
Peaks (minimum elevation of 8,000 ft / 2,400 m):
    Mt. Huascaran: ●located in the Andes ●highest point in Peru
Plateau Regions:
    Altiplano: ●located in southeastern Peru ●extends into Bolivia ● basin in
    the Andes
Rain forests:
    Amazon: ●covers much of northern and eastern Peru ●extends into Ecuador,
    Colombia, Brazil, and Bolivia ●largest rain forest in the world

Deserts:
Atacama: •located in southeastern Peru •extends into Chile •driest place in the world
Sechura: •located in northwestern Peru
Oceans:
Pacific: •forms most of the western and southern coasts of Peru
Gulfs:
Gulf of Guayaquil: •forms part of the northwestern coast of Peru •feeds into the
Pacific Ocean
Lakes:
Lake Titicaca: •located in southeastern Peru •on the Altiplano near the slopes of
the Andes •extends into Bolivia •largest lake in South America
Rivers:
Amazon: •has its source in the Andes •forms part of the Peru-Colombia border
•extends into Brazil •longest river in South America
Jurua: •has its source in the Andes •extends into Brazil
Maranon: •tributary of the Amazon River •has its source in the Andes
Pastaza: •tributary of the Maranon River •extends into Ecuador
Purus: •has its source in the Andes •extends into Brazil
Putumayo: •forms part of the Peru-Colombia border •extends into Colombia
Ucayali: •tributary of the Amazon River •has its source in the Andes

POLITICAL:
Independence: July 28, 1821 (from Spain)
Bordering Countries: Brazil, Colombia, Ecuador, Bolivia, Chile (5)
Administrative Divisions: Amazonas, Ancash, Apurimac, Arequipa, Ayacucho,
Cajamarca, Cusco, Huancavelica, Huanuco, Ica, Junin, La Libertad, Lambayeque,
Lima, Loreto, Madre de Dios, Moquegua, Pasco, Piura, Puno, San Martin, Tacna,
Tumbes, Ucayali (24 departments) •Callao (1 constitutional province)
Ethnic/Racial Groups: Amerindian, mestizo, white
Religion: Christianity (primarily Roman Catholic)
Languages: Spanish, Quechua, Aymara
Currency: nuevo sol
Current President: Alejandro Toledo Manrique
Cities (capital, largest, or with at least a million people):
Lima: •located in western Peru •in the Lima department and the Callao constitu-
tional province •capital of Peru •most populated city in Peru (8,180,000 people)
•on the edge of the Andes

ENVIRONMENTAL/ECONOMIC:
Climate: tropical in the east; dry desert in the west; temperate to frigid in the Andes
Natural Resources: copper, silver, gold, petroleum, timber
Agricultural Products: coffee, cotton, sugarcane, rice, poultry
Major Exports: fish and fish products, gold, copper, zinc, crude petroleum
and by-products
Natural Hazards: earthquakes, tsunamis, floods, landslides, volcanoes

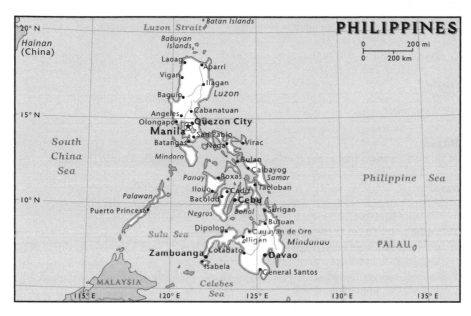

PHILIPPINES

Country Name: Republic of the Philippines
Continent: Asia
Area: 115,831 sq mi / 300,000 sq km
Population: 81,578,000
Population Density: 704 people per sq mi / 272 people per sq km
Capital: Manila

PHYSICAL:
Highest Point: Mount Apo 9,692 ft / 2,954 m
Lowest Point: Philippine Sea 0 ft / 0 m (sea level)
Peaks (minimum elevation of 8,000 ft / 2,400 m):
 Mount Apo: •located on the island of Mindanao •highest point in the Philippines
Seas:
 Bohol: •forms part of the inner coast of the Philippines •feeds into the Sulu and
  Philippine Seas
 Celebes: •forms most of the southern coast of Mindanao •feeds into the Philippine Sea
 Philippine: •forms most of the eastern coast of the Philippines •feeds into the
  Pacific Ocean
 Sibuyan: •forms part of the inner coast of the Philippines •feeds into the Sulu and
  Philippine Seas
 South China: •forms most of the western coast of the Philippines •feeds into the
  Philippine and Java Seas

Sulu: •forms part of the inner coast of the Philippines •feeds into the South China and Celebes Seas

Visayan: •forms part of the inner coast of the Philippines •feeds into the Sulu and Philippine Seas

Gulfs:

Davao: •forms part of the southeastern coast of Mindanao •feeds into the Philippine Sea

Moro: •forms part of the southern coast of Mindanao •feeds into the Celebes Sea

Bays:

Manila: •forms part of the southwestern coast of Luzon •feeds into the South China Sea

Straits:

Luzon: •forms much of the northern coast of Luzon •separates the Philippines from the island of Taiwan •connects the South China and Philippine Seas

Islands:

Cebu: •island between Negros and Leyte •bordered by the Visayan and Bohol Seas

Leyte: •island between Samar and Cebu •bordered by the Visayan and Bohol Seas

Luzon: • largest island in the Philippines •bordered by the South China, Sibuyan, and Philippine Seas

Mindanao: •second largest island in the Philippines •bordered by the Sulu Sea, Bohol Sea, Philippine Sea, Celebes Sea, Moro Gulf, and Davao Gulf

Mindoro: •island off the southern coast of Luzon •bordered by the South China, Sulu, and Sibuyan Seas

Negros: •island between Panay and Cebu •bordered by the Sulu, Visayan, and Bohol Seas

Palawan: •island between the South China and Sulu Seas

Panay: •island between Negros and Mindoro •bordered by the Sulu, Sibuyan, and Visayan Seas

Samar: •island off the southeastern coast of the Philippines •bordered by the Philippine Sea

POLITICAL:

Independence: July 4, 1946 (from the United States)

Administrative Divisions: Abra, Agusan del Norte, Agusan del Sur, Aklan, Albay, Antique, Apayao, Aurora, Basilan, Bataan, Batanes, Batangas, Benguet, Biliran, Bohol, Bukidnon, Bulacan, Cagayan, Camarines Norte, Camarines Sur, Camiguin, Capiz, Catanduanes, Cavite, Cebu, Compostela, Davao del Norte, Davao del Sur, Davao Oriental, Eastern Samar, Guimaras, Ifugao, Ilocos Norte, Ilocos Sur, Iloilo, Isabela, Kalinga, Laguna, Lanao del Norte, Lanao del Sur, La Union, Leyte, Maguindanao, Marinduque, Masbate, Mindoro Occidental, Mindoro Oriental, Misamis Occidental, Misamis Oriental, Mountain, Negros Occidental, Negros Oriental, North Cotabato, Northern Samar, Nueva Ecija, Nueva Vizcaya, Palawan, Pampanga, Pangasinan, Quezon, Quirino, Rizal, Romblon, Samar, Sarangani, Siquijor, Sorsogon, South Cotabato, Southern Leyte, Sultan Kudarat, Sulu, Surigao del Norte, Surigao del Sur, Tarlac, Tawi-Tawi, Zambales, Zamboanga del Norte, Zamboanga del Sur, Zamboanga Sibugay (79 provinces) ●Alaminos, Angeles, Antipolo, Bacolod, Bago, Baguio, Bais, Balanga, Batangas, Bayawan, Bislig, Butuan, Cabanatuan, Cadiz, Cagayan de Oro, Calamba, Calapan, Calbayog, Candon, Canlaon, Cauayan, Cavite, Cebu, Cotabato, Dagupan, Danao, Dapitan, Davao, Digos, Dipolog, Dumaguete, Escalante, Gapan, General Santos, Gingoog, Himamayan, Iligan, Iloilo, Iriga, Isabela, Kabankalan, Kalookan, Kidapawan, Koronadal, La Carlota, Laoag, Lapu-Lapu, Las Pinas, Legazpi, Ligao, Lipa, Lucena, Maasin, Makati, Malabon, Malaybalay, Malolos, Mandaluyong, Mandaue, Manila, Marawi, Markina, Masbate, Munoz, Muntinlupa, Naga, Olongapo, Ormoc, Oroquieta, Ozamis, Pagadian, Palayan, Panabo, Paranaque, Pasay, Pasig, Passi, Puerto Princesa, Quezon, Roxas, Sagay, Samal, San Carlos (in Negros Occidental), San Carlos (in Pangasinan), San Fernando (in La Union), San Fernando (in Pampanga), San Jose, San Jose del Monte, San Pablo, Santiago, Silay, Sipalay, Sorsogon, Surigao, Tabaco, Tacloban, Tacurong, Tagaytay, Taghilaran, Tagum, Talisay (in Cebu), Talisay (in Negros Oriental), Tanauan, Tangub, Tanjay, Tarlac, Toledo, Trece Martires, Tuguegarao, Urdaneta, Valencia, Valenzuela, Victorias, Vigan, Zamboanga (115 chartered cities)

Ethnic/Racial Groups: Christian Malay, Muslim Malay, Chinese
Religions: Christianity (Roman Catholic, Protestant), Islam, Buddhism
Languages: Filipino (based on Tagalog), English, 8 major dialects
Currency: Philippine peso
Current President: Gloria Macapagal-Arroyo
Cities (capital, largest, or with at least a million people):
Manila: ●located on the island of Luzon ●city in the Manila chartered city ●capital of the Philippines ●most populated city in the Philippines (10,677,000 people) ●chief port on Manila Bay

ENVIRONMENTAL/ECONOMIC:
Climate: tropical marine with monsoons
Natural Resources: timber, petroleum, nickel, cobalt, silver
Agricultural Products: rice, coconuts, corn, sugarcane, pork
Major Exports: electronic equipment, machinery and transport equipment, garments, coconut products
Natural Hazards: typhoons, cyclones, landslides, volcanoes, earthquakes, tsunamis

POLAND
Country Name: Republic of Poland
Continent: Europe
Area: 120,728 sq mi / 312,685 sq km
Population: 38,599,000
Population Density: 320 people per sq mi / 123 people per sq km
Capital: Warsaw

PHYSICAL:

Highest Point: Rysy 8,199 ft / 2,499 m
Lowest Point: near Raczki Elblaskie 7 ft / 2 m below sea level
Mountain Ranges:
   Carpathian: •cover much of southern Poland •extend into Czech Republic, Slovakia, and Ukraine
   Sudeten: •located in southwestern Poland •extend into Czech Republic
Peaks (minimum elevation of 8,000 ft / 2,400 m):
   Rysy: •located in the Carpathian Mountains •on the Poland-Czech Republic border •highest point in Poland
Seas:
   Baltic: •forms part of the northern coast of Poland •feeds into the Kattegat
Gulfs:
   Gulf of Gdansk: •forms the northeastern coast of Poland •feeds into the Baltic Sea
Bays:
   Pomeranian: •forms part of the northwestern coast of Poland •feeds into the Baltic Sea
Rivers:
   Odra (Oder): •has its mouth in the Stettiner Haff •forms part of the Poland-Germany border •extends into Czech Republic
   Wista (Vistula): •has its mouth in the Gulf of Gdansk •has its source in the Carpathian Mountains
   Warta: •tributary of the Oder River •has its source in southern Poland
Lagoons:
   Stettiner Haff: •feeds into the Baltic Sea •on the Poland-Germany border
Regions:
   Beskids: •mountainous region that covers much of southern Poland •includes part of the Carpathian Mountains

POLITICAL:

Independence: November 11, 1918 (proclaimed an independent republic)
Bordering Countries: Czech Republic, Ukraine, Germany, Slovakia, Belarus, Russia (Kaliningrad province), Lithuania (7)
Regions:
   Galicia: •region in southeastern Poland •includes part of the Carpathian Mountains •extends into Ukraine
   Masuria: •region in northeastern Poland
   Pomerania: •region that covers much of northern Poland •south of the Baltic Sea •extends into Germany
   Silesia: •region in southwestern Poland •north of the Sudeten Mountains
Administrative Divisions: Dolnoslaskie, Kujawsko-Pomorskie, Lodzkie, Lubelskie, Lubuskie, Malopolskie, Mazowieckie, Opolskie, Podkarpackie, Podlaskie, Pomorskie, Slaskie, Swietokrzyskie, Warminsko-Mazurskie, Wielkopolskie, Zachodniopomorskie (16 provinces)
Ethnic/Racial Groups: predominantly Polish
Religion: Christianity (primarily Roman Catholic)

POLAND

Language: Polish
Currency: zloty
Current President: Aleksander Kwasniewski
Cities (capital, largest, or with at least a million people):
   Warsaw: •located in eastern Poland •city in the Mazowieckie province •capital of
      Poland •most populated city in Poland (2,200,000 people) •chief port on the
      Wista (Vistula) River
   Lodz: •located in central Poland •city in the Lodzkie province

ENVIRONMENTAL/ECONOMIC:
Climate: temperate wet; cold winters/mild summers
Natural Resources: coal, sulfur, copper, natural gas, silver
Agricultural Products: potatoes, fruits, vegetables, wheat, poultry
Major Exports: machinery and transport equipment, intermediate manufactured goods
Natural Hazards: floods

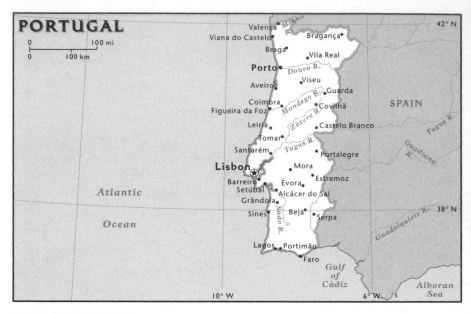

PORTUGAL

Country Name: Portuguese Republic
Continent: Europe
Area: 35,655 sq mi / 92,345 sq km
Population: 10,446,000
Population Density: 293 people per sq mi / 113 people per sq km
Capital: Lisbon

PHYSICAL:

Highest Point: Ponta do Pico (in the Azores) 7,713 ft / 2,351 m
Lowest Point: Atlantic Ocean 0 ft / 0 m (sea level)
Oceans:
  Atlantic: •forms the western coast of Portugal
Gulfs:
  Gulf of Cadiz: •forms the southeastern coast of Portugal •feeds into the Atlantic Ocean
Rivers:
  Guadiana: •has its mouth in the Gulf of Cadiz •forms part of the Portugal-Spain
    border •extends into Spain
  Tagus: •has its mouth in the Atlantic Ocean •forms part of the Portugal-Spain
    border •extends into Spain
Islands:
  Azores: •island group in the middle of the Atlantic Ocean
  Madeira: •island group in the eastern Atlantic Ocean •off the coast of Morocco

POLITICAL:

Independence: 1140 (established as an independent kingdom; declared an independent republic October 5, 1910)

Bordering Country: Spain (1)

Administrative Divisions: Aveiro, Beja, Braga, Braganca, Castelo Branco, Coimbra, Evora, Faro, Guarda, Leiria, Lisboa, Portalegre, Porto, Santarem, Setubal, Viana do Castelo, Vila Real, Viseu (18 districts) ●Azores, Madeira (2 autonomous regions)

Ethnic/Racial Groups: predominantly Portuguese

Religion: Christianity (primarily Roman Catholic)

Languages: Portuguese, Mirandese

Currency: euro

Current President: Jorge Sampaio

Cities (capital, largest, or with at least a million people):

Lisbon: ●located in southwestern Portugal ●city in the Lisboa district ●capital of Portugal ●most populated city in Portugal (1,962,000 people) ●chief port on the Tagus River and Atlantic Ocean

ENVIRONMENTAL/ECONOMIC:

Climate: temperate marine, cool and rainy in the north; warmer and drier in the south

Natural Resources: fish, forests (cork), iron ore, copper, zinc

Agricultural Products: grain, potatoes, olives, grapes, sheep

Major Exports: clothing and footwear, machinery, chemicals, cork and paper products, hides

Natural Hazards: earthquakes (in the Azores)

QATAR

Country Name: State of Qatar
Continent: Asia
Area: 4,448 sq mi / 11,521 sq km
Population: 629,000
Population Density: 141 people per sq mi / 55 people per sq km
Capital: Doha

PHYSICAL:

Highest Point: Tuwayyir al Hamir 338 ft / 103 m
Lowest Point: Persian Gulf 0 ft / 0 m (sea level)
Deserts:

Rub al Khali: •covers most of the country •extends into Saudi Arabia

Gulfs:

Gulf of Bahrain: •forms most of the western coast of Qatar •feeds into the
Persian Gulf

Persian: •forms the northern and eastern coasts of Qatar •feeds into the Gulf
of Oman

POLITICAL:

Independence: September 3, 1971 (from the United Kingdom)

Bordering Country: Saudi Arabia (1)

Administrative Divisions: Ad Dawhah, Al Ghuwayriyah, Al Jumayliyah, Al Khawr, Al Wakrah, Ar Rayyan, Jarayan al Batinah, Madinat ash Shamal, Umm Said, Umm Salal (10 municipalities)

Ethnic Groups: Arab, Pakistani, Indian, Iranian

Religion: primarily Islam

Languages: Arabic, English

Currency: Qatari rial

Current Prime Minister: Abdallah bin Khalifa Al Thani

Cities (capital, largest, or with at least a million people):

Doha: •located in eastern Qatar •city in the Ad Dawhah municipality •capital of Qatar •most populated city in Qatar (286,000 people) •chief port on the Persian Gulf

ENVIRONMENTAL/ECONOMIC:

Climate: arid with mild winters/hot and humid summers

Natural Resources: petroleum, natural gas, fish

Agricultural Products: fruits, vegetables, poultry, dairy products, beef

Major Exports: petroleum products, fertilizers, steel

Natural Hazards: haze, dust storms, sandstorms

Q

ROMANIA

Country Name: Romania
Continent: Europe
Area: 92,043 sq mi / 238,391 sq km
Population: 21,622,000
Population Density: 235 people per sq mi / 91 people per sq km
Capital: Bucharest

PHYSICAL:
Highest Point: Moldoveanu 8,346 ft / 2,544 m
Lowest Point: Black Sea 0 ft / 0 m (sea level)
Mountain Ranges:
> Carpathian: ●cover much of northern Romania ●extend into Ukraine
> Transylvanian Alps: ●cover much of central Romania

Peaks (with minimum elevation of 8,000 ft / 2,400 m):
> Moldoveanu: ●located in the Transylvanian Alps ●highest point in Romania

Grasslands/Prairies:
> Black Sea Lowland: ●located in southeastern Romania ●extends into Moldova and Ukraine
> Great Alfold: ●covers much of western Romania ●extends into Ukraine, Hungary, and Serbia and Montenegro

Seas:
> Black: ●forms the southeastern coast of Romania ●feeds into the Sea of Marmara

Rivers:
> Danube: ●has its mouth in the Black Sea ●forms most of the Romania-Bulgaria border ●forms part of Romania's border with Serbia and Montenegro and Ukraine ●extends into Hungary and Serbia and Montengero
> Prut: ●tributary of the Danube River ●forms all of the Romania-Moldova border ●forms part of the Romania-Ukraine border ●extends into Ukraine

Deltas:
> Delta of the Danube: ●mouth of the Danube River ●feeds into the Black Sea ●borders Ukraine

POLITICAL:
Independence: 1878 (independence from Turkey officially recognized)
Bordering Countries: Bulgaria, Ukraine, Serbia and Montenegro, Moldova, Hungary (5)

ROMANIA

SLOVAKIA
UKRAINE
HUNGARY
MOLDOVA
CROATIA
BOSNIA &
HERZEGOVINA
SERBIA AND
MONTENEGRO
BULGARIA
Black Sea

0 50 mi
0 50 km

48° N
44° N
20° E   24° E   28° E

•Darabani
•Satu Mare
•Carei •Baia Mare   •Botoşani
•Marghita   Suceava•   Iaşi•
•Oradea
Piatra Neamţ•   Vaslui•
•Ineu   •Cluj-Napoca   Bacău•
•Curtici   Tîrgu Mureş
•Arad   Mureş R.
Sînnicolau Mare   •Blaj   Adjud•   •Tecuci
Cugir•   •Sibiu   •Braşov   Galaţi•
•Timişoara   Buzău•   Brăila•   •Tulcea
Reşiţa•   Vulcan•
Rîmnicu Vîlcea•   •Pitesti   •Ploieşti   •Babadag
Drobeta-
Turnu Severin   ⊛ Bucharest
Craiova•   Videle•   Călăraşi•   Constanţa
Alexandria•   •Giurgiu

Danube R.   Tisza R.   Drava R.   Mureş R.   Morava R.   Olt R.   Argeş R.   Danube R.   Dnister R.   Prut R.   Siret R.   Danube R.

Regions:

    Dobruja: •region in southeastern Romania •west of the Black Sea •east and south of the Danube River •extends into Bulgaria

    Moldavia: •region in eastern Romania •east of the Carpathian Mountains •west of the Prut River

    Transylvania: •region in northwestern Romania •west of the Carpathian Mountains •north of the Transylvanian Alps

    Walachia: •region in southern Romania •south of the Transylvanian Alps •north of the Danube River

Administrative Divisions: Alba, Arad, Arges, Bacau, Bihor, Bistrita-Nasaud, Botosani, Braila, Brasov, Buzau, Calarasi, Caras-Severin, Cluj, Constanta, Covasna, Dimbovita, Dolj, Galati, Giurgiu, Gorj, Harghita, Hunedoara, Ialomita, Iasi, Ilfov, Maramures, Mehedinti, Mures, Neamt, Olt, Prahova, Salaj, Satu Mare, Sibiu, Suceava, Teleorman, Timis, Tulcea, Vaslui, Vilcea, Vrancea (41 counties) •Bucuresti (1 municipality)

Ethnic/Racial Groups: Romanian, Hungarian, Roma

Religion: Christianity (Eastern Orthodox, Protestant, Roman Catholic)

Languages: Romanian, Hungarian, German

Currency: leu

Current President: Ion Iliescu

Cities (capital, largest, or with at least a million people):

    Bucharest: •located in southern Romania •city in the Bucuresti municipality •capital of Romania •most populated city in Romania (1,853,000 people)

R

ENVIRONMENTAL/ECONOMIC:
Climate: temperate with cold and snowy winters/sunny summers with occasional heavy rains
Natural Resources: petroleum, timber, natural gas, coal, iron ore
Agricultural Products: wheat, corn, barley, sugar beets, eggs
Major Exports: textiles and footwear, metals and metal products, machinery and equipment, minerals and fuels
Natural Hazards: earthquakes, landslides

RUSSIA
Country Name: Russian Federation
Continent: Asia/Europe (most of the land area is in Asia; the capital city and most of the population is in Europe)
Area: 6,592,850 sq mi / 17,075,400 sq km (largest country in the world)
Population: 145,546,000
Population Density: 22 people per sq mi / 8.5 people per sq km
Capital: Moscow

PHYSICAL:
Highest Point: Mount Elbrus 18,510 ft / 5,642 m
Lowest Point: Caspian Sea 92 ft / 28 m below sea level
Mountain Ranges:
   Altay: ●located in southern Russia ●extend into Kazakhstan, China, and Mongolia
   Caucasus: ●located in southwestern Russia ●extend into Georgia and Azerbaijan
   Cherskiy Range: ●located in northeastern Russia
   Eastern Sayan: ●located in southern Russia ●extend into Mongolia
   Kolyma Range: ●located in northeastern Russia
   Ural: ●located in western Russia ●form part of what is sometimes recognized as the boundary between the continents of Asia and Europe
   Western Sayan: ●located in southern Russia
   Yablonovyy Range: ●located in southern Russia
Peaks (with minimum elevation of 8,000 ft / 2,400 m):
   Mount Elbrus: ●located in the Caucasus ●highest point in Russia ●highest point in Europe
Grasslands/Prairies:
   North Siberian Lowland: ●located in northern Russia
   West Siberian Plain: ●covers much of central Russia
Plateau Regions:
   Aldan Plateau: ●located in eastern Russia
   Central Siberian Plateau: ●covers much of central Russia
Depressions:
   Caspian Depression: ●located in southwestern Russia ●extends into Kazakhstan
   Caspian Sea: ●located in southwestern Russia ●lowest point in Europe

Oceans:

Arctic: •forms much of the northern coast of Russia

Pacific: •forms much of the eastern coast of Russia

Seas:

Barents: •forms part of the northwestern coast of Russia •feeds into the Arctic Ocean

Bering: •forms part of the northeastern coast of Russia •feeds into the Pacific Ocean

Black: •forms part of the southwestern coast of Russia •feeds into the Sea of Marmara

Chukchi: •forms part of the northeastern coast of Russia •feeds into the Arctic Ocean

East Siberian: •forms part of the northeastern coast of Russia •feeds into the Arctic Ocean

Kara: •forms part of the northern coast of Russia •feeds into the Arctic Ocean

Laptev: •forms part of the northern coast of Russia •feeds into the Arctic Ocean

Sea of Azov: •forms part of the southwestern coast of Russia •feeds into the Black Sea

Sea of Japan: •forms part of the southeastern coast of Russia •feeds into the Sea of Okhotsk, Pacific Ocean, and East China Sea

Sea of Okhotsk: •forms part of the eastern coast of Russia •feeds into the Pacific Ocean

White: •forms part of the northwestern coast of Russia •feeds into the Barents Sea

Gulfs:

Gulf of Anadyr: •forms part of the northeastern coast of Russia •feeds into the Bering Sea

Gulf of Finland: •forms part of the western coast of Russia •feeds into the Baltic Sea

Gulf of Ob: •forms part of the northern coast of Russia •feeds into the Kara Sea

Shelikhov: •forms part of the eastern coast of Russia •feeds into the Sea of Okhotsk

Straits:
   Bering: •forms part of the northeastern coast of Russia •separates Russia from
      the United States •connects the Chukchi and Bering Seas
   La Perouse: •forms part of the southeastern coast of Sakhalin Island •separates
      Sakhalin Island from Japan •connects the Sea of Japan and Sea of Okhotsk
   Tatar: •forms part of the southeastern coast of Russia •separates Sakhalin Island
      from mainland Russia •connects the Sea of Okhotsk and Sea of Japan
Lakes:
   Caspian Sea: •located in southwestern Russia •extends into Azerbaijan and
      Kazakhstan •largest lake in the world •lowest point in Europe
   Lake Baikal: • located in southern Russia •on the edge of the Eastern Sayan Mountains
      •largest lake entirely in Asia
   Lake Ladoga: •located in northwestern Russia •largest lake entirely in Europe
   Lake Onega: •located in northwestern Russia
   Lake Peipus: •located in western Russia •on the Russia-Estonia border
   Lake Pskov: •located in western Russia •on the Russia-Estonia border
   Rybinsk Reservoir: •located in western Russia •fed by the Volga River
Rivers:
   Aldan: •tributary of the Lena River •has its source in the Aldan Plateau
   Amur: •has its mouth in the Tatar Strait •forms part of the Russia-China border
   Angara: •tributary of the Yenisey River
   Dnieper: •has its source in western Russia •extends into Belarus and Ukraine
   Don: •has its mouth in the Sea of Azov •has its source in western Russia
   Donets: •tributary of the Don River •has its source in southwestern Russia •extends
      into Ukraine
   Irtysh (Ertis): • tributary of the Ob •extends into Kazakhstan and China
   Kolyma: •has its mouth in the East Siberian Sea •has its source in the
      Cherskiy Range
   Lena: •has its mouth in the Laptev Sea •has its source in southern Russia
   Ob: • has its mouth in the Gulf of Ob • has its source in the Altay Mountains
   Pechora: • has its mouth in the Barents Sea • has its source in the Ural Mountains
   Volga: •has its mouth in the Caspian Sea •has its source in western Russia •flows
      through the Rybinsk Reservoir •longest river in Europe
   Western Dvina: • has its source in western Russia •extends into Belarus and Latvia
   Yenisey: •has its mouth in the Kara Sea
Deltas:
   Volga River Delta: •mouth of the Volga River •feeds into the Caspian Sea
Peninsulas:
   Chukchi: •bordered by the Chukchi Sea, Bering Sea, Gulf of Anadyr, and Bering Strait
   Kamchatka: •bordered by the Pacific Ocean, Sea of Okhotsk, Bering Sea, and
      Shelikhov Gulf
   Kola: •bordered by the White and Barents Seas
   Taymyr: •bordered by the Kara and Laptev Seas

Islands:

Franz Josef Land: •island group between the Arctic Ocean and Barents Sea

Kuril: • island chain between the Sea of Okhotsk and Pacific Ocean

New Siberian: •island group off the coast of northeastern Russia •bordered by the Arctic Ocean, Laptev Sea and East Siberia Sea

Novaya Zemlya: •island group off the northwestern coast of Russia •bordered by the Barents and Kara Seas

Sakhalin: •island separated from the mainland by the Tatar Strait •bordered by the Sea of Okhotsk, Tatar Strait, and La Perouse Strait

Severnaya Zemlya: •island group off the coast of the Taymyr Peninsula •bordered by the Arctic Ocean, Kara Sea, and Laptev Sea

Regions:

Siberia: •covers much of northern and central Russia •south of the Kara Sea, Laptev Sea, East Siberian Sea, Chukchi Sea, and Gulf of Ob •west of the Bering Sea, Shelikhov Gulf, and Pacific Ocean •east of the Ural Mountains •north of the Altay Mountains, Western Sayan Mountains, Eastern Sayan Mountains, Aldan Plateau, Sea of Okhotsk, and Shelikhov Gulf •includes the Cherskiy Range, Kolyma Range, Central Siberian Plateau, West Siberian Plain, North Siberian Lowland, Taymyr Peninsula, Chukchi Peninsula, and Kamchatka Peninsula

POLITICAL:

Independence: August 24, 1991 (from the Soviet Union)

Former Names: Russian Empire, Russian Soviet Federated Socialist Republic

Bordering Countries: Kazakhstan, China, Mongolia, Ukraine, Finland, Belarus, Georgia, Estonia, Azerbaijan, Lithuania, Latvia, Poland, Norway, North Korea (14)

Administrative Divisions: Amurskaya (Blagoveshchensk), Arkhangel'skaya, Astrakhanskaya, Belgorodskaya, Bryanskaya, Chelyabinskaya, Chitinskaya, Irkutskaya, Ivanovskaya, Kaliningradskaya, Kaluzhskaya, Kamchatskaya (Petropavlovsk-Kamchatskiy), Kemerovskaya, Kirovskaya, Kostromskaya, Kurganskaya, Kurskaya, Leningradskaya, Lipetskaya, Magadanskaya, Moskovskaya, Murmanskaya, Nizhegorodskaya, Novgorodskaya, Novosibirskaya, Omskaya, Orenburgskaya, Orlovskaya (Orel), Penzenskaya, Permskaya, Pskovskaya, Rostovskaya, Ryazanskaya, Sakhalinskaya (Yuzhno-Sakhalinsk), Samarskaya, Saratovskaya, Smolenskaya, Sverdlovskaya (Yekaterinburg), Tambovskaya, Tomskaya, Tul'skaya, Tverskaya, Tyumenskaya, Ul'yanovskaya, Vladimirskaya, Volgogradskaya, Vologodskaya, Voronezhskaya, Yaroslavskaya (49 oblasts) •Adygeya, Altay, Bashkortostan, Buryatiya, Chechnya, Chuvashiya, Dagestan, Ingushetiya, Kabardino-Balkariya, Kalmykiya, Karachayevo-Cherkesiya, Kareliya, Khakasiya, Komi, Mariy-El, Mordoviya, Sakha, Severnaya Osetiya-Alaniya, Tatarstan, Tyva, Udmurtiya (21 republics) •Aginskiy Buryatskiy, Chukotskiy, Evenkiyskiy, Khanty-Mansiyskiy, Komi-Permyatskiy, Koryakskiy, Nenetskiy, Taymyrskiy, Ust'-Ordynskiy Buryatskiy, Yamalo-Nenetskiy (10 autonomous okrugs) •Altayskiy (Barnaul), Khabarovskiy, Krasnodarskiy, Krasnoyarskiy, Primorskiy (Vladivostok), Stavropolskiy (6 krays) •Moscow, Saint Petersburg (2 federal cities) •Yevreyskaya (1 autonomous oblast)

Ethnic/Racial Groups: Russian, Tatar, Ukrainian
Religions: Christianity (Russian Orthodox), Islam, other
Language: Russian
Currency: Russian ruble
Current President: Vladimir Putin
Cities (capital, largest, or with at least a million people):
Moscow: • located in western Russia • city in the Moscow federal city division • capital of Russia • most populated city in Russia (10,672,000 people)
Saint Petersburg: • located in northwestern Russia • city in the Saint Petersburg federal city division • chief port on the Gulf of Finland
Novosibirsk: • located in southern Russia • city in the Novosibirskaya oblast
Yekaterinburg: • located in western Russia • city in the Sverdloskaya oblast
Nizhniy Novgorod: • located in western Russia • city in the Nizhegorodskaya oblast • chief port on the Volga River
Samara: • located in western Russia • city in the Samarskaya oblast
Omsk: • located in southern Russia • city in the Omskaya oblast
Kazan: • located in western Russia • city in the Tatarstan republic
Rostov na Donu: • located in western Russia • city in the Rostovskaya oblast
Chelyabinsk: • located in western Russia • city in the Chelyabinskaya oblast
Volgograd: • located in western Russia • city in the Volgogradskaya oblast
Ufa: • located in western Russia • city in the Bashkortostan republic

ENVIRONMENTAL/ECONOMIC:
Climate: steppe in the south; humid continental in Europe; subarctic to tundra in Siberia; polar in the north; cool winters along the Black Sea; frigid winters in Siberia/warm summers in the steppes and cool along the Arctic coast
Natural Resources: oil, natural gas, coal, minerals, timber
Agricultural Products: grain, sugar beets, sunflower seeds, vegetables, beef
Major Exports: petroleum and petroleum products, natural gas, wood and wood products, metals, fur
Natural Hazards: permafrost, volcanoes, earthquakes, floods, forest fires

RWANDA
Country Name: Republic of Rwanda
Continent: Africa
Area: 10,169 sq mi / 26,338 sq km
Population: 8,306,000
Population Density: 817 people per sq mi / 315 people per sq km
Capital: Kigali

PHYSICAL:
Highest Point: Mount Karisimbi 14,787 ft / 4,507 m
Lowest Point: Ruzizi River 3,117 ft / 950 m

Mountain Ranges:
Virunga: •cover most of western and central Rwanda •extend into Democratic
Republic of the Congo and Burundi
Peaks (with minimum elevation of 8,000 ft / 2,400 m):
Mount Karisimbi: •located in the Virunga Mountains •on the Rwanda-Democratic
Republic of the Congo border •highest point in Rwanda
Valleys:
Great Rift: •located in western Rwanda •extends into Democratic Republic of the
Congo, Uganda, and Burundi
Lakes:
Lake Kivu: •located in western Rwanda •on the slopes of the Virunga Mountains •in the
Great Rift Valley •on the Rwanda-Democratic Republic of the Congo border

POLITICAL:
Independence: July 1, 1962 (from Belgian administration)
Former Name: Ruanda
Bordering Countries: Burundi, Democratic Republic of the Congo, Tanzania,
Uganda (4)
Administrative Divisions: Butare, Byumba, Cyangugu, Gikongoro, Gisenyi, Gitarama,
Kibungo, Kibuye, Kigali Rurale, Kigali-ville, Ruhengeri, Umutara, (12 prefectures)
Ethnic/Racial Groups: Hutu, Tutsi, Twa
Religions: Christianity (Roman Catholic, Protestant), Islam
Languages: Kinyarwanda, French, English, Kiswahili

Currency: Rwandan franc
Current President: Paul Kagame
Cities (capital, largest, or with at least a million people):
>   Kigali: •located in central Rwanda •city in the Kigali-ville prefecture •capital of
>   Rwanda •most populated city in Rwanda (656,000 people) •on the edge of the
>   Virunga Mountains

ENVIRONMENTAL/ECONOMIC:
Climate: temperate with rainy/dry seasons; mild in the mountains with some snow
Natural Resources: gold, tin ore, tungsten ore, methane, hydropower
Agricultural Products: coffee, tea, pyrethrum, bananas, livestock
Major Exports: coffee, tea, hides, tin ore
Natural Hazards: droughts, volcanoes

SAINT KITTS AND NEVIS

Country Name: Federation of Saint Kitts and Nevis
Continent: North America
Area: 104 sq mi / 269 sq km (smallest in North America)
Population: 46,000 (smallest in North America)
Population Density: 442 people per sq mi / 171 people per sq km
Capital: Basseterre

PHYSICAL:
Highest Point: Mount Liamuiga 3,793 ft / 1,156 m
Lowest Point: Caribbean Sea 0 ft / 0 m (sea level)
Oceans:
  Atlantic: ●forms the eastern coast of Saint Kitts and Nevis
Seas:
  Caribbean: ●forms the western coast of Saint Kitts and Nevis ●feeds into the
    Atlantic Ocean
Islands:
  Nevis: ●second largest island in Saint Kitts and Nevis ●bordered by the Atlantic
    Ocean and Caribbean Sea

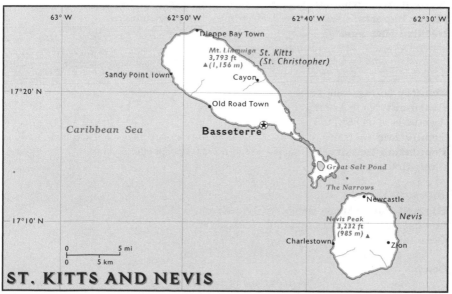

Saint Kitts: •largest island in Saint Kitts and Nevis •bordered by the Atlantic Ocean and Caribbean Sea

POLITICAL:
Independence: September 19, 1983 (from the United Kingdom)
Former Name: Federation of Saint Christopher and Nevis
Administrative Divisions: Christ Church Nichola Town, Saint Anne Sandy Point, Saint George Basseterre, Saint George Gingerland, Saint James Windward, Saint John Capesterre, Saint John Figtree, Saint Mary Cayon, Saint Paul Capesterre, Saint Paul Charlestown, Saint Peter Basseterre, Saint Thomas Lowland, Saint Thomas Middle Island, Trinity Palmetto Point (14 parishes)
Ethnic/Racial Groups: black, British, Portuguese, Lebanese
Religion: Christianity (Anglican, other Protestant)
Language: English
Currency: East Caribbean dollar
Current Prime Minister: Denzil Douglas
Cities (capital, largest, or with at least a million people):
Basseterre: •located on the island of Saint Kitts •city in the Saint George Basseterre parish •capital of Saint Kitts and Nevis •most populated city in Saint Kitts and Nevis (13,000 people) •chief port on the Caribbean Sea

ENVIRONMENTAL/ECONOMIC:
Climate: tropical, moderated by sea breezes; little temperature variation; rainy/dry seasons
Natural Resources: arable land
Agricultural Products: sugarcane, rice, yams, vegetables, fish
Major Exports: machinery, food, electronics, beverages, tobacco
Natural Hazards: hurricanes

SAINT LUCIA
Country Name: Saint Lucia
Continent: North America
Area: 238 sq mi / 616 sq km
Population: 162,000
Population Density: 681 people per sq mi / 263 people per sq km
Capital: Castries

PHYSICAL:
Highest Point: Mount Gimie 3,117 ft / 950 m
Lowest Point: Atlantic Ocean 0 ft / 0 m (sea level)
Oceans:
Atlantic: •forms the eastern coast of Saint Lucia
Seas:
Caribbean: •forms the western coast of Saint Lucia •feeds into the Atlantic Ocean

Islands:
  Saint Lucia: • main island in Saint Lucia • bordered by the Atlantic Ocean and
    Caribbean Sea

POLITICAL:
Independence: February 22, 1979 (from the United Kingdom)
Administrative Divisions: Anse-la-Raye, Castries, Choiseul, Dauphin, Dennery,
  Gros-Islet, Laborie, Micoud, Praslin, Soufriere, Vieux-Fort (11 quarters)
Ethnic/Racial Groups: black, mixed, East Indian, white
Religion: Christianity (Roman Catholic, Protestant)
Languages: English, French patois
Currency: East Caribbean dollar
Current Prime Minister: Kenneth Davis Anthony
Cities (capital, largest, or with at least a million people):
  Castries: • located in northwestern Saint Lucia • city in the Castries quarter • capital
    of Saint Lucia • most populated city in Saint Lucia (14,000 people) • chief port
    on the Caribbean Sea

ENVIRONMENTAL/ECONOMIC:
Climate: tropical, moderated by northeast trade winds; dry/rainy seasons
Natural Resources: forests, sandy beaches, minerals, mineral springs, geothermal potential
Agricultural Products: bananas, coconuts, vegetables, citrus
Major Exports: bananas, clothing, cacao, vegetables
Natural Hazards: hurricanes, volcanoes

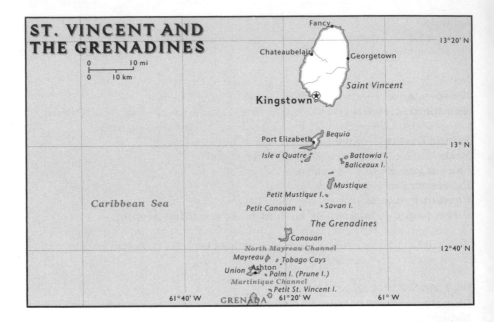

SAINT VINCENT AND THE GRENADINES

Country Name: Saint Vincent and the Grenadines
Continent: North America
Area: 150 sq mi / 389 sq km
Population: 110,000
Population Density: 733 people per sq mi / 283 people per sq km
Capital: Kingstown

PHYSICAL:

Highest Point: Soufriere volcano 4,049 ft / 1,234 m
Lowest Point: Atlantic Ocean 0 ft / 0 m (sea level)
Oceans:
  Atlantic: •forms the eastern coast of Saint Vincent and the Grenadines
Seas:
  Caribbean: •forms the western coast of Saint Vincent and the Grenadines
Islands:
  The Grenadines: •island group south of Saint Vincent •bordered by the Atlantic
    Ocean and Caribbean Sea
  Saint Vincent: •largest island in Saint Vincent and the Grenadines •bordered by the
    Atlantic Ocean and Caribbean Sea

Independence: October 27, 1979 (from the United Kingdom)
Administrative Divisions: Charlotte, Grenadines, Saint Andrew, Saint David, Saint George, Saint Patrick (6 parishes)
Ethnic/Racial Groups: African American, mixed, East Indian, Carib Amerindian
Religion: Christianity (Anglican, Methodist, Roman Catholic, other Protestant)
Languages: English, French patois
Currency: East Caribbean dollar
Current Prime Minister: Ralph Gonsalves
Cities (capital, largest, or with at least a million people):
Kingstown: •located on the island of Saint Vincent •city in the Saint George parish •capital of Saint Vincent and the Grenadines •most populated city in Saint Vincent and the Grenadines (29,000 people) •chief port on the Caribbean Sea

ENVIRONMENTAL/ECONOMIC:
Climate: tropical with little temperature variation; rainy/dry seasons
Natural Resources: hydropower, cropland
Agricultural Products: bananas, coconuts, sweet potatoes, spices, cattle
Major Exports: bananas, eddoes and dasheen (taro), arrowroot starch, tennis racquets
Natural Hazards: hurricanes, volcanoes

SAMOA
Country Name: Independent State of Samoa
Continent: Australia/Oceania
Area: 1,093 sq mi / 2,831 sq km
Population: 172,000
Population Density: 157 people per sq mi / 61 people per sq km
Capital: Apia

PHYSICAL:
Highest Point: Mount Silisili 6,096 ft / 1,858 m •on the island of Savaii
Lowest Point: Pacific Ocean 0 ft / 0 m (sea level)
Oceans:
Pacific: •forms most of the coast of Samoa
Islands:
Savaii: •largest island in Samoa •surrounded by the Pacific Ocean
Upolu: •second largest island in Samoa •surrounded by the Pacific Ocean

POLITICAL:
Independence: January 1, 1962 (from New Zealand administration)
Former Name: Western Samoa
Administrative Divisions: Aana, Aiga-i-le-Tai, Atua, Faasaleleaga, Gagaemauga, Gagaifomauga, Palauli, Satupaitea, Tuamasaga, Vaa-o-Fonoti, Vaisigano (11 districts)

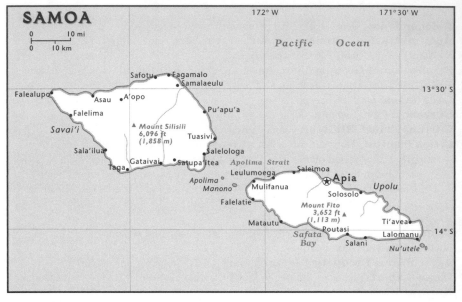

SAMOA

172° W   171°30' W

Pacific Ocean

Safotu • Fagamalo
• Samalaeulu

Falealupo •
Asau • A'opo
• Falelima
Pu'apu'a

Savai'i
▲ *Mount Silisili*
6,096 ft
(1,858 m)
Tuasivi •

Sala'ilua •
Salelologa •

Taga • Gataivai • Satupa'itea *Apolima Strait*
Leulumoega • Saleimoa
Apolima ○ ⊛ **Apia**
Manono ○ Mulifanua *Upolu*
Falelatie • Solosolo
Mount Fito
3,652 ft ▲
Matautu • *(1,113 m)* Ti'avea •
Poutasi • Lalomanu
Safata Salani
Bay Nu'utele ○ 0

13°30' S

14° S

Ethnic/Racial Groups: Samoan, Euronesian
Religion: predominantly Christian faiths
Languages: Samoan, English
Currency: tala
Current Chief: Tanumafili II Malietoa
Cities (capital, largest, or with at least a million people):
  Apia: •located on the island of Upolu •city in the Tuamasaga district •capital of
  Samoa •most populated city in Samoa (40,000 people) •chief port on the
  Pacific Ocean

ENVIRONMENTAL/ECONOMIC:
Climate: tropical with rainy/dry seasons
Natural Resources: hardwood forests, fish, hydropower
Agricultural Products: coconuts, bananas, taro, yams
Major Exports: fish, coconut oil and cream, copra, taro
Natural Hazards: typhoons, volcanoes

SAN MARINO
Country Name: Republic of San Marino
Continent: Europe
Area: 24 sq mi / 61 sq km
Population: 30,000
Population Density: 1,250 people per sq mi / 492 people per sq km
Capital: San Marino

PHYSICAL:
Highest Point: Monte Titano 2,425 ft / 739 m
Lowest Point: Torrente Ausa 180 ft / 55 m
Mountain Ranges:
   Apennines: •cover much of the country •extend into Italy

POLITICAL:
Independence: September 3, 301(established as an independent republic)
Bordering Country: Italy (1)
Administrative Divisions: Acquaviva, Borgo Maggiore, Chiesanuova, Domagnano,
   Faetano, Fiorentino, Monte Giardino, San Marino, Serravalle (9 municipalities)
Ethnic/Racial Groups: Sammarinese, Italian
Religion: Christianity (Roman Catholic)
Language: Italian
Currency: euro
Current Leader: Fiorenzo Stolfi
Cities (capital, largest, or with at least a million people):
   Serraville: •located in northeastern San Marino •city in the Serraville municipality
      •most populated city in San Marino (9,000 people) •on the edge of the Apennines
   San Marino: •located in western San Marino •in the San Marino municipality
      •capital of San Marino (5,000 people)

Climate: Mediterranean with mild to cool winters/warm and sunny summers
Natural Resources: building stone
Agricultural Products: wheat, grapes, corn, olives, cattle
Major Exports: building stone, lime, wood, chestnuts, wheat
Natural Hazards: landslides

SAO TOME AND PRINCIPE

Country Name: Democratic Republic of Sao Tome and Principe
Continent: Africa
Area: 386 sq mi / 1,001 sq km
Population: 176,000
Population Density: 456 people per sq mi / 176 people per sq km
Capital: Sao Tome

PHYSICAL:
Highest Point: Pico de Sao Tome 6,640 ft / 2,024 m
Lowest Point: Atlantic Ocean 0 ft / 0 m (sea level)
Oceans:
  Atlantic: •forms the southern coast of Sao Tome
Gulfs:
  Gulf of Guinea: •forms all but the southern coast of Sao Tome and Principe •feeds
    into the Atlantic Ocean

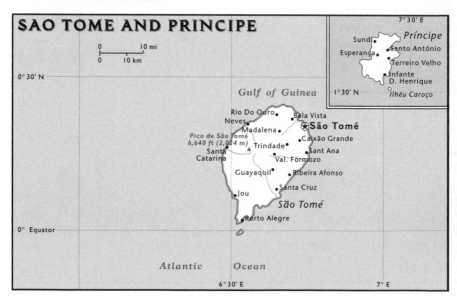

Islands:
    Principe: •second largest island in Sao Tome and Principe •surrounded by the
        Gulf of Guinea
    Sao Tome: •largest island in Sao Tome and Principe •bordered by the Atlantic
        Ocean and the Gulf of Guinea

POLITICAL:
Independence: July 12, 1975 (from Portugal)
Administrative Divisions: Principe, Sao Tome (2 provinces)
Ethnic/Racial Groups: mestizo, black, Portuguese
Religion: Christianity (Roman Catholic, Evangelical, Protestant)
Language: Portuguese
Currency: dobra
Current President: Fradique de Menezes
Cities (capital, largest, or with at least a million people):
    Sao Tome: •located on the island of Sao Tome •city in the Sao Tome province
    •capital of Sao Tome and Principe •most populated city in Sao Tome and
    Principe (54,000 people) •chief port on the Gulf of Guinea

ENVIRONMENTAL/ECONOMIC:
Climate: tropical hot and humid with rainy/dry seasons
Natural Resources: fish, hydropower
Agricultural Products: cacao, coconuts, palm kernels, copra, poultry
Major Exports: cacao, copra, coffee, palm oil
Natural Hazards: floods

SAUDI ARABIA
Country Name: Kingdom of Saudi Arabia
Continent: Asia
Area: 756,985 sq mi / 1,960,582 sq km
Population: 24,070,000
Population Density: 32 people per sq mi / 12 people per sq km
Capital: Riyadh

PHYSICAL:
Highest Point: Jabal Sawda 10,279 ft / 3,133 m
Lowest Point: Red Sea 0 ft / 0 m (sea level)
Mountain Ranges:
    Jabal al Hijaz: •cover much of western Saudi Arabia •extend into Yemen
Peaks (minimum elevation of 8,000 ft / 2,400 m):
    Jabal Sawda: •located in the Jabal al Hijaz •highest point in Saudi Arabia

Plateau Regions:
    Najd: •covers much of central Saudi Arabia •desert basin west of the Jabal al Hijaz •north of the Rub al Khali
Deserts:
    Rub al Khali: •covers much of southern Saudi Arabia •extends into Yemen, Oman, United Arab Emirates, and Qatar
Seas:
    Red: •forms most of the western coast of Saudi Arabia •feeds into the Gulf of Aden
Gulfs:
    Gulf of Aqaba: •forms part of the northwestern coast of Saudi Arabia •feeds into the Red Sea
    Gulf of Bahrain: •forms part of the eastern coast of Saudi Arabia •feeds into the Persian Gulf
    Persian: •forms most of the eastern coast of Saudi Arabia •feeds into the Gulf of Oman

POLITICAL:
Independence: September 23, 1932 (date of unification of the kingdom)
Bordering Countries: Yemen, Iraq, Jordan, Oman, United Arab Emirates, Kuwait, Qatar (7)
Regions:
    Asir: •region in southwestern Saudi Arabia •includes part of the Jabal al Hijaz •west of the Rub al Khali
Administrative Divisions: Al Bahah, Al Hudud ash Shamaliyah, Al Jawf, Al Madinah, Al Qasim, Ar Riyad, Ash Sharqiyah (Eastern Province), Asir, Hail, Jizan, Makkah, Najran, Tabuk (13 provinces)

Ethnic/Racial Groups: Arab, Afro-Asian
Religion: predominantly Islam
Language: Arabic
Currency: Saudi riyal
Current King: Fahd bin al-Aziz Al Saud
Cities (capital, largest, or with at least a million people):

Riyadh: •located in central Saudi Arabia •city in the Ar Riyad province •capital of Saudi Arabia •most populated city in Saudi Arabia (5,126,000 people) •on the eastern edge of the Najd

Jeddah: •located in southwestern Saudi Arabia •city in the Makkah province •chief port on the Red Sea

Mecca: •located in southwestern Saudi Arabia •city in the Makkah province •on the edge of the Jabal al Hijaz

ENVIRONMENTAL/ECONOMIC:
Climate: dry desert with extreme temperatures
Natural Resources: petroleum, natural gas, iron ore, gold, copper
Agricultural Products: wheat, barley, tomatoes, melons, mutton
Major Exports: petroleum and petroleum products
Natural Hazards: sandstorms, dust storms

SENEGAL

Country Name: Republic of Senegal
Continent: Africa

Area: 75,955 sq mi / 196,722 sq km
Population: 10,580,000
Population Density: 139 people per sq mi / 54 people per sq km
Capital: Dakar

PHYSICAL:
Highest Point: near Nepen Diakha 1,906 ft / 581 m
Lowest Point: Atlantic Ocean 0 ft / 0 m (sea level)
Grasslands/Prairies:
Sahel: •covers most of the country •extends into the Gambia, Mauritania, Mali, Guinea, and Guinea-Bissau
Oceans:
Atlantic: •forms the western coast of Senegal
Rivers:
Gambie (Gambia): •extends into Guinea and the Gambia
Senegal: •has its mouth in the Atlantic Ocean •forms all of the Senegal-Mauritania border •extends into Mali

POLITICAL:
Independence: April 4, 1960 (from France)
Bordering Countries: Mauritania, Gambia, Mali, Guinea-Bissau, Guinea (5)
Administrative Divisions: Dakar, Diourbel, Fatick, Kaolack, Kolda, Louga, Matam, Saint-Louis, Tambacounda, Thies, Ziguinchor (11 regions)
Ethnic/Racial Groups: Wolof, Pular, Serer, Joia, Mandinka
Religions: Islam, Christianity
Languages: French, Wolof, Pulaar, Diola, Jola, Mandinka
Currency: Communaute Financiere Africaine franc
Current President: Abdoulaye Wade
Cities (capital, largest, or with at least a million people):
Dakar: •located in western Senegal •city in the Dakar region of Senegal •capital of Senegal •most populated city in Senegal (2,167,000 people) •chief port on the Atlantic Ocean

ENVIRONMENTAL/ECONOMIC:
Climate: tropical hot and humid with rainy/dry seasons
Natural Resources: fish, phosphates, iron ore
Agricultural Products: peanuts, millet, corn, sorghum, cattle
Major Exports: fish, groundnuts, petroleum products, phosphates, cotton
Natural Hazards: floods, droughts

SERBIA AND MONTENEGRO

Country Name: Serbia and Montenegro
Continent: Europe
Area: 39,450 sq mi / 102,173 sq km
Population: 10,684,000
Population Density: 271 people per sq mi / 105 people per sq km
Capitals: Belgrade (administrative capital), Podgorica (judicial capital)

PHYSICAL:

Highest Point: Daravica 9,698 ft / 2,656 m
Lowest Point: Adriatic Sea 0 ft / 0 m (sea level)
Mountain Ranges:
  Balkan: • in southeastern Serbia and Montenegro •extend into Bulgaria
  Dinaric Alps: •located in southwestern Serbia and Montenegro •extend into Bosnia and Herzegovina and Croatia
Peaks (minimum elevation of 8,000 ft / 2,400 m):
  Daravica: •located in the Dinaric Alps •highest point in Serbia and Montenegro •near the Serbia and Montenegro-Albania border
Grasslands/Prairies:
  Great Alfold: •covers most of northern Serbia and Montenegro •extends into Croatia, Hungary, and Romania
Seas:
  Adriatic: •forms the southwestern coast of Serbia and Montenegro •feeds into the Ionian Sea

Lakes:
   Lake Scutari: •located in southwestern Serbia and Montenegro •on the Serbia and
      Montenegro-Albania border
Rivers:
   Danube: •forms part of Serbia and Montenegro's border with Croatia and Romania
      •extends into Hungary, Romania, and Bulgaria
   Sava: •tributary of the Danube River•forms part of the Serbia and Montenegro-Bosnia
      and Herzegovina border •extends into Croatia
   Tisa: •tributary of the Danube River •extends into Hungary and Romania

POLITICAL:
Independence: April 27, 1992 (from Yugoslavia)
Former Name: Yugoslavia
Bordering Countries: Bosnia and Herzegovina, Romania, Bulgaria, Albania,
   Croatia, Macedonia, Hungary (7)
Regions:
   Serbia: •region that covers most of the country •includes part of the Balkan Mountains
Administrative Divisions: Montenegro, Serbia (2 republics) •Kosovo, Vojvodina
   (2 nominally autonomous provinces)
Ethnic/Racial Groups: Serb, Albanian, Montenegrin, Hungarian
Religions: Christianity (Orthodox, Roman Catholic), Islam
Languages: Serbian, Albanian
Currency: new Yugoslav dinar, euro
Current President: Svetozar Marovic
Cities (capital, largest, or with at least a million people):
   Belgrade •located in central Serbia and Montenegro •city in the Serbia republic
      •administrative capital of Serbia and Montenegro •most populated city in Serbia
      and Montenegro (1,118,000 people) •chief port on the Danube and Sava Rivers
   Podgorica •located in southwestern Serbia and Montenegro •judicial capital of
      Serbia and Montenegro •largest city in the Montenegro republic (163,493 people)

ENVIRONMENTAL/ECONOMIC:
Climate: continental in the north with cold winters/hot and rainy summers; continental/
   Mediterranean in the central region; mild along the coast with hot and dry summers/cold
   and snowy winters
Natural Resources: oil, natural gas, coal, iron ore, bauxite
Agricultural Products: cereals, fruits, vegetables, tobacco, cattle
Major Exports: manufactured goods, food and live animals, raw materials
Natural Hazards: earthquakes

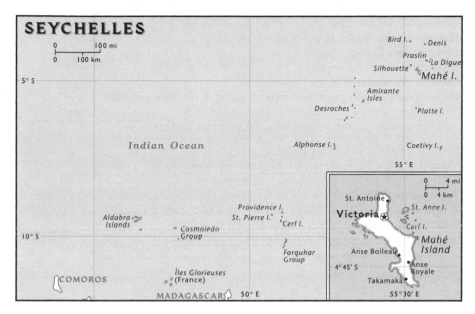

SEYCHELLES

Country Name: Republic of Seychelles
Continent: Africa
Area: 176 sq mi / 455 sq km (smallest country in Africa)
Population: 87,000 (smallest in Africa)
Population Density: 494 people per sq mi / 191 people per sq km
Capital: Victoria

PHYSICAL:
Highest Point: Morne Seychellois 2,969 ft / 905 m
Lowest Point: Indian Ocean 0 ft / 0 m (sea level)
Oceans:
   Indian: •surrounds the Seychelles
Islands:
   Seychelles: •group of islands extending northeast of Madagascar and Comoros
   Mahe: •largest island in Seychelles •surrounded by the Indian Ocean

POLITICAL:
Independence: June 29, 1976 (from the United Kingdom)
Administrative Divisions: Anse aux Pins, Anse Boileau, Anse Etoile, Anse Louis, Anse Royale, Baie Lazare, Baie Sainte Anne, Beau Vallon, Bel Air, Bel Ombre, Cascade, Glacis, Grand' Anse (on Mahe), Grand' Anse (on Praslin), La Digue, La Riviere Anglaise, Mont Buxton, Mont Fleuri, Plaisance, Pointe La Rue, Port Glaud, Saint Louis, Takamaka (23 administrative districts)

Ethnic/Racial Groups: predominantly Seychellois (mix of French, African, and Asian)
Religion: Christianity (Roman Catholic, Anglican)
Languages: English, French, Creole
Currency: Seychelles rupee
Current President: James Michel
Cities (capital, largest, or with at least a million people):
  Victoria: •city on Mahe Island •capital of Seychelles •most populated city in Seychelles (25,000 people) •chief port on the Indian Ocean

ENVIRONMENTAL/ECONOMIC:
Climate: tropical humid marine with warmer/cooler seasons
Natural Resources: fish, copra, cinnamon trees
Agricultural Products: coconuts, cinnamon, vanilla, sweet potatoes, broiler chickens
Major Exports: canned tuna, frozen fish, cinnamon bark, copra, petroleum products
Natural Hazards: droughts

SIERRA LEONE

Country Name: Republic of Sierra Leone
Continent: Africa
Area: 27,699 sq mi / 71,740 sq km
Population: 5,733,000
Population Density: 207 people per sq mi / 80 people per sq km
Capital: Freetown

PHYSICAL:
Highest Point: Durukonko 6,391 ft / 1,948 m
Lowest Point: Atlantic Ocean 0 ft / 0 m (sea level)
Oceans:
    Atlantic: •forms the western and southern coasts of Sierra Leone

POLITICAL:
Independence: April 27, 1961 (from the United Kingdom)
Bordering Countries: Guinea, Liberia (2)
Administrative Divisions: Eastern, Northern, Southern (3 provinces) •Western (1 area)
Ethnic/Racial Groups: Temne, Mende, other indigenous tribes, Creole
Religions: Islam, indigenous beliefs, Christianity
Languages: English, Mende, Temne, Krio
Currency: leone
Current President: Ahmad Tejan Kabbah
Cities (capital, largest, or with at least a million people):
    Freetown: •located in western Sierra Leone •city in the Western area •capital of
    Sierra Leone •most populated city in Sierra Leone (921,000 people) •chief port
    on the Atlantic Ocean

ENVIRONMENTAL/ECONOMIC:
Climate: tropical hot and humid with rainy/dry seasons
Natural Resources: diamonds, titanium ore, bauxite, iron ore, gold
Agricultural Products: rice, coffee, cacao, palm kernels, poultry
Major Exports: diamonds, rutile, cacao, coffee
Natural Hazards: harmattan winds, sandstorms, dust storms

SINGAPORE
Country Name: Republic of Singapore
Continent: Asia
Area: 255 sq mi / 660 sq km
Population: 4,372,000
Population Density: 17,145 people per sq mi / 6,624 people per sq km (most dense
    in Asia)
Capital: Singapore

PHYSICAL:
Highest Point: Timah Hill 531 ft / 162 m
Lowest Point: South China Sea 0 ft / 0 m (sea level)
Straits:
    Singapore: •forms the southern coast of Singapore •separates Singapore from
    Indonesia •connects the Strait of Malacca and South China Sea

Johore: •forms the northern coast of Singapore •separates Singapore from Malaysia
•feeds into the Singapore Strait

Islands:
Singapore: •main island in Singapore •bordered by the Singapore Strait

POLITICAL:
Independence: August 9, 1965 (from the United Kingdom)
Ethnic/Racial Groups: Chinese, Malay, Indian
Religions: Buddhism, Islam, Christianity, Hinduism, Sikh, Taoism, Confucianism
Languages: Chinese, Malay, Tamil, English
Currency: Singapore dollar
Current President: Sellapan Rama Nathan
Cities (capital, largest, or with at least a million people):
Singapore: •located in southern Singapore •capital of Singapore •most populated
city in Singapore (4,185,200 people) •chief port on the Singapore Strait

ENVIRONMENTAL/ECONOMIC:
Climate: tropical hot and humid with monsoon rains
Natural Resources: fish, deep-water ports
Agricultural Products: rubber, copra, fruit, orchids, poultry
Major Exports: machinery and equipment, consumer goods, chemicals, mineral fuels
Natural Hazards: floods, thunderstorms, haze

SLOVAKIA

Country Name: Slovak Republic
Continent: Europe
Area: 18,932 sq mi / 49,035 sq km
Population: 5,355,000
Population Density: 283 people per sq mi / 109 people per sq km
Capital: Bratislava

PHYSICAL:
Highest Point: Gerlachovsky Stit 8,710 ft / 2,655 m
Lowest Point: Bodrok River 308 ft / 94 m
Mountain Ranges:
   Carpathian: ●cover much of central Slovakia ●extend into Czech Republic, Poland, and Ukraine
Peaks (minimum elevation of 8,000 ft / 2,400 m):
   Gerlachovsky Stit: ●located in the Carpathian Mountains ●highest point in Slovakia
Grasslands/Prairies:
   Great Alfold: ●located in southeastern Slovakia ●extends into Ukraine and Hungary
Rivers:
   Danube: ●forms part of Slovakia-Hungary border ●extends into Austria and Hungary
   Vah: ●tributary of the Danube River ●has its source in the Carpathian Mountains

Independence: January 1, 1993 (from Czechoslovakia)
Bordering Countries: Hungary, Poland, Czech Republic, Ukraine, Austria (5)
Administrative Divisions: Banskobystricky, Bratislavsky, Kosicky, Nitriansky, Presovsky, Trenciansky, Trnavsky, Zilinsky (8 regions)
Ethnic/Racial Groups: Slovak, Hungarian, Roma
Religion: Christianity (Roman Catholic, Protestant, Orthodox)
Languages: Slovak, Hungarian
Currency: Slovak koruna
Current President: Ivan Gasparovic
Cities (capital, largest, or with at least a million people):
　　Bratislava: ●located in southwestern Slovakia ●city in the Bratislavsky region ●capital of Slovakia ●most populated city in Slovakia (425,000 people) ●chief port on the Danube River

ENVIRONMENTAL/ECONOMIC:

Climate: temperate with cool summers/cold winters
Natural Resources: brown coal, lignite, iron ore, copper ore, manganese ore
Agricultural Products: grains, potatoes, sugar beets, hops, pigs
Major Exports: machinery and transport equipment, manufactured goods
Natural Hazards: floods, thunderstorms, landslides

SLOVENIA
Country Name: Republic of Slovenia
Continent: Europe
Area: 7,827 sq mi / 20,273 sq km
Population: 1,999,000
Population Density: 255 people per sq mi / 99 people per sq km
Capital: Ljubljana

PHYSICAL:

Highest Point: Triglav 9,393 ft / 2,863 m
Lowest Point: Gulf of Trieste 0 ft / 0 m (sea level)
Mountain Ranges:
　　Julian Alps: ●cover much of western Slovenia ●extend into Italy, Austria, and Croatia
Peaks (minimum elevation of 8,000 ft / 2,400 m):
　　Triglav: ●located in the Julian Alps ●highest point in Slovenia
Gulfs:
　　Gulf of Trieste: ●forms the southwestern coast of Slovenia ●feeds into the Gulf of Venice
Rivers:
　　Drava: ●extends into Austria, Croatia, and Hungary
　　Sava: ●has its source in the Julian Alps ●extends into Croatia

Independence: June 25, 1991 (from Yugoslavia)
Former Names: People's Republic of Slovenia, Socialist Republic of Slovenia
Bordering Countries: Croatia, Austria, Italy, Hungary (4)
Administrative Divisions: Ajdovscina, Beltinci, Benedikt, Bistrica ob Sotli, Bled,
Bloke, Bohinj, Borovnica, Bovec, Braslovce, Brda, Brezice, Brezovica, Cankova, Cerklje
na Gorenjskem, Cerknica, Cerkno, Cerkvenjak, Crensovci, Crna na Koroskem,
Crnomelj, Destrnik, Divaca, Dobje, Dobrepolje, Dobrna, Dobrova-Horjul-Polhov
Gradec, Dobrovnik-Dobronak, Dolenjske Toplice, Dol pri Ljubljani, Domzale,
Dornava, Dravograd, Duplek, Gorenja Vas-Poljane, Gorisnica, Gornja Radgona, Gornji
Grad, Gornji Petrovci, Grad, Grosuplje, Hajdina, Hoce-Slivnica, Hodos-Hodos, Horjul,
Hrastnik, Hrpelje-Kozina, Idrija, Ig, Ilirska Bistrica, Ivancna Gorica, Izola-Isola,
Jesenice, Jezersko, Jursinci, Kamnik, Kanal, Kidricevo, Kobarid, Kobilje, Kocevje,
Komen, Komenda, Kostel, Kozje, Kranjska Gora, Krizevci, Krsko, Kungota, Kuzma,
Lasko, Lenart, Lendava-Lendva, Litija, Ljubno, Ljutomer, Logatec, Loska Dolina,
Loski Potok, Lovrenc na Pohorju, Luce, Lukovica, Majsperk, Markovci, Medvode,
Menges, Metlika, Mezica, Miklavz na Dravskem Polju, Miren-Kostanjevica, Mirna Pec,
Mislinja, Moravce, Moravske Toplice, Mozirje, Muta, Naklo, Nazarje, Odranci,
Oplotnica, Ormoz, Osilnica, Pesnica, Piran-Pirano, Pivka, Podcetrtek, Podlehnik,
Podvelka, Polzela, Postojna, Prebold, Preddvor, Prevalje, Puconci, Race-Fram, Radece,
Radenci, Radlje ob Dravi, Radovljica, Ravne na Koroskem, Razkrizje, Ribnica, Ribnica
na Pohorju, Rogaska Slatina, Rogasovci, Rogatec, Ruse, Salovci, Selnica ob Dravi,
Semic, Sempeter-Vrtojba, Sencur, Sentilj, Sentjernej, Sentjur pri Celju, Sevnica, Sezana,
Skocjan, Skofja Loka, Skofljica, Slovenska Bistrica, Slovenske Konjice, Smarje pri Jelsah,

Smartno ob Paki, Smartno pri Litiji, Sodrazica, Solcava, Sostanj, Starse, Store, Sveta Ana, Sveti Andraz v Slovenskih Goricah, Sveti Jurij, Tabor, Tisina, Tolmin, Trbovlje, Trebnje, Trnovska Vas, Trzic, Trzin, Turnisce, Velika Polana, Velike Lasce, Verzej, Videm, Vipava, Vitanje, Vodice, Vojnik, Vransko, Vrhnika, Vuzenica, Zagorje ob Savi, Zalec, Zavrc, Zelezniki, Zetale, Ziri, Zirovnica, Zuzemberk, Zrece (182 municipalities)
•Celje, Koper-Capodistria, Kranj, Ljubljana, Maribor, Murska Sobota, Nova Gorica, Nova Mesto, Ptuj, Slovenj Gradec, Velenje (11 urban municipalities)

Ethnic/Racial Groups: Slovene, Croat, Serb, Bosniak
Religion: Christianity (primarily Roman Catholic)
Languages: Slovenian, Serbo-Croatian
Currency: tolar
Current President: Janez Drnovsek
Cities (capital, largest, or with at least a million people):
Ljubljana: •located in central Slovenia •city in the Ljubljana urban municipality •capital of Slovenia •most populated city in Slovenia (256,000 people) •on the edge of the Julian Alps •chief port on the Sava River

ENVIRONMENTAL/ECONOMIC:

Climate: Mediterranean along the coast; continental in the mountains and valleys with hot summers/cold winters
Natural Resources: lignite coal, lead, zinc, mercury, uranium
Agricultural Products: potatoes, hops, wheat, sugar beets, cattle
Major Exports: manufactured goods, machinery and transport equipment, chemicals, food
Natural Hazards: floods, earthquakes

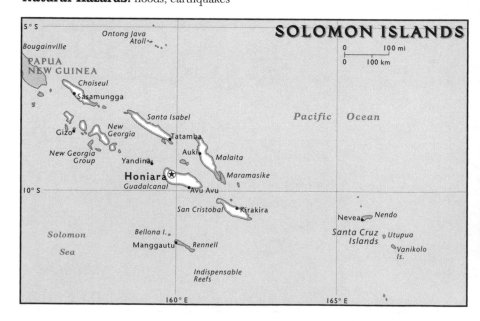

SOLOMON ISLANDS

Country Name: Solomon Islands
Continent: Australia/Oceania
Area: 10,954 sq mi / 28,370 sq km
Population: 491,000
Population Density: 45 people per sq mi / 17 people per sq km
Capital: Honiara

PHYSICAL:

Highest Point: Mount Makarakomburu 8,028 ft / 2,447 m
Lowest Point: Pacific Ocean 0 ft / 0 m (sea level)

Peaks (minimum elevation of 8,000 ft / 2,400 m):
Mount Makarakomburu: •located on the island of Guadalcanal •highest point in Solomon Islands
Oceans:
Pacific: •forms most of the northern coast of Solomon Islands
Seas:
Solomon: •forms most of the southern coast of Solomon Islands •feeds into the Coral Sea and Pacific Ocean
Coral: •forms part of the southern coast of Solomon Islands •feeds into the Pacific Ocean
Islands:
Guadalcanal: •largest island in Solomon Islands •bordered by the Solomon Sea

POLITICAL:

Independence: July 7, 1978 (from the United Kingdom)
Former Name: British Solomon Islands
Administrative Divisions: Central, Choiseul (Lauru), Guadalcanal, Isabel, Makira, Malaita, Rennell/Bellona, Temotu, Western (9 provinces) •Honiara (1 capital territory)
Ethnic/Racial Groups: Melanesian, Polynesian, Micronesian, European
Religion: Christianity (Protestant, Roman Catholic)
Languages: Melanesian pidgin, indigenous languages, English
Currency: Solomon Islands dollar
Current Prime Minister: Allan Kemakeza
Cities (capital, largest, or with at least a million people):
Honiara: •located on the island of Guadalcanal •city in the Honiara capital territory •capital of Solomon Islands •most populated city in Solomon Islands (56,000 people) •chief port on the Solomon Sea

ENVIRONMENTAL/ECONOMIC:

Climate: tropical monsoon
Natural Resources: fish, forests, gold, bauxite, phosphates

SOMALIA

Agricultural Products: cacao, coconuts, palm kernels, rice, cattle
Major Exports: timber, fish, copra, palm oil
Natural Hazards: typhoons, earthquakes, volcanoes

SOMALIA
Country Name: Somalia
Continent: Africa
Area: 246,201 sq mi / 637,657 sq km
Population: 8,025,000
Population Density: 33 people per sq mi / 13 people per sq km
Capital: Mogadishu

PHYSICAL:
Highest Point: Buuraha Surud Cad 7,900 ft / 2,408 m
Lowest Point: Indian Ocean 0 ft / 0 m (sea level)
Oceans:
 Indian: •forms the eastern coast of Somalia
Gulfs:
 Gulf of Aden: •forms the northern coast of Somalia •feeds into the Arabian Sea
 and Indian Ocean

Rivers:
   Webi Shabeelle: •has its mouth in the Indian Ocean •extends into Ethiopia
Regions:
   Haud: •lowland, desert region that stretches across northern Somalia •extends
      into Ethiopia

POLITICAL:
Independence: July 1, 1960 (from United Kingdom and Italian administration)
Former Names: Somali Republic, Somali Democratic Republic, British Somaliland,
   Italian Somaliland
Bordering Countries: Ethiopia, Kenya, Djibouti (3)
Regions:
   Somaliland •mountainous region in northern Somalia •declared independence
      from Somalia in 1991
Administrative Divisions: Awdal, Bakool, Banaadir, Bari, Bay, Galguduud, Gedo,
   Hiiraan, Jubbada Dhexe, Jubbada Hoose, Mudug, Nugaal, Sanaag, Shabeellaha
   Dhexe, Shabeellaha Hoose, Sool, Togdheer, Woqooyi Galbeed (18 regions)
Ethnic/Racial Groups: Somali, Bantu
Religion: Islam (primarily Sunni)
Languages: Somali, Arabic, Italian, English
Currency: Somali shilling
Current President: Abdullahi Yusuf Ahmed
Cities (capital, largest, or with at least a million people):
   Mogadishu: •located in southeastern Somalia •city in the Banaadir region •capital of
      Somalia •most populated city in Somalia (1,175,000 people) •chief port on the
      Indian Ocean

ENVIRONMENTAL/ECONOMIC:
Climate: mainly desert with mild to hot temperatures and two monsoon seasons
Natural Resources: uranium, iron ore, tin, gypsum, bauxite
Agricultural Products: bananas, sorghum, corn, coconuts, cattle
Major Exports: livestock, bananas, hides, fish, charcoal
Natural Hazards: droughts, dust storms, floods

SOUTH AFRICA
Country Name: Republic of South Africa
Continent: Africa
Area: 470,693 sq mi / 1,219,090 sq km
Population: 44,024,000
Population Density: 94 people per sq mi / 36 people per sq km
Capitals: Pretoria (administrative capital), Cape Town (legislative capital), Bloemfontein
   (judicial capital)

PHYSICAL:
Highest Point: Mafadi 11,306 ft / 3,446 m
Lowest Point: Atlantic Ocean 0 ft / 0 m
Mountain Ranges:
Drakensberg: •cover an area from southern to northeastern South Africa
Peaks (minimum elevation of 8,000 ft / 2,400 m):
Mafadi: •located in the Drakensberg •on the South Africa-Lesotho border (just north of Giant's Castle) •highest point in South Africa
Plateau Regions:
Great Karoo: •located in southern South Africa •basin at the western end of the Drakensberg
Deserts:
Kalahari: •located in northern and western South Africa •extends into Namibia and Botswana
Oceans:
Atlantic: •forms part of the western coast of South Africa
Indian: •forms the eastern coast and most of the southern coast of South Africa
Rivers:
Limpopo: •has its source in the Drakensberg •forms all of the South Africa-Zimbabwe border •forms part of the South Africa-Botswana border •extends into Mozambique
Orange: •has its mouth in the Atlantic Ocean •forms much of the South Africa-Namibia border •extends into Lesotho
Vaal: •tributary of the Orange River •has its source in the Drakensberg

Capes:
    Cape Agulhas: •bordered by the Indian Ocean •southernmost point in Africa
    Cape of Good Hope: •bordered by the Atlantic and Indian Oceans

POLITICAL:
Independence: May 31, 1910 (from the United Kingdom)
Former Name: Union of South Africa
Bordering Countries: Botswana, Namibia, Lesotho, Mozambique, Swaziland, Zimbabwe (6)
Regions:
    Bushmanland: •region in western South Africa •east of the Atlantic Ocean
    Zululand: •region in eastern South Africa •west of the Indian Ocean
Administrative Divisions: Eastern Cape, Free State, Gauteng, KwaZulu-Natal, Limpopo, Mpumalanga, Northern Cape, North-West, Western Cape (9 provinces)
Ethnic/Racial Groups: black, white, mixed, Indian
Religions: Christianity, indigenous beliefs, Islam, Hinduism
Languages: Afrikaans, English, Ndebele, Pedi, Sotho, Swazi, Tsonga, Tswana, Venda, Xhosa, Zulu
Currency: rand
Current President: Thabo Mbeki
Cities (capital, largest, or with at least a million people):
    Johannesburg: •located in northeastern South Africa •city in the Gauteng province •most populated city in South Africa (5,271,000 people)
    Cape Town: •located in southwestern South Africa •city in the Western Cape province •legislative capital of South Africa (3,103,000 people) •a major port on the Atlantic Ocean
    Durban: •located in eastern South Africa •city in the KwaZulu-Natal province •on the edge of the Drakensberg •a major port on the Indian Ocean
    Pretoria: •located in northeastern South Africa •city in the Gauteng province •administrative capital of South Africa (1,209,000 people)
    Soweto: •located in northeastern South Africa •city in the Gauteng province
    Bloemfontein: •located in central South Africa •city in the Free State province •judicial capital of South Africa (381,000 people)

ENVIRONMENTAL/ECONOMIC:
Climate: mostly semi-arid; subtropical on the east coast
Natural Resources: gold, chromium, antimony, coal, iron ore
Agricultural Products: corn, wheat, sugarcane, fruits, beef
Major Exports: gold, diamonds, platinum, other metals and minerals, machinery and equipment
Natural Hazards: droughts

SPAIN

Country Name: Kingdom of Spain
Continent: Europe
Area: 195,363 sq mi / 505,988 sq km
Population: 41,334,000
Population Density: 212 people per sq mi / 82 people per sq km
Capital: Madrid

PHYSICAL:
Highest Point: Pico de Teide (on Tenerife) 12,198 ft / 3,718 m
Lowest Point: Atlantic Ocean 0 ft / 0 m (sea level)
Mountain Ranges:
  Cordillera Cantabrica (Cantabrian): •cover much of northern Spain
  Pyrenees: •located in northeastern Spain •extend into France and Andorra
  Sierra Morena: •cover much of southern Spain
Peaks (minimum elevation of 8,000 ft / 2,400 m):
  Pico de Teide: •located on the island of Tenerife in the Canary Islands •highest
    point in Spain
Oceans:
  Atlantic: •forms part of the western coast of Spain
Seas:
  Alboran (sometimes considered part of the Mediterranean): •forms much of the
    southern coast of Spain •feeds into the Atlantic Ocean

Balearic: •forms much of the eastern coast of Spain •feeds into the Mediterranean Sea
Mediterranean: •forms much of the eastern and southern coasts of Spain •feeds into the Atlantic Ocean

Gulfs:
Gulf of Cadiz: •forms part of the southwestern coast of Spain •feeds into the Atlantic Ocean
Gulf of Valencia: •forms part of the eastern coast of Spain •feeds into the Balearic Sea

Bays:
Bay of Biscay: •forms most of the northern coast of Spain •feeds into the Atlantic Ocean

Straits:
Strait of Gibraltar: •forms part of the southwestern coast of Spain •separates Spain from Morocco •connects the Alboran Sea and the Atlantic Ocean

Rivers:
Duero (Douro): •has its source in northern Spain •forms part of the Spain-Portugal border •extends into Portugal
Ebro: •has its mouth in the Balearic Sea •has its source in the Cordillera Cantabrica
Guadiana: •has its mouth in the Gulf of Cadiz •has its source in central Spain •forms part of the Spain-Portugal border •extends into Portugal
Tagus: •has its source in eastern Spain •forms part of the Spain-Portugal border •extends into Portugal

Islands:
Balearic: • island group between the Mediterranean and Balearic Seas
Canary: •island group off the the coast of Western Sahara (claimed by Morocco) •surrounded by the Atlantic Ocean
Gran Canaria: •island in the Canary Islands •surrounded by the Atlantic Ocean
Majorca: •largest island in Spain •island in the Balearic Islands •bordered by the Mediterranean and Balearic Seas
Tenerife: •second largest island in Spain •island in the Canary Islands •surrounded by the Atlantic Ocean

POLITICAL:
Independence: 1492 (final victory over the Moors)
Bordering Countries: Portugal, France, Andorra, Morocco, Gibraltar (dependency of the United Kingdom)(5)
Administrative Divisions: Andalucia, Aragon, Asturias, Baleares (Balearic Islands), Canarias (Canary Islands), Cantabria, Castilla-La Mancha, Castilla y Leon, Cataluna, Ceuta (along north coast of Morocco), Communidad Valencian, Extremadura, Galicia, La Rioja, Madrid, Melilla (along north coast of Morocco), Murcia, Navarra, Pais Vasco (Basque Country) (19 autonomous communities)
Ethnic/Racial Groups: Castilian, Catalan, Basque, Galician
Religion: Christianity (primarily Roman Catholic)
Languages: Castilian Spanish, Catalan, Galician, Basque
Currency: euro

Current Prime Minister: Jose Luis Rodriguez Zapatero
Cities (capital, largest, or with at least a million people):
Madrid: •located in central Spain •city in the Madrid autonomous community
•capital of Spain •most populated city in Spain (5,145,000 people)
Barcelona: •located in northeastern Spain •city in the Cataluna autonomous
community •chief port on the Mediterranean Sea
Valencia: •located in eastern Spain •city in the Communidad Valencian autonomous
community •chief port on the Gulf of Valencia
Seville: •located in southern Spain •city in the Andalucia autonomous community

ENVIRONMENTAL/ECONOMIC:
Climate: temperate with hot summers/cold winters in the interior and moderate
summers/cool winters along the coast
Natural Resources: coal, lignite, iron ore, copper, lead
Agricultural Products: grain, vegetables, olives, wine grapes, beef
Major Exports: machinery, motor vehicles, foodstuffs, other consumer goods
Natural Hazards: droughts

SRI LANKA
Country Name: Democratic Socialist Republic of Sri Lanka
Continent: Asia
Area: 25,299 sq mi / 65,525 sq km
Population: 19,273,000
Population Density: 762 people per sq mi / 294 people per sq km
Capital: Colombo

PHYSICAL:
Highest Point: Pidurutalagala 8,281 ft / 2,524 m
Lowest Point: Indian Ocean 0 ft / 0 m (sea level)
Peaks (minimum elevation of 8,000 ft / 2,400 m):
Pidurutalagala: •located in southern Sri Lanka •highest point in Sri Lanka
Oceans:
Indian: •forms the southern coast of Sri Lanka
Gulfs:
Gulf of Mannar: •forms much of the western coast of Sri Lanka •feeds into the
Indian Ocean
Bays:
Bay of Bengal: •forms much of the eastern coast of Sri Lanka •feeds into the
Indian Ocean
Straits:
Palk: •forms much of the northwestern coast of Sri Lanka •separates the island of
Sri Lanka from India •connects the Gulf of Mannar and the Bay of Bengal

Islands:

Sri Lanka: •main island in Sri Lanka •bordered by the Indian Ocean, Gulf of Mannar, Bay of Bengal, and Palk Strait

POLITICAL:

Independence: February 4, 1948 (from the United Kingdom)

Former Names: Serendib, Ceylon

Administrative Divisions: Central, North Central, North Eastern, North Western, Sabaragamuwa, Southern, Uva, Western (8 provinces)

Ethnic/Racial Groups: Sinhalese, Tamil, Moor

Religions: Buddhism, Hinduism, Christianity, Islam

Languages: Sinhala, Tamil, English

Currency: Sri Lankan rupee

Current President: Chandrika Bandaranaike Kumaratunga

Cities (capital, largest, or with at least a million people):

Colombo: •located in southwestern Sri Lanka •city in the Western province •capital of Sri Lanka •most populated city in Sri Lanka (648,000 people) •chief port on the Indian Ocean

ENVIRONMENTAL/ECONOMIC:

Climate: tropical monsoon with two monsoon seasons

Natural Resources: limestone, graphite, mineral sands, gems, phosphates

Agricultural Products: rice, sugarcane, grains, pulses, milk

Major Exports: textiles and apparel, tea, diamonds, coconut products, petroleum products

Natural Hazards: cyclones, tornadoes

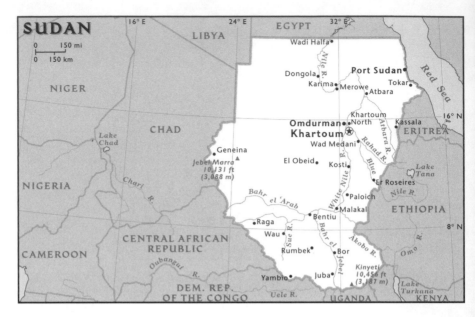

SUDAN

Country Name: Republic of the Sudan
Continent: Africa
Area: 967,500 sq mi / 2,505,813 sq km (largest in Africa)
Population: 38,114,000
Population Density: 39 people per sq mi / 15 people per sq km
Capital: Khartoum

PHYSICAL:
Highest Point: Kinyeti 10,456 ft / 3,187 m
Lowest Point: Red Sea 0 ft / 0 m (sea level)
Peaks (minimum elevation of 8,000 ft / 2,400 m):
    Kinyeti: •located in southeastern Sudan •highest point in Sudan
Grasslands/Prairies:
    Sahel: •covers much of central Sudan •extends into Chad and Central African
        Republic
Deserts:
    Libyan: •located in northwestern Sudan •extends into Egypt, Libya, and Chad
    Nubian: •covers much of northern Sudan •extends into Egypt
    Sahara: •covers most of northern Sudan •extends into Chad, Libya, and Egypt
        •largest desert in the world
Swamps:
    Sudd: •located in southern Sudan

Seas:

Red: •forms the eastern coast of Sudan •feeds into the Gulf of Aden

Lakes:

Lake Nasser: •also known in Sudan as Lake Nubia •located in northern Sudan •fed by the Nile River •formed by the Aswan High Dam •on the edge of the Nubian Desert •surrounded by the Sahara •extends into Egypt

Rivers:

Blue Nile: •tributary of the Nile River •extends into Ethiopia

Nile: •extends into Egypt •longest river in the world (including its White Nile tributary)

White Nile: •tributary of the Nile River •extends into Uganda

POLITICAL:

Independence: January 1, 1956 (from Egypt and the United Kingdom)

Former Name: Anglo-Egyptian Sudan

Bordering Countries: Ethiopia, Chad, Egypt, Central African Republic, Democratic Republic of the Congo, Eritrea, Uganda, Libya (8)

Administrative Divisions: A'ali an Nil, Al Bahr al Ahmar, Al Buhayrat, Al Jazirah, Al Khartum, Al Qadarif, Al Wahdah, An Nil al Abyad, An Nil al Azraq, Ash Shamaliyah, Bahr al Jabal, Gharb al Istiwa'iyah, Gharb Bahr al Ghazal, Gharb Darfur, Gharb Kurdufan, Janub Darfur, Janub Kurdufan, Junqali, Kassala, Nahr an Nil, Shamal Bahr al Ghazal, Shamal Darfur, Shamal Kurdufan, Sharq al Istiwa'iyah, Sinnar, Warab (26 states)

Ethnic/Racial Groups: black, Arab, Beja

Religions: Islam (primarily Sunni), indigenous beliefs, Christianity

Languages: Arabic, Nubian, Ta Bedawie, many local dialects

Currency: Sudanese dinar

Current President: Umar Hassan al-Bashir

Cities (capital, largest, or with at least a million people):

Khartoum: •located in eastern Sudan •city in the Al Khartum state •capital of Sudan •most populated city in Sudan (4,286,000 people) •chief port on the Nile, White Nile, and Blue Nile Rivers

ENVIRONMENTAL/ECONOMIC:

Climate: tropical in the south; arid desert in the north; rainy/dry seasons

Natural Resources: petroleum, iron ore, copper, chromium ore, zinc

Agricultural Products: cotton, groundnuts, sorghum, millet, wheat

Major Exports: oil and petroleum products, cotton, sesame, livestock, groundnuts

Natural Hazards: dust storms, droughts

SURINAME

Country Name: Republic of Suriname

Continent: South America

Area: 63,037 sq mi / 163,265 sq km (smallest in South America)

Population: 444,000 (smallest in South America)

Population Density: 7.0 people per sq mi / 2.7 people per sq km (least dense in South America)
Capital: Paramaribo

PHYSICAL:
Highest Point: Juliana Top 4,035 ft / 1,230 m
Lowest Point: unnamed location 7 ft / 2 m below sea level
Mountain Ranges:
　　Guiana Highlands: ●cover much of southern Suriname ●extend into Guyana, Brazil, and French Guiana (overseas territory of France)
Oceans:
　　Atlantic: ●forms the northern coast of Suriname
Lakes:
　　Van Blommestein Meer: ●located in eastern Suriname ●reservoir of the Suriname River ●formed by the Afobaka Dam
　　Wonotobo Vallen: ●located in western Suriname ●on the edge of the Guiana Highlands

POLITICAL:
Independence: November 25, 1975 (from the Netherlands)
Former Names: Netherlands Guiana, Dutch Guiana
Bordering Countries: Guyana, Brazil, French Guiana (French overseas territory) (3)
Administrative Divisions: Brokopondo, Commewijne, Coronie, Marowijne, Nickerie, Para, Paramaribo, Saramacca, Sipaliwini, Wanica (10 districts)

Ethnic/Racial Groups: East Indian, Creole, Javanese, Maroons, Amerindian, Chinese
Religions: Hinduism, Christianity (Protestant, Roman Catholic), Islam
Languages: Dutch, English, Sranang Tongo, Hindustani, Javanese
Currency: Surinamese guilder
Current President: Runaldo Ronald Venetiaan
Cities (capital, largest, or with at least a million people):
> Paramaribo: •located in northern Suriname •city in the Paramaribo district •capital of Suriname •most populated city in Suriname (253,000 people) •chief port on the Atlantic Ocean

ENVIRONMENTAL/ECONOMIC:
Climate: tropical, moderated by trade winds
Natural Resources: timber, hydropower, fish, kaolin, shrimp
Agricultural Products: paddy rice, bananas, palm kernels, beef, forest products
Major Exports: alumina, crude oil, lumber, shrimp and fish, rice
Natural Disasters: floods, forest fires

SWAZILAND
Country Name: Kingdom of Swaziland
Continent: Africa
Area: 6,704 sq mi / 17,363 sq km
Population: 1,161,000
Population Density: 173 people per sq mi / 67 people per sq km
Capitals: Mbabane (administrative capital), Lobamba (legislative and royal capital)

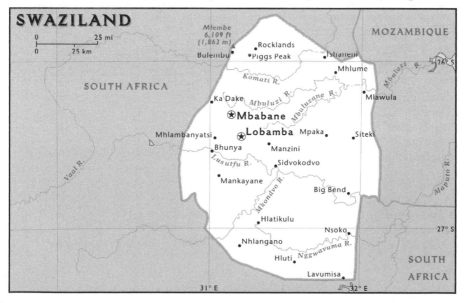

PHYSICAL:
Highest Point: Mlembe 6,109 ft / 1,862 m
Lowest Point: Great Usutu River 69 ft / 21 m
Mountain Ranges:
    Drakensberg: •cover much of western Swaziland •extend into South Africa

POLITICAL:
Independence: September 6, 1968 (from the United Kingdom)
Bordering Countries: South Africa, Mozambique (2)
Administrative Divisions: Hhohho, Lubombo, Manzini, Shiselweni (4 districts)
Ethnic/Racial Groups: native African, European
Religions: indigenous beliefs, Christianity (Roman Catholic), Islam
Languages: English, siSwati
Currency: lilangeni
Current King: Mswati III
Cities (capital, largest, or with at least a million people):
    Mbabane: •located in northwestern Swaziland •in the Hhohho district •judicial
        capital of Swaziland (70,000 people)
    Lobamba: •in the Hhohho district • legislative and royal capital of Swaziland (4,400
        people)

ENVIRONMENTAL/ECONOMIC:
Climate: tropical to temperate
Natural Resources: asbestos, coal, clay, cassiterite, hydropower
Agricultural Products: sugarcane, cotton, corn, tobacco, cattle
Major Exports: soft drink concentrates, sugar, wood pulp, cotton yarn
Natural Hazards: droughts

SWEDEN
Country Name: Kingdom of Sweden
Continent: Europe
Area: 173,732 sq mi / 449,964 sq km
Population: 8,960,000
Population Density: 52 people per sq mi / 20 people per sq km
Capital: Stockholm

PHYSICAL:
Highest Point: Kebnekaise 6,926 ft / 2,111 m
Lowest Point: Lake Hammarsjon 8 ft / 2.41 m below sea level
Mountain Ranges:
    Kjolen: •cover an area from northern to southwestern Sweden •extend into
        Norway and Finland
Seas:
    Baltic: •forms much of the southern coast of Sweden •feeds into the Kattegat

Gulfs:

Gulf of Bothnia: •forms part of the eastern coast of Sweden •feeds into the
  Baltic Sea

Kattegat: •forms part of the southwestern coast of Sweden •feeds into the North Sea

Straits:

Kalmar: •forms much of the southeastern coast of Sweden •separates the island of
  Oland from Sweden

Oresund: •forms part of the southwestern coast of Sweden •separates Sweden from
  Denmark •connects the Baltic Sea and the Kattegat

Channels:

Skagerrak: •forms part of the southwestern coast of Sweden •separates Sweden and
  Norway from Denmark •connects the Kattegat and the North Sea

Lakes:

Vanern: •located in southwestern Sweden •largest lake in Sweden

Vattern: •located in southern Sweden

Islands:

Gotland: •island in the Baltic Sea •off the southeastern coast of Sweden

Oland: •island off the coast of southeastern Sweden •bordered by the Baltic Sea
  and the Kalmar Strait

POLITICAL:

Independence: June 6, 1523 (date Gustav Vasa became king)

Bordering Countries: Norway, Finland (2)

Regions:

    Gotaland: •region that covers much of southern Sweden •east of the Skagerrak, Kattegat, and Oresund •west of the Baltic Sea and Kalmar Strait •includes parts of Lakes Vanern and Vattern

    Lapland: •region located in northern Sweden •includes part of the Kjolen •extends into Norway and Finland

    Norrland: •region that covers much of northern and central Sweden •includes part of the Kjolen • west of the Gulf of Bothnia

    Svealand: •region that covers much of central Sweden •includes part of the Kjolen •west of the Gulf of Bothnia and Baltic Sea •includes parts of Lakes Vanern and Vattern

Administrative Divisions: Blekinge, Dalarnas, Gavleborgs, Gotlands, Hallands, Jamtlands, Jonkopings, Kalmar, Kronobergs, Norrbottens, Orebro, Ostergotlands, Skane, Sodermanlands, Stockholms, Uppsala, Varmlands, Vasterbottens, Vasternorrlands, Vastmanlands, Vastra Gotalands (21 counties)

Ethnic/Racial Groups: Swedish, Finnish, Sami

Religion: Christianity (Lutheran, Roman Catholic)

Language: primarily Swedish

Currency: Swedish krona

Current Prime Minister: Goran Persson

Cities (capital, largest, or with at least a million people):

    Stockholm: •located in southeastern Sweden •city in Stockholms county •capital of Sweden •most populated city in Sweden (1,697,000 people) •chief port on the Baltic Sea

ENVIRONMENTAL/ECONOMIC:

Climate: temperate in the south; sub-arctic in the north; cold winters/cool summers

Natural Resources: iron ore, copper, lead, zinc, gold

Agricultural Products: barley, wheat, sugar beets, meat

Major Exports: machinery, motor vehicles, paper products, pulp and wood, iron and steel products

Natural Hazards: sea ice

SWITZERLAND

Country Name: Swiss Confederation

Continent: Europe

Area: 15,940 sq mi / 41,284 sq km

Population: 7,341,000

Population Density: 461 people per sq mi / 178 people per sq km

Capital: Bern

PHYSICAL:

Highest Point: Dufourspitze 15,203 ft / 4,634 m

Lowest Point: Lake Maggiore 640 ft / 195 m

Mountain Ranges:
    Alps: •cover much of the country •extend into France, Italy, Germany,
        Liechtenstein, and Austria
    Jura: •cover an area from southwestern to northern Switzerland •extend into France

Peaks (minimum elevation of 8,000 ft / 2,400 m):
    Dom: •located in the Alps
    Dufourspitze: •located in the Alps •on the Switzerland-Italy border just east of the
        Matterhorn•highest point in Switzerland
    Matterhorn: •located in the Alps •on the Switzerland-Italy border

Passes:
    Great Saint Bernard: •located in the Alps •crosses the border into Italy

Lakes:
    Lake Constance: •located in northeastern Switzerland •on the border with Germany
        and Austria •on the edge of the Alps •fed by the Rhine River
    Lake of Geneva: •located in southwestern Switzerland •on the Switzerland-France
        border •between the Jura Mountains and the Alps •fed by the Rhone River
    Lake of Lucerne: •located in central Switzerland •on the edge of the Alps
    Lake Maggiore: •located in southern Switzerland •on the Switzerland-Italy border
        •on the edge of the Alps
    Lake Neuchatel: •located in western Switzerland •on the edge of the Jura Mountains

Rivers:
    Inn: •has it source in the Alps •extends into Austria
    Rhine: •has its source in the Alps •forms much of Switzerland's border with

Germany and Liechtenstein •forms part of the Switzerland-Austria border
•extends into Austria and Germany
Rhone: •has its source in the Alps •extends into France

POLITICAL:
Independence: August 1, 1291 (founding of the Swiss Confederation)
Bordering Countries: Italy, France, Germany, Austria, Liechtenstein (5)
Administrative Divisions: Aargau, Appenzell Ausser-Rhoden, Appenzell Inner-Rhoden, Basel-Landschaft, Basel-Stadt, Bern, Fribourg, Geneve, Glarus, Graubunden, Jura, Luzern, Neuchatel, Nidwalden, Obwalden, Sankt Gallen, Schaffhausen, Schwyz, Solothurn, Thurgau, Ticino, Uri, Valais, Vaud, Zug, Zurich (26 cantons)
Ethnic/Racial Groups: German, French, Italian, Romanche
Religion: Christianity (Roman Catholic, Protestant)
Languages: German, French, Italian, Romanisch
Currency: Swiss franc
Current President: Joseph Deiss
Cities (capital, largest, or with at least a million people):
Zurich: •located in northern Switzerland •city in the Zurich canton •most populated city in Switzerland (979,000 people)
Bern: •located in western Switzerland •capital of Switzerland (320,000 people) •in the Bern canton

ENVIRONMENTAL/ECONOMIC:
Climate: temperate that varies with altitude; cold and snowy winters/cool to warm summers
Natural Resources: hydropower potential, timber, salt
Agricultural Products: grains, fruits and vegetables, meat
Major Exports: machinery, chemicals, metals, watches, agricultural products
Natural Hazards: avalanches, landslides, flash floods

SYRIA
Country Name: Syrian Arab Republic
Continent: Asia
Area: 71,498 sq mi / 185,180 sq km
Population: 17,537,000
Population Density: 245 people per sq mi / 95 people per sq km
Capital: Damascus

PHYSICAL:
Highest Point: Mount Hermon 9,232 ft / 2,814 m
Lowest Point: Mediterranean Sea 0 ft / 0 m (sea level)
Mountain Ranges:
Anti-Lebanon: •located in southwestern Syria •extend into Lebanon

Peaks (minimum elevation of 8,000 ft / 2,400 m):
   Mount Hermon: ●located in the Anti-Lebanon Mountains ●on the Syria-Lebanon border ●highest point in Syria
Deserts:
   Syrian: ●covers much of the country ●extends into Jordan and Iraq
Seas:
   Mediterranean: ●forms the western coast of Syria ●feeds into the Atlantic Ocean
Rivers:
   Euphrates: ●extends into Turkey and Iraq
   Orontes: ●has its source in the Anti-Lebanon Mountains ●extends into Lebanon and Turkey

POLITICAL:
Independence: April 17, 1946 (from French administration)
Former Name: United Arab Republic (with Egypt)
Bordering Countries: Turkey, Iraq, Jordan, Lebanon, Israel (5)
Regions:
   Mesopotamia: ●ancient region that covers much of eastern Syria ●extends into Iraq
Administrative Divisions: Al Hasakah, Al Ladhiqiyah, Al Qunaytirah, Ar Raqqah, As Suwayda, Dara, Dayr az Zawr, Dimashq, Halab, Hamah, Hims, Idlib, Rif Dimashq, Tartus (14 provinces)
Ethnic/Racial/Racial Groups: Arabs, Kurds, Armenians
Religions: Islam (Sunni, Alawite, Druze, other Muslim sects), Christianity
Languages: Arabic, Kurdish, Armenian, Aramaic, Circassian, French, English

Currency: Syrian pound
Current President: Bashar al-Asad
Cities (capital, largest, or with at least a million people):
   Aleppo: ●located in northwestern Syria ●city in the Halab province
      ●most populous city in Syria (2,569,000 people)
   Damascus: ●located in southwestern Syria ●city in the Dimashq province
      ●capital of Syria (2,228,000 people) ●between the Anti-Lebanon Mountains
      and the Syrian Desert

ENVIRONMENTAL/ECONOMIC:

Climate: mostly desert with hot and dry summers/mild and rainy winters along the
   coast; occasional snow or sleet around Damascus
Natural Resources: petroleum, phosphates, chrome ore, manganese ore, asphalt
Agricultural Products: wheat, barley, cotton, lentils, beef
Major Exports: crude oil, petroleum products, fruits and vegetables, cotton fiber,
   clothing
Natural Hazards: dust storms, sandstorms

TAJIKISTAN

Country Name: Republic of Tajikistan
Continent: Asia
Area: 55,251 sq mi / 143,100 sq km
Population: 6,574,000
Population Density: 119 people per sq mi / 46 people per sq km
Capital: Dushanbe

PHYSICAL:

Highest Point: Qullai Ismoili Somoni 24,590 ft / 7,495 m
Lowest Point: Syr Darya (river) 984 ft / 300 m
Mountain Ranges:
    Pamirs: •located in eastern Tajikistan •extend into Afghanistan, China, and
        Kyrgyzstan
Peaks (minimum elevation of 8,000 ft / 2,400 m):
    Qullai Ismoili Somoni •located in the Pamirs •highest point in Tajikistan
Rivers:
    Amu Darya: •has its source in the Pamirs •forms part of the Tajikistan-Afghanistan
        border •extends into Afghanistan and Uzbekistan
    Syr Darya: •extends into Uzbekistan and Kyrgyzstan •forms part of the Tajikistan-
        Uzbekistan border

POLITICAL:

Independence: September 9, 1991 (from the Soviet Union)
Former Name: Tajik Soviet Socialist Republic
Bordering Countries: Afghanistan, Uzbekistan, Kyrgyzstan, China (4)
Administrative Divisions: Viloyati Khatlon, Viloyati Sughd (2 provinces) •Viloyati
    Mukhtori Kuhistoni Badakhshon (1 autonomous province)
Ethnic/Racial Groups: Tajik, Uzbek, Russian
Religion: Islam (Sunni, Shiite)
Languages: Tajik, Russian
Currency: somoni
Current President: Emomali Rahmonov
Cities (capital, largest, or with at least a million people):
    Dushanbe: •located in western Tajikistan •city in the Viloyati Khatlon province
        •capital of Tajikistan •most populated city in Tajikistan (554,000 people)

TAJIKISTAN

ENVIRONMENTAL/ECONOMIC:
Climate: Midlatitude continental with hot summers/mild winters; semi-arid to polar in the east
Natural Resources: hydropower, petroleum, uranium, mercury, brown coal
Agricultural Products: cotton, grain, fruits, grapes, vegetables
Major Exports: aluminum, electricity, cotton, fruits, vegetable oil, textiles
Natural Hazards: earthquakes, floods

TANZANIA
Country Name: United Republic of Tanzania
Continent: Africa
Area: 364,900 sq mi / 945,087 sq km
Population: 35,363,000
Population Density: 97 people per sq mi / 37 people per sq km
Capitals: Dar es Salaam (administrative capital), Dodoma (legislative capital)

PHYSICAL:
Highest Point: Kilimanjaro 19,341 ft / 5,895 m
Lowest Point: Indian Ocean 0 ft / 0 m (sea level)
Mountain Ranges:
    Pare: •located in northeastern Tanzania

Peaks (minimum elevation of 8,000 ft / 2,400 m):
Kilimanjaro: •located in the Pare Mountains •highest point in Africa
Valleys:
Great Rift: •covers an area from northern to southern Tanzania •extends into Kenya, Burundi, Democratic Republic of the Congo, Zambia, and Malawi
Grasslands/Prairies:
Serengeti Plain: •located in northern Tanzania •extends into Kenya
Oceans:
Indian: •forms the eastern coast of Tanzania
Lakes:
Lake Eyasi: •located in northern Tanzania •in the Great Rift Valley

Lake Malawi: •forms most of Tanzania's border with Malawi •extends into Malawi and Mozambique

Lake Natron: •located in northern Tanzania •in the Great Rift Valley •extends into Kenya

Lake Rukwa: •located in western Tanzania •in the Great Rift Valley

Lake Tanganyika: •located in western Tanzania •in the Great Rift Valley •on the border with Democratic Republic of the Congo, Burundi, and Zambia

Lake Victoria: •located in northwestern Tanzania •extends into Uganda and Kenya •largest lake in Africa •third largest lake in the world
Islands:
Zanzibar: •largest island off the coast of Tanzania •surrounded by the Indian Ocean

POLITICAL:
Independence: April 26, 1964 (from the United Kingdom)
Former Name: United Republic of Tanganyika and Zanzibar
Bordering Countries: Kenya, Mozambique, Malawi, Democratic Republic of the
Congo, Burundi, Uganda, Zambia, Rwanda (8)
Administrative Divisions: Arusha, Dar es Salaam, Dodoma, Iringa, Kagera,
Kigoma, Kilimanjaro, Lindi, Manyara, Mara, Mbeya, Morogoro, Mtwara, Mwanza,
Pemba North, Pemba South, Pwani, Rukwa, Ruvuma, Shinyanga, Singida, Tabora,
Tanga, Zanzibar Central/South, Zanzibar North, Zanzibar Urban/West (26 regions)
Ethnic/Racial Groups: predominantly Bantu on the mainland; Arab, African, mixed
on Zanzibar
Religions: Christianity, Islam, indigenous beliefs
Languages: Kiswahili, Kiungujo, English, Arabic, many local languages
Currency: Tanzanian shilling
Current President: Benjamin William Mkapa
Cities (capital, largest, or with at least a million people):
Dar es Salaam: •located in eastern Tanzania •city in the Dar es Salaam region
•administrative capital of Tanzania •most populated city in Tanzania
(2,683,000 people) •chief port on the Indian Ocean
Dodoma: •located in central Tanzania •city in the Dodoma region •legislative
capital of Tanzania (155,000 people)

ENVIRONMENTAL/ECONOMIC:
Climate: tropical along the coast; temperate in the highlands
Natural Resources: hydropower, tin, phosphates, iron ore, coal
Agricultural Products: coffee, sisal, tea, cotton, cattle
Major Exports: gold, coffee, cashew nuts, manufactures, cotton
Natural Hazards: floods, droughts

THAILAND
Country Name: Kingdom of Thailand
Continent: Asia
Area: 198,115 sq mi / 513,115 sq km
Population: 63,063,000
Population Density: 318 people per sq mi / 123 people per sq km
Capital: Bangkok

PHYSICAL:
Highest Point: Doi Inthanon 8,415 ft / 2,565 m
Lowest Point: Gulf of Thailand 0 ft / 0 m (sea level)
Peaks (minimum elevation of 8,000 ft / 2,400 m):
Doi Inthanon: •located in northwestern Thailand •highest point in Thailand

Plateau Regions:
    Khorat Plateau: •covers much of eastern Thailand
Seas:
    Andaman: •forms much of the southwestern coast of Thailand •feeds into the
        Indian Ocean
Gulfs:
    Gulf of Thailand: •forms the southeastern coast of Thailand •feeds into the South
        China Sea
Straits:
    Strait of Malacca: •forms part of the southwestern coast of Thailand •separates the
        Malay Peninsula from Indonesia •connects the Andaman and South China Seas
Rivers:
    Chao Phraya: •has its mouth in the Gulf of Thailand •has its source in northwestern
        Thailand
    Mekong: •forms part of the Thailand-Laos border •extends into Laos, Cambodia,
        and Myanmar
    Salween (Thanlwin): •forms part of the Thailand-Myanmar border •extends into
        Myanmar
Peninsulas:
    Malay: •bordered by the Gulf of Thailand, South China Sea, Strait of Malacca, and
        Andaman Sea •forms the southernmost part of Thailand •includes part of Malaysia

POLITICAL:
Independence: 1238 (never colonized; traditional date for founding of the country)
Former Name: Siam

Bordering Countries: Myanmar, Laos, Cambodia, Malaysia (4)

Administrative Divisions: Amnat Charoen, Ang Thong, Buriram, Chachoengsao, Chai Nat, Chaiyaphum, Chanthaburi, Chiang Mai, Chiang Rai, Chon Buri, Chumphon, Kalasin, Kamphaeng Phet, Kanchanaburi, Khon Kaen, Krabi, Krung Thep Mahanakhon (Bangkok), Lampang, Lamphun, Loei, Lop Buri, Mae Hong Son, Maha Sarakham, Mukdahan, Nakhon Nayok, Nakhon Pathom, Nakhon Phanom, Nakhon Ratchasima, Nakhon Sawan, Nakhon Si Thammarat, Nan, Narathiwat, Nong Bua Lamphu, Nong Khai, Nonthaburi, Pathum Thani, Pattani, Phangnga, Phatthalung, Phayao, Phetchabun, Phetchaburi, Phichit, Phitsanulok, Phra Nakhon Si Ayutthaya, Phrae, Phuket, Prachin Buri, Prachuap Khiri Khan, Ranong, Ratchaburi, Rayong, Roi Et, Sa Kaeo, Sakon Nakhon, Samut Prakan, Samut Sakhon, Samut Songkhram, Sara Buri, Satun, Sing Buri, Sisaket, Songkhla, Sukhothai, Suphan Buri, Surat Thani, Surin, Tak, Trang, Trat, Ubon Ratchathani, Udon Thani, Uthai Thani, Uttaradit, Yala, Yasothon (76 provinces)

Ethnic/Racial Groups: Thai, Chinese

Religions: Buddhism, Islam

Languages: Thai, English, ethnic and regional dialects

Currency: baht

Current Prime Minister: Thaksin Chinnawat

Cities (capital, largest, or with at least a million people):
Bangkok: •located in central Thailand •city in the Krung Thep Mahanakhon (Bangkok) province •capital of Thailand •most populated city in Thailand (6,604,000 people) •chief port on the Chao Phraya River

ENVIRONMENTAL/ECONOMIC:

Climate: tropical with two monsoon seasons; hot and humid in the south

Natural Resources: tin, rubber, natural gas, tungsten, tantalum

Agricultural Products: rice, cassava (tapioca), rubber, corn

Major Exports: computers, transistors, seafood, clothing, rice

Natural Hazards: land subsidence, droughts

TIMOR-LESTE see East Timor

TOGO

Country Name: Republic of Togo

Continent: Africa

Area: 21,925 sq mi / 56,785 sq km

Population: 5,429,000

Population Density: 248 people per sq mi / 96 people per sq km

Capital: Lome

PHYSICAL:

Highest Point: Mont Agou 3,235 ft / 986 m

Lowest Point: Bight of Benin 0 ft / 0 m (sea level)

TOGO

0   50 mi
0   50 km

White Volta R.
Volta R.
Oti R.
Kara R.
Duka R.
Lake Volta
Mono R.
Oti R.
Ouémé R.
Ogun R.
Niger R.
Kainji Reservoir

•Dapaong
•Tandjouaré
Mango•
•Kanté
Guérin-Kouka•
•Lama-Kara
•Bafilo
•Bassar
Sokodé• •Tchamba
•Blitta
•Yégué
Kpèssi•
•Atakpamé
Badou•
Notsé•
•Kpalimé
•Tabligbo
Tsévié•
Lomé ⊛ •Aného
Volta R.

BENIN
GHANA
NIGERIA
CÔTE D'IVOIRE

Gulf of Guinea

10° N
8° N
6° N
2° W   0°   2° E   4° E

Bays:
> Bight of Benin: •forms the southern coast of Togo •feeds into the Gulf of Guinea

POLITICAL:
Independence: April 27, 1960 (from French administration)
Former Name: French Togoland
Bordering Countries: Ghana, Benin, Burkina Faso (3)
Administrative Divisions: Central, Kara, Maritime, Plateaux, Savanes (5 regions)
Ethnic/Racial Groups: Ewe, Mina, Kabre, and other African tribes
Religions: indigenous beliefs, Christianity, Islam
Languages: French, Ewe, Mina, Kabye, Dagomba
Currency: Communaute Financiere Africaine franc
Current President: Gnassingbe Eyadema
Cities (capital, largest, or with at least a million people):
> Lome: •located in southern Togo •city in the Maritime region •capital of Togo
> •most populated city in Togo (799,000 people) •chief port on the Bight of Benin

ENVIRONMENTAL/ECONOMIC:
Climate: tropical; hot and humid in the south; semi-arid in the north
Natural Resources: phosphates, limestone, marble, arable land
Agricultural Products: coffee, cacao, cotton, yarns, livestock
Major Exports: re-exports, cotton, phosphates, coffee, cacao
Natural Hazards: harmattan winds, droughts

TONGA

```
0        50 mi
0      50 km
```

Vava'u Group   Vava'u
                Neiafu
Late
                                    Pacific Ocean
19° S

Ha'apai
Group

Kao   Ha'ano
Tofua   Foa
        Lifuka
        Uiha

Fonuafo'ou   Nomuka
         Nomuka 'Otu Tolu
         Group   Group

Pacific Ocean

Nuku'alofa   21° S
Tongatapu
Fua'amotu   Ohonua
Tongatapu Group   'Eua

174° W   172° W

TONGA

Country Name: Kingdom of Tonga
Continent: Australia/Oceania
Area: 289 sq mi / 748 sq km
Population: 107,000
Population Density: 370 people per sq mi / 143 people per sq km
Capital: Nukualofa

PHYSICAL:
Highest Point: unnamed location 3,389 ft / 1,033 m
Lowest Point: Pacific Ocean 0 ft / 0 m (sea level)
Oceans:
    Pacific: ●surrounds Tonga
Islands:
    Tongatapu: ●largest island in Tonga ●surrounded by the Pacific Ocean

POLITICAL:
Independence: June 4, 1970 (from the United Kingdom)
Former Name: Friendly Islands
Administrative Divisions: Haapai, Tongatapu, Vavau (3 island groups)
Ethnic/Racial Groups: Polynesian
Religion: Christianity
Languages: Tongan, English

Currency: paanga
Current King: Taufaahau Tupou IV
Cities (capital, largest, or with at least a million people):
  Nukualofa: ●located on the island of Tongatapu ●city in the Tongatapu island group ●capital of Tonga ●most populated city in Tonga (35,000 people) ●chief port on the Pacific Ocean

ENVIRONMENTAL/ECONOMIC:
Climate: tropical, modified by trade winds with warm/cool seasons
Natural Resources: fish, fertile soil
Agricultural Products: squash, coconuts, copra, bananas, fish
Major Exports: squash, fish, vanilla beans, root crops
Natural Hazards: cyclones, earthquakes, volcanoes

TRINIDAD AND TOBAGO
Country Name: Republic of Trinidad and Tobago
Continent: North America
Area: 1,980 sq mi / 5,128 sq km
Population: 1,309,000
Population Density: 661 people per sq mi / 255 people per sq km
Capital: Port-of-Spain

PHYSICAL:
Highest Point: El Cerro del Aripo 3,084 ft / 940 m
Lowest Point: Atlantic Ocean 0 ft / 0 m (sea level)
Oceans:
  Atlantic: ●forms the eastern and southern coast of Trinidad and Tobago
Seas:
  Caribbean: ●forms the northern coast of Trinidad ●forms the western and southern coasts of Tobago ●feeds into the Atlantic Ocean
Gulfs:
  Gulf of Paria: ●forms the western coast of Trinidad ●separates Trinidad and Venezuela
Islands:
  Tobago: ●second largest island in Trinidad and Tobago ●bordered by the Atlantic Ocean and Caribbean Sea
  Trinidad: ●largest island in Trinidad and Tobago ●bordered by the Atlantic Ocean, Caribbean Sea, and Gulf of Paria

POLITICAL:
Independence: August 31, 1962 (from the United Kingdom)
Administrative Divisions: Caroni, Mayaro, Nariva, Saint Andrew, Saint David, Saint George, Saint Patrick, Victoria (8 counties) ●Arima, Port-of-Spain, San Fernando (3 municipalities) ● Tobago (1 ward)

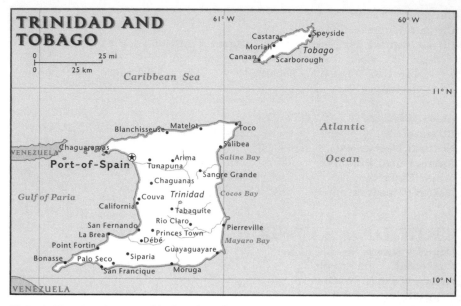

TRINIDAD AND TOBAGO

0 ——— 25 mi
0 ——— 25 km

Ethnic/Racial Groups: black, East Indian, mixed
Religions: Christianity (Roman Catholic, Anglican), Hindu
Languages: English, Hindi, French, Spanish
Currency: Trinidad and Tobago dollar
Current President: George Maxwell Richards
Cities (capital, largest, or with at least a million people):
   Port-of-Spain: •located on the island of Trinidad •city in the Port-of-Spain
      municipality •capital of Trinidad and Tobago •most populated city in Trinidad
      and Tobago (55,000 people) •chief port on the Gulf of Paria

ENVIRONMENTAL/ECONOMIC:
Climate: Tropical with a rainy season
Natural Resources: petroleum, natural gas
Agricultural Products: cacao, sugarcane, rice, citrus
Major Exports: petroleum and petroleum products, chemicals, steel
Natural Hazards: tropical storms

TUNISIA

Country Name: Republic of Tunisia
Continent: Africa
Area: 63,170 sq mi / 163,610 sq km
Population: 9,898,000
Population Density: 157 people per sq mi / 60 people per sq km
Capital: Tunis

PHYSICAL:

Highest Point: Jebel ech Chambi 5,066 ft / 1,544 m

Lowest Point: Shott el Gharsa 56 ft / 17 m below sea level

Mountain Ranges:

Atlas: •located in northwestern Tunisia •extend into Algeria

Deserts:

Grand Erg Oriental: •covers much of western Tunisia •extends into Algeria

Sahara: •covers much of southern and central Tunisia •extends into Algeria and
Libya •largest desert in the world

Seas:

Mediterranean: •forms much of the northern and eastern coasts of Tunisia •feeds
into the Atlantic Ocean

Gulfs:

Gulf of Gabes: •forms part of the eastern coast of Tunisia •feeds into the
Mediterranean Sea

Gulf of Tunis: •forms much of the northeastern coast of Tunisia •feeds into the
Mediterranean Sea

Lakes:

Shott el Jerid: •located in western Tunisia •on the edge of the Grand Erg Oriental

POLITICAL:

Independence: March 20, 1956 (from France)

Bordering Countries: Algeria, Libya (2)

Administrative Divisions: Al Kaf, Al Mahdiyah, Al Munastir, Al Qasrayn, Al Qayrawan, Aryanah, Bajah, Banzart, Bin Arus, Jundubah, Madanin, Manouba, Nabul, Qabis, Qafsah, Qibili, Safaqis, Sidi Bu Zayd, Silyanah, Susah, Tatawin, Tawzar, Tunis, Zaghwan (24 governorates)

Ethnic/Racial Groups: Arab, European

Religion: predominantly Islam

Languages: Arabic, French

Currency: Tunisian dinar

Current President: Zine El Abidine Ben Ali

Cities (capital, largest, or with at least a million people):

Tunis: ●located in northern Tunisia ●city in the Tunis governorate ●capital of Tunisia ●most populated city in Tunisia (1,996,000 people) ●chief port on the Gulf of Tunis

ENVIRONMENTAL/ECONOMIC:

Climate: temperate in the north with mild and rainy winters/hot and dry summers; desert in the south

Natural Resources: petroleum, phosphates, iron ore, lead, zinc

Agricultural Products: olives, olive oil, grain, dairy products

Major Exports: textiles, mechanical goods, phosphates and chemicals, agricultural products

Natural Hazards: droughts

TURKEY

Country Name: Republic of Turkey

Continent: Asia/Europe

Area: 300,948 sq mi / 779,452 sq km

Population: 71,224,000

Population Density: 237 people per sq mi / 91 people per sq km

Capital: Ankara

PHYSICAL:

Highest Point: Mount Ararat 16,853 ft / 5,137 m

Lowest Point: Mediterranean Sea 0 ft / 0 m (sea level)

Mountain Ranges:

Lesser Caucasus: ●located in northeastern Turkey ●extend into Georgia and Armenia

Taurus: ●cover an area from southern to eastern Turkey

Zagros: ●cover much of eastern Turkey ●extend into Iran and Iraq

Peaks (minimum elevation of 8,000 ft / 2,400 m):

Mount Ararat: ●located in the Zagros Mountains ●highest point in Turkey

Seas:

Aegean: ●forms part of the western coast of Turkey ●feeds into the Mediterranean Sea and Sea of Crete

Black: •forms most of the northern coast of Turkey •feeds into the Sea of Marmara

Mediterranean: •forms most of the southern coast of Turkey •feeds into the Atlantic Ocean

Sea of Marmara: •forms part of the northwestern coast of Turkey •feeds into the Aegean Sea

Gulfs:

Gulf of Antalya: •forms part of the southwestern coast of Turkey •feeds into the Mediterranean Sea

Straits:

Bosporus: •forms part of the northwestern coast of Turkey •separates European Turkey from Asian Turkey •connects the Black Sea and Sea of Marmara

Dardanelles: •forms part of the northwestern coast of Turkey •separates European Turkey from Asian Turkey •connects the Sea of Marmara and Aegean Sea

Lakes:

Atatürk Reservoir: •located in southern Turkey •on the edge of the Taurus Mountains •fed by the Euphrates River •formed by the Atatürk Dam

Lake Tuz: •located in central Turkey

Lake Van: •located in eastern Turkey •on the edge of the Zagros Mountains

Rivers:

Aras: •has its source in the Taurus Mountains •forms part of the Turkey-Armenia border

Euphrates: •has its source in the Zagros Mountains •extends into Syria and Iraq

Evros: •has its mouth in the Aegean Sea •forms the Turkey-Greece border

Orontes: •has its mouth in the Mediterranean Sea •extends into Syria

Tigris: •has its source in the Taurus Mountains •extends into Iraq
Dams:
Ataturk: •located in southern Turkey •on the Euphrates River •forms the Ataturk Reservoir
Regions:
Anatolia: •mountainous region that covers most of Turkey •includes the Taurus Mountains and much of the Zagros Mountains •east of the Aegean Sea and Sea of Marmara •south of the Black Sea •north of the Mediterranean Sea and the Gulf of Antalya

POLITICAL:
Independence: October 29, 1923 (from the Ottoman Empire)
Bordering Countries: Syria, Iran, Iraq, Armenia, Georgia, Bulgaria, Greece, Azerbaijan (8)
Regions:
Cappadocia: •region that covers much of central Turkey •includes part of the Taurus Mountains
Kurdistan: •region in southeastern Turkey •south of the Taurus Mountains •includes part of the Zagros Mountains •extends into Iran and Iraq
Thrace: •region that covers most of European Turkey •south of the Black Sea and north of the Sea of Marmara •extends into Bulgaria and Greece
Administrative Divisions: Adana, Adiyaman, Afyon, Agri, Aksaray, Amasya, Ankara, Antalya, Ardahan, Artvin, Aydin, Balikesir, Bartin, Batman, Bayburt, Bilecik, Bingol, Bitlis, Bolu, Burdur, Bursa, Canakkale, Cankiri, Corum, Denizli, Diyarbakir, Duzce, Edirne, Elazig, Erzincan, Erzurum, Eskisehir, Gaziantep, Giresun, Gumushane, Hakkari, Hatay, Igdir, Isparta, Istanbul, Izmir, Kahramanmaras, Karabuk, Karaman, Kars, Kastamonu, Kayseri, Kilis, Kirikkale, Kirklareli, Kirsehir, Kocaeli, Konya, Kutahya, Malatya, Manisa, Mardin, Mersin, Mugla, Mus, Nevsehir, Nigde, Ordu, Osmaniye, Rize, Sakarya, Samsun, Sanliurfa, Siirt, Sinop, Sirnak, Sivas, Tekirdag, Tokat, Trabzon, Tunceli, Usak, Van, Yalova, Yozgat, Zonguldak (81 provinces)
Ethnic/Racial Groups: Turkish, Kurdish
Religion: predominantly Islam
Languages: Turkish, Kurdish, Arabic, Armenian, Greek
Currency: Turkish lira
Current President: Ahmet Necdet Sezer
Cities (capital, largest, or with at least a million people):
Istanbul: •located in northwestern Turkey •city in the Istanbul province •most populated city in Turkey (9,592,000 people) •chief port on the Sea of Marmara and the Bosporus Strait
Ankara: •located in central Turkey •city in the Ankara province •capital of Turkey (3,428,000 people)
Izmir: •located in western Turkey •city in the Izmir province •chief port on the Aegean Sea
Bursa: •located in northwestern Turkey •city in the Bursa province

Adana: •located in southern Turkey •city in the Adana province •on the edge of the Taurus Mountains

Gaziantep: •located in southern Turkey •city in the Gaziantep province

ENVIRONMENTAL/ECONOMIC:

Climate: temperate with hot, dry summers/mild, wet winters; harsher in the mountains

Natural Resources: coal, iron ore, copper, chromium, antimony

Agricultural Products: tobacco, cotton, grain, olives, livestock

Major Exports: apparel, foodstuffs, textiles, metal manufactures, transport equipment

Natural Hazards: earthquakes

TURKMENISTAN

Country Name: Turkmenistan
Continent: Asia
Area: 188,456 sq mi / 488,100 sq km
Population: 5,703,000
Population Density: 30 people per sq mi / 12 people per sq km
Capital: Ashgabat

PHYSICAL:

Highest Point: Gora Ayrıbaba 10,299 ft / 3,139 m

Lowest Point: Vpadina Akchanaya 266 ft / 81 m below sea level

Peaks (minimum elevation of 8,000 ft / 2,400 m):
  Gora Ayribaba: ●located in eastern Turkmenistan ●on the Turkmenistan-Uzbekistan border ●highest point in Turkmenistan
Depressions:
  Vpadina Akchanaya: ●located in northern Turkmenistan ●lowest point in Turkmenistan
  Caspian Sea: ●forms the western coast of Turkmenistan
Desert:
  Garagum: ●covers most of Turkmenistan
Lakes:
  Caspian Sea: ●forms most of western coast of Turkmenistan ●extends into Kazakhstan and Iran ●largest lake in the world
Rivers:
  Amu Darya: ●forms part of Turkmenistan's border with Uzbekistan and Afghanistan ●extends into Uzbekistan

POLITICAL:
Independence: October 27, 1991 (from the Soviet Union)
Former Name: Turkmen Soviet Socialist Republic
Bordering Countries: Uzbekistan, Iran, Afghanistan, Kazakhstan (4)
Administrative Divisions: Ahal, Balkan, Dasoguz, Lebap, Mary (5 provinces)
Ethnic/Racial Groups: Turkmen, Uzbek, Russian, Kazakh
Religions: Islam, Christianity (primarily Eastern Orthodox)
Languages: Turkmen, Russian, Uzbek
Currency: Turkmen manat
Current President: Saparmurat Niyazov
Cities (capital, largest, or with at least a million people):
  Ashgabat: ●located in southen Turkmenistan ●city in the Ahal province ●capital of Turkmenistan ●most populated city in Turkmenistan (574,000 people) ●on the edge of the Garagum desert

ENVIRONMENTAL/ECONOMIC:
Climate: subtropical desert
Natural Resources: petroleum, natural gas, coal, sulfur, salt
Agricultural Products: cotton, grains, livestock
Major Exports: gas, oil, cotton fiber, textiles
Natural Hazards: droughts, sandstorms

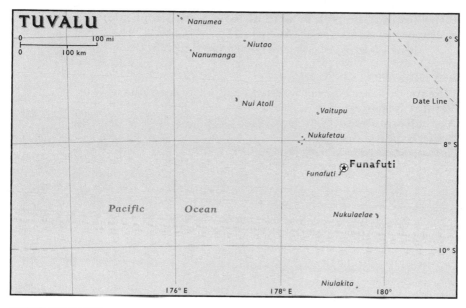

TUVALU

Country Name: Tuvalu
Continent: Australia/Oceania

Area: 10 sq mi / 26 sq km
Population: 10,000 (smallest in Australia/Oceania)
Population Density: 1,000 people per sq mi / 385 people per sq km
Capital: Funafuti

PHYSICAL:
Highest Point: unnamed location 16 ft / 5 m
Lowest Point: Pacific Ocean 0 ft / 0 m (sea level)
Oceans:
 Pacific: •surrounds Tuvalu

POLITICAL:
Independence: October 1, 1978 (from the United Kingdom)
Former Name: Ellice Islands
Ethnic/Racial Groups: Polynesian, Micronesian
Religion: Christianity; predominantly Church of Tuvalu (Congregationalist)
Languages: Tuvaluan, English, Samoan
Currency: Australian dollar, Tuvaluan dollar
Current Prime Minister: Maatia Toafa

Cities (capital, largest, or with at least a million people):
    Funafuti: •located on an island in central Tuvalu •capital of Tuvalu •most populated
    city in Tuvalu (6,000 people) •chief port on the Pacific Ocean

ENVIRONMENTAL/ECONOMIC:
Climate: tropical, moderated by easterly trade winds; heavy rains in winter
Natural Resources: fish
Agricultural Products: coconuts, fish
Major Exports: copra, fish
Natural Hazards: cyclones, high sea levels

UGANDA
Country Name: Republic of Uganda
Continent: Africa
Area: 93,104 sq mi / 241,139 sq km
Population: 25,262,000
Population Density: 271 people per sq mi / 105 people per sq km
Capital: Kampala

PHYSICAL:
Highest Point: Margherita Peak (on Mount Stanley) 16,763 ft / 5,109 m
Lowest Point: Lake Albert 2,037 ft / 621 m
Mountain Ranges:
    Bleus: •cover much of western Uganda •extend into Democratic Republic of the Congo
    Mitumba: •located in southwestern Uganda •extend into Democratic Republic of the Congo and Rwanda

Peaks (minimum elevation of 8,000 ft / 2,400 m):
    Mount Stanley: •located in the Bleus Mountains •on the Uganda-Democratic Republic of the Congo border •highest point in Uganda (see map page 91)

Lakes:
    Lake Albert: •located in western Uganda •on the edge of the Bleus Mountains •fed by the Victoria Nile River •on the Uganda-Democratic Republic of the Congo border
    Lake Edward: •located in southwestern Uganda •on the edge of the Bleus Mountains •on the Uganda-Democratic Republic of the Congo border
    Lake Kyoga: •located in central Uganda •fed by the Victoria Nile River
    Lake Victoria: •covers much of southern Uganda •Owens Falls Dam on the Victoria Nile River makes the lake a reservoir •extends into Tanzania and Kenya •largest lake in Africa •third largest lake in the world

Rivers:
    Albert Nile: •extends into Sudan
    Victoria Nile: •tributary of the Albert Nile River •flows into Lake Albert •has its source in Lake Victoria •Owens Falls Dam creates hydroelectric power from the river

Dams:
    Owen Falls: •located in southeastern Uganda •crosses the Victoria Nile River •makes Lake Victoria a reservoir

POLITICAL:
Independence: October 9, 1962 (from the United Kingdom)

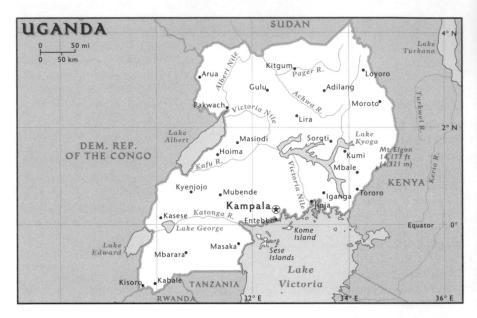

Bordering Countries: Kenya, Democratic Republic of the Congo, Sudan, Tanzania, Rwanda (5)

Administrative Divisions: Adjumani, Apac, Arua, Bugiri, Bundibugyo, Bushenyi, Busia, Gulu, Hoima, Iganga, Jinja, Kabale, Kabarole, Kaberamaido, Kalangala, Kampala, Kamuli, Kamwenge, Kanungu, Kapchorwa, Kasese, Katakwi, Kayunga, Kibale, Kiboga, Kisoro, Kitgum, Kotido, Kumi, Kyenjojo, Lira, Luwero, Masaka, Masindi, Mayuge, Mbale, Mbarara, Moroto, Moyo, Mpigi, Mubende, Mukono, Nakapiripirit, Nakasongola, Nebbi, Ntungamo, Pader, Pallisa, Rakai, Rukungiri, Sembabule, Sironko, Soroti, Tororo, Wakiso, Yumbe (56 districts)

Ethnic/Racial Groups: Baganda, Ankole, Basoga, Itesco, Bakiga, other indigenous groups

Religions: Christianity (Roman Catholic, Protestant), indigenous beliefs, Islam

Languages: English, Ganda or Luganda, many local languages

Currency: Ugandan shilling

Current President: Yoweri Kaguta Museveni

Cities (capital, largest, or with at least a million people):
Kampala: •located in southern Uganda •city in the Kampala district •capital of Uganda •most populated city in Uganda (1,246,000 people) •chief port on Lake Victoria

ENVIRONMENTAL/ECONOMIC:

Climate: tropical with rainy/dry seasons; semi-arid in the northeast

Natural Resources: copper, cobalt, hydropower, limestone, salt

Agricultural Products: coffee, tea, cotton, tobacco, beef

Major Exports: coffee, fish and fish products, tea, gold, cotton
Natural Hazards: floods, lalndslides, thunderstorms

UKRAINE

Country Name: Ukraine
Continent: Europe
Area: 233,090 sq mi / 603,700 sq km (largest country completely in Europe)
Population: 47,793,000
Population Density: 205 people per sq mi / 79 people per sq km
Capital: Kiev

PHYSICAL:
Highest Point: Hora Hoverla 6,762 ft / 2,061 m
Lowest Point: Black Sea 0 ft / 0 m (sea level)
Mountain Ranges:
　Carpathian: ●located in western Ukraine ●extend into Poland, Slovakia, and
　　Romania
Grasslands/Prairies:
　Great Alfold: ●located in western Ukraine ●extends into Slovakia, Hungary, and Romania
　Black Sea Lowland: ●covers most of southern Ukraine ●extends into Moldova and
　　Romania
Swamps:
　Pinsk Marshes: ●located in northwestern Ukraine ●extend into Belarus

Seas:
   Black: •forms part of the southern coast of Ukraine •feeds into the Sea of Marmara
   Sea of Azov: •forms part of the southeastern coast of Ukraine •feeds into the Black Sea
Rivers:
   Danube: •has its mouth in the Black Sea •forms part of the Ukraine-Romania border
      •extends into Romania and Hungary
   Dnieper: •has its mouth in the Black Sea •forms part of the Ukraine-Belarus border
      •extends into Belarus and Russia
   Dniester (Nistru): •has its mouth in the Black Sea •has its source in the Carpathian
      Mountains •forms part of the Ukraine-Moldova border •extends into Moldova
   Donets: •extends into Russia
   Prut: •has its source in the Carpathian Mountains •forms part of the Ukraine-
      Romania border
   Tisza: •has its source in the Carpathian Mountains •forms part of the Ukraine-
      Romania border •extends into Hungary
Peninsulas:
   Crimean: •bordered by the Black Sea and Sea of Azov

POLITICAL:
Independence: August 24, 1991 (from the Soviet Union)
Former Names: Ukrainian National Republic, Ukrainian State, Ukrainian Soviet
   Socialist Republic
Bordering Countries: Russia, Moldova, Belarus, Romania, Poland, Hungary,
   Slovakia (7)
Regions:
   Bessarabia: •region in southwestern Ukraine •includes part of the Black Sea
      Lowland •northwest of the Black Sea •extends into Moldova
Administrative Divisions: Cherkaska, Chernihivska, Chernivetska,
   Dnipropetrovska, Donetska, Ivano-Frankivska, Kharkivska, Khersonska,
   Khmelnytska, Kirovohradska, Kyyivska, Luhanska, Lvivska, Mykolayivska, Odeska,
   Poltavska, Rivnenska, Sumska, Ternopilska, Vinnytska, Volynska, Zakarpatska,
   Zaporizka, Zhytomyrska (24 oblasti) •Avtonomna Respublika Krym (1 autonomous
   republic) •Kiev, Sevastopol (2 municipalities)
Ethnic/Racial Groups: Ukrainian, Russian
Religions: Christianity (Ukrainian Orthodox, Ukrainian Catholic, Protestant), Judaism
Languages: Ukrainian, Russian, Romanian, Polish, Hungarian
Currency: hryvnia
Current President: Viktor Yushenko
Cities (capital, largest, or with at least a million people):
   Kiev: •located in northern Ukraine •city in the Kiev municipality •capital of Ukraine
      •most populated city in Ukraine (2,618,000 people) •chief port on the Dnieper River
   Kharkiv: •located in northeastern Ukraine •city in the Kharkivska oblast
   Odesa: •located in southwestern Ukraine •city in the Odeska oblast •on the edge
      of the Black Sea Lowland •chief port on the Black Sea

Dnipropetrovsk: •located in eastern Ukraine •city in the Dnipropetrovs'ka oblast •a major port on the Dnieper River

ENVIRONMENTAL/ECONOMIC:
Climate: temperate continental; Mediterranean on the south Crimean coast, wettest in the north and west, cool/cold winters, warm/hot summers
Natural Resources: iron ore, coal, manganese, natural gas, oil
Agricultural Products: grain, sugar beets, sunflower seed, beef
Major Exports: ferrous and nonferrous metals, fuel and petroleum products, chemicals, machinery and transport equipment
Natural Hazards: floods, landslides, hail, snowstorms

UNITED ARAB EMIRATES
Country Name: United Arab Emirates
Continent: Asia
Area: 30,000 sq mi / 77,700 sq km
Population: 3,888,000
Population Density: 130 people per sq mi / 50 people per sq km
Capital: Abu Dhabi

PHYSICAL:
Highest Point: Jabal Yibir 5,010 ft / 1,527 m
Lowest Point: Persian Gulf 0 ft / 0 m (sea level)

Deserts:
  Rub al Khali: ●covers most of the country ●extends into Saudi Arabia and Oman
Gulfs:
  Gulf of Oman: ●forms part of the eastern coast of United Arab Emirates ●feeds
    into the Arabian Sea
  Persian: ●forms most of the coast of United Arab Emirates ●feeds into the Gulf
    of Oman

POLITICAL:
Independence: December 2, 1971 (from the United Kingdom)
Former Names: Trucial Oman, Trucial States
Bordering Countries: Saudi Arabia, Oman (2)
Administrative Divisions: Abu Dhabi, Ajman, Al Fujayrah, Dubayy Ras al
    Khaymah, Sharjah, Umm al Qaywayn (7 emirates)
Ethnic/Racial Groups: Arab, Iranian, Indian
Religions: Islam (Sunni and Shiite), Christianity, Hinduism
Languages: Arabic, Persian, English, Hindi, Urdu
Currency: Emirati dirham
Current President: Sheikh Khalifa bin Zayed al-Nahyan
Cities (capital or with at least a million people):
  Dubayy: ●located in northeastern United Arab Emirates ●city in the Dubayy
    emirate ●most populated city in United Arab Emirates (1,570,000 people)
    ●on the edge of the Rub al Khali ●chief port on the Persian Gulf
  Abu Dhabi: ●located on an island in central United Arab Emirates ●city in the Abu
    Dhabi emirate ●capital of the United Arab Emirates (475,000 people) ●a major
    port on the Persian Gulf

ENVIRONMENTAL/ECONOMIC:
Climate: desert; cooler in the mountains
Natural Resources: petroleum, natural gas
Agricultural Products: dates, vegetables, watermelons, poultry, fish
Major Exports: crude oil, natural gas, re-exports, dried fish, dates
Natural Hazards: sandstorms, dust storms

UNITED KINGDOM
Country Name: United Kingdom of Great Britain and Northern Ireland
Continent: Europe
Area: 93,788 sq mi / 242,910 sq km
Population: 59,200,000
Population Density: 631 people per sq mi / 244 people per sq km
Capital: London

PHYSICAL:
Highest Point: Ben Nevis 4,408 ft / 1,344 m
Lowest Point: The Fens 13 ft / 4 m below sea level
Mountain Ranges:
    Cambrian: ●located in central Wales on the island of Great Britain
    Grampian Hills: ●located in Scotland on the island of Great Britain ●forms a
        boundary between the Scottish Highlands and the Scottish Lowlands ●includes
        Ben Nevis, highest peak in the United Kingdom
    Pennines: ●located on the island of Great Britain ●extend from the Scotland-
        England border into central England
Valleys:
    Glen Mor: ●located on the island of Great Britain ●on the edge of the Grampian Hills
Grasslands/Prairies:
    Salisbury Plain: ●located in southwestern England ●on the island of Great Britain
        ●site of Stonehenge
Oceans:
    Atlantic: ●forms part of the western and northern coasts of the United Kingdom
Seas:
    Celtic: ●forms part of the southwestern coast of the United Kingdom ●feeds into
        the Atlantic Ocean
    Irish: ●forms part of the inner coast of the United Kingdom ●feeds into the Celtic
        Sea and Atlantic Ocean
    North: ●forms most of the eastern coast of the United Kingdom ●feeds into the
        Atlantic Ocean

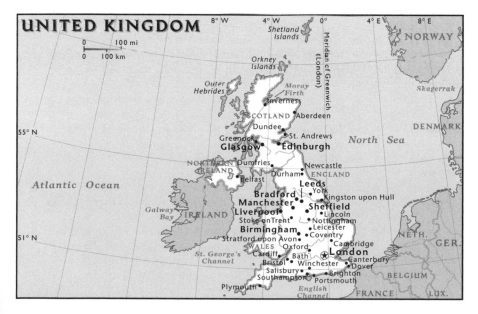

Sea of the Hebrides: •forms part of the northwestern coast of the United Kingdom •feeds into the Atlantic Ocean

Bays:
Cardigan Bay: •forms part of the western coast of Great Britain •feeds into the Irish Sea
Firth of Clyde: •forms part of the western coast of the island of Great Britain •feeds into the North Channel
Firth of Forth: •forms part of the northeastern coast of the island of Great Britain •feeds into the North Sea
Moray Firth: •forms part of the northern coast of the island of Great Britain •feeds into the North Sea

Straits:
Strait of Dover: •forms part of the southeastern coast of the island of Great Britain •separates the island of Great Britain from France •connects the English Channel and the North Sea

Channels:
Bristol: •forms part of the southwestern coast of the island of Great Britain •feeds into the Celtic Sea
English: •forms much of the southern coast of the island of Great Britain •separates the island of Great Britain and France •connects the North Sea and the Atlantic Ocean
North: •forms part of the inner coast of the United Kingdom •separates the island of Great Britain from the island of Ireland •connects the Irish Sea and the Atlantic Ocean
Saint George's: •forms part of the southwestern coast of the island of Great Britain •separates the island of Great Britain and Ireland •connects the Irish and Celtic Seas

Passages:
The Minch: •forms part of the northwestern coast of the United Kingdom •separates the Outer Hebrides from the island of Great Britain •connects the Sea of the Hebrides and Atlantic Ocean

Lakes:
Loch Lomond: •located on the island of Great Britain •on the edge of the Grampian Hills
Lough Foyle: •located in northern Northern Ireland •on the United Kingdom-Ireland border
Lough Neagh: •located in central Northern Ireland

Rivers:
Mersey: •has its mouth in the Irish Sea •has its source in the Pennines
Severn: •has its mouth in the Bristol Channel •has its source in the Cambrian Mountains
Thames: •has its mouth in the North Sea •has its source in southern England
Trent: •has its mouth in the Humber Estuary •has its source in the Pennines

Deltas:
Humber Estuary: •mouth of the Trent River •feeds into the North Sea

Capes:
  Land's End: •bordered by the Celtic Sea, Atlantic Ocean, and English Channel
    •southwesternmost point in the United Kingdom
Islands:
  Great Britain: •largest island in the United Kingdom •bordered by the Atlantic
    Ocean, Sea of the Hebrides, North Sea, Irish Sea, Celtic Sea, Moray Firth, Firth
    of Clyde, Firth of Forth, Cardigan Bay, Strait of Dover, North Channel, Saint
    George's Channel, Bristol Channel, English Channel, and The Minch
  Inner Hebrides: •island group off the northwestern coast of the United Kingdom
    •bordered by the Atlantic Ocean and Sea of the Hebrides
  Ireland: •second largest island in the United Kingdom •bordered by the Atlantic
    Ocean, Irish Sea, North Channel, and St. George's Channel •made up of the
    country of Ireland and Northern Ireland (part of the United Kingdom)
  Isle of Lewis: •largest island in the Outer Hebrides •bordered by the Atlantic
    Ocean and The Minch
  Orkney: •island group off the northern coast of the United Kingdom •bordered by
    the Atlantic Ocean and North Sea
  Outer Hebrides: •island group off the northwestern coast of the United Kingdom
    •bordered by the Atlantic Ocean and The Minch
  Shetland: •island group north of the Orkney Islands •bordered by the Atlantic
    Ocean and North Sea

POLITICAL:
Independence: 10th century (England), 1536 (union of England and Wales formalized),
  1707 (union of England and Scotland as Great Britain), 1801 (union of Great Britain
  and Ireland), 1927 (present name adopted)
Bordering Country: Ireland (1)
Regions:
  Ulster: •region that covers Northern Ireland •extends into Ireland
Administrative Divisions: England, Northern Ireland, Scotland, Wales (4 countries)
External Territories: Anguilla, Bermuda, British Indian Ocean Territory, British
  Virgin Islands, Cayman Islands, Channel Islands, Falkland Islands, Gibraltar, Isle of
  Man, Montserrat, Pitcairn Islands, Saint Helena, South Georgia and the South
  Sandwich Islands, Turks and Caicos Islands (14)
Ethnic/Racial Groups: English, Scottish, Irish, Welsh, Ulster
Religions: Christianity (Anglican, Roman Catholic, other Protestant), Islam
Languages: English, Welsh, Scottish form of Gaelic
Currency: British pound
Current Prime Minister: Tony Blair
Cities (capital, largest, or with at least a million people):
  London: •located on the island of Great Britain •city in southeastern England
    •capital of the United Kingdom •most populated city in the United Kingdom
    (7,615,000 people) •chief port on the River Thames

Manchester-Liverpool: ● located on the island of Great Britain ● metropolitan area in central England
Glasgow: ● located on the island of Great Britain ● city in western Scotland
Birmingham: ● located on the island of Great Britain ● city in central England

ENVIRONMENTAL/ECONOMIC:
Climate: temperate, moderated by the North Atlantic Current
Natural Resources: coal, petroleum, natural gas, iron ore, lead
Agricultural Products: cereals, oilseed, potatoes, vegetables, cattle
Major Exports: manufactured goods, fuels, chemicals, food, beverages
Natural Hazards: winter windstorms, floods

UNITED STATES

Country Name: United States of America
Continent: North America
Area: 3,794,083 sq mi / 9,826,630 sq km
Population: 291,512,000 (largest in North America)
Population Density: 77 people per sq mi / 30 people per sq km
Capital: Washington, D.C.

PHYSICAL:
Highest Point: Mount McKinley 20,320 ft / 6,194 m
Lowest Point: Death Valley 282 ft / 86 m below sea level

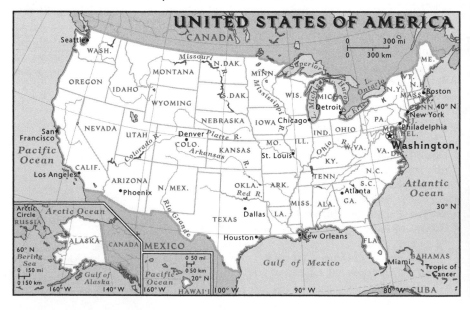

Mountain Ranges:
  Alaska: •located in southern Alaska •includes Mount McKinley (Denali) highest point in North America
  Aleutian: •located in southwestern Alaska on the Aleutian Peninsula
  Appalachian: •stretch north-south across the eastern United States •extend into Canada
  Brooks: •located in northern Alaska
  Cascade: •located near the Pacific Coast •east of the Coast Ranges •extends from northern California to Washington •has many volcanic peaks •includes Mount St. Helens
  Coast: •located along the western coast of the contiguous United States •extend from California to Washington •continue along the southern coast of Alaska
  Rocky : •cover much of the western United States •just west of the Great Plains •extend into Canada •form a continental divide
  Saint Elias: •located in southeastern Alaska •extend from Alaska into Canada
  Sierra Nevada: •located in eastern California in the western United States

Peaks (minimum elevation of 8,000 ft / 2,400 m):
  Mount McKinley: •located in the Alaska Range •highest point in North America •also called Denali
  Mount Whitney: •located in the Sierra Nevada •highest point in the contiguous United States

Passes:
  Chilkoot: •located in the Coast Mountains of Alaska •crosses the border into Canada

Valleys:
  San Joaquin: •located in California between the Coast Ranges and the Sierra Nevada

Grasslands/Prairies:
  Great Plains: •cover much of the central United States •located between the Rocky Mountains and the Mississippi River •extend into Canada
  Coastal Plain: •extends from the Gulf Coast of the United States northeast along the Atlantic Coast

Plateau Regions:
  Colorado Plateau: •located in the southwestern United States •between the Great Basin and the Rocky Mountains
  Columbia Plateau: •located in the northwestern United States •between the Cascade Range and Rocky Mountains
  Great Basin: •covers much of the western United States •desert region between the Sierra Nevada and Rocky Mountains
  Ozark Plateau: •forested plateau in the south-central United States •covers much of Arkansas •extends into Missouri

Depressions:
  Death Valley: •located in southwestern United States •in California near the Nevada border •part of the Mojave Desert •lowest point in North America

Swamps:
  The Everglades: •located in southeastern United States •cover much of the southern part of the Florida Peninsula

Deserts:

    Chihuahuan: •located in the southwestern United States •in Texas and New Mexico •extends into Mexico

    Mojave: •located in the southwestern United States •primarily in southern California and Nevada

    Sonoran: •located in the southwestern United States •primarily in Arizona •extends into Mexico

Oceans:

    Arctic: •forms much of the northern coast of Alaska

    Atlantic: •forms most of the eastern coast of the United States

    Pacific: •forms most of the western coast of the United States

Seas:

    Beaufort: •forms part of the northeastern coast of Alaska •feeds into the Arctic Ocean

    Bering: •forms part of the western coast of Alaska •feeds into the Pacific Ocean

    Chukchi: •forms part of the northwestern coast of Alaska •feeds into the Arctic Ocean

Gulfs:

    Gulf of Alaska: •forms part of the southern coast of Alaska •feeds into the Pacific Ocean

    Gulf of Maine: •forms part of the northeastern coast of the United States •feeds into the Atlantic Ocean

    Gulf of Mexico: •forms much of the southern coast of the United States •feeds into the Caribbean Sea and Atlantic Ocean

Bays:

    Chesapeake: •forms part of the eastern coast of the United States •feeds into the Atlantic Ocean •estuary of the Susquehanna River •separates the eastern and western portions of Maryland and Virginia

Sounds:

    Puget: •forms part of the northwestern coast of the United States •feeds into the Pacific Ocean •located in Washington

Straits:

    Bering : •forms part of the northwestern coast of Alaska •separates Alaska and Russia •connects the Chukchi and Bering Seas

    Strait of Juan de Fuca: •forms part of the northwestern coast of the United States •separates the United States from Canada •connects Puget Sound and the Pacific Ocean

    Straits of Florida: •form part of the southeastern coast of the United States •separate the Florida Peninsula and Cuba •connect the Gulf of Mexico and Atlantic Ocean

Lakes:

    Great Salt: •located in the state of Utah •between the Rocky Mountains and the Great Basin •largest lake in Utah

    Lake Erie: •located in the northeastern United States between Lake Huron and Lake Ontario •on the United States-Canada border •fourth largest of the Great Lakes in surface area

Lake Huron: •located on the United States-Canada border •third largest of the
   Great Lakes in surface area •located between Lake Erie and Lake Michigan
Lake Michigan: •located in the north-central United States between Lake Huron
   and Lake Superior •second largest of the Great Lakes in surface area •only one
   of the Great Lakes entirely in the United States
Lake Okeechobee: •located in the southeastern United States •largest lake in
   Florida •on the edge of the Everglades
Lake Ontario: •located in the northeastern United States •on the United States-
   Canada border •easternmost and smallest of the Great Lakes in surface area
   •empties into the St. Lawrence River
Lake Pontchartrain: •located in the southern United States •on the Gulf Coastal
   Plain •largest lake in Louisiana
Lake Superior: •located on the United States-Canada border •westernmost and
   largest of the Great Lakes •largest lake in North America

Rivers:

Arkansas: •tributary of the Mississippi River •has its source in the Rocky Mountains
Colorado: •has its source in the Rocky Mountains •empties into the Gulf of
   California •extends into Mexico •forms the Grand Canyon
Columbia: •forms much of the Washington-Oregon border •has its mouth in the
   Pacific Ocean •extends into Canada •a major source of hydroelectric power for
   the Pacific Northwest
Mississippi: •has its mouth in the Gulf of Mexico •has its source in Lake Itasca in
   Minnesota •including its tributary the Missouri River, the Mississippi forms the
   longest river in North America
Missouri: •tributary of the Mississippi River •has its source in the Rocky Mountains
   •along with the Mississippi River, it forms the longest river in North America
Ohio: •tributary of the Mississippi River •has its source in the Appalachian Mountains
Rio Grande: •has its mouth in the Gulf of Mexico •has its source in the Rocky
   Mountains •forms much of the United States-Mexico border
Saint Lawrence: •has its mouth in the Gulf of Saint Lawrence •forms part of the
   United States-Canada border
Snake: •tributary of the Columbia River •has its source in the Rocky Mountains
   •forms part of the Idaho-Oregon border •forms Hells Canyon, deepest gorge in
   the United States

Deltas:

Mississippi River Delta: •mouth of the Mississippi River •feeds into the Gulf of
   Mexico •located in Louisiana

Waterfalls:

Niagara: •located in northeastern United States •part of the Niagara River •on the
   United States-Canada border (between New York State and Ontario)
Yosemite: •located in western United States •in the Sierra Nevada

Dams:

Glen Canyon: •located on the Colorado River •near the Arizona-Utah border
   •creates Lake Powell •a hydroelectric dam

Grand Coulee: ●located in Washington State ●on the Columbia River ●a hydroelectric dam

Hoover: ●located on the Colorado River ●on the Arizona-Nevada border●creates Lake Mead ●a hydroelectric dam

Peninsulas:

Alaska: ●bordered by the Bering Sea and Pacific Ocean

Florida: ●bordered by the Atlantic Ocean, Gulf of Mexico, and Straits of Florida

Olympic: ●bordered by the Pacfic Ocean, Strait of Juan de Fuca, and Puget Sound

Seward: ●borders the Chukchi Sea, Bering Sea, and Bering Strait

Capes:

Cape Cod: ●bordered by the Gulf of Maine and the Atlantic Ocean

Cape Flattery: ●bordered by the Pacific Ocean and the Strait of Juan de Fuca ●located at the northwestern tip of the Olympic Peninsula ●in Washington

Cape Hatteras: ●chain of barrier islands in the Atlantic Ocean ●off the coast of North Carolina

Islands:

Aleutian: ●chain of volcanic islands ●extend west from Alaska across the 180-degree meridian ●bordered by the Bering Sea and Pacific Ocean

Hawaiian: ●island group surrounded by the Pacific Ocean ●Hawaii, Kauai, Oahu, Molokai, and Maui are the main islands in the group ●volcanic in origin ●make up the only island U.S. state

Long: ●located off the northeastern coast of the United States ●bordered by the Atlantic Ocean and Long Island Sound ●part of New York

POLITICAL:

Independence: July 4, 1776 (from Great Britain)

Bordering Countries: Canada, Mexico (2)

Administrative Divisions: Alabama, Alaska, Arizona, Arkansas, California, Colorado, Connecticut, Delaware, Florida, Georgia, Hawaii, Idaho, Illinois, Indiana, Iowa, Kansas, Kentucky, Louisiana, Maine, Maryland, Massachusetts, Michigan, Minnesota, Mississippi, Missouri, Montana, Nebraska, Nevada, New Hampshire, New Jersey, New Mexico, New York, North Carolina, North Dakota, Ohio, Oklahoma, Oregon, Pennsylvania, Rhode Island, South Carolina, South Dakota, Tennessee, Texas, Utah, Vermont, Virginia, Washington, West Virginia, Wisconsin, Wyoming (50 states) ●District of Columbia (1 federal district)

External Territories: American Samoa, Baker Island, Guam, Howland Island, Jarvis Island, Johnston Atoll, Kingman Reef, Midway Islands, Navassa Island, Northern Mariana Islands, Palmyra Atoll, Puerto Rico, U.S. Virgin Islands, Wake Island (14)

Ethnic/Racial Groups: white, Hispanic, black, Asian, Amerindian

Religions: Christianity (Protestant, Roman Catholic), Judaism

Languages: English, Spanish

Currency: U.S. dollar

Current President: George W. Bush

Cities (capital, largest, or with at least a million people):

New York: •located in the northeastern United States •city in New York State •most populated city in the United States (8,092,000 people) •chief port on the Atlantic Ocean

Los Angeles: •located in the southwestern United States •largest city in California •on the edge of the Coast Ranges •a major port on the Pacific Ocean

Chicago: •located in the midwestern United States •largest city in Illinois •chief port on Lake Michigan

Houston: •located in the southern United States •city in Texas •a major port on the Gulf of Mexico

Philadelphia: •located in eastern United States •city in Pennsylvania •a major river port on the East Coast

Phoenix: •located in the southwestern United States •city in Arizona •on the edge of the Sonoran Desert

San Diego: •located in the southwestern United States •city in California •a major ocean port and military base on the Pacific Ocean

San Antonio: •located in the south-central United States •city in Texas

Dallas: •located in the south-central United States •city in Texas •on the edge of the Great Plains

Washington, D.C.: •located in the eastern United States •city between Maryland and Virginia •capital of the United States (570,898 people)

ENVIRONMENTAL/ECONOMIC:

Climate: mostly temperate; tropical in Hawaii and Florida, arctic in Alaska, semi-arid in the Great Plains, arid in the Great Basin

Natural Resources: coal, copper, lead, molybdenum, phosphates

Agricultural Products: wheat, corn, other grains, fruits, beef

Major Exports: capital goods, automobiles, industrial supplies and raw materials, consumer goods, agricultural products

Natural Hazards: hurricanes, tornadoes, mudslides, forest fires, floods, volcanoes, earthquakes, tsunamis, permafrost (in Alaska)

URUGUAY

Country Name: Oriental Republic of Uruguay
Continent: South America
Area: 68,037 sq mi / 176,215 sq km
Population: 3,380,000
Population Density: 50 people per sq mi / 19 people per sq km
Capital: Montevideo

PHYSICAL:

Highest Point: Cerro Catedral 1,686 ft / 514 m
Lowest Point: Atlantic Ocean 0 ft / 0 m (sea level)

Oceans:
   Atlantic: ●forms the eastern coast of Uruguay
Rivers:
   Negro: ●tributary of the Uruguay River ●extends into Brazil
   Uruguay: ●forms all of the Uruguay-Argentina border ●feeds into the Rio de la
     Plata estuary ●extends into Brazil
Lakes:
   Lago Rincon del Bonete: ●located in central Uruguay ●fed by the Negro River
   Lagoa Mirim: ●located in eastern Uruguay ●extends into Brazil
Deltas:
   Rio de la Plata estuary: ●mouth of the Uruguay River ●ends in the Atlantic
     Ocean ●forms most of the southern coast of Uruguay ●borders Uruguay
     and Argentina

POLITICAL:
Independence: August 25, 1825 (from Brazil)
Former Names: Banda Oriental, Cisplatine Province
Bordering Countries: Brazil, Argentina (2)
Administrative Divisions: Artigas, Canelones, Cerro Largo, Colonia, Durazno,
   Flores, Florida, Lavalleja, Maldonado, Montevideo, Paysandu, Rio Negro, Rivera,
   Rocha, Salto, San Jose, Soriano, Tacuarembo, Treinta y Tres (19 departments)
Ethnic/Racial Groups: white, mestizo, black
Religion: Christianity (primarily Roman Catholic)
Languages: Spanish, Portunol, Brazilero

Currency: Uruguayan peso
Current President: Jorge Batlle Ibanez
Cities (capital, largest, or with at least a million people):
Montevideo: •located in southern Uruguay •city in the Montevideo department •capital of Uruguay •most populated city in Uruguay (1,341,000 people) •chief port on the Rio de la Plata estuary

ENVIRONMENTAL/ECONOMIC:

Climate: warm temperate; temperature almost never falls below freezing
Natural Resources: arable land, hydropower, minor minerals, fisheries
Agricultural Products: rice, wheat, corn, barley, livestock
Major Exports: meat, rice, leather products, wool, vehicles
Natural Hazards: pamperos (violent winds), droughts, floods

UZBEKISTAN

Country Name: Republic of Uzbekistan
Continent: Asia
Area: 172,742 sq mi / 447,400 sq km
Population: 25,672,000
Population Density: 149 people per sq mi / 57 people per sq km
Capital: Tashkent

PHYSICAL:

Highest Point: Adelunga Toghi 14,111 ft / 4,301 m
Lowest Point: Sarygamysh Koli 39 ft / 12 m below sea level
Peaks (minimum elevation of 8,000 ft / 2,400 m):
    Adelunga Toghi: ●located in eastern Uzbekistan ●on the Uzbekistan-Kyrgyzstan border ●highest point in Uzbekistan
Plateau Regions:
    Ustyurt: ●located in northwestern Uzbekistan ●extends into Kazakhstan
Deserts:
    Qizilqum: ●covers much of central Uzbekistan ●extends into Kazakhstan
Lakes:
    Aral Sea: ●located in northwestern Uzbekistan ●extends into Kazakhstan ●east of the Ustyurt Plateau and west of the Qizilqum desert
Rivers:
    Amu Darya: ●has its mouth in the Aral Sea ●forms all of the Uzbekistan-Afghanistan border ●forms part of the Uzbekistan-Turkmenistan border ●extends into Turkmenistan and Afghanistan
    Syr Darya: ●extends into Tajikistan and Kazakhstan

POLITICAL:

Independence: September 1, 1991 (from the Soviet Union)
Former Name: Uzbek Soviet Socialist Republic
Bordering Countries: Kazakhstan, Turkmenistan, Tajikistan, Kyrgyzstan, Afghanistan (5)
Administrative Divisions: Andijon, Buxoro, Fargona, Jizzax, Namangan, Navoiy, Qashqadaryo, Samarqand, Sirdaryo, Surxondaryo, Toshkent, Xorazm(12 provinces) ●Qoraqalpogiston (1 autonomous republic) ●Tashkent (1 city)
Ethnic/Racial Groups: Uzbek, Russian, Tajik, Kazakh, Karakalpak, Tatar
Religions: Islam, Christianity (primarily Eastern Orthodox)
Languages: Uzbek, Russian, Tajik
Currency: Uzbekistani sum
Current President: Islom Karimov
Cities (capital, largest, or with at least a million people):
    Tashkent: ●located in eastern Uzbekistan ●city in the Tashkent city division ●capital of Uzbekistan ●most populated city in Uzbekistan (2,155,000 people)

ENVIRONMENTAL/ECONOMIC:

Climate: mostly midlatitude desert; hot summers/mild winters; semi-arid grassland in the east
Natural Resources: natural gas, petroleum, coal, gold, uranium
Agricultural Products: cotton, vegetables, fruits, grain, livestock
Major Exports: cotton, gold, energy products, mineral fertilizers, ferrous metals
Natural Hazards: droughts, sandstorms

VANUATU

Country Name: Republic of Vanuatu
Continent: Australia/Oceania
Area: 4,707 sq mi / 12,190 sq km
Population: 214,000
Population Density: 45 people per sq mi / 18 people per sq km
Capital: Port-Vila

PHYSICAL:
Highest Point: Tabwemasana 6,158 ft / 1,877 m
Lowest Point: Pacific Ocean 0 ft / 0 m (sea level)
Oceans:
  Pacific: •forms the eastern coast of Vanuatu
Seas:
  Coral: •forms the western coast of Vanuatu •feeds into the Pacific Ocean
Islands:
  Espiritu Santo: •largest island in Vanuatu •bordered by the Pacific Ocean and Coral Sea

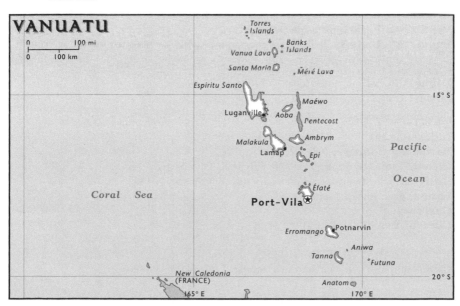

POLITICAL:
Independence: July 30, 1980 (from France and the United Kingdom)
Former Name: New Hebrides
Administrative Divisions: Malampa, Penama, Sanma, Shefa, Tafea, Torba (6 provinces)
Ethnic/RacialGroups: predominantly Melanesian
Religions: Christianity (Protestant, Roman Catholic), indigenous beliefs
Languages: English, French, more than 100 local languages
Currency: vatu
Current President: Kalkot Matas Kelekele
Cities (capital, largest, or with at least a million people):
   Port-Vila: •located on Efate Island in central Vanuatu •city in the Shefa province
      •capital of Vanuatu •most populated city in Vanuatu (31,000 people) •chief port
      on the Pacific Ocean and the Coral Sea

ENVIRONMENTAL/ECONOMIC:
Climate: tropical, moderated by southeast trade winds
Natural Resources: manganese, hardwood forests, fish
Agricultural Products: copra, coconuts, cocoa, coffee
Major Exports: copra, beef, cacao, timber, kava
Natural Hazards: typhoons, volcanoes, earthquakes, tsunamis

VATICAN CITY
Country Name: State of the Vatican City (The Holy See)
Continent: Europe
Area: 0.2 sq mi / 0.4 sq km (smallest country in the world)
Population: 1,000 (smallest in the world)
Population Density: 5,000 people per sq mi / 2,500 people per sq km

PHYSICAL:
Highest Point: unnamed location 246 feet / 75 meters
Lowest Point: unnamed location 62 feet / 19 meters

POLITICAL:
Independence: February 11, 1929 (from Italy)
Bordering Country: Italy (1)
Ethnic/RacialGroups: predominantly Italian and Swiss
Religion: Christianity (predominantly Roman Catholic)
Languages: Italian, Latin, French
Currency: euro
Current Pope: John Paul II

ENVIRONMENTAL/ECONOMIC:
Climate: temperate; mild and rainy winters/hot and dry summers

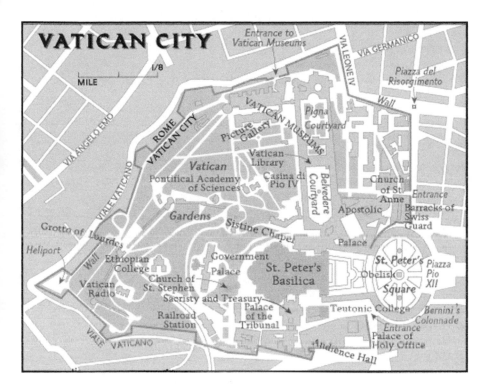

1/8
MILE

Entrance to
Vatican Museums

VIA LEONE IV

VIA GERMANICO

Piazza del
Risorgimento

VIA ANGELO EMO

ROME
VATICAN CITY

VATICAN MUSEUMS

Pigna
Courtyard

Wall

VIA LE VATICANO

Picture
Gallery

Vatican
Library

Vatican
Pontifical Academy
of Sciences

Casina di
Pio IV

Belvedere
Courtyard

Church
of St
Anne

Entrance

Grotto of Lourdes

Gardens

Sistine Chapel

Apostolic

Barracks of
Swiss
Guard

Heliport

Wall

Palace

Ethiopian
College

Government
Palace

St. Peter's
Basilica

St. Peter's
Square

Piazza
Pio
XII

Vatican
Radio

Church of
St. Stephen

Sacristy and Treasury

Obelisk

Bernini's
Colonnade

VIALE VATICANO

Railroad
Station

Palace
of the
Tribunal

Teutonic College

Entrance

Andience Hall

Palace of
Holy Office

VENEZUELA

Country Name: Bolivarian Republic of Venezuela
Continent: South America
Area: 352,144 sq mi / 912,050 sq km
Population: 25,698,000
Population Density: 73 people per sq mi / 28 people per sq km
Capital: Caracas

PHYSICAL:
Highest Point: Pico Bolivar 16,427 feet / 5,007 meters
Lowest Point: Atlantic Ocean 0 feet / 0 meters (sea level)
Mountain Ranges:
    Cordillera de Merida: •located in northwestern Venezuela
    Guiana Highlands: •cover much of southern and central Venezuela •extend into
        Brazil and Guyana
Peaks (minimum elevation of 8,000 ft / 2,400 m):
    Pico Bolivar: •located in the Cordillera de Merida •highest point in Venezuela

Grasslands/Prairies:
    Llanos: ●cover much of western Venezuela ●extend into Colombia
Rain forests:
    Amazon: ●covers part of southern Venezuela ●extends into Colombia and Brazil
Oceans:
    Atlantic: ●forms most of the northeastern coast of Venezuela
Seas:
    Caribbean: ●forms most of the northern coast of Venezuela ●feeds into the
        Atlantic Ocean
Gulfs:
    Gulf of Paria: ●forms part of the northeastern coast of Venezuela ●feeds into the
        Caribbean Sea and the Atlantic Ocean
    Gulf of Venezuela: ●forms part of the northwestern coast of Venezuela ●feeds into
        the Caribbean Sea ●southern part is called Lake Maracaibo
Lakes:
    Lake Maracaibo: ●located in northwestern Venezuela ●southernmost part of the Gulf
        of Venezuela
Rivers:
    Meta: ●tributary of the Orinoco River ●forms part of the Venezuela-Colombia border
        ●extends into Colombia
    Orinoco: ●has its mouth in the Atlantic Ocean ●has its source in the Guiana Highlands
        ●forms part of the Venezuela-Colombia border
Deltas:
    Orinoco: ●mouth of the Orinoco River ●feeds into the Atlantic Ocean

Waterfalls:
Angel: •located in eastern Venezuela • located in the Guiana Highlands •highest
waterfall in the world

POLITICAL:
Independence: July 5, 1811 (from Spain)
Bordering Countries: Brazil, Colombia, Guyana (3)
Administrative Divisions: Amazonas, Anzoategui, Apure, Aragua, Barinas,
Bolivar, Carabobo, Cojedes, Delta Amacuro, Falcon, Guarico, Lara, Merida,
Miranda, Monagas, Nueva Esparta, Portuguesa, Sucre, Tachira, Trujillo, Vargas,
Yaracuy, Zulia (23 states) •Distrito Federal (1 federal district) •Dependencias
Federales (1 federal dependency)
Ethnic/Racial Groups: Spanish, Italian, Portuguese, Arab, German, black, indigenous
Religion: Christianity (primarily Roman Catholic)
Languages: Spanish, indigenous dialects
Currency: bolivar
Current President: Hugo Chavez Frias
Cities (capital, largest, or with at least a million people):
Caracas: •located in northern Venezuela •city in the Distrito Federal and the Miranda
state •capital of Venezuela •most populated city in Venezuela (3,226,000 people)
Maracaibo: •located in northwestern Venezuela •city in the Zulia state •chief port
on Lake Maracaibo and the Gulf of Venezuela
Valencia: •located in northern Venezuela •city in the Carabobo state

ENVIRONMENTAL/ECONOMIC:
Climate: tropical hot and humid; more moderate in the highlands
Natural Resources: petroleum, natural gas, iron ore, gold, bauxite
Agricultural Products: corn, sorghum, sugarcane, rice, beef
Major Exports: petroleum, bauxite, aluminum, steel, chemicals
Natural Hazards: floods, rockslides, mudslides, droughts

VIETNAM
Country Name: Socialist Republic of Vietnam
Continent: Asia
Area: 127,844 sq mi / 331,114 sq km
Population: 80,786,000
Population Density: 632 people per sq mi / 244 people per sq km
Capital: Hanoi

PHYSICAL:
Highest Point: Fan Si Pan 10,308 feet / 3,142 meters
Lowest Point: South China Sea 0 feet / 0 meters (sea level)

Mountain Ranges:
　Annam Cordillera: ●covers much of Vietnam
Peaks (minimum elevation of 8,000 ft / 2,400 m):
　Fan Si Pan: ●located in northwestern Vietnam ●highest point in Vietnam
Seas:
　South China: ●forms much of the southern and eastern coasts of Vietnam ●feeds
　　into the Philippine and Java Seas
Gulfs:
　Gulf of Thailand: ●forms part of the southwestern coast of Vietnam ●feeds into the
　　South China Sea
　Gulf of Tonkin: ●forms the northeastern coast of Vietnam ●feeds into the South
　　China Sea
Rivers:
　Mekong: ●has its mouth in the South China Sea ●extends into Cambodia, Laos,
　　and China
　Red: ●has its mouth in the Gulf of Tonkin ●forms part of the Vietnam-China border
　　●extends into China
Deltas:
　Mekong River Delta: ●mouth of the Mekong River ●feeds into the South China Sea

POLITICAL:
Independence: September 2, 1945 (from France)
Former Names: North Vietnam, South Vietnam
Bordering Countries: Laos, China, Cambodia (3)

Administrative Divisions: An Giang, Bac Giang, Bac Kan, Bac Lieu, Bac Ninh, Ba Ria-Vung Tau, Ben Tre, Binh Dinh, Binh Duong, Binh Phuoc, Binh Thuan, Ca Mau, Can Tho, Cao Bang, Dac Lak, Dac Nong, Dien Bien, Dong Nai, Dong Thap, Gia Lai, Ha Giang, Hai Duong, Ha Nam, Ha Tay, Ha Tinh, Hau Giang, Hoa Binh, Hung Yen, Khanh Hoa, Kien Giang, Kon Tum, Lai Chau, Lam Dong, Lang Son, Lao Cai, Long An, Nam Dinh, Nghe An, Ninh Binh, Ninh Thuan, Phu Tho, Phu Yen, Quang Binh, Quang Nam, Quang Ngai, Quang Ninh, Quang Tri, Soc Trang, Son La, Tay Ninh, Thai Binh, Thai Nguyen, Thanh Hoa, Thua Thien-Hue, Tien Giang, Tra Vinh, Tuyen Quang, Vinh Long, Vinh Phuc, Yen Bai (60 provinces) ● Can Tho, Da Nang, Haiphong, Hanoi, Ho Chi Minh (5 municipalities)

Ethnic/Racial Groups: Vietnamese, Chinese, Hmong, Thai, Khmer, Cham

Religions: Buddhism, Hoa Hao, Cao Dai, Christianity, indigenous beliefs, Islam

Languages: Vietnamese, English, French, Chinese, Khmer, local languages

Currency: dong

Current President: Tran Duc Luong

Cities (capital, largest, or with at least a million people):

Ho Chi Minh City: ● located in southern Vietnam ● city in the Ho Chi Minh municipality ● most populated city in Vietnam (6,063,000 people)

Hanoi: ● located in northern Vietnam ● city in the Hanoi municipality ● capital of Vietnam (3,977,000 people) ● chief port on the Red River

ENVIRONMENTAL/ECONOMIC:

Climate: tropical in the south; monsoonal in the north; rainy/dry seasons

Natural Resources: phosphates, coal, manganese, bauxite, chromate

Agricultural Products: paddy rice, corn, potatoes, rubber, poultry

Major Exports: crude oil, marine products, rice, coffee, rubber

Natural Hazards: typhoons, floods

YEMEN

Country Name: Republic of Yemen
Continent: Asia
Area: 207,286 sq mi / 536,869 sq km
Population: 19,350,000
Population Density: 93 people per sq mi / 36 people per sq km
Capital: Sanaa

PHYSICAL:

Highest Point: Mount Nabi Shuayb 12,336 ft / 3,760 m
Lowest Point: Arabian Sea 0 ft / 0 m (sea level)
Mountain Ranges:

Hadramawt: •covers much of southern Yemen
Jabal al Hijaz: •covers much of western Yemen •extends into Saudi Arabia

Peaks (minimum elevation of 8,000 ft / 2,400 m):

Mount Nabi Shuayb: •located in the Jabal al Hijaz •highest point in Yemen

Deserts:

Rub al Khali: •covers much of northern Yemen •extends into Saudi Arabia and Oman

Seas:

Arabian: •forms part of the eastern coast of Yemen •feeds into the Indian Ocean

Red: •forms much of the western coast of Yemen •feeds into the Gulf of Aden

Gulfs:

Gulf of Aden: •forms most of the southern coast of Yemen •feeds into the Arabian Sea

Straits:

Bab al Mandab: •forms part of the southwestern coast of Yemen •separates Yemen from Eritrea and Djibouti •connects the Red Sea and Gulf of Aden

Islands:

Socotra: •island at the eastern end of the Gulf of Aden •bordered by the Arabian Sea and Gulf of Aden

POLITICAL:

Independence: May 22, 1990 (unification of North and South Yemen)

Former Names: North Yemen, South Yemen

Bordering Countries: Saudi Arabia, Oman (2)

Administrative Divisions: Abyan, Adan, Ad Dali, Al Bayda, Al Hudaydah, Al Jawf, Al Mahrah, Al Mahwit, Amran, Dhamar, Hadramawt, Hajjah, Ibb, Lahij, Marib, Sadah, Sana, Shabwah, Taizz (19 governorates)

Ethnic/Racial Groups: predominantly Arab

Religion: Islam (Sunni, Shiite)

Language: Arabic

Currency: Yemeni rial

Current President: Ali Abdallah Salih

Cities (capital, largest, or with at least a million people):

Sanaa: •located in western Yemen •city in the Sana governorate •capital of Yemen •most populated city in Yemen (1,469,000 people) •located in the Jabal al Hijaz

ENVIRONMENTAL/ECONOMIC:

Climate: mostly desert; hot and humid along the coast; temperate in the western mountains; hot and dry desert in the east

Natural Resources: petroleum, fish, rock salt, marble, coal

Agricultural Products: grain, fruits, vegetables, pulses, dairy products

Major Exports: crude oil, coffee, dried and salted fish

Natural Hazards: sandstorms, dust storms

ZAMBIA

Country Name: Republic of the Zambia
Continent: Africa
Area: 290,586 sq mi / 752,614 sq km
Population: 10,896,000
Population Density: 37 people per sq mi / 14 people per sq km
Capital: Lusaka

PHYSICAL:

Highest Point: location in the Mafinga Hills 7,549 ft / 2,301 m
Lowest Point: Zambezi River 1,079 ft / 329 m
Mountain Ranges:
Muchinga: located in eastern Zambia
Lakes:
Lake Bangweulu: located in northern Zambia
Lake Kariba: located in southern Zambia formed by the Kariba Dam fed by the Zambezi River on the Zambia-Zimbabwe border
Lake Mweru: located in northern Zambia on the Zambia-Democratic Republic of the Congo border
Lake Tanganyika: located in northern Zambia extends into the Democratic Republic of the Congo and Tanzania
Rivers:
Luangwa: tributary of the Zambezi River has its source in the Muchinga Mountains forms part of the Zambia-Mozambique border
Zambezi: has its source in northwestern Zambia forms all of Zambia's border with Zimbabwe and Botswana forms much of the Zambia-Namibia border extends into Angola and Mozambique
Waterfalls:
Victoria: located in southern Zambia on the Zambezi River on the Zambia-Zimbabwe border
Dams:
Kariba: located in southeastern Zambia forms Lake Kariba on the Zambezi River on the Zambia-Zimbabwe border

POLITICAL:

Independence: October 24, 1964 (from the United Kingdom)
Former Name: Northern Rhodesia

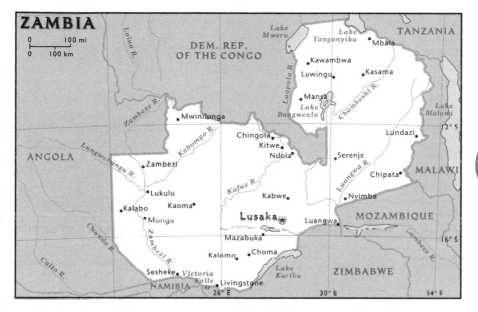

Bordering Countries: Democratic Republic of the Congo, Angola, Malawi, Zimbabwe, Mozambique, Tanzania, Namibia, Botswana (8)

Administrative Divisions: Central, Copperbelt, Eastern, Luapula, Lusaka, Northern, North-Western, Southern, Western (9 provinces)

Ethnic/Racial Groups: more than 70 indigenous groups, including Bamba, Tonga, Ngoni, Lozi

Religions: Christianity, Islam, Hinduism

Languages: English, indigenous languages

Currency: Zambian kwacha

Current President: Levy Mwanawasa

Cities (capital, largest, or with at least a million people):
   Lusaka: •located in south-central Zambia •city in the Lusaka province •capital of
   Zambia •most populated city in Zambia (1,394,000 people)

ENVIRONMENTAL/ECONOMIC:

Climate: tropical, modified by altitude; rainy/dry seasons

Natural Resources: copper, cobalt, zinc, lead, coal

Agricultural Products: corn, sorghum, rice, peanuts, cattle

Major Exports: copper, cobalt, electricity, tobacco, flowers

Natural Hazards: droughts, tropical storms

ZIMBABWE

Country Name: Republic of Zimbabwe
Continent: Africa
Area: 150,872 sq mi / 390,757 sq km
Population: 12,577,000
Population Density: 83 people per sq mi / 32 people per sq km
Capital: Harare

PHYSICAL:

Highest Point: Inyangani 8,504 ft / 2,592 m
Lowest Point: Runde/Save River junction 531 ft / 162 m
Peaks (minimum elevation of 8,000 ft / 2,400 m):
　　Inyangani: ●located in eastern Zimbabwe ●highest point in Zimbabwe
Lakes:
　　Lake Kariba: ●located in northwestern Zimbabwe ●formed by the Kariba Dam ●on
　　　the Zambezi River ●on the Zimbabwe-Zambia border
Rivers:
　　Limpopo: ●forms all of the Zimbabwe-South Africa border ●extends into Mozambique
　　Zambezi: ●forms all of the Zimbabwe-Zambia border ●extends into Zambia and
　　　Mozambique
Waterfalls:
　　Victoria: ●located in western Zimbabwe ●on the Zambezi River ●on the Zimbabwe-
　　　Zambia border
Dams:
　　Kariba: ● located in northwestern Zimbabwe ●forms Lake Kariba ●on the Zambezi
　　　River ●on the Zimbabwe-Zambia border

POLITICAL:

Independence: April 18, 1980 (from the United Kingdom)
Former Names: Rhodesia, Southern Rhodesia
Bordering Countries: Mozambique, Botswana, Zambia, South Africa (4)
Administrative Divisions: Manicaland, Mashonaland Central, Mashonaland East,
　　Mashonaland West, Masvingo, Matabeleland North, Matabeleland South, Midlands
　　(8 provinces) ●Bulawayo, Harare (2 cities)
Ethnic/Racial Groups: Shona, Ndebele
Religions: syncretic (part Christian and part indigenous beliefs), Christianity,
　　indigenous beliefs
Languages: English, Shona, Sindebele
Currency: Zimbabwean dollar
Current Presidents: Robert Gabriel Mugabe and Joseph Msika
Cities (capital, largest, or with at least a million people):
　　Harare: ●located in northern Zimbabwe ●city in the Harare city division ●capital of
　　　Zimbabwe ●most populated city in Zimbabwe (1,469,000 people)
　　Bulawayo: ●located in southwestern Zimbabwe ●city in the Bulawayo city division

ZIMBABWE

ENVIRONMENTAL/ECONOMIC:

Climate: tropical, moderated by altitude; rainy/dry seasons
Natural Resources: coal, chromium ore, asbestos, gold, nickel
Agricultural Products: corn, cotton, tobacco, wheat, cattle
Major Exports: tobacco, gold, ferroalloys, textiles, clothing
Natural Hazards: droughts, floods, severe storms

Geographic Extremes

Largest in area: Russia
North America: Canada
South America: Brazil
Europe: Russia (Ukraine is the largest country entirely in Europe.)
Asia: Russia (China is the largest country entirely in Asia.)
Africa: Sudan
Australia/Oceania: Australia

Smallest in area: Vatican City
North America: St. Kitts and Nevis
South America: Suriname
Europe: Vatican City
Asia: Maldives
Africa: Seychelles
Australia/Oceania: Nauru

Largest in population: China
North America: United States
South America: Brazil
Europe: Russia (Germany is the most populated country entirely in Europe.)
Asia: China
Africa: Nigeria
Australia/Oceania: Australia

Smallest in population: Vatican City
North America: St. Kitts and Nevis
South America: Suriname
Europe: Vatican City
Asia: Maldives
Africa: Seychelles
Australia/Oceania: Tuvalu

Densest in population: Monaco
North America: Barbados
South America: Ecuador
Europe: Monaco
Asia: Singapore
Africa: Mauritius
Australia/Oceania: Nauru

Least dense in population: Mongolia
North America: Canada
South America: Suriname
Europe: Iceland
Asia: Mongolia
Africa: Namibia
Australia/Oceania: Australia

Highest point: Mount Everest
(Nepal/China)
North America: Mount McKinley (U.S.)
South America: Aconcagua (Argentina)
Europe: Mount Elbrus (Russia)
Asia: Mount Everest (Nepal/China)
Africa: Kilimanjaro (Tanzania)
Australia/Oceania: Mt. Wilhelm (Papua
New Guinea)

Lowest point: Dead Sea (Israel/Jordan)
North America: Death Valley (U.S.)
South America: Valdes Peninsula
(Argentina)
Europe: Caspian Sea (Russia)
Asia: Dead Sea (Israel/Jordan)
Africa: Lake Assal (Djibouti)
Australia/Oceania: Lake Eyre (Australia)

Largest grassland: Eurasian steppe
(Europe/Asia)

Largest plateau: Tibetan (China)

Largest rain forest: Amazon
(South America

Largest swamp: Pantanal
(South America)

Largest desert: Sahara (Africa)

Largest lake: Caspian Sea (Russia/
Azerbaijan/Iran/Turkmenistan/
Kazakhstan)
North America: Lake Superior
(U.S./Canada)
South America: Lake Titicaca°
(Peru/Bolivia)
Europe: Caspian Sea (Russia); Lake
Ladoga (Russia) is the largest lake
entirely in Europe.

Asia: Caspian Sea (Azerbaijan/Iran/
Turkmenistan/Kazakhstan); Lake
Baikal (Russia) is the largest lake
entirely in Asia.
Africa: Lake Victoria (Kenya/Tanzania/
Uganda)
Australia/Oceania: Lake Eyre (Australia)

Longest river: Nile (Africa)
North America: Mississippi-Missouri
South America: Amazon
Europe: Volga
Asia: Chang Jiang (Yangtze)
Africa: Nile
Australia/Oceania: Murray-Darling

Largest river discharge: Amazon
(South America)

Tallest waterfall: Angel Falls
(Venezuela)

Largest dam: Three Gorges Dam
(China)

Largest island: Greenland

° Lake Maracaibo, although called
a lake, is actually an extension of the
Gulf of Venezuela

Glossary

Amerindian: a term for the native peoples of the Americas

animism: the belief that natural objects, such as trees, mountains, and rivers, are inhabited by spirits

Austronesian: people of mixed Australian and Polynesian, Melanesian, Micronesian, Malaysian, or Formosan ancestry

capital goods: tools, machinery, and other equipment or items used to produce goods and services

Carib: a descendant of Amerindian people who formerly lived in certain islands of the West Indies and in northern South America; also the language of these people

CIS: an acronym for the Commonwealth of Independent States, an alliance established in 1991 and made up of republics of the former Soviet Union (Web site: www.cis.minsk.by)

continental climate: a midlatitude climate occurring on large landmasses in the Northern Hemisphere; characterized by great variations in temperature seasonally and between day and night

Coptic: the native Christian religion of Egypt and Ethiopia

creole: a person of European heritage, especially French, born in the West Indies, Central America, tropical South America, or the U.S. Gulf States

erg: a huge desert area characterized by deep sand dunes

estuary: the broadened seaward end of a river that usually has a mixture of fresh and salt water that rises and falls with the tides

ethnic group: a group of people with a common ancestry and cultural tradition; examples include Irish, Hispanic, and Russian

Euronesian: people of mixed European and Polynesian, Micronesian, or Melanesian ancestry

ferroalloy: an alloy of iron used in the manufacture of steel, such as chromium and manganese

foehn: a warm, dry wind blowing into mountain valleys, especially in the European Alps

geothermal energy: heat energy generated from Earth's interior

harmattan: a hot, dusty wind that blows from the Sahara to the Atlantic coast of Africa, primarily from November to March

manufactured goods: raw materials that have been made into marketable goods by the use of industrial equipment

Melanesian: people indigenous to Melanesia, the part of Oceania that includes the islands of Fiji, New Guinea, Vanuatu, the Solomon Islands, and New Caledonia

mestizo: a person, especially in Latin America, whose ancestry is a mix of Spanish or Portuguese and American Indian

Micronesian: people indigenous to Micronesia, the part of Oceania that includes Guam, Kiribati, the Mariana Islands, Palau, and the Federated States of Micronesia

mistral: a violent wind blowing south to the Mediterranean coast of France, most often in winter and spring, that can last for a hundred days each year

monsoon: a seasonal change in the direction of prevailing winds that causes wet and dry seasons in some areas

mulatto: a person of mixed black and white ancestry

Negrito: a term for any dark-skinned person of short stature living in Oceania or Southeast Asia

nonferrous metals: metals that contain no iron

Oceania: name for the widely scattered islands of Polynesia, Micronesia, and Melanesia; often includes Australia and New Zealand

patois: a form of a language that differs from the accepted standard; a local dialect

permafrost: a permanently frozen layer of soil, gravel, and sand bound together by ice; found below Earth's surface at high latitudes or elevations

pidgin English: a form of English that is a mix of English and one or more local languages

Polynesian: people indigenous to Polynesia, the part of Oceania that includes the Hawaiian Islands, the Society Islands, Samoa, and French Polynesia

precious metals: relatively scarce but valuable metals, including gold, silver, platinum, and iridium

racial group: a group of people defined by its genetic makeup; examples include whites, blacks, and Amerindians

re-exports: foreign goods that are exported by a nation in the same form in which they were originally imported into that nation

Sahel: a semiarid region of short, tropical grassland that lies between the Sahara and the tropical wet region of equatorial Africa and that is prone to frequent droughts

sirocco: a hot, usually springtime wind blowing from the Sahara to the Mediterranean coast of Africa

Soviet Union: an abbreviated name for the former Union of Soviet Socialist Republics (U.S.S.R.) that consisted of 15 republics, the largest of which was the Russian Soviet Federated Socialist Republic (Russia); ceased to exist in 1991

steppe: a Slavic word for the relatively flat, mostly treeless temperate grasslands that stretch across much of central Europe and central Asia

steppe climate: associated with midlatitude grasslands; characterized by hot summers, cold winters, and moderate rainfall

tsunami: powerful and potentially destructive ocean waves triggered by an earthquake or volcanic eruption

Bibliography

National Geographic Atlas of the World, 8th Edition. National Geographic Society, Washington, D.C., 2004.

National Geographic Xpeditions Atlas. National Geographic Society, Washington, D.C., www.nationalgeographic.com/xpeditions/atlas/

Wikipedia—The Free Encyclopedia. October 2004. en.wikipedia.org/wiki/Main_Page.

The World Factbook. Central Intelligence Agency, Washington, D.C. www.cia.gov/cia/publications/factbook/index.html

The World Gazetteer. 21 Jun 2004 www.world-gazetteer.com/home.htm

About the
Author

Andrew Wojtanik is a 15-year-old ninth grader who enjoys looking at maps, charting out territory, and wondering what life is like in different places. Of all the places he has been, his favorite is the Grand Canyon. He hopes one day to experience the awe and beauty of all of America's national parks. He would also like to travel around the world and eventually get a job that will allow him to use his geography skills. Andrew also enjoys track, baseball, and golf. He lives with his family in Overland Park, Kansas.

One of the world's largest nonprofit scientific and educational organizations, the National Geographic Society was founded in 1888 "for the increase and diffusion of geographic knowledge." Fulfilling this mission, the Society educates and inspires millions every day through its magazines, books, television programs, videos, maps and atlases, research grants, the National Geographic Bee, teacher workshops, and innovative classroom materials. The Society is supported through membership dues, charitable gifts, and income from the sale of its educational products. This support is vital to National Geographic's mission to increase global understanding and promote conservation of our planet through exploration, research, and education.

For more information, please call 1-800-NGS LINE (647-5463)
or write to the following address:

National Geographic Society
1145 17th Street N.W.
Washington, D.C. 20036-4688 U.S.A.

Visit the Society's Web site at www.nationalgeographic.com.

Your Notes

. . . .

Your Notes

. . . .